CIM
TUTORIAL TEXT

**Professional
Postgraduate
Diploma**

Case study
Strategic Marketing in Practice

**by Juanita Cockton
and Angela Hatton**

In this September 2006 Tutorial Text

This text contains:
- Revision and self-testing material
- A teaching case covering a variety of skills
- Interactive action programmes to build skills
- Analysis of cases representing recent exams and a variety of industry contexts

---

First edition 1999
Eighth edition September 2006

ISBN 0 7517 2743 1 (Previous edition 0 7517 2390 8)

British Library Cataloguing-in-Publication Data
A catalogue record for this book
is available from the British Library

Published by

BPP Professional Education
Aldine House, Aldine Place
London W12 8AW

www.bpp.com

Printed in Great Britain by W M Print
45-47 Frederick Street
Walsall, West Midlands
WS2 9NE

We are grateful to the Chartered Institute of Marketing for permission to reproduce in this text the syllabus, tutor's guidance notes, past cases, examination questions and extracts from the examiner's reports.

Preface

The exam

The Postgraduate Diploma awarded by the Chartered Institute of Marketing is a management qualification which puts a major emphasis on the practical understanding of marketing activities. At the same time, the Institute's examinations recognise that the marketing professional works in a fast changing organisational, economic and social environment. Knowledge and skills in analysis and decision, together with an appreciation of the strategic role of marketing in the corporate structure of an understanding of the challenges of implementation, are essential ingredients of managerial competence in this field.

The secret of exam success is effective study material which is focused and relevant to the exam *you* will be sitting. This is the philosophy underpinning this *Tutorial Text*, which has been especially written for candidates sitting this case study examination. It is divided into four parts.

This *Tutorial Text* starts in Part A with a description of the case study and a health-check to cover your knowledge of the planning process. We apply a detailed 10-step process to a 'teaching case', *Biocatalysts* (Part B), selected as it is good example of the processes you have to go through. Part C consists of the December 2005 case, Signifo Expenses and the June 2006 case based on the retail sector, for you to work through on your own and compare with the suggested solutions. Part D, the final part gives advice on exam preparation.

Help us to help you

Your feedback will help us improve this *Tutorial Text*, so please complete and return the Review Form at the end of this *Tutorial Text;* you will be entered automatically in a free prize draw.

A final word

This *Tutorial Text* offers a professional solution to your needs in preparing for this challenging exam.

BPP Professional Education
September 2006

For information about all the products and services offered by the BPP Holdings plc group, visit our website. The address is: *www.bpp.com*

How to use this Tutorial Text

1 What is the CIM case study?

There is no formal syllabus for the CIM's case study examination Strategic Marketing in Practice. Instead the syllabus is based on all the knowledge gained in your Professional Postgraduate Diploma studies. It is examined by a case study, normally comprising 40 to 70 pages of narrative, charts and tables and issued to examinees by post about **four weeks in advance of the examination**. The issue of the case study some four weeks in advance allows time for in depth analysis and discussion.

The case study is a **practical** test of the candidates' knowledge of marketing at a strategic level gained across their Postgraduate Diploma studies and their ability to apply it. Normally candidates will also have some practical experience in marketing to bring to bear. At the same time, some **background knowledge** is necessary.

Whilst case study methods vary according to the institution and lecturer concerned, a particular model embodying a comprehensive approach is detailed in this *Tutorial Text*.

2 Discussing the case study

Students are strongly advised to conduct in-depth discussion with colleagues on the case study analysis and its issues. This is often accomplished at colleges by the forming of **syndicate groups** of four to six people and the holding of frequent **plenary sessions** where all candidates gather together. In this way, a syndicate member not only hears the view of his or her syndicate, but also those of other syndicates. In this way a much more balanced, integrated and secure approach can be developed. Of course, whilst classroom discussion may be the best for obtaining this sort of feedback, you may benefit from using the Internet if you cannot attend class. How about conducting a discussion with another person using instant messenger?

Although you have the case study four weeks in advance you are not allowed to take all your analysis notes into the exam with you. This prevents the reproduction of preprepared answers. It is useful to work with others on the analysis if possible but the decisions made need to be your own. You must believe in your recommendations and be able to justify them in order to come across credibly in the exam.

3 Practice

The case is a challenging assessment method. Knowledge and understanding are tested but so are your practical skills of analysis and decision-making. Your recommendations must be presented persuasively to influence your audiences of the **examiner** and the **organisation** you are advising.

Like any exam, practice is key to success. In this text, you have three whole CIM cases to work with. The first case Biocatalyst is a 'teaching case'. It walks you through the ten steps of the case process with complete analysis so you can follow the 'thought' process for yourself. Complete the activities and take your time but remember it is the 'process' of case analysis that we are focusing on.

Two further cases are provided for you to take on an increasingly large part of the analysis work and to build your confidence with the process. The first, Signifo, was the subject of the December 2005 exam. It explores how an SME can harness Internet technology to grow its business. Finally you have the chance to work the June 2006 case, based on W H Smith as a well known organisation trying to revive a flagging brand in the competitive retail sector.

Use the materials here to build up a structure for tackling the exam case irrespective of its focus and theme, sector or geographic location. You will find this preparation integrates and consolidates your learning from the other three Postgraduate Diploma papers.

A note on pronouns

On occasions in this *Tutorial Text*, 'he' is used for 'he or she', 'him' for 'him or her' and so forth. Whilst we try to avoid this practice, it is sometimes necessary for reasons of style. No prejudice or stereotyping according to sex is intended or assumed.

Syllabus overview

Strategic Marketing in Practice (Professional Postgraduate Diploma)

Aims and objectives

Marketing has to be firmly rooted in both theory and practice. Practice informs theory and vice versa. Strategic Marketing in Practice is designed to allow participants to put strategic marketing into practice. As the final subject in this qualification, it not only builds on the knowledge and skills developed in all the preceding modules, but also looks for an overall competence in marketing that encompasses all the various subject areas covered in the lower qualification levels. As marketing is constantly evolving, continuously informed by both academic and business research, one of the aims of this module is to explore the latest trends and innovations relevant to marketers who are operating at a strategic level within organisations. One of the other aims is to understand marketing as an activity, which is important in all contexts (profit, not-for-profit, societal, global). It is expected that participants will be able to add value to both their marketing experience and marketing knowledge.

Learning outcomes

Participants will be able to:

■ Identify and critically evaluate marketing issues within various environments, utilising a wide range of marketing techniques, concepts and models.

■ Assess the relevance of, and opportunities presented by, contemporary marketing issues within any given scenario including innovations in marketing.

■ Identify and critically evaluate various options available within given constraints and apply competitive positioning strategies, justifying any decisions taken.

■ Formulate and present a creative, customer-focused and innovative competitive strategy for any given context, incorporate relevant investment decisions, appropriate control aspects and contingency plans.

■ Demonstrate an understanding of the management of marketing activities as part of the implementation of strategic direction, taking into account business intelligence requirements, marketing processes, resources, markets and the company vision.

■ Promote and facilitate the adoption and maintenance of a strong market and customer orientation with measurable marketing metrics.

■ Synthesise various strands of knowledge and skills from the different syllabus modules effectively in developing an effective solution for any given context.

Knowledge and skill requirements

The essential skills assessed as part of this subject are:

- Analysis, interpretation, evaluation and synthesis of information, including the ability to draw conclusions.

- Identification, exploration and evaluation of strategic options.

- Selection and justification of appropriate options using decision criteria.

- Establishing the activities, resources and schedule needed to implement the chosen strategy.

- Managing, implementing, co-ordinating and controlling the strategy.

Participants will be expected to demonstrate their awareness of current issues and an ability to make recommendations for a given context. From time to time CIM will publish a list of trends and innovations to guide tutors and participants in their preparation for assessment. Participants will be expected to read widely in the area of strategic marketing as part of their studies at this level.

Senior Examiner's view of the paper

1 Overview of the area

The case paper is the culmination of all the marketing subjects covered at all levels, but especially the Diploma and the Postgraduate Diploma. For this reason, there is no specific syllabus for this paper. The syllabuses for the other three papers give a clear strategic focus. This type of expertise will be needed to tackle the case study paper. It will not be possible to tackle the case study without a strong grasp of the fundamentals of marketing communications and international marketing. In this sense, for all students, the case study is a culmination of the application of all the marketing knowledge they have gained over several years.

2 The changing focus of the paper

- Marketing as a subject area is undergoing major changes. These changes are taking place as a result of dramatic shifts in technology, demographics, globalisation, systems of production, logistics and ecological issues. In future, therefore, the paper will be designed to reflect more of these contemporary issues in addition to the knowledge base mentioned above.

- The case studies will also be designed to develop strategic marketing issues which can be operationalised and implemented within realistic constraints. It is often forgotten that marketing is not just about positioning and growth, but also about **effectiveness** within **given constraints** within most organisations. These constraints mean that strategies have to be sensibly evaluated and chosen, with hard decisions being made. When particular strategies are chosen, it is clear that the constraints could be many and varied. Constraints, for instance could be financial, organisational (both employee and culture related), marketing (image, size of markets, branding, distribution systems, networks) and, if the organisation is a division of a large entity, headquarter-imposed constraints.

Globalisation

- The rapid changes in technology are far reaching as they are changing the normal paradigms of marketing. The four P's cannot be discussed with certainty. The nature and direction of marketing strategies, necessarily have to take into account the massive computing power available and the advent of business on the Internet. Many multi-nationals have operated globally for decades, but technology is changing the patterns of production and consumption.

- For instance, global brands are available anywhere and production facilities may be located in a myriad of different countries. For smaller companies, the Internet holds the promises and pitfalls of operating in a global arena.

- The introduction of the Euro has meant that Pan-European marketing strategies have to be thought through in a different manner. The changing nature and the growth of south Asian markets has an enormous impact on the marketing strategies of organisations. The nature and strength of the American market is often forgotten in many marketing cases. The case studies will reflect these changes and will embrace many different sectors of industry.

Organisational issues

- When developing marketing strategies it is important that the culture and nature of the organisation is taken into account. Marketing strategies often succeed and fail as a result of inappropriate personnel, inappropriate structures or climates within organisations. Organisations are therefore always striving to create the appropriate structures and develop appropriate cultures to meet the demands of the market place.

- The customer is king and marketing strategists have to place the level of market orientation at the centre of their thinking.

Sustainability

- Marketing literature has for a time long been concerned with growth and market share. It is important that issues surrounding the constraints imposed by the environment are taken into account. The world is facing an enormous challenge in terms of the availability of resources and the needs of the population. In some respects a challenge posed to marketing strategists is the need to consider constraints and responsibility – corporate social responsibility is increasingly a requirement not an option.

Financial issues

- Financial issues will also play a key role in developing strategies.

- A good knowledge of basic financial statements such as profit and loss accounts, balance sheets and cashflow statements is required.

Knowledge of contemporary marketing issues

- Each case is different and will therefore test some knowledge of contemporary issues. Students need to be encouraged to read journal articles pertaining to the case study.

Application of previous knowledge

- The need to apply models for analysis will continue. However, a more critical approach in applying these techniques will be needed. The paper will reflect the need for both academic and practical knowledge as a true marketer needs to have experience of both areas for developing sensible strategies.

Issues of implementation and control

- An awareness of the clear decision-making and implementation strategies will be tested. As will be strategic positioning, innovation and branding in the context of implementation and control

3   Links with other papers

The paper is the culmination of all the knowledge gained at all CIM levels. The foundations laid by the marketing syllabuses underpin this paper. The fundamental underpinning knowledge needed is the ability to undertake strategic analysis. In tutoring and preparing students for this paper, tutors need to be aware of the linkages with other areas and they need to be able to draw from a variety of literature sources in order to enhance and improve their analytic and decision-making skills. In each case there is an emphasis on understanding international issues as well as communications issues.

The examiners are looking for candidates to demonstrate analytical ability, interpretive skills, insight, innovation and creativity in answering questions. They are also looking for candidates to take clear and sensible decisions within the context of the case study. A critical awareness of the specific issues involved, relevant theoretical underpinning, attention to detail, coherence and justification of strategies adopted will also be assessed.

To perform well on the paper, candidates will have to exhibit the following.

■   A need to concentrate on the strategic aspects of marketing underpinned by the necessary detail

■   The ability to identify 'gaps' in the case study and to outline the assumptions made

■   The ability to critically apply relevant models for case analysis

■   The ability to draw and synthesise from any of the diploma subject areas as relevant

■   Concentration on the question set rather than the pre-prepared answer

■   The ability to answer in the report format with comprehensive sentences rather than providing simplistic lists

■   The judicious use of diagrams for illustrative purposes

■   The ability to draw disparate links together and give coherent answers

■   Innovation and creativity in answering the questions

■   Demonstration of practical applications of marketing knowledge

■   Sensible use of time and an ability to plan the answer within the set time

■   A good understanding of the case study set

■   The ability to draw up a comprehensive and convincing marketing plan with accompany costs and schedules

■   The ability to suggest appropriate control mechanisms and contingency plans

Part A

Introducing Case Study

Why a Case Study? 1

Chapter Topic List	
1	What the Case Study is and how it differs from other CIM papers
2	The value of Case Study in the work place
3	Case problems and challenges
4	How to get the most from this *Tutorial Text*
5	CIM's expectations
6	The characteristics of an excellent case candidate and the secret of winning examiner support

1 What the Case Study is and how it differs from other CIM papers

1.1 The final paper for the CIM qualification is the case study. The Case Study paper requires that you **integrate** all your previous studies and it provides a realistic assessment of whether you have acquired the knowledge and skills to tackle a practical marketing challenge in a commercially credible way.

1.2 The case study is distinctly different from other CIM exams, both in terms of its assessment and its syllabus.

1.3 The Examiner can call upon any aspect of the eleven CIM subjects. CIM expects you to be conversant with the breadth and depth of these other papers either through previous studies or on the basis of the exemptions you have been awarded.

1.4 You should **not** attempt to tackle this case study paper until you have studied the other three Postgraduate Diploma papers.

1.5 Case studies represent **real organisations** and describe the marketing challenges they face. Often, cases are also set in real time and so you may well be faced with a very topical issue. In the sample case we are using in the first part of this manual, **Biocatalysts**, the issue was GM products and biotechnology. At the time of the case, GM crop trials were headline news. You will be given management and marketing data in the form of a narrative with various appendices. This may well include financial data.

1.6 You are sent a copy of the exam case study about four weeks prior to the exam date. You then have time to complete your analysis of the case data and to think through your strategic recommendations.

1.7 In the exam room, you will be faced with specific questions, you will be expected to present and justify your decisions.

1.8 You are allowed to take into the exam a limited number of pre-prepared pages of analysis summary. We will say more about how to prepare for these later in this manual.

1.9 There are few short cuts when it comes to tackling a case study and it is a time-consuming exercise, but you will find the process extends your knowledge and improves skills which have immediate relevance to your work.

2 The value of Case Study in the work place

2.1 Case Study is a very **practical** examination. A knowledge of marketing theory on its own will not be sufficient to gain you an exam pass. You have to be able to apply that theory in the context of a real business issue and situation. This means that you must:

(a) Know the framework for developing both strategic marketing and operational marketing plans

(b) Be able to apply the various tools of analysis, recognising and acknowledging the limitations of these where appropriate

(c) Be able to make decisions, in a way which reflects customer needs and be able to justify those decisions

(d) Be able to explain broader implications to the business

(e) Have the skills to present your views and ideas in a convincing way

2.2 Even experienced marketers often pay little more than lip service to the marketing planning process. Faced with the pressure of an impending examination, many candidates are amazed at the depth and quality of strategic thinking possible, even with the limited information supplied in a case. This experience can be a useful benchmark for marketing planning in your own business.

2.3 Some students get concerned about not being expert in the sector of the exam case study. It can seem daunting if you have B2C experience and are suddenly faced with a B2B challenge, like Biocatalysts. This may seem unrealistic and less representative of life in the business world. However, in our experience as consultants, it is a very real reflection of the situations we face. Our expertise is marketing, and the disciplines and concepts of marketing travel well between sectors. If anything, lack of detailed industry or product knowledge makes it easier to avoid the myopia so often characteristic of those who are product focused.

2.4 Besides the chance to practise analysis and decision-making skills, the case study also provides the opportunity further to develop **team-work skills**. Unless you are studying independently, you will probably be tackling the case as part of a formal syndicate or study group. This is an excellent idea as it provides a time efficient way of tackling analysis as well as providing a forum for brainstorming and creative thinking. However, to make a syndicate work, you need to have and use team working skills and be disciplined in how you communicate with other members. Again, these are practical skills highly valued in the workplace.

3 Case problems and challenges

3.1 Case study brings with it its own set of problems and challenges which you need to be aware of before beginning your studies.

3.2 In practice, relatively few candidates fail examinations because of lack of knowledge. **Much more common is a lack of exam technique**. This results in any one of a number of common problems including failing to **manage time** or answer the question set. Similarly, with the Case Study exam, it is often a failure of technique not knowledge which causes exam failure. Exam technique is rather different for a case exam, but none the less requires practice and the development of a wide range of skills already alluded to, from analysis to persuasive communication, skills which you would expect to find in a **competent, practising marketing manager**.

3.3 Exam technique for the case study starts when the exam case is **issued**. Finding enough time for preparation and using that time effectively is all part of case technique. The seeds of success or failure are sown during this important preparation time, so **preparation is key**.

Valuable information

3.4 The exams may seem like a long way off, but it is never too early to start planning for them. Check out the date of your Case Study exam. This will be on the first or second Friday of December or June, but the **exact date should be available on the CIM website**. Calculate back four weeks from this date. This is the latest date the case should be issued to you. By this date, you want to have broadly completed any work on other examination subjects, so you have the maximum time available for the case study. You will need to find about 40 hours preparation time during these weeks. Where will it come from?

- Avoid planning too many events for those pre-exam weekends
- Talk to your employer about taking some study leave
- Book holiday time for study if necessary

3.5 **Using your preparation time well** is the next case challenge. **Sharing the workload** by being part of a study group is to be advised whenever possible. There is no doubt that cracking a case study alone is hard and lonely work, but, whether working alone or as part of a group, you need a timetable and plan of action. In this Tutorial Text, we are going to work through a sample case in detail, showing you what must be done and providing you with a recommended framework, but you will need the self-discipline to apply that to the exam case.

3.6   Some candidates fail to meet the challenge of analysis. They do too little or too much. Both are recipes for failure. Watch out for indications of which trap you are most likely to fall into.

The Too Little Analysis Candidate	The Too Much Analysis Candidate

The Reader. Confuses reading the case with analysis of it. Does not see the importance of analysing appendices and cross referencing findings.	**The Analysis Addict**. Suffers from the complaint we know as **Analysis Paralysis**. The symptoms are fear of decision-making and finding comfort in the safe activity of analysis.
The Too Little Analysis Candidate	The Too Much Analysis Candidate

The Juggler. Typically puts off tackling the analysis till the week before the exam. With so many other things to do, it is easy to not take this paper seriously. Sadly what might seem straightforward and obvious at the first read often proves much more complex after detailed analysis.	**The Detail Fanatic**. It is easy to get hung upon calculations to the third decimal place, or be brought to a halt by inconsistencies in a case. There will be inconsistencies and discrepancies but successful candidates do not let this distract them. They keep focused on the bigger picture, and where necessary, they make assumptions and move on.

3.7   Adequate analysis will ensure you have a sound grasp of the case issues and have the facts and figures needed to support your recommendations and convince the examiner of their commercial credibility.

3.8   **Moving on from analysis to decision-making** is another exam challenge for case students. Analysis **can be comforting**; you are busy doing something and there is almost always something else that could be done. Case tutors tend to despair when, despite all our warnings, a student phones the week of the exam and says 'you know the figures in table 3...'. This candidate has been paralysed by analysis and is unlikely to do very well in the exam. They have failed to move on.

(a)   The examiner does not want to be told to 'choose a profitable segment.' What he/she does want is to be told how to go about choosing a profitable segment, specific advice on the criteria to be applied and the decision framework to be used. If enough data exists, the examiner wants you to apply the criteria and come up with the recommendation of which segment to target.

(b)   Advice which is a generality will not gain marks. 'Set a quantified objective' will not do. You need to set detailed objectives which are underpinned by quantitative measures.

> 'I recommend that an ambitious growth objective is set, with profit reaching £10 million by 2008 (a £4 million increase). I believe this is achievable because:
>
> (i)   The key competitor is tied up in merger talks.
> (ii)   The overall market is forecast to grow by 20% pa.
> (iii)   Our new service level package will provide us a strong competitive advantage'

It is this clarity of advice and strong justification which the examiner will be looking for. You can see how a grasp of the facts and figures can help you.

3.9 Before the examination day, you will need to have a broad picture of the strategic options open to the business and which options you would support in what circumstances.

3.10 The focus and level for this paper can also cause problems. It is a **strategic** level focus, where the emphasis is on helping the organisation to determine:

(a)   Which products and markets to serve
(b)   The competitive strategy likely to be most effective in winning business from these markets
(c)   Which segments of the selected markets to target
(d)   How best to deploy the marketing mix to gain a competitive advantage within these segments
(e)   The implications for the organisation and management
(f)   The challenges of implementation
(g)   Contemporary issues

3.12 **Questions for this paper must be answered in the order set**. Consider mark allocation to ensure you manage your time effectively. Remember that **how** you communicate your answer is critical and that there are two aspects to this.

(a)   **Presentation**, report formats and clear lay out play a key role and make an important first impression.

(b)   The **style and tone** of your work needs to be appropriate to the case role you have been allocated and your arguments need to be persuasive.

3.13 As you work through this *Tutorial Text*, we will help you improve your exam technique and case skills, but it is helpful if you have an honest evaluation of your likely strengths and weaknesses in terms of case exam skills and techniques. Once you have identified your weaknesses, you will be able to take positive steps to tackle them.

3.14 Take time now to identify your strengths and weaknesses against the following.

	Strengths	Weaknesses
Prioritising case and managing the four weeks prior to the exam		
Handling the analysis: ■ Quantitative data ■ Qualitative data		

	Strengths	Weaknesses
Focusing at strategic not tactical level		
Moving on to decision-making		
Making clear decisions		
Organising your thinking		
Presentation and communication		
Managing time in the exam		
Being flexible in the light of additional information		
Using data to justify decisions		

4 How to get the most from this *Tutorial Text*

4.1 Objectives of this *Tutorial Text*

(a)   Provide you with a simple to follow case process

(b)   Ensure you are familiar with the examiner's expectations in terms of level, tone and focus

(c)   Demonstrate a sample case analysed in a step by step process

(d)   Give you the opportunity to practise case technique in the context of past cases prior to the exam to help you build skills and confidence

(e)   Alert you to the most common mistakes made by unsuccessful case students

(f)   Help you review your knowledge and develop the skills needed to apply these tools and frameworks to deliver a coherent and integrated set of plans from the strategic to the operational

(g)   Encourage you to review your presentation and communication skills so that your work has maximum impact

4.2   What this *Tutorial Text* will not do is teach you the tools and frameworks of the other CIM subjects – we assume you have studied these, but in the next chapter we will help you audit that knowledge and identify any gaps.

4.3   This *Tutorial Text* has been developed in three sections,

(a)   Introducing Case Study
(b)   A sample case
(c)   Two further practice cases

4.4   It is tempting to try and speed up the process by missing out sections, in particular the practice cases in section C. We strongly advise you **not** to do this. You cannot pass a case exam simply by reading about the process; you **must** give yourself some hands on practice.

4.5   To get the most out of this *Tutorial Text*, you should use it as a guide through your preparation. We will provide you with signposts to help you assess your progress and will identify places where you might do additional work and practice. It is, however, important to recognise you are learning about the case process. Every case study is different and, like you, we will not know about the sector or industry of the case until the exam month.

4.6 In Section A, we will show you a generic process for tackling a case study. In Section B, we will apply that process to a past CIM Case. In Section C, you will have two more recent CIM exams on which to build your own skills in applying the process.

Time

4.7 Remember when planning your case study preparation that the exam case will be issued four weeks in advance, so you need to have completed your work through this text by then. We recommend you allow:

	Minimum	Maximum	
Part A of this *Tutorial Text*	2 hours	4 hours	Introduction to the subject
Part B	20 hours	40 hours	Guided tour of the case process
Part C	40 per case	60 per case	Individual practice cases: time varies according to the depth you work these
Exam Case preparation	40 hours	60 hours	

5 CIM's expectations

5.1 You will perhaps have already gathered that the case study is treated as something of a jewel in the crown. This final paper is the **last hurdle** to your official recognition as a professionally qualified marketer and it is seen as being the acid test of your commercial credibility.

5.2 In fact **commercial credibility** has, for a number of years, been one of the **key measures** the **examiners have used in assessing case candidates.**

(a) Does the proposed strategy make sense – can it be substantiated from the analysis?
(b) Is the proposal convincing?

5.3 Remember that, for the CIM examiner, the case study is simply a vehicle for assessing your commercial competence. Every six months the scenario changes but the **characteristics CIM are looking for in a successful candidate remain the same.**

(a) Does the candidate **appreciate the context** of the case scenario? Is the strategy realistic in terms of the available resources and are constraints such as time frames recognised?

(b) Is there evidence of an appreciation of the **broader business implications** of proposals in terms of the impact on profitability, the resources and budgets needed for implementation and the effect of any proposed changes on people within the organisation?

(c) Are **plans supported by specific strategies** to ensure implementation and do they incorporate proposals for **measuring performance** and progress.

Action Programme 1

If you have the opportunity, take time to review a marketing plan you have worked on or which has been developed within your organisation. How would you implement it based on the comments above?

5.4 **CIM expect you to spend up to 60 hours preparing for a case examination.** You have plenty of time to present well-thought out and sensible arguments. One acid test of commercial credibility is to ask yourself, 'If you worked for the company in question, would your script be taken seriously?'

Action Programme 2

In the *Sunday Times Business News* there is often a featured company – their situation described and a number of experts asked their views. This is essentially a case study in action. Make a point of looking at these and in particular assess the experts. Who impresses you and why? Which of them would you be prepared to pay as a consultant?

What advice could you give to the business?

5.5 It is easy to get so involved in the case scenario that you forget that the real challenge is to **pass the exam**. You must make certain that you make the right impression. Irrespective of the quality of your strategy your paper tells the examiner a lot about you.

Symptom	What it says about you
Failure to finish the questions	A poor resource manager. The exam task was clear and the resource available predicted
Poor presentation	A careless, unprofessional approach
Lack of quantification in the form of objectives, budgets etc	A fear of financial aspects
Unconvincing arguments	A poor communicator
Too much attention to the detail	A lack of strategic overview

5.6 The examiners are looking only for evidence of the characteristics you would expect in a competent marketing professional. We will be considering these required skills in detail in Chapter 2. Before you move on you might like to spend five minutes thinking through what you would expect these to be.

6 The characteristics of an excellent case candidate and the secret of winning examiner support

6.1 The excellent candidate is well prepared. Case study is a long process and careful preparation helps ensure precious study time is used both efficiently and effectively.

6.2 The best candidates are well organised. They have an action plan which they keep to and where possible they involve other people in the process.

6.3 Their analysis is thorough and is used as a basis for strategy and decision-making, not as an end in its own right.

6.4 The successful candidate presents a script that wins examiner support – building on 3Ps of presentation, perspective and persuasion.

- **Presentation**

  Well written in report format with clear structure. Lots of white space, diagrams and use of colour help to present information quickly and effectively.

The Wall of Words Examiners do not want to be confronted by whole pages of written narrative, unbroken and unstructured – the horror of a wall of words	**Successful scripts** **Structure** Clear headings and sub headings make structure clear **White space and colour** Add interest to draw attention to key points

- **Perspective** is incorporated to ensure the audience is convinced you have thought about the commercial realities

A major above the line communication strategy for a small regional player	x
Acknowledgement of the profit pressure and likely demands of the shareholders	✓
Product development suggested for the firm with limited time or money	x
Product development for the cash-rich player with a dated portfolio	✓

- **Persuasion** is incorporated to ensure the audience is convinced.

I recommend we adopt a differentiated strategy and target European customers first.	In this highly competitive sector a differentiated strategy rolled out across Europe would give us the opportunity to: ■ Win a premium price ■ Reflect the very real buyer behaviour – differences evidenced by our research ■ Learn from each successive launch

6.5 The best candidates know the case well enough to be able to respond flexibly in the exam room changing emphasis, and even strategy, in light of the questions.

Chapter Roundup

- This chapter provided the context for your case study preparations.

    You should now be aware of the characteristics of a good candidate and understand how CIM has positioned the case study examination.

- You should be able to explain to others the value of the case process and identify a list of skills which both the successful case candidate and the experienced marketing practitioner need to demonstrate.

Quick Quiz

1   Case study differs from other CIM exams in two significant ways. What are they? (see paras 1.2, 1.3 and 1.6)

2   How long before the exam day can you expect to receive your case study? (1.6)

3   Case study is a very practical examination. Identify how the examiners might test whether you have the ability to apply the theory in the context of a case study. (2.1)

4   What do we mean if we described a case candidate as suffering from Analysis paralysis? (3.6)

5   Why do students sometimes find it difficult to move on from analysis to decisions? (3.8)

6   How would you describe to someone the focus and level which characterise how CIM has positioned this paper? (3.10)

7   What are the two levels of communication which are critical to the successful case candidate? (3.12)

8   Where will you get a knowledge of the planning tools essential for this paper? (4.2)

9   Identify four ways in which an examiner might assess the commercial credibility of a case candidate. (5.3)

10 How much should you be prepared to invoice the case client for at the end of the examination? (5.4)

11 Identify four ways in which your approach to the exam paper gives the examiner an insight into your performance as a manager. (5.5)

12 What characteristics would you look for in a successful marketer? (5.6)

13 Three P's are important in a successful script. What are they? (6.4)

14 Why is flexibility an important characteristic for the case student and the practising manager? (6.5)

The Tools and Knowledge Needed: a healthcheck

2

1 Key skills

1.1 You have already considered the key skills a marketing manager should have. Our list includes:

Characteristics	Evidence
1 Structured thinking	Uses frameworks and presents data in clear report format
2 Knowledgeable	Working command of the marketer's tools, the confidence to adapt them and understand their limitations
3 Financially aware	Confident to use and include numbers. Clear appreciation that marketing decisions will impact on profitability
4 Analytical	Decisions made on the basis of analysis not hunch
5 Creative	Able to look at problems in a different way, innovative ideas and approaches encouraged
6 Decisive	Criteria for decisions laid out but clear decisions then made – no procrastination: in today's fast moving markets, speed is often of the essence
7 An Implementer	Anyone can write plans, but it takes real skill to implement them from internal marketing plans to contingency plans and timetables. The examiners will be looking for evidence that you can go from paper to action
8 A Resource Manager	Budgets and appreciation of costs is key here. Control measures demonstrate your understanding of the value of resources… and remember the evidence you provide through your own time management

BPP
PROFESSIONAL EDUCATION

2 Knowledge check

Test yourself on the knowledge check questions, without referring to notes or books.

As you work your way through this text, identify and address any knowledge gaps. Keep 'Notes to Self' as a way of ensuring that anything you are unfamiliar with, or need to revise, is dealt with. You do not want to be doing this with the exam case study.

There are nearly 50 questions for you to tackle in the Action Programme below so you need to give yourself time: at least 1 hour if you just going to do a mental Q&A or 2 hours if you intend to make notes. You might find it helps to do a block of 12 questions and then check the feedback.

Action Programme

1   What is the purpose of analysis, and what is the desired outcome?

2   What are the key components of an internal and external corporate or business audit?

3   Name four models the marketer can use during the analysis process. Briefly explain their purpose.

4   What is the role of the vision and mission statements? Distinguish between them.

5   What is planning gap analysis?

6   What are strategic options/business strategies and how might they be evaluated?

7   What competitive positions might a business adopt? What are their implications?

8   Note common methods of consumer and business to business segmentation.

9   What is the Decision Making Unit (DMU) and why is it important to marketers?

10   How can marketing research help in the analysis, planning and control processes?

11   What does the term 'Balanced Scorecard' mean?

12   What are the key components of a marketing information system (MkIS)?

Check your answers with the feedback now if you prefer to tackle this in learning bites.

13   What contexts affect marketing communications?

14   What factors affect customers' purchase decision making?

15   What is the decision making process (DMP)?

16   What types of perceived risk are involved in purchase decisions and how can marketers reduce perceived risk?

17   What internal factors affect communications with an organisation's external audiences?

18   What internal factors influence corporate image and reputation?

19   What models are there for establishing communication objectives?

20   A brand is made up of many parts, both tangible and intangible. What are the components of a brand?

21   How can a brand help to build loyalty?

22   Briefly define the meaning of push, pull and profile communication strategies.

23   How can marketers change attitudes?

24   What does 'share of voice' (SOV) mean?

You might find it helps to check feedback again now.

25   Name three World Institutions that have helped to promote world trade.

26   What are market agreements and what types of agreements are there?

27   What is an economic trading bloc and name three?

28   What do NIC and LDC stand for?

29   What are the currents and cross currents referred to by Porter?

30   What are tariffs?

31   What are Harmonised Tariff System (HTS)?

32   What does high context and low context culture mean?

33   What is critical dissonance, often found in international marketing?

34   What is the process of internationalisation?

35   What direct methods of entry are available to exporters?

36   What are the four dimensions Hofstede uses to describe different national cultural characteristics?

Check your answers with ours at the end of the chapter.

37   Compare and contrast the problems you might encounter managing knowledge in a power culture and a role culture.

38   What are the three key functions of Adair's action centred leadership?

39   Name three styles of leadership and an advantage and disadvantage of each. What are the most reliable sources of leadership power?

40   What five key factors need to be taken into account when designing a team and what are the key issues of managing teams through stages of development?

41   What are typical symptoms of poor motivation and causes of poor motivation? Name and briefly explain three theories of motivation.

42   What two key factors affect an organisation's ability to develop good standards of customer service? How do these and other factors contribute to customer expectations being formed?

43   What is the customer's chain of experience?

44   What broad markets/stakeholders do relationship marketing strategies target?

45   What are the stages people might go through during periods of change?

46   Why would you segment your internal market during management of change and what might these segments be?

47   What are the key factors in effective management of change?

48   Quantitative measures are a very narrow way of measuring organisation performance, what other models of measurement might be more appropriate?

Check your answers with ours at the end of the chapter.

How did you get on?

2.8 Make sure you take the time to review your answers thoroughly and honestly. The run up to a case exam is the wrong time to discover knowledge gaps. None of us knows it all, so don't be surprised if you have identified content you need to brush up on.

2.9 **Make a list of topics for review or revision.** Tick off one or two a week until you are confident with your underpinning knowledge.

Notes to Self

Topics for Review	Deadline date
1	
2	
3	
4	
5	
6	
7	
8	
9	
10	

3 Integrating the Postgraduate Diploma subjects

3.1 The aims and objectives of *Strategic Marketing in Practice* are to convert theory and knowledge into practice. Throughout this *Tutorial Text* and the practice case studies, you will have the opportunity to test your knowledge further and to practise your marketing skills. At each stage, you will be encouraged to use models and techniques on the case study to help you establish the current situation and develop credible solutions.

Introduction to the case study

3.2 Your practical experience will be immensely important in this exercise. If you **treat the case study** as though it was **another project at work** and your **exam preparation** as though you were getting ready for a **presentation to senior management**, then you will have an idea of the level, depth and degree of detail which is needed.

3.3 The case study is a vehicle for the examiners to assess your marketing management competence. It is critical to your success in this paper that you remember that the **problems of the case are not the central focus for the examiner**. Your skills, the processes you go through, and the tools and techniques you use are what are being assessed.

A typical case study

3.4 CIM supplies the examination case in the form of an A4 booklet, printed on both sides of the page. You make a working copy of the exam case for use in preparation. Do not write on your original copy until you are ready to annotate it.

3.5 You will only be allowed to take the original case study into the exam with you and this may be notated. You will want to leave it to the end of your preparation to add the most useful notes to your case study – so **work on a copy**.

3.6 Typically, the CIM case will be 40 to 70 pages long. It will consist of 5 to 10 pages of text followed by appendices. The case study data is likely to include some or all of the following.

- Background and historical data on the company featured
- Corporate and group organisation
- Marketing and sales operations
- Strengths, weaknesses, opportunities and threats (indicative only)
- Market size, segments, competitors, trends
- Environmental factors
- Marketing mix
- Marketing research
- Consolidated accounts (profit and loss, balance sheet)

3.7 As is usual in most management case studies, the CIM case will:

- Include information which is not particularly useful
- Exclude data which you might feel is essential

3.8 This is to test your ability to discern information needs and also to design a marketing research plan and/or improvements to the marketing information system. You are likely to find some anomalies and contradictions in the case study, obliging you to make assumptions. Do not be distracted by these. This is usual and has never caused problems. In reality often it is difficult to obtain information, check its validity or comparability, so the case experience is reflecting real life.

3.9 On the inside front cover of the case you will find **important notes** for candidates, followed by a page **candidate's brief**, which you must of course read thoroughly and have in mind when interpreting the subsequent data in the case itself.

4 Going forward

4.1 In this *Tutorial Text* we are going to show you a number of case studies.

(a) Firstly, Biocatalysts, where we will take you step by step through the process of analysing case material and developing decisions. Biocatalysts is a particularly good teaching case as it remains current and stretches the marketers who think they can throw money at problems. The case will be used to introduce principal concepts and demonstrate key aspects of analysis. Remember the analysis given in examples is not exhaustive and is not the only way to conduct analysis.

(b) The remaining cases will bring you up to date with the latest case studies, provide further examples, give you the opportunity to practise further and allow you to see the variety of industries, companies and problems you will encounter. These cases also provide a reminder that in some industries short, medium and long term can be a matter of months while in others it can be years and that some companies have immediate short term problems while others face the challenge of a longer term vision for the future.

4.2 There are a number of ways you can use the material in this *Tutorial Text*. The **least** effective is to simply turn the pages. Reading other people's analysis will not give you the experience and practice you need when it comes to the exam.

You can work all the cases completely, using our analysis or comments as prompts and feedback: to do this thoroughly will take time and effort, but your reward will be increasing confidence and valuable marketing skills.

Between these two extremes are many variations. You can use Biocatalysts as a guided tour for you to see what is expected and then work the next case in depth.

Think about the time you have available and then use the material in the most appropriate way for you.

Action Programme review

1 The purpose of analysis is to establish the effectiveness of business performance in the environment in which it operates and the business's position in the market. This includes establishing internal strengths and weaknesses of the business and external opportunities and threats offered by market conditions, competition and customer behaviour.

2 The internal audit identifies the strengths and weaknesses of business activities. The components of the internal audit include evaluating the effectiveness of the business's structure, culture, financial performance, people (and management), business operations (processes and technology used), strategic purpose and planning and its market position. The external audit identifies the opportunities and threats in the business environment. The components of the external audit includes evaluating macro factors (PEST) and micro factors (competition, customers, suppliers, distribution etc).

3 Examples of models the marketer can use during the analysis process include:

■ Product life cycle (PLC) – used to establish the stage of the product (eg introduction, growth, maturity, decline) and to provide indicators of investment needs and how the marketer should manage the product (eg heavy competition likely during maturity so differentiation important)

■ Boston matrix (BCG) – used to evaluate products (and SBUs) for their cash generation and cash requirements. Helps the marketer make decisions about investing, harvesting

■ Multifactor matrices – GE matrix used to evaluate business strengths and market attractiveness

■ Porter's Five Forces – provides a framework for identifying the forces that affect the competitive structure of an industry and potential sources of profitability. The marketer is encouraged to consider new entrants into the market and barriers to entry, suppliers and supplier power, buyers and buyer power, potential or actual substitute products and possible unsatisfied needs.

4 The vision and mission statements are important communication statements that inform stakeholders of future intentions and the purpose of the business. The mission clarifies the purpose of the business by communicating what the business does, who for and how. The vision signals future aspirations, for example a future desired position in the market.

5   Planning gap analysis establishes the gap between the forecast of what the business can achieve if it carries on with its current strategies and performance in the predicted market conditions, and its desired corporate goals. The gap is the financial shortfall between forecast and target that will need to be filled by new and/or different strategies and performance.

6   The Ansoff matrix is a very useful model for identifying strategic options/business strategies. These are the broad product market opportunities identified during analysis. The GE matrix is one of the models that might be used to evaluate which options to select.

7   The best known theory on competitive position is Porter's generic competitive strategies. The positions are:

Cost leadership advantage: aims to achieve overall cost leadership being low cost provider requires:

- Cost and efficient objectives
- Tight cost and overhead control
- Pursuit of high value customers only
- Cost minimisation in all areas
- Achieving critical mass
- Achieving economies of scale

Implications

Usually requires high relative market share certainly requires volume
Possibly favourable access to raw materials
Investment up front and heavy investment in latest technology
Continued re-investment to maintain low cost leadership position

Differentiation advantage: aims to create unique offering (something perceived as different from rest) and requires:

- Design or brand image
- Technology
- Features
- Customer service
- Dealer network
- Combination of these to differentiate

Implications

Can preclude high market share if differentiation built on exclusivity
Balance between high costs of providing differentiation and profits
Need for professional marketing skills and ability to attract skilled people
Product engineering and capability in R and D, creativity/innovation
Needs corporate reputation for quality or technological expertise
Needs strong co-operation from channels
Needs strong co-ordination of R & D, marketing
Qualitative measurements

Focus advantage: aims to focus on needs of a particular buyer group, area of product line or geographic market and to do so more efficiently/effectively than competition. Requires:

- Cost leadership
- Differentiation, or
- Both the above

Implications

Vulnerability of niche approach
Doubts regarding profit potential
Implications as covered in cost and differentiation

8   Segmentation methods available to the marketer include:

Geographic: postcode, city, town, village, rural, coastal, county, region, country, continent, climate

Demographic: age, sex, family life cycle, family size, religion, income, occupation, ethnic origin, socio economic group

Behavioural: benefits sought, purchase behaviour, purchase occasion, usage

Psychographic: personality, attitude, lifestyle

Geodemographic: combines geographic and demographic **plus** overlay of psychographic **and** patterns of purchasing behaviour

Business to business: SIC codes, process or product, geographic, size of company, operating variables, circumstances, purchase methods; increasingly DMUs and behavioural factors are used

9   The Decision Making Unit (DMU) is the unit made of those people involved in the decision to buy. It is a model that has become most helpful in organisation buying (although also relevant in some consumer markets). It is important to marketers because it is a useful framework for ensuring that all members of the buying process are identified and their needs addressed.

10 Marketing research can help throughout the analysis, planning and control process.

Marketing research can help during **analysis** by gathering information that establishes the current situation. The business can establish its current position against competitors, customer perceptions and the likely impact of market forces.

Marketing research can help the **planning process** by ensuring decisions are informed. Decisions can be made on customer groups to serve, positioning and the development and design of the marketing mix to ensure efficient and effective use of resources.

Marketing research can help the **control process** in measuring business and marketing effectiveness and performance. This can be done using questionnaires, focus groups etc to ask customers, distribution channels and other stakeholders for their assessment of the business and its marketing mix.

11 The balanced scorecard refers to the linking of objective-setting to measuring performance and is a balance of both quantitative and qualitative measures. Customer feedback and input is an important part of measuring effectiveness as well as measuring business operations at a broader level. Measuring the effectiveness of the organisation in terms of its learning, innovation and continuous improvement is also important.

12   The key components of a marketing information systems are:

Marketing Information System MkIS

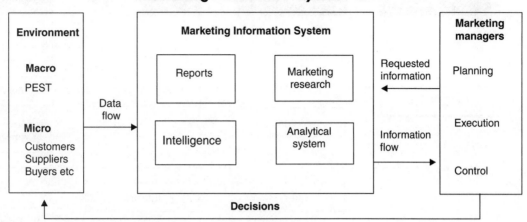

Knowledge check answers for integrated communications issues

13   The external contexts that affect marketing communications include legislative, economic, societal, corporate responsibility, technology (information and communications).

14   Factors that affect customers' purchase decision making include segmentation factors (eg geographic, demographic, behavioural, psychographic), involvement with purchase (high or low involvement), decision making process, wants, needs and motives, attitudes and beliefs.

15   The decision making process (DMP) refers to the process consumers go through when deciding to buy. This process most typically, but not always, is:

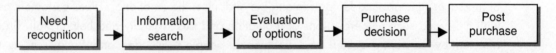

16   Perceived risk involved in purchase decisions include performance, financial, physical, social, ego and time. Marketers can try to reduce perceived risk by providing information, building brand loyalty, guarantees, endorsements, money back/exchange and samples.

17   Internal factors that affect communications with an organisation's external audiences include corporate vision, mission and strategy, culture and ethics, management and leadership style, employee attitudes and behaviour.

18   Internal factors that influence corporate image and reputation include corporate personality (culture, attitudes, values and beliefs) and corporate identity (cues and signals that are real indicators evident in product, place, communications and behaviour).

19   Some of the better known models for establishing communication objectives include:

STAGE	AIDA	ADOPTION	DAGMAR
			Unaware
COGNITIVE		Awareness	Awareness
	Attention		[Comprehension]
	Interest	Interest	
AFFECTIVE	Desire	Evaluation	Conviction
		Trial	
CONATIVE	Action	Adoption	Action

20   A brand is made up of tangible attributes: product components eg reliability, durability and measurable business and marketing mix, and performance e.g. accessibility of place, timeliness of messages. It is also made up of intangible attributes: the emotional values customers associate with the brand such as perceptions of reputation and trust, friendly and helpful staff. Brands are affected by corporate culture and behaviour, people's attitudes and behaviour as well as marketing mix performance.

21   Every purchase is a risk for the customer and they are looking for clues of what they can expect. A successful brand is a very effective way of reassuring customers of quality and reliability and of reducing risk. Providing the organisation continues to deliver what the customer wants and achieve high satisfaction levels, the brand can be very effective in building loyalty.

22   A push strategy is designed to encourage the organisation's channels or outlets to take products. A pull strategy is designed to attract customers into the organisation's channels or outlets. A profile strategy deals with the overall image and positioning of the company.

23   Marketers can change attitudes by changing beliefs, changing order of importance, changing attributes of product or service, changing associations, changing attitudes to comparable products.

24   Share of voice (SOV) refers to the total advertising spend in the market by all advertisers.

Knowledge check answers for international marketing issues

25   World Institutions that have helped to promote world trade are the World Trade Organisation, WTO; International Monetary Fund, IMF: World Bank, IBRD: United Nations Conference on Trade & Development, UNCTAD; Group of 8, G8; OECD.

26   A market agreement is a trading agreement between countries on the exchange goods and broader business operations. The types of agreements are free trade area, customs union, common market, economic union and political union.

27   An economic trading bloc is a group of countries that come together to form a trading area offering favourable conditions to member countries. Examples include APEC (Australia, Brunei, Canada, Chile, China, HK, Indonesia, Japan, South Korea, Malaysia, Mexico, New Zealand, Papua New Guinea, Philippines, Singapore, Taiwan, Thailand, US), Southern Common Market MerCoSur (Argentina, Brazil, Paraguay, Uruguay) as well as NAFTA, EU and ASEAN.

28   NIC stands for Newly Industrialised Country; LDC for Less Developed Country. They are examples of economic stages of development. Other terms include Advanced Industrialised Countries, Newly Emerging Economies, Big Emerging Economies.

29   Currents are primary macro forces affecting competition; cross currents are evolving trends driving international competition to behave differently.

30   Tariffs are rules, duties, rate schedules, regulations of trade. Examples include customs duties (% value of goods), preferential tariff (in certain circumstances eg historical preference arrangements), specific duty (amount per weight, volume etc), countervailing (additional duties levied to offset subsidies granted in exporting country) variable import levies (levies on imported goods costing less than domestic}, temporary surcharges) anti dumping regulations.

31   Harmonised tariff system (HTS) has been developed by importers and exporters to determine the correct classification number for product/service that will cross borders. With HT Schedule B export classification number is same as import number.

32   Extent to which language and communication is diffuse/implicit – high context [culture depends heavily on external environment, situation, non verbal behaviour in creating and interpreting communications] specific/explicit – low context [environment less important, non verbal behaviour often ignored, directness/bluntness valued, ambiguity disliked]). Example of a country with a high context culture is Japan and of a country with a low context culture is Switzerland.

33   Criticality dissonance refers to respondents transforming/disguising responses for fear of how responses will be used.

34   The process of internationalisation is when an organisation moves from indirect exporting to a global business, from being uninterested in exporting through to formulating long term strategies for international markets. An organisation might move through various stages including domestic marketing, experimental involvement, active involvement and finally to committed involvement.

35   Direct methods of entry include agents, distributors, licensing, franchise, JVs, SBAs, wholly owned subsidiaries.

36   Hofstede's four dimensions used to describe different national cultural characteristics are:

■   Power distance – the extent of equality between management and subordinates
■   Uncertainty avoidance – attitudes to risk and change
■   Masculinity – traditional definition of sex roles
■   Individualism – extent of recognition of the individual or the group

Knowledge check answers for managing marketing performance

37   *Power culture*

■   Information gathering processes are unlikely to be formalised and the informality may result in lack of connections between separate pieces of information being made

■   There is unlikely to be formalised analysis of information allowing interpretation and objective evaluation

■   There may be selectivity and filtering of information by those closest to the central figure if this information does not fit with desired ambitions regardless of outcomes

Role culture

- Bureaucratic processes and systems would result in a lack of selectivity in information gathering

- Information gathered would tend to be over complicated and may involve many unnecessary procedures

- Information gathering would be a slow process and may result in information being out of date before its significance is recognised.

38
- Building the team
- Achieving the task
- Developing the individual

39
- *Autocratic*

   Advantage: decisive, get things done quickly

   Disadvantage: Employees lack motivation, commitment

- *Democratic*

   Advantage: Employees involved so motivated, committed

   Disadvantage: can slow down decision making, and action taking

- *Lassez faire*

   Advantage: Employees take responsibility for decisions, fully involved

   Disadvantage: Manager can lose control, can become chaotic

Most reliable sources of leadership power

- Respect and trust
- Teams

40   *Key factors in designing a team*

- Assessing team knowledge and skills – audit
- Deciding on structure of team – balance of functional (technical) skills and team role skills
- Ensuring team size is appropriate to the task and managing and controlling the team
- Functional roles
- Team roles

Key issues of managing teams through stages

Getting the team to performing stage as soon as possible.

- Forming – design introductions and activities that allow people to get to know each other quickly – focus on positive aspects

- Storming – allow differences to emerge, encourage people to deal openly with conflicts – focus on strengths people bring to the team

- Norming – formalisation of tasks and procedures/processes for carrying out work– focus on skills that are needed

- Performing – clarify objectives and tasks, planning and implementation – focus on performance and recognition for achievement of objectives and contribution to team effectiveness

41 *Symptoms of poor motivation*

- Absenteeism, possibly symptoms of stress

- Reduction in productivity and a refusal or reluctance to do anything except the minimum that has to be done

- Behaviour reflecting non co-operation, withdrawal, aggression or defensiveness

- Increasing complaints about work loads, routines and conditions and opposition to any new ideas, changes etc.

- Poor time keeping and a general sense of "it can wait"

- Increasing staff turnover

Causes of poor motivation include:

- Poor management – eg criticism, threats, lack of interest in employees

- Poor working conditions

- Poor pay – inequality in pay structures or bonuses

- Poor communications – lack of information, one way

- Poor training and development – people poorly equipped to carrying out their tasks and responsibilities

- Unreasonable targets and lack of explanation of expected standards

Three theories of motivation

Maslow's hierarchy of needs

A description of human needs that should be satisfied if people are to be happy and work productively. These needs are arranged in order of importance with the most basic needs physiological, security and safety being the most important and social, esteem and self fulfilment less important until basic needs are met. The hierarchy indicates that basic needs must be satisfied before other needs higher up the hierarchy become important and can be satisfied. If circumstances change and basic needs are under threat eg. changes in the work place or redundancy, the higher needs become less important again and lower needs become important and are defended.

Hertzberg's hygiene factors and motivators

- Hygiene factors are lower order needs which do not motivate but can cause dissatisfaction if they are missing or wrong eg salary, status, working conditions, working relationships, supervision, job security

- Motivators are higher order needs that do motivate but can only do so (or it is difficult for them to do so) if lower order needs are missing eg achievement, recognition, job interest, responsibility, advancement

McClelland's three motivation needs

- Need for achievement – being able to take responsibility for design and development that results in successful outcomes

- Need for power – to have control and influence over events and people

- Need for affiliation – to have relationships and belong

Vroom's theory of motivation

Expectancy theory – people are motivated by what they value and different people value different things. The reward must be easily understood and be perceived as of value to the person receiving the reward, so for example one person might be motivated by promotion, another by recognition for achievement. People will interpret the route to achieving the reward differently and therefore will put in the effort and performance they believe appropriate to achieving the reward.

McGregor's theory X and theory Y

- Theory X assumptions – people are lazy, untrustworthy and dislike work or responsibilities. They therefore require high levels of supervision and control and will be uninterested in the organisation or its activities.

- Theory Y assumptions – people are willing to work and interested in work and personal development and growth. They are prepared to take responsibility, are self disciplined and creative. They require minimal levels of supervision and control and should be encouraged to use their creativity in improving the organisation's performance

42
- Organisation culture – its values, beliefs and attitudes to people
- People – their attitudes to customers and what represents good customer service

You may also have included eg training, management skills, which are relevant and important, but customer service cannot be developed without the right culture and people.

What contributes to customer expectations being formed?

- The organisation's own activities which include promotional activities, product/service performance and reputation

- Other influences such as press coverage, customer's own experience and background (of the industry, other companies, products etc.)

43 The customer's chain of experience or moments of truth is the process the customer goes through when buying from an organisation. It involves the people and processes the customer comes in contact with and the nature of that contact. This process can be a poor or good experience.

44 Seven markets:

- Customers
- Referral markets
- Employees (internal)
- Distribution channels
- Suppliers
- Prospective employees
- Influence eg institutions such as financial, trade, education

45
- Shock and denial – difficulty in coming to terms with changes and refusal to accept what is happening

- There can be a danger of hopelessness and a feeling of being out of control

- Acceptance – providing they are supported

- Experimentation – to allow understanding and to build confidence

- Commitment – engaging in work routines again and focusing on goals

46　Internal markets need to be understood if resistance to change and perceptions of threats are to be minimised. Change can only be successful if the people responsible for managing and implementing change accept the change.

To understand these internal markets we need to understand how people perceive the intended changes and what affect it will have on them. Different people will be affected in different ways and if we know how they are affected we can set up support systems and training programmes that will help them come to terms with the change and take on their new tasks and responsibilities.

47
- Clear objective of the purpose of change
- Planning for change
- Communications – internal marketing
- Segmenting internal market
- Involving people – project and design teams
- Training and development
- Support systems

48　**Balanced scorecard –** Traditional measures have tended to focus on finances and volumes and draw on historical data to enable measurement to take place. The balanced scorecard goes beyond purely financial measures and attempts to evaluate, anticipate and inform the measurement process on current and future drivers of performance.

The balanced scorecard takes a far broader and more comprehensive approach to measurement and informing strategic development and embraces strategic as well as tactical performance.

- Customer – satisfaction, loyalty, value, complaints, repeat purchases

- Financial performance – Profitability, ROCE etc.

- Culture (innovation and learning) – NPD success, idea generation/transference into success

- People and management – staff morale, staff contribution to new ideas, staff turnover, absence,

It requires effective information systems, essential for measurement. The balanced scorecard objectives are derived from a top-down process driven by the mission, vision, corporate objectives and strategies, which are translated into tangible objectives and measures. The measures represent a balance between external measures for shareholders and customers, and internal measures of critical business processes, innovation, learning and growth. The measures are balanced between the outcome measures (past performance) and measures that drive future performance. The scorecard is balanced between objective easily-quantified outcome measures and subjective, somewhat-judgemental performance drivers of the outcome measures.

Part B

The Sample Case: Biocatalysts

BPP
PROFESSIONAL EDUCATION

The process case:
the ten steps
3

Chapter Topic List	
1	The Case Study process
2	What are we trying to achieve? The output of the case process
3	Working the maxi case
4	Introducing the ten-step case process
5	Team work and the importance of your own work
6	Introducing the Biocatalysts case

1 The Case Study process

1.1 In the previous chapter, you checked your underpinning knowledge from the other diploma papers. This provides you with critical foundations on which you can build your case skills.

1.2 However, **knowledge** is not enough to ensure a pass in this paper. You must **understand** the **process and techniques of case study** and have the practical **skills** to apply those recognised frameworks to the case scenario in a commercially credible way.

1.3 It is important that you recognise there are two aspects to the case or planning process:

(a) The stages that make up the process

(b) The outcomes of those stages recorded as decisions and actions in the planning document and supported by analysis

1.4 The stages you will go through will be familiar.

- Where are we now? analysis and auditing
- Where do we want to be? corporate decisions
- What are the implications? organisation and management
- How are we going to get there? marketing decisions and implementation policy
- How do we ensure we arrive? control decisions

BPP
PROFESSIONAL EDUCATION

2 What are we trying to achieve? The output of the case process

2.1 Professionally qualified and trained marketing managers can make a significant difference to an organisation, given a chance! In today's competitive environment, few organisations have the luxury of not needing marketing. Marketing is not just a matter of survival: the challenge for marketers is to ensure their organisations are successful.

2.2 To do this requires using to the organisation's advantage the analytical and decision making skills we have been discussing.

2.3 Too often business success is measured by today's bottom line: 'how much profit did we make this quarter'. It is short sighted, often short-term, and usually tactical. Sooner or later the lack of strategic perspective and customer focus will result in the organisation failing. You have seen in your studies how a focus on short-term profit often erodes long term shareholder value.

2.4 The desired outcome for business is success and this can be measured as profitability (in the broader sense if a non profit making organisation shareholder aspirations).

2.5 Success can be short-term survival, medium-term market development and/or long-term achievement of the vision. It should also be measured as:

- High customer satisfaction, value and loyalty
- High employee morale, productivity and loyalty
- Excellent and strong working partnerships with other stakeholders
- A strong and powerful brand
- A strong and distinct competitive position in the market
- Continued sustainable growth

2.6 The desired outcome of the case study process is the same but with an important additional goal, that of passing the exam.

2.7 Your goal is therefore to ensure you add value by **providing insights** into the current situation through your analysis and, through **effective decision making**, develop **credible** plans that will ensure organisation success. As has already been mentioned, exam technique is as important as your analysis and decision skills. The exam is your opportunity to demonstrate to the examiner your ability to communicate convincingly and persuasively.

2.8 To ensure you adopt a professional approach to working the case study process the following steps are recommended.

3 Working the maxi case

3.1 Tackling the case study requires a systematic and methodical approach. The amount of data you will be presented with provides you with ample opportunity to get lost. The skill you are required to demonstrate is that you can **sort**, **organise** and **analyse** this data, **disregarding** data that cannot help in the planning process and converting the rest into marketing intelligence that is useful for decision making purposes. (In other words, what good marketing professionals should be doing for their organisations.) One of the factors that separates successful managers and companies from the mediocre is their ability to gather, analyse and use information to inform decision making.

3.2 The case is first analysed to determine the **current situation**. Decisions that will solve problems and ensure success can then be made. Each stage of the planning process is covered by working the case study.

(a) **Where are we now?** Analysis tools and models are used to help establish current business performance and market conditions.

(b) **Where do we want to be?** Corporate decisions: tools and models are used to help determine future direction.

(c) **What are the implications?** Organisation and management implementation issues.

(d) **How can we get there?** Marketing decisions: further planning techniques and frameworks help to formulate marketing plans.

(e) **How can we ensure we arrive?** Control models and techniques are used to establish standards and measure and evaluate performance.

3.3 One of the difficulties experienced by many students, and by many marketing managers in their jobs, is that of knowing where to start and how to proceed. The following framework has proved to be a successful way of working the case study and ensuring a methodical and systematic approach that delivers results.

3.4 It is worth remembering that in reality a company does not stop what it is doing to start an audit. There is often a logical sequence of events but **many activities can and would be carried out simultaneously**. However, for simplicity, we will be describing the auditing process step by step.

3.5 We will give guidelines on how long each stage may take. These are guidelines only as everyone works at a different pace and each case study is different, but the guidelines will help give you some idea of the time you should allocate.

4 Introducing the ten-step process

Ten-step process

You can see how the three other papers combine to create this ten step process.

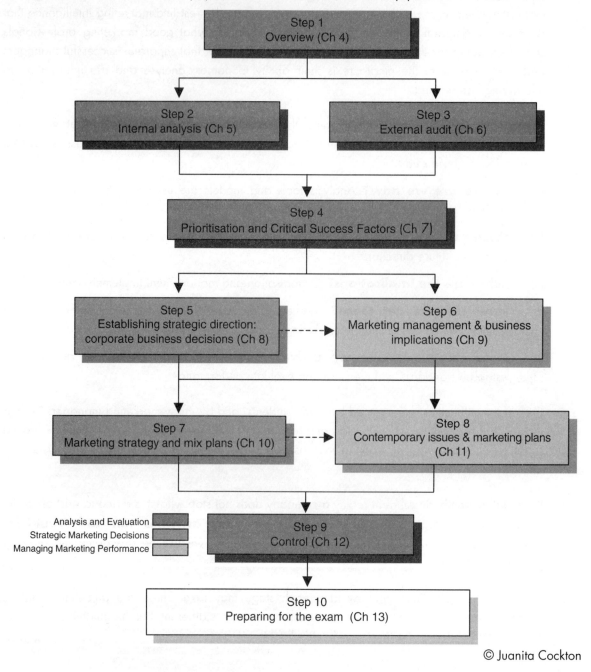

© Juanita Cockton

Step 1. Overview

4.1 When you are ready to start work on the practice case study, wait until you have a quiet hour or two and **read it through once and put aside.** When you have more time, read through again and this time begin making notes. tidied

(a) **Consider your focus: who are you, (position, responsibility) and what have you been asked to do?** You are getting into **role** and tackling the case study from the perspective of either an employee of the company or an external consultant to the company. This initial acknowledgement of your task is important. From time to time, when perhaps you are overwhelmed by the case, you can return to your initial thoughts to focus you on the important issues.

(b) **Begin your marketing research shopping list** – start identifying information gaps. **Identifying information needs from the start is important**. You will add to this list throughout your working of the case study, but sometimes the obvious gaps you notice at the beginning can be forgotten as you make assumptions and start thinking of your information gaps in terms of the strategies you are developing.

(c) **Establish an overview of the industry you are operating in.** You may not work in this industry, and need to get a sense of what is going on. Experience shows that those who do work in the industry that the case study is set in are often more disadvantaged than those who do not because of the wealth of information they have. These people have to be very disciplined at staying within the case study and not allowing their knowledge to distract them from the scenario set.

(d) **Establish, broadly, the challenges facing the organisation.** At this stage you are not trying to identify every problem and challenge but rather impressions of what this organisation is doing. You will sort out the available information into themes or functional areas like sales information or competitor data.

> Step 1 will take you approximately 2 – 4 hours.

Step 2. Analysis: internal audit

4.2 Now the real work starts.

(a) From this point on, your analysis will be in **depth** and needs to produce results of value.

(b) The intention is to establish the **organisation's strengths and weaknesses**.

  (i) The case material and appendices are analysed to determine, where possible, what the organisation is doing well and where it is under performing.

  (ii) A structured approach ensures we do not miss anything out that could impact on current and future performance.

  (iii) We will need to do this in detail for the marketing activity and then for the whole business. This requires the marketer to put on the hats of others in the organisation to review the financial, HR or operational dimensions of the business.

Step 3. Analysis: external audit

4.3 This step requires analysis of both the micro and macro external environments.

(a) **Micro**: The market, its dynamics, customers, competitors, suppliers, distributors and stakeholders.

(b) **Macro**: Analysis of the external environment provides insights into the macro factors affecting the business (eg PEST). We may have information on market conditions such as value of markets, stage of growth, maturity or decline or be left with no more than assumptions and impressions.

BPP
PROFESSIONAL EDUCATION

> Steps 2 and 3 will take you approximately 23 – 33 hours. (It is difficult to break up the hours between the steps sometimes because of a lot of the information on the organisation is required for two or more steps. You may break some of this work down by sharing analysis with others if you are working in syndicate groups.

Step 4. Critical Success Factors (CSFs) and summarising analysis

4.4 (a) The danger of the analysis process is that you end up with long lists of strengths, weaknesses, opportunities and threats which, while useful, will not focus management on what needs to be done. Before moving on to decisions, the final stage of analysis is to **prioritise our findings**. There are models and techniques to help do this.

The conclusion of analysis will be to prioritise the factors that are critical to the organisation's success and implementation of plans. Each CSF will have key issues associated with it. Terminology varies between companies. You may have your own terminology.

> Step 4, a review of your analysis, prioritising and reaching conclusions, will take you approximately 1 – 2 hours. In case study, this step is particularly important as the case questions are often drawn from these critical success factors. Additionally you will be making a start on your analysis summary.

(b) Having worked through the process of analysis you are now able to summarise this analysis for taking into the exam room. You will not finish this task until you have worked through decisions. You need to complete a draft, possibly a second draft of your analysis and then move on to consider decisions. The reason for this is that by thinking through solutions you are better able to refine your summary in light of possible decisions.

> The analysis summary will take longer but you will work at this over a period of time while considering decisions.

Step 5. Corporate/business decisions

4.5 We now move into the decision stage. From this point on, you are exploring alternative solutions/ideas in **outline only**. You will not be developing written out plans.

(a) The future desired, and/or necessary, direction of the organisation is determined and expressed through a **vision** (if applicable) and the **mission statements**. **Corporate objectives** are considered if none exist, and the planning gap established. These will have to be quantified.

(b) **Strategic options**, identified during analysis, are reviewed and criteria to evaluate them are developed. Selected strategies must be able to fill the identified gap.

(c) The strategic role of the **brand** and **competitive positioning** will need to be agreed.

> Step 5 will take you approximately 4 – 5 hours.

Step 6. Marketing management & implications

4.6 Often an important aspect of developing and implementing a new strategic direction is the organisation's **current business operations**. The plans may require a **change in, for example, organisational culture or structure.** There may be implications for managing the brand strategically or improving international management.

Management and leadership style, and the management of marketing teams, influence the way in which an organisation delivers value and satisfaction to stakeholders. They are part of the challenge of improving overall organisation performance.

Your internal analysis will have established what changes need to take place if the business is to succeed, for example adopting a marketing orientation, and at this stage you need to consider the issues.

> Step 6 will take you approximately 2 – 3 hours.

Step 7. Marketing strategy & marketing mix plans

4.7 When decisions on strategic direction have been considered, and product market opportunities and competitive positioning have been evaluated, decisions on **marketing objectives and strategy** can be explored. These decisions include **translating the business objective** into a **marketing objective**, segmenting markets identified, and selecting those segments the organisation should target, the positioning statement and targeting strategy. This work needs to be done for every selected business strategy.

Marketing mix plans (the 7Ps) are considered to implement marketing strategies. These plans must be consistent with the organisation's overall competitive positioning and help to differentiate the business in a meaningful way.

Marketing research needs are identified.

> Step 7 will take you approximately 6 – 8 hours.

Step 8. Contemporary issues and management plans

4.8 Each case study has its own specific issues, for example customer relationship management, supply chain management, brand building and so on. Most decisions, whether strategic or operational, will have an impact on the wider business and its management. Training in customer relationship management is an example. In Step 8, we identify what these issues are, and evaluate solutions to address them.

Step 9. Implementation and control

4.9 Solutions are only of value if they are implemented, and thoughts about not only who must do what but how you will sell the strategy to senior manager colleagues and teams will earn you credit with the examiners. Control is an important factor in successful marketing planning. It ensures we use our resources effectively and that plans will be delivered on time. Budgets, timetable of activities, targets and measurement all need to be considered and agreed.

> Step 9 will take you approximately 1 – 3 hours.

Step 10. Managing your material and preparing for exam

4.10 Review solutions for consistency. Have the business, financial and human resource implications been considered and included? Are solutions consistent and integrated?

For your analysis and solutions to be sound, consistent and credible, you need to organise yourself to manage large amounts of paperwork. We provide tips on how you can organise your case materials and yourself. This will become your checklist to help you manage your case material.

> Step 10 will take you approximately 1 – 2 hours.

Action Programme 1

Look ahead to when you are taking the exam. During the four weeks leading up to the exam, where are you going to find those 40 – 60 hours? Do a timetable and identify who you need to negotiate time with (employer, partner, friends etc). Log that time and protect it; it will be essential to passing. As you work through the practice cases, note how long each step takes and amend your time planner as appropriate.

5 Team work and the importance of your own work

5.1 All those sitting the case study are required to work the case study individually and 'own' the analysis and decision. There are of course tempting short cuts 'a quick read through will do it', someone else's analysis etc and these are usually a short cut to failure.

5.2 There are a number of problems in working the case study alone, all of which can be overcome. It is important to acknowledge these early on and have strategies for overcoming them. For example, a lack of confidence that you are interpreting material correctly or a personal weakness in some area – for marketers the favourite is financial! – are problems that can be resolved, and any good marketing professional will review and utilise appropriate resources available.

5.3 Some students of case study work in groups, either in colleges or companies.

(a) There are obvious advantages of group work, particularly that of dealing with the quantity of work that will be generated. More importantly, if you have the advantage of working in a team, make sure you recognise and play to each others' strengths. In particular try not to duplicate effort. Work can be broken down between team members to make the most of the limited time available. Good communications, participation and support are vital ingredients for effective teams.

(b) However you cannot abdicate responsibility for the analysis. You need to review work generated by others, understand it and agree with it. You cannot simply **use** it, as you will not be able to adapt your thinking in the light of extra information in the exam room.

5.4 Whilst it is perfectly acceptable to share analysis in this way, you cannot work together after you move onto decision making. The examiner does **not** want group answers, each student repeating the same mission and strategy.

5.5 If you do not have the advantage of a case study group, you can still 'recruit' help in the form of, for example, a marketing manager who develops marketing plans, a financial manager who understands ratios. Do not expect these people to do the job for you. The intention is to gain their support in helping you understand and interpret, or develop a new skill that will enable you to analyse the case material and arrive at credible solutions.

5.6 Particularly during the practice case, there will never be a better opportunity for you to experiment and learn by applying the theory in a practice case scenario.

6 Introducing the Biocatalysts case

Action Programme 2

To finish this chapter, we would like you to familiarise yourself with a typical CIM case – Biocatalysts.

You will need to find half an hour and some peace and quiet. You need to read through the narrative to get a feel for the case. This can be quite a quick read through, rather as you would a magazine article. **Do not** at this stage try and do anything with the material you are certainly not about to make any decisions at this stage. Treat it like a story. What is the setting, the business context? Can you spot the contemporary issues? Who are the key players and what is happening?

Only read to page 16, the end of the narrative.

Tutor Tip

To make it easier for you to refer to the case material as we work though the next section, you may find it helpful to copy or remove the case pages so you have a separate case document to work on. You need to work a case study in the time frame it is set in – so don't add up to date information.

CASE STUDY
TEACHING CASE

Strategic Marketing in Practice

Biocatalysts Ltd

This case was used in a past CIM examination

BPP
PROFESSIONAL EDUCATION

Candidate's Brief

You are Joseph Mendes, a Marketing Consultant of some repute, who has been appointed by Biocatalysts Ltd. to undertake the development of a marketing report, prior to undertaking a strategic exercise. Joseph's previous work ranged across many industry sectors, but he had not undertaken any work in the biotechnology sector. He is keen to understand the sector and the company profile before he develops any plans. As part of his internal and external research he has prepared the following report. At the end of this report are appendices relating to the main body of the text. Joseph has prepared this report for the Managing Director, Stewart North, ready for the next Board Meeting.

Important Notice

This case material is based on an actual organisation and existing market conditions. However, the information provided and some real data has been disguised to preserve commercial confidentiality.

Candidates are strictly instructed not to contact Biocatalysts Ltd. or other companies in the industry. Additional information will be provided at the time of the examination. Further copies may be obtained from The Chartered Institute of Marketing, Moor Hall, Cookham, Maidenhead, Berkshire, SL6 9QH, UK.

Report by Joseph Mendes

Private and Confidential

Biocatalysts Ltd.

Background Information

Biocatalysts Ltd. is an independent speciality enzyme company operating in the low-volume high-value end of the industrial enzyme market. Biocatalysts Ltd. started trading in 1986 as a wholly owned subsidiary of Grand Metropolitan. It occupies a large factory unit in Wales. Following a management buyout from Shell Ventures in 1991 it is now a totally independent company.

The company is one of the UK's leading developers and producers of speciality enzymes (natural proteins which act as catalysts). It produces enzymes in one of two ways. For the food and textile industries it produces speciality enzyme complexes complete with additional chemicals which are sold for moderate margins; for the diagnostic and pharmaceutical industries it has developed its own unique enzymes which it manufactures and sells at higher margins. The development costs of these higher margin manufactured enzymes are paid for by the profit and from Government/European grants which the company has so far been successful in obtaining.

Biocatalysts' customers use enzymes to improve the efficiency and convenience of processes in a wide range of industries, including flavour production, brewing, fruit processing, baking and textiles (enzyme fading of denim jeans). In addition, some of the higher value enzymes currently available and under development are used in diagnostic kits, used for testing for abnormalities in humans and pharmaceutical manufacturing. This broad spread of markets and wide geographical sales gives the company a balanced portfolio with steady, profitable income streams.

Enzyme Technology

Enzymes are nature's biological catalysts. They accelerate rates of reaction, helping the conversion of substances into other types of chemicals more useful for industrial processes. In the commercial arena, enzymes have two broad kinds of use: process aids and active ingredients. Enzymes have been used by mankind for at least 4,000 years in the form of natural microbial fermentations for making beer, wine, cheese and many other products. However, the recognition of enzymes as entities only began 170 years ago. In Germany, in 1830, a paper was first published which discussed the isolation of an enzyme which could convert starch to sugar. The substance is now known as amylase. By 1860, many other enzymes were recognised and isolated. Among these were pepsin, polyphenol oxidase, peroxidase and invertase.

Refined enzymes were first commercialised by a Danish chemist, Christian Hansen, who produced the first isolated preparation of rennet from dried calf stomach. It was primarily used for cheesemaking and the original company Danisco is currently a major supplier of enzymes for the dairy industry. In 1900, a Japanese scientist, Takamine, developed a fermentation for the industrial production of a fungal amylase for making soy sauce and other oriental seasonings. The Takamine laboratories are now part of CPC International. The early 1900s saw the development of a heat stable bacterial amylase in textile production, used for 'desizing', a process used to remove starch from fibres after completion of the weaving process. The use of this enzyme stopped the use of dilute acid in water which often damaged the textiles. Otto Rohm, a German chemist, developed the use of digestive enzymes for leather curing. Before this, dog and pigeon excrement was used for curing leather. The Rohm company is now a significant player in the enzyme business (see Appendix 1.).

After the Second World War, enzyme technology received a boost from developments which were taking place in the antibiotic field. The method of growing cultures in liquid media was adopted by the enzyme industry, increasing yields and lowering costs.

In essence, enzymes can be described as the catalysts of the living world. For example, enzymes are responsible for nearly all the metabolic processes taking place in the human body. These processes have been harnessed by industry so that a small amount of enzyme can enable a large scale chemical reaction to take place under very mild conditions. This increases the cost effectiveness of the production of a number of food and other products (see Appendix 2.). The enzymes are highly specific in their catalytic power and their ability to transform chemicals.

Page 4 of Biocatalysts

World Market

The estimated sales of value of the sales of industrial enzymes was estimated to be in excess of $1 billion in 1994 – Figure 1. (about $1.3 billion in 1997). Sales growth is increasing in the more speciality applications sectors ('other' in pie chart) and tending to level out in the commodity sectors (Figure 2.). Technical research, however, continues to develop large volume enzymes for existing applications such as paper and pulp, textiles and in the longer term, waste treatment and environmental maintenance. Industry analysts (Enzymology, 1998), see the market for enzymes expanding from $1.7 billion to $2 billion by 2005. The Russian market is as yet undeveloped, owing to economic pressures, but could be large. The Chinese market is quite large, especially for food enzymes, but again this market is relatively 'closed' and full scale Western style processes have yet to be adopted.

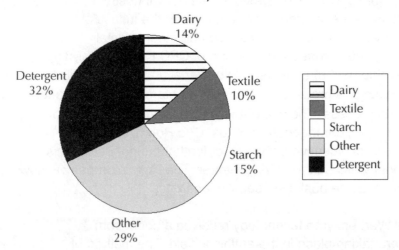

Distribution of Enzyme Sales (1994)

Dairy 14%
Detergent 32%
Textile 10%
Starch 15%
Other 29%

Legend: Dairy, Textile, Starch, Other, Detergent

Figure 1.

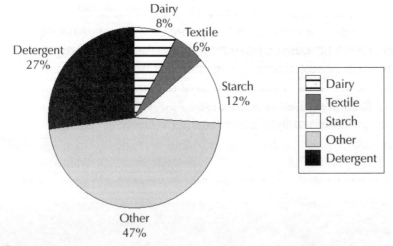

Forecast Distribution of Enzyme Sales (2005)

Dairy 8%
Textile 6%
Detergent 27%
Starch 12%
Other 47%

Legend: Dairy, Textile, Starch, Other, Detergent

Figure 2.

There are now approximately 12 major global producers, with increasingly distinct separate product ranges between them. This number of key producers helps to reduce total domination by any one of them. At the same time, it shows a trend towards a reduction in customer choice of producer for a particular enzyme type. Approximately another 60 companies produce substantial amounts of a smaller range, and there are around 400 companies producing industrial quantities of a very limited range of enzyme types. Essentially all these companies are selling into a global market. For many companies that are producing enzymes in 15-40m^3 fermenters, difficult decisions have to be made regarding economies of scale. For them it is a classic case of 'being stuck in the middle'. They will either have to expand their facilities (costly) to compete with the market leaders or specialise in niche markets where they may not have the requisite expertise (see Figure 3.).

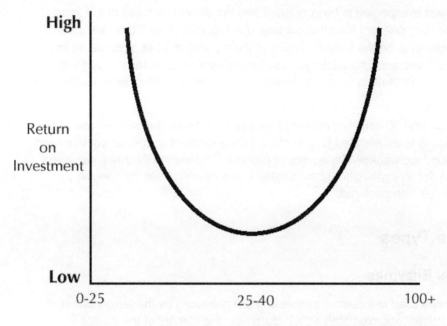

Figure 3.

The estimates show that nearly 60 per cent of the total world supply of enzymes is prepared in Europe, mainly within the European Community. Another 15 per cent is produced in North America, primarily 'in-house' for large scale application by large scale processors of natural materials, such as alcohol and sugar syrup. Numerous Japanese companies produce many, but not all, types of commercial enzyme, contributing another 12 to 15 per cent of the world production. The Russian and the Chinese markets probably use a wide variety of enzyme types for indigenous use, but are not yet active commercially. It is likely that their active entry into the market will expand the global market by a considerable degree.

Enzyme Types and Sources

Proteinases are a very important enzyme type because of their enormous use in the dairy (coagulants) and detergent industries, and collectively they account for approximately 40 per cent of all enzyme sales. Carbohydrases which are used in baking, brewing, distilling, starch and textiles, form the second largest group. The conventional approach to the division of world sales of enzymes is to assess them by their sectoral applications (detergent, dairy, textiles, starch, and 'other') as shown in Figure 1. It is useful to examine the 'other' section as it helps to determine the possible composition of the future markets. Currently the 12 main sectors under the 'other' market are alcohol, animal feed, baking, chemical biotransformations, diagnostics, fats and oils, flavour, fruit and wine, leather, protein (other than for milk coagulation, flavour and detergents), pulp and paper and water. These are the sectors that Biocatalysts Ltd. mainly operates in. Growth in these areas is expected to be very rapid and the division of sales in the year 2005 will be very different from that portrayed in Figure 1. This 'other' sector is likely collectively to be the largest section of the enzyme market, accounting for over 47% of the sales. This sector is expected to exceed $500 million worth of sales by 2005, accounting for approximately 70% of the growth of all industrial enzymes.

Out of the original 30 common enzyme types used in 1983, the number used has doubled, owing to accelerated Research and Development in both universities and biotechnology companies. The advent of Genetic Engineering Techniques, (see Appendix 3. for an explanation) has created many opportunities for specific enzymes to be manufactured.

Enzyme Types

Microbial Enzymes

Most enzymes used in industrial processing are produced by the fermentation of micro-organisms (approximately 90%). Currently, the identity of the source microbe is very important in the assessment of permitted use for food processing in most countries. The use of genetically modified organisms in the production of enzymes means that these have to be approved by food agencies, as 'novel' foods are supposedly created. These then have to be tested differently for approval. All information has to be open and transparent. In many cases too, a new enzyme preparation is likely to have a different compositional spectrum from the one produced in the traditional manner, with differing side activities. It could be that critical components of the customer's process were not identified when GMOs (Genetically Modified Organisms) were used. In some cases some side activities may well be absent, even if critical. Therefore in any new development, the customer has to be kept aware of the changes. For instance, previously all insulin (for diabetics) originated from pigs, with an enzyme used to convert the insulin to human insulin. A by-product from this process was sold cheaply for leather curing. As a result of the use of biotechnology, 50% of human insulin is now produced directly by fermentation and does not contain the by-product enzyme. This has meant that the by-product, used in the leather industry, has now become the *main product,* increasing the costs of leather curing. The advent of the new technology has created considerable problems in that industry sector. Nonetheless, producers are using sophisticated purification and recovery techniques to build up stocks of enzymes. These stock levels can pose problems, depending on supply/demand situations. Production changes usually take 6 weeks to implement and different applications may need differing purity standards. For many bulk produced enzymes, such as the ones used in detergents, dairy, starch and textiles, the systems produce enzymes continuously and the prices are effectively half those of about ten years ago.

Plant Enzymes

These include proteases such as papain, bromelain and ficin, enzymes of cereals and soya beans and the more specialised enzymes from citrus fruits. Increased supplies of plant enzyme are very dependent on growth cycles, climate, new long-term suppliers and world political and agricultural policies. This area is particularly ripe for the use of GMOs. The shortage of papain in recent years has been a good example of these particular issues affecting this market.

Animal Enzymes

These include pancreatic, lipases and proteinases, pepsins, pregastric esterases and rennets. These can be produced as ultra-refined entities or in bulk. The supply and demand of these enzymes depends on food and agricultural policies which control the numbers of livestock available for slaughter. Owing to viral and other problems such as BSE[1], there is a need for potential purchasers to take considerable safety measures. Consumers too are becoming more aware of the end products they consume. Owing to this, companies are increasingly purchasing enzymes that have been produced microbially or through genetic engineering processes. There is also an increasing demand for producing kosher certified enzymes for food production (see Appendix 4.).

---

1   BSE stands for Bovine Spongiform Encephalopathy, passed on to humans through ingestion of beef products which contain the disease. Humans suffer Creutzfeldt-Jakob Disease (CJD), leading to brain deterioration and death. Currently in the UK no-one is sure of the extent or prevalence of this disease in the general population. It is possible that the disease is prevalent in many other developed countries.

Page 8 of Biocatalysts

Factors Customers Need to Consider when Purchasing Enzymes for Industrial Processes

For companies purchasing enzymes, it is important that they get a clear indication of how specific the chemical reactions are, the optimum level of acidity or alkalinity (pH) at which the enzymes perform, and the temperature range of performance. Activators and inhibitors are also of vital importance, as certain food processes need enzymes to be 'switched off' at the end of a particular process. Currently research is directed at producing molecules which can do this safely in food production, as it can be difficult to 'switch off' enzymes easily (enzymes often catalyse reactions, and continue to be effective until another chemical which stops the reactivity is introduced). Customers need to have similar analytical techniques to those used by the suppliers, so that the strength of an enzyme is clearly understood by both parties. The other key factors which purchasers take into consideration are availability with consistency in quality and activity in a particular enzyme type, together with a track record for safety. A supplier who is prepared to disseminate information actively on new and current developments is not only educating the customer (and potential customers), but possibly offering new and better processing methods. Finally price is always an issue and suppliers are required to establish enzyme purity and activity levels which are consistent with the price set.

Bulk enzymes are being produced more and more from GMOs (Genetically Modified Organisms) mainly by two European companies and one US company, Gist Brocades, Novo Nordisk and Genencor. Japan is weak in bulk enzyme production but strong in speciality enzymes, particularly for medical diagnostics. Its exports of bulk enzymes to Europe and the USA are consequently relatively low, but beginning to grow. In the UK, Biocatalysts Ltd., Rhone-Poulenc, Biozyme and Genzyme (the last two, diagnostics only) are the manufacturers of speciality enzymes. The research leading to this method of production has cost millions of dollars, with much of the development work taking place in the 1980s. The costs of developing GMO production for new enzymes range from tens to hundreds of thousands of dollars. Many, but not all speciality enzymes will be produced increasingly by GMOs, and will be cheaper and purer.

Non-GMO trade is expected to continue for some time. There are certain food manufacturers who will not use GMO produced enzymes, owing to the 'bad' publicity received in general by GMOs (see Appendices 3. and 4.). 'Other' processes justify the need for the 'side' (extra) activities of bulk enzymes, made traditionally for efficient performance. GMO produced enzymes do not contain side activities which are usually vital for the optimum performance of enzymes within the food industry. Companies like Biocatalysts Ltd. are in the market to purchase these enzymes, from which they can reprocess some of the enzymes they need.

Biocatalysts' Place in the Enzyme Industry

Biocatalysts Ltd. is rather special in that it offers a full technical service to present and potential customers, including giving clients access to a database of non-competing enzymes available commercially. As part of this service, Biocatalysts Ltd. offers valid cost comparisons between products whose performance is measured on different scales, as there is no internationally accepted scale. Enzymes, for instance, can be produced in different strengths, offering different levels of activity.

The pricing ranges reflect these differences; however, consumers may only be aware of prices and not strength and efficacy. In this sense, Biocatalysts Ltd. attempts to provide a high level of technical support to its customers. Biocatalysts Ltd. sells its products (see Appendix 9.) into the following markets:

Food

Many parts of the food industry use enzymes, mainly as processing aids. Examples include baking, brewing, protein modification, fruit processing and flavour production. Most bulk enzymes, as produced by the big manufacturers, are usable in many food processes but are not optimum for each particular process. Biocatalysts Ltd. specialises in producing optimum performing products for the food industry, which outperform (in function and price) the competing bulk enzymes. Examples of this are specific enzymes for apple and pear juice extraction, as opposed to using just one enzyme for both types of fruit.

Textiles

Most stone washed denim jeans are now enzyme washed. This is almost a commodity business, where a small percentage of a large market can be readily picked up by supplying special blends of enzymes and chemicals that produce specific types of styles of faded jeans. As faded jeans are going out of fashion, this is not seen as a long-term business, but this sector generates very useful short-term margins.

Diagnostics

All babies born in developed countries are tested for a genetic disorder, PKU (phenylketonurea). A test involving the Biocatalysts enzyme Phenylalanine Dehydrogenase can be undertaken in minutes, replacing a slow labour-intensive method of detecting phenylalanine in the blood. Twenty-four million tests are done every year. Biocatalysts Ltd. is the only producer of this enzyme. Quanatase and ICN have received FDA (Food and Drug Administration) approval in the USA for this system. This means that the growth will now be very rapid over the next few years. The margins are good in this area. Customers are often tied into this market as, once a kit has been approved, they are very loath to change any of the components.

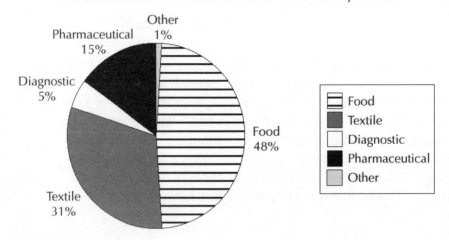

Market Breakdown of Sales for 1997 for Biocatalysts Ltd.

Figure 4.

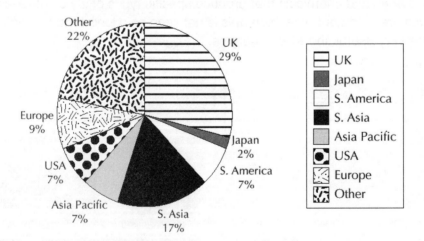

Biocatalysts Ltd. Geographical Sales for 1997

Figure 5.

Figures 4. and 5. show the market and geographical breakdown of the main areas of sales for Biocatalysts Ltd.

Customer Focus

Biocatalysts Ltd is unique amongst the world's enzyme companies. Its willingness to supply custom-tailored products for its clients means that the whole company focus is directed towards customers, attempting to provide total customer satisfaction. This customer focus has resulted in Biocatalysts Ltd. growing at more than twice the industry average over the past ten years. The company has many exclusive agreements with blue-chip companies around the world, who value the product and technical services that Biocatalysts Ltd. provides. Small- and medium-sized companies are also offered a competing range of services. Biocatalysts Ltd. does not make or sell high-volume commodity enzymes, such as those used in the detergent or starch processing industries. They operate in selected parts of the enzyme market where their technical support and willingness to work with customers on a one-to-one basis is highly valued. These enzyme sectors usually require, not single enzyme entities, but enzyme complexes, where the ratios of each of the components are crucial to the efficacy of the whole enzyme product and the customer's process. Biocatalysts Ltd. does not believe in the customers 'making do' with compromise enzyme products, just because that is the way they came off the fermenter. In order to be more customer focused, the fermentation for the manufacture of Biocatalysts is sub-contracted out. This allows for more flexibility and a focus on investment on enzyme technology, not in capital intensive massive stainless steel vats for large batches of production.

Research and Development

Much of the Research and Development programme is focused on the development of new enzymes and enzyme complexes, mainly identified by the customers. New application ideas and opportunities for the current range of blended enzymes are identified from contacts with clients. The development of these is mainly handled by technical sales staff (see Appendix 5.). Sales of current products (or variants of current products) for these new applications, accounts for much of the short-term growth in sales. Biocatalysts Ltd. has many allegiances with leading UK universities, where most of the basic research into new enzymes is carried out (see Figure 6.). This allows the company to focus its in-house scientists on the needs of its customers and keeping fully up-to-date with the latest developments in bio-research.

R&D Cycle/Sales Cycle

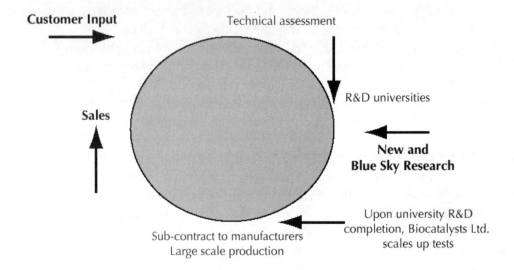

Production

The production plant and laboratory take up around 8,000 square feet of a modern factory unit. The plant includes equipment for liquid and powder blending, fermentation (small scale) and filtration and pilot chromatographic purification and drying. Large scale fermentation is contracted out. The intention of the company is to continue sub-contracting fermentation as there is general over-capacity in the marketplace and to continue investing in downstream processing equipment. Additional investment of around £1 million would be needed to carry out all fermentation in-house, covering all the volume forecasts for the next five years.

The laboratory has all the necessary technical equipment, which is fully depreciated and can still function for at least a further five years. Quality control tests are carried out in-house on all incoming materials and finished products. The company has received the ISO 9000[2] accreditation. The factory is not fully utilised and it is estimated that sales could double with small additions to the existing plant and by employing one or two more production personnel. Batch sizes are flexible and most stock is kept as raw materials or work in progress to maximise flexibility.

---

2   ISO 9000 stands for Quality Accreditation of processes and products on a worldwide basis.

Marketing

The sales and marketing for the company is carried out by 5 people (see organisation chart in Appendix 5.), including the Managing Director. This team looks at the possibilities for new product development and sets out the long-term strategy for the company. The three active sales staff are either home or office based and they spend 80 per cent of their time on sales. The products are sold all around the world and 70 per cent of the products are exported. Most of the exports are generated by agents or distributors who often carry a range of imported products in their portfolio. Biocatalysts Ltd. has a presence in 35 countries. The sales team in the UK supports the agents in the other countries. Agents are used extensively by Biocatalysts Ltd. as their products can be classified as mainly being business to business. The use of agents is not without its problems, as in many cases the range of products offered by Biocatalysts Ltd. may form just a small amount of a particular agent's product portfolio. Unlike selling other products, the agents in the enzyme business need constant updating. The biggest issue facing the company therefore is the quality of the agents and the way they undertake sales. For example, Biocatalysts Ltd. has an enzyme for olive oil processing, so that yields can be increased. In Italy, there are numerous family farms with small olive oil processors. In this instance the agent needs to know something about that sector and also needs to 'educate' the farmers. In order to improve the sales focus, the company is now looking to recruit an agent who actually sells olive oil processing equipment to the farmers. Biocatalysts Ltd. produces a newsletter every six months. This is sent to all its distributors and customers and helps to update them on the current Research and Development activities of the company and any further developments in their current products.

As price is often an issue with many buyers, it is important to Biocatalysts Ltd. that it has the following factors in place:

a. The right agent, i.e. an agent who understands the different sectors well.

b. An agent who is working efficiently and effectively.

c. That the agent is selling the 'right' product.

The last issue of selling the 'right' product is very important, as enzymes come in differing strengths, and often customers may choose one brand over another simply on price, without realising the efficacy of the product(s). The agents are on a 5 per cent commission. Agents are a useful way of expanding the market, but Biocatalysts Ltd. is aware that there is no substitute for having its own sales marketing staff in the marketplace. However, the sales need to take off considerably before the company can justify recruiting another marketer. Most agents are difficult to control and the company relies a lot on their market research and knowledge of country specific issues. Agents mainly carry a range of products which they sell into different markets. Their motivation is often financial and they are therefore more willing to sell products which may offer greater returns. In many cases, they may not be adept at gauging incipient markets in enzymes. Currently therefore the quality of the agents is clearly an issue. Each year the company pays for all its agents to come for a few days' training sessions at the company headquarters. However, not all the agents attend these sessions. The training is particularly important as the markets have narrowed and niche markets require a greater degree of customer focus.

Marketing Issues

Targeting

It is important that Biocatalysts Ltd. develops a marketing strategy for the new products it introduces into the marketplace. One particular strategy could be the way in which innovators are targeted and then followed through with the early adopters. This strategy requires a sustained and expensive marketing effort. The other way in which markets could be opened up would be to bring in a big end-user from the outset, so that application trials could be carried out on an exclusive basis. This would probably mean lower margins, but guaranteed sales and income. More generally exhibitions and mailshots play an important part in the company's targeting strategy. The exhibitions also provide a forum for discussion for the agents. Targeting users is important if marketing effort is not to be dissipated. In order to target effectively, a considerable amount of market research needs to be undertaken for each country. This is costly and difficult, as the statistics and secondary information for many countries can be quite poor.

Web Site

Many biotechnology based companies offer excellent web sites which are both educational and interactive. Currently Biocatalysts Ltd. does not have a web site (but it does have an email address) and is looking to develop a fully interactive site, which can be used for both the agents as well as potential and existing customers. An added benefit would also be good links with its suppliers and the university R&D teams, providing them with updates on product availability, trialling results and scale-up problems or successes. However, the development of such a site will need resourcing and ongoing commitment with regular updating.

Pricing

Enzymes usually form a small part of most customers' product costs. The reliability of the product and service from the supplier is usually more important to customers than finding the cheapest source. In addition, alternative enzyme supplies cannot be identified from paper cost studies. The only way to find out whether an enzyme works and if it is cost-effective is to undertake a trial production run. If potential cost savings are small, many food manufacturers will be unwilling to do the test runs. Pricing therefore can be complex and needs to be customised according to the needs of the customers' product and process costs.

The Future

Food is arguably the most important product of consumption for the average person. Food is vital for sustaining life. At the same time it can be, certainly in well-developed economies and the wealthier sections of communities in most countries, a significant symbol of culture and refinement. The marketing of GMOs presents a new challenge in marketing communications. Currently many companies producing GMOs advertise discreetly. However, many companies, such as Monsanto, have created a very powerful web site devoted to the subject. There are many arguments about risks and benefits to the consumer and the need for open debate, whereas many pressure groups such as Friends of the Earth question the ethics of the production of GMOs in general. The whole debate is now out in the open and many newspaper articles are devoted to the subject. Given the sensitive nature of food and the adverse publicity generated by the BSE crisis, it is important to consider in a rational manner the main communication and advertising strategies that GMO producers could possibly adopt. In this respect Biocatalysts Ltd. has been open in its discussions on the subject (see Appendix 3.). In some instances, GMOs are likely to have positive benefits for the consumer, especially in the production of rennet or porcine based enzymes which would then be granted 'kosher' status as they are not animal derived (see Appendix 4.). This would then provide Biocatalysts Ltd. with a positive positioning strategy in niche markets. Most companies in this sector are likely to be considering effective ways of developing their communications strategies, so that the customers and downline consumers have a clear and rational picture of the issues involved.

Page 16 of Biocatalysts

Summary

Biocatalysts Ltd. has a range of different business markets with a 'near commodity' business in textiles, which needs little or no R&D. The 'New Technology' business is mainly in the food market and represents 50 per cent of the sales (see Figure 4.). The diagnostics (hi-tech) side of the business accounts for 10 per cent of the sales, but the margins are above average, as high development costs have to be met. The company is growing at 20 per cent per annum at a conservative estimate (see Appendix 6.). Biocatalysts Ltd. is generally quite well prepared for the advent of the Euro (see Appendix 7.). It is clear that there is considerable market potential within the enzyme industry; however, the advent of new genetic engineering techniques and the growth of new applications create their own marketing problems. Biocatalysts Ltd. has to consider how well it can grow into being an important, but respected, niche player in the marketplace.

Appendix 1.

Some Competitor Profiles

As described in the text, the enzyme business is quite complex and fragmented; nonetheless it is useful to consider some of the other companies in the business.

Some Suppliers of Enzymes for Biocatalysts Ltd.

Supplier	Country	Supplier	Country
Alko	Finland	Grinsted Products	Denmark
Amano Int.	Japan (UK)	Kyowa Hakko Europe	Germany
Biocatalysts Ltd.	UK	Larbus S. A.	Spain
Biopole	France	Meito Sangyo	Japan
Biocon (part of ICI Quest)	Ireland	Miles Laboratories	USA
Biozyme	UK	**Novo Nordisk**	**Denmark**
Boehringer	Germany	Oriental Yeast	Japan
Boll	France	Recordati	Italy
Calbiochem	USA	Rohm	Germany
Cultor	Finland	Rhone-Poulenc-ABM Brewing	France
Dafa S. A.	France	SAF-ISIS	France
E. Merck	Germany	Sigma Chemicals	USA
Fluka	Switzerland	Solvay Enzymes GmbH	Germany
Genencor International	**USA (Finland)**	Stern Enzymes GmbH	Germany
Genzyme	USA (UK)	Toyo Jozo	Japan
Girona S. A.	Spain	Viobin Corporation	USA
Gist Brocades	**The Netherlands**	Worthington	USA

Despite many companies producing enzymes, the market as a whole is dominated by three major suppliers: Novo Nordisk (50% of the world enzyme sales) with Gist Brocades and Genencor International having substantial market shares (together around 25%).

Japanese Companies

The Japanese companies tend to be complex with the enzyme business 'hidden' amongst the general shareholding. Also it is worth remembering that a lot of Japanese enzyme production is food related and is produced by 'surface' fermentation, giving poorer yields than their European counterparts.

Nagase & Co. Ltd.

Figures for 1997	US Dollars
Net Sales (Total Trading Transactions)	4,608,766
Dyestuffs	414,301
Chemicals	1,714,671
Plastics	1,590,662
Electronic systems and materials	745,078
Healthcare and others	144,054
Net income	45,839
Net income per share	0.30
At Year End:	
Total assets	2,664,674
Shareholders' equity	958,217

Nagase has a subsidiary which is called Nagase Biochemical Sales Co. Ltd.

Amano Pharmaceuticals Co. Ltd.

With subsidiaries in Europe (Amano Enzymes Europe Ltd., Milton Keynes, UK) and the USA (Amano Enzyme USA Co. Ltd., Lombard, Illinois).

The company calls itself the 'World No. 1 Speciality Enzyme Producer Founded in 1899'. The company also produces Kosher certified enzymes.

Employees: 420, Products: 400, Patents: 50, Turnover: $92m.

Amano Sales Breakdown

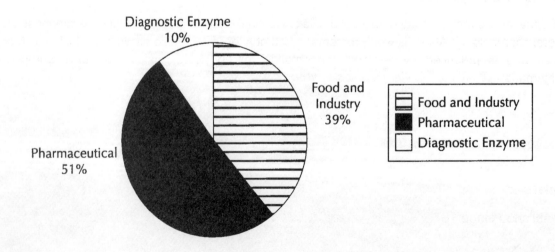

Pharmaceutical Enzyme Area

Business Unit	Products
Digestive Enzymes	Regular type (Amylase, Protease, Lipase, Cellulase), Speciality type (Lactase, ∝-Galactosidase).
Anti-inflammation	Microbial protease (Crystalline protease).
Chiral Synthesis	Lipase, Esterase.
Others	OTC Medicines.

Food Industry Enzyme Area

Amano is focused on the production of speciality enzymes, with worldwide acceptance for food processing.

Business Unit	Application
Baking	Bread, Crackers.
Protein Hydrolysis	Flavour, Functionality, Dietary needs,
Fats/Oils	Hypo-allergenicity.
Starch Processing	Flavour, Functionality.
Brewing	Glucose, Maltose, Maltotriose, Isomaltose
	Oligosaccharides, Cyclodextrin.
	Japanese Sake Wine, Beer, Spirits.

The diagnostic area is growing and Amano are actively seeking new enzymes to improve the effective detection of diseases.

Tests	Items
Substrate determination	Glucose, Cholesterol, Triglyceride, Bilirubin, Free fatty acids, Others. (Used for health checks and individuals with cholesterol problems).

Key European and US Based Companies

Rohm

Produces high quality enzymes for baking and other food uses.

Danisco

Established since 1872. Food ingredients, sweeteners. Sales DKK 25 billion.

Novo Nordisk

Novo Nordisk's two core business areas are healthcare and enzymes.
Novo Nordisk has about half of the world market for industrial enzymes. The enzyme business employs 3,000 people worldwide.

Key Strengths

A large company with a good R&D facility; internationally based with regional and local business development centres. The regional centres are based as follows:

Europe, Middle East and Africa	Paris, France
North America	Franklinton, NC, USA
Latin America	Curitiba, Brazil
Asia Pacific	Hong Kong, China

These RBDCs ensure that markets receive customer service matched to their own specific regional characteristics. They give Novo Nordisk the flexibility to adapt to local conditions and needs.

Financial Statement for the First Nine Months of 1998 (Unaudited)

	1998	1997	% Change
Net turnover	2,053	1,938	6
Operating income	422	346	22
Net financials	16	15	6
Income before tax	438	361	21
Tax	153	131	17
Net income	285	230	24
Employees at end of period	14,770	13,916	6
Earnings per share of DKK 10	3.82	3.09	24

Report on Enzyme Business (EB) Alone

EB sales rose by 1% in the first nine months of 1998. The modest sales increase is due in particular to a decrease in sales of technical enzymes. The market for industrial enzymes continues to be negatively affected by two factors. Firstly the situation in Asia has hit sales of industrial enzymes harder than previously expected and, as a result, sales in the region, including the textile area, are approximately 13% lower than in the same period last year. Around half of the decrease is due to weaker currency exchange rates in the region. Secondly, the value of the market for enzymes for the textile industry has decreased significantly as a result of a considerable decline in the number of blue jeans sales towards darker garments. Sales to the textile industry are thus 38% lower than last year. Exclusive of sales to Asia and to the textile industry, enzyme sales in the first nine months of 1998 increased 7% compared with the same period last year.

Against this background, the world market for industrial enzymes in 1998 is now expected to remain at the same level as in 1997. This also applies to Novo Nordisk's sales of industrial enzymes. It is anticipated that the financial impact of the reduced sales expectations will be countered by outgoing productivity improvements and cost-cutting measures in EB.

Biozyme

Established in 1971. The company is based in the UK and the USA.

Genzyme

This company is one of the oldest in biotechnology and was formed in 1981. The company is based in Cambridge, Massachusetts. It is mainly a healthcare company with much of the enzyme production developed for tissue repairs, therapeutics, surgical use and diagnostic tests. For the first nine months of 1998 its turnover was around $490 million. The revenues reflected higher sales of Ceredase and Cerezyme enzymes.

Gist Brocades

This company has worldwide operations, but the headquarters are in the Netherlands. The company is the world's largest antibiotics manufacturer within the pharmaceuticals sector. In the food market it offers baking, cheese and yoghurt making, brewing and fruit juice processing. Flavours and flavouring are another growth area. The company also produces enzymes for the animal feed industry, so that pigs and poultry can digest their foods better. Gist Brocades is very active in the growth markets of Asia and Latin America. The company is very active on the patent front. It employs 7,000 people in 70 locations, in more than 25 countries. Three quarters of all employees are based outside the Netherlands.

Genencor International

The company is based in the USA. It is the world's largest company dedicated exclusively to industrial biotechnology; through its new genetic engineering techniques, it develops and markets enzymes and biocatalysts. The company has hundreds of successful products, with more than 1,200 worldwide patents. The company has a $60 million facility in Stanford, California. Genencor International revolutionised industrial biotechnology with the world's first industrial-scale recombinant enzyme, and the world's first protein engineered industrial enzyme. These innovations introduced state-of-the-art genetic engineering techniques into the industry.

Appendix 2.

Major Industrial Enzyme Types and their Applications

Enzyme	Application
∝-Amylase	Corn syrup, baking, textile sizing, paper sizing, fuel alcohol, detergents, lens cleaners.
β-Amylase (Malt)	Beer, fuel alcohol, starch, production of maltose.
D-amino oxidase	Purification of L-amino acids.
Glucoamylase	Corn syrup, fuel alcohol.
Catalase	Egg desugaring, fruit and vegetable conservation.
Cellulase	Wine, beer, fruit juice.
Glucose isomerase	High-fructose corn syrup.
Glucose oxidase	Egg desugaring, oxygen scavenging, fruit conservation.
Invertase	Invert sugar.
Lactase	Dairy.
Lipase	Cheese.
Amyglycosidase	Starch, conversion of dextrin to glucose.
Proteinase	Protein (milk), production of peptone (soya bean), pre-treatment of soy sauce.
Papain, Proteases	Protein in beer, removal of turbidity, tenderising meat, cheese and flavour production.
Rennin (chymosin), Rennet	Casein, production of cheese.
Pectinase	Pectin, production of fruit juice, wine, beer, coffee.
Triacylglycerol lipase	Lipid, hydrolysis of lipid, flavour modification, cheese ripening, fat degradation.
Penicillin acylase	Semisynthetic Penicillin based antibiotics.
Pregrastric esterase	Cheese, butter flavour.
Protease	Detergents, lens cleaners.
Trypsin	Leather tanning.
β-Fructofuranosidase	Sucrose, production of inverted sugar.
β-Galactosidase	Lactose, decomposition of lactose.
α-Galactosidase	Raffinose, decomposition of raffinose.
Anthocyanase	Anthocyan, decolouration of anthocyan.
AMP deaminase	Adenylic acid, production of L-amino acid.
Aminoacylase	D, L-Acyl amino acid, production of L-amino acid.
Lysozyme	Egg white, against chlostridia in cheesemaking.
Lactase	Yeast, production of lactic acid, decomposition of whey.
Invertase	Sucrose, dethickening in chocolate.

Many industrial enzymes have multiple applications, as it makes good business sense to extend the utility of a product to as many applications as possible. This helps to increase sales and reduces the risk of having only a few customers. For example, alpha-amylase (α-amylase) is used in corn syrup manufacture, baking, textile sizing, fuel alcohol production, and an alkaline type, alpha-amylase, is used in detergents and lens cleaners.

Microbial Enzymes Legally used in Food Processing in the USA

Amyloglucosidase from *Rhizopuis juveus*	Degradation of gelatinised starch into constituent sugars, in the production of distilled spirits and vinegar.
Carbohydrase from *Aspergillus ginger*	a. Removal of visceral mass (bellies) in clam processing. b. Aid in the removal of shell in shrimp processing.
Carbohydrase from *Rhizopus, oryzae*	Production of dextrose from starch.
Catalase from *Micrococcus lysodeiktus*	Destruction and removal of hydrogen peroxides in the manufacture of cheese.
Esterase (lipase) from Mucor miehei	Flavour enhancer in cheeses, fats and oils and milk products.
α-Galactosidase from *Mortierella vinaceae* (free enzyme and mycelia) (var. raffinoseutilizer)	Production of sucrose from sugar beets, by addition as mycelia pellets to the molasses to increase the yield of sucrose, followed by the removal of the spent mycellial pellets by filtration.
Microbial Milk-clotting Enzymes from *Endothia parasitica bacillus cereus* *Mucor pusillus (var. Lindt)* *Mucor miehei (var. Cooney et emerson)*	Production of cheese if the enzyme was obtained from a pure culture fermentation.

Appendix 3.

Genetically Modified Organisms

Genetically Modified Organisms (GMOs) are increasingly being used for production. There are many reasons for this, but some of them are:

- The production of purer enzyme products.

- Shorter development times for new enzymes.

- Reduced usage of energy and raw materials for production, giving reduced production costs.

In some countries, such as Germany, there has been a large negative reaction to GMOs. From a scientific point of view, there are no reasons for this negative response to GMOs for enzyme production.

The actual enzyme itself is identical whether it is produced by a wild-type organism or a GMO, although the end product will contain less impurities. In addition, enzyme end products do not contain any of the production organism, so the consumer is not exposed in any way to the GMO.

At the moment Biocatalysts Ltd. does not manufacture any of its enzyme products from GMOs, although it has several new enzymes under development which will be produced from GMOs. The first enzyme produced from a GMO is expected to be launched in 1999. These new enzymes will need special literature and a clear policy for communications.

The use of GMOs for enzyme production appears to offer many benefits; they are safe and efficient to use, and pose no threat to the environment or the end consumer. The end-user should be fully informed and promotional literature

should clearly state if the production organism is a GMO.

Diagram to Show how GMOs are Made:

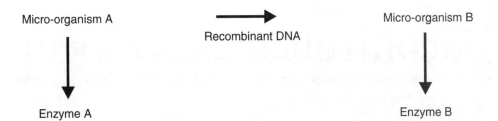

Micro-organism A

Recombinant DNA

Micro-organism B

Enzyme A

Enzyme B

A Typical Genetic Engineering Sequence

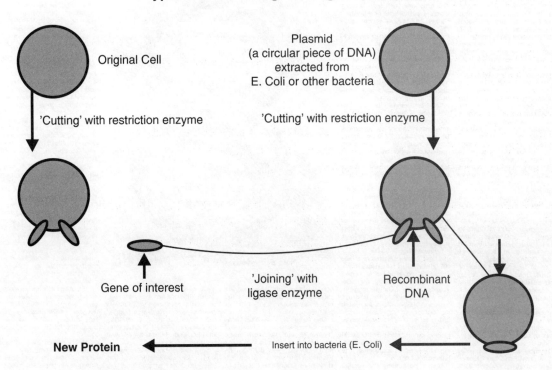

Original Cell

Plasmid
(a circular piece of DNA)
extracted from
E. Coli or other bacteria

'Cutting' with restriction enzyme

'Cutting' with restriction enzyme

Gene of interest

'Joining' with
ligase enzyme

Recombinant
DNA

New Protein

Insert into bacteria (E. Coli)

One trait of living matter is the presence of genes which give a particular set of individual characteristics. Most genes are composed of DNA – deoxyribonucleic acid – which has a highly complex structure, consisting of the amino acids adenine, cytosine, guanine and thiamine, together with carbohydrate and phosphate groups, arranged in the pattern of a double helix. It is now possible to extract a fragment of DNA from one living micro-organism (e.g. plant cell or bacterial culture) to a second micro-organism, thus altering the genetic properties of the second micro-organism. Popularly this process is known as 'genetic engineering'; a technically more accurate term is 'recombinant DNA research'.

The new altered micro-organism would naturally possess different characteristics and, more importantly, different enzymatic properties. The way in which this is achieved is shown above.

FINANCIAL TIMES   WEEKEND FEBRUARY 13/FEBRUARY 14 1999

COMMENT & ANALYSIS

An uncontrolled experiment

Concern is growing over genetically modified food, write **Clive Cookson** and **Vanessa Houlder**

Might genetically modified foods become the next mad-cow crisis? Plants with altered genes are already pervasive in the food chain (see below). The view of mainstream scientists is clear: genetically modified foods that have been approved for human consumption are extremely unlikely to damage your health.

But the scientific wisdom was just as clear 10 years ago about mad-cow disease: the risk of BSE infecting people was negligible. The few maverick scientists who warned that the infection might cross the species barrier from cattle to people were attacked as irresponsible and received little attention. Unfortunately, they have turned out to be right.

The spectre of BSE haunts the current debate over genetic foods. Again, the vast majority of scientists pooh-pooh the view that eating genetically modified crops could pose any threat.

But this time consumer groups and politicians are listening to the minority who claim that added genes and the proteins they produce could pose a danger both to the environment and to human health.

"BSE has made people in Europe very sensitive to new technologies in the food supply industry, and very wary of scientists and government attempts to reassure them," says John Durant, professor of public understanding of science at Imperial College, London.

"It could be that the price of the BSE fiasco will be even greater outside the beef industry than inside it, if it makes the European public resist GM crops."

Public concern intensified yesterday after 20 international scientists signed a memorandum in support of controversial research that showed rats fed with an experimental kind of genetically modified potato suffered damage to their immune systems and changes to the size of their livers, hearts and brains.

Some of the findings were rapidly disowned by the Rowett Research Institute in Aberdeen, the institute where the work was carried out. It described the presentation of the work as "misleading" and asked Arpad Pusztai, the scientist involved, to retire.

The scientists who this week rallied round Dr Pusztai say his concerns are justified. Stanley Ewen, a pathologist at Aberdeen University medical school, says the work might even have disturbing implications for modified crops already in use, such as maize. Vivyan Howard, toxicopathologist at Liverpool University, says the growth retardation seen in young rats at the Rowett has serious implications, since underweight babies might show behavioural problems.

The researchers challenge the adequacy of the existing regulatory system in the UK and, by extension, the rest of the world. Dr Howard says: "The regulatory process needs to be more thorough, more objective and to ask the right questions." He and other scientists are calling for a moratorium on the use of genetically modified foods.

However, the fact is that such concerns remain those of a minority. Other scientists vigorously defend the existing system which, they say, involves detailed, case-by-case studies including feeding trials where necessary.

Professor Derek Burke, a biologist and former chairman of the UK government's advisory committee on novel foods, is "absolutely confident" about the safeguards in the existing system. The suggestion that the findings have any implications for existing GM crops is "absolute rubbish", he says. There was never any question that the particular genetic modification in the Rowett experiment – the potato contained a toxin – would enter the human food chain.

Lastly, he claims, the British regulatory system is more safety-conscious than that of the US.

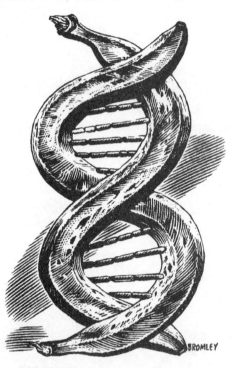

BROMLEY

"On medicine and drugs we are more relaxed. On food it is the other way round. It's a different attitude to risk."

One reason why the Europeans may be risk-averse is widespread ignorance both of how much genetically modified food there is and what has been done to the plants. While genetically modified plants are restricted in Europe to experimental field trials, commercial crops are marching across the fields of North and South America and east Asia, facing little consumer or political resistance. The total area planted worldwide has risen from 2.8m hectares in 1996 to 12.8m hectares in 1997 and an estimated 30m hectares last year.

Soya and maize are leading the way. The main modifications introduced so far enable plants either to kill insect pests or to resist a specific herbicide (so the farmer can spray the field with it to kill all the weeds without harming the crop).

Apart from the uncertainty over the facts, another barrier to public acceptance has arisen: all the benefits so far seem to have accrued to the farmers and the companies supplying them, while all the risks are born by consumers and the environment. More obvious public benefits – such as improved food qualities and gigantic improvements in productivity – remain promises.

Large-scale public surveys, such as those conducted by Prof Durant at Imperial College with George Gaskell at the London School of Economics, consistently show far more consumer opposition to genetically modified food in Europe than in North America. But the contrary is true of medical biotechnology; more Americans than Europeans express opposition to genetic testing. "We should avoid the stereotyped view that Americans are gung-ho about new technology and Europeans are not," Prof Durant says.

Besides BSE, which has not affected the US, he cites the very different views of agriculture on opposite sides of the Atlantic. "When Europeans think of wildlife and the rural environment, they think of farmland, and for them GM technology appears to be the next step in an unwelcome intensification of agriculture," he says. "Americans, in contrast, think of the wilderness areas in their national parks; they regard their farmland as part of the industrial system."

Whether the European concern or the American enthusiasm for crop engineering is more justified may not become clear for decades. Dr Howard says it will be extremely difficult to monitor the public for ill effects from GM food.

"Maybe, after 20 to 30 years, things might come to the fore," he says. "But you won't have any unexposed population against which to measure it. It is an uncontrolled experiment."

A fridge full of modified genes

John Willman reports on what vegetables, fruits and foods life science groups have altered

A wide variety of genetically modified crops has been developed by the leading life sciences groups, ranging from potatoes and cauliflowers to lettuces and raspberries. They offer benefits such as better insect resistance, tolerance to chemical spray, better nutritional content and longer shelf lives after harvesting.

Only four are in use in the UK food industry and two of these have relatively restricted applications.

One is the genetically modified enzyme used to make vegetarian cheese, replacing rennet which is extracted from calves' stomachs. It is now increasingly used in making hard cheeses for general consumption.

The second is the genetically modified tomatoes used to make tomato paste. These tomatoes are less likely to rot on the plant and remain firmer after picking, producing a higher yield when turned into purée. As a result, the paste is cheaper and – according to Safeway, the supermarket chain – scores higher in consumer taste tests.

The other two are soyabeans and maize, both of which largely originate from the US. They are used much more widely – and in the case of soya increasingly hard to find in a non-modified form.

Soya is an ingredient in many products, including cakes and biscuits, chilled foods and vegetarian textured meat products as well as soya sauce and cooking oil. It is used in about 60 per cent of processed foods, though in some cases in very small quantities.

Most of the soya used in the UK comes from the US where genetically modified crops made up about a third of the harvest last year and the share is rising rapidly. Bulk shipments routinely mix modified and non-modified, and any food product that may contain modified ingredients must be labelled as such in Europe.

Maize is also used as a basic ingredient in many food and drink products, including breakfast cereals, crisps and snacks, petfood and processed foods. It is also a source of fructose used in soft drinks and confectionery. Europe is able to produce much of its maize needs so it is easier to keep genetically modified grain out of the UK food chain.

Under EU rules, a food using any genetically modified ingredient must be labelled accordingly. The only exception is derivatives of soya that contain none of the protein – such as oil.

The real question, however, is whether food manufacturers always know whether GM ingredients are in their products. One food company – which does not want to be identified – found traces of genetic modification in 14 out of 20 products it believed to be GM-free.

Genetically modified products

Ingredient	Used in
Enzyme to replace animal rennet	Vegetarian cheese and other cheeses
Tomatoes	Tomato paste
Soya	Chilled foods, cakes and biscuits, vegetarian textured meat products, processed foods
Maize	Crisps and snacks, cereals, pet food, processed foods

Appendix 4.

Vegetarian Enzyme Modified Cheese

Important changes in the dairy industry over the last ten years or so, have seen a significant move away from animal derived enzymes, such as calf stomach rennet, used in cheese manufacture, to microbially derived rennets. A similar, but more recent move has also occurred in the production of cheese derived flavour ingredients, such as Enzyme Modified Cheese (EMC) – an important and growing sector of the flavours market. The move away from animal derived products allows the cheeses and EMCs to be offered with both vegetarian, and kosher status – important and growing niche markets in the food industry.

Extra impetus has been given by recent concerns over possible BSE and swine fever transmissions. Many food and flavour suppliers are now starting to look for non-animal alternatives. However, much processed cheese is still made containing EMC, manufactured with animal derived enzymes. It is now generally agreed that there is a pronounced change occurring in the demand for EMC with vegetarian (and kosher) status, requiring the use of microbially derived enzymes in its manufacture. Of course, EMC is not only used in processed cheese but can be found as a flavour ingredient in a rapidly expanding selection of cheese flavoured snacks and convenience foods. It is even used in some pet foods!

Biocatalysts Ltd. is at the forefront of these changes, especially in EMC production. Whilst Biocatalysts Ltd. offers the conventional animal derived enzymes, it has always specialised in microbially derived enzyme products for vegetarian and kosher status EMC. Biocatalysts Ltd. offers a comprehensive range of well-developed formulations for a variety of cheese flavours, and has an active R&D programme for the introduction of new, microbially derived enzymes for new flavours. Biocatalysts Ltd. also offers a unique tailor-made formulation service if a customer has specific requirements that standard products do not fully satisfy.

Appendix 5.

Biocatalysts Ltd. Organisation Chart

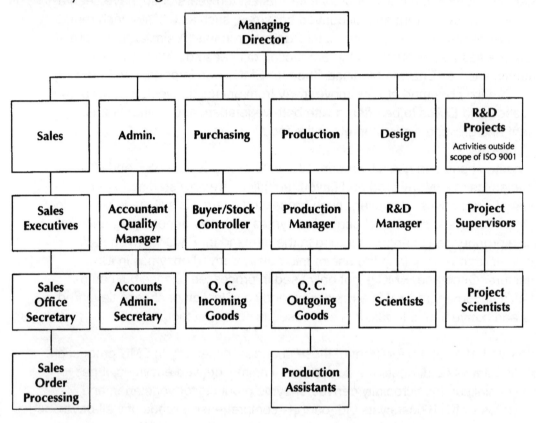

Q. C. = Quality Control
R&D = Research and Development

Appendix 6.

Biocatalysts Ltd.
Abbreviated Balance Sheet

	1997		1996	
	£	£	£	£
Fixed assets				
Tangible assets		177,667		173,671
Investments		2		3
		177,669		173,674
Current assets				
Stocks	157,877		188,466	
Debtors	783,623		517,462	
Cash at bank and in hand	12,122		30,987	
	953,622		736,915	
Creditors: amounts falling due within one year	(508,073)		(399,078)	
Net current assets		445,549		337,837
Total assets less current liabilities		623,218		511,511
Deferred assets		10,138		10,138
Net assets		633,356		521,649
Capital and reserves				
Called up share capital		500,000		405,511
Capital reserve		–		7,089
Profit and loss account		133,356		109,049
Total shareholders funds		633,356		521,649
Attributable to:				
Equity shareholders		633,356		521,649

These financial statements are prepared in accordance with the special provisions of Part VII of the Companies Act, 1985, relating to small companies.

(Information supplied by Biocatalysts Ltd.)

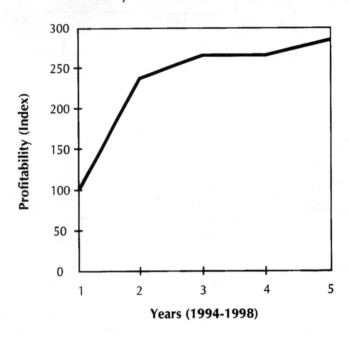

Profitability 1994-1998 (1994 = 100)

The company turnover is approximately £2.5 million.

Previous Years' Business Ratios

	1994	1995
Current Ratio	2.3	2.2
Acid Test	1.4	1.5
Stock Turn	4.9	4.8
Stock Holding (Days)	75	72
Payment Period	75	72
% Profit	4.9	8.2

The company is growing at 20-30% per annum. The sales profile follows the normal Pareto effect with 80% of the customers providing only 20% of the sales.

Appendix 7.

Biocatalysts Ltd. and Trading

Trading in the Euro (€), £s and $s

There is strong worldwide interest in how the new European money system based on the Euro €, is actually working (even if it is only how to get a computer keyboard with the new Euro symbol as part of the standard layout!).

More than two thirds of Biocatalysts' annual turnover is from export sales and it is used to working with different currencies. Biocatalysts Ltd. appears to be fully prepared for trading in the Euro. Biocatalysts Ltd. is able to offer quotations, take orders and, most importantly, accept payment in the Euro (€), American Dollars ($), and UK Pounds Sterling (£). All other currency transactions are usually 'translated' into one of the above three currencies.

BPP
PROFESSIONAL EDUCATION

Appendix 8.

Management Buyout History

1983 Biocatalysts Ltd. name registered.

1985 Work started on a new enzyme facility in South Wales.

1986 Biocatalysts Ltd. starts trading under the ultimate ownership of Grand Metropolitan.

1987 Management buyout financed by the Welsh Development Authority and Welsh Venture Capital Fund when Grand Metropolitan started to divest non-core businesses.

Collaboration with Universities

Biocatalysts Ltd. collaborates with around 8 different UK universities (Food and Biochemistry) and several European universities. In general, basic research is done at the universities (screening, gene cloning, new enzyme developments) before the laboratory processes are brought in for scale-up applications work. In addition, Biocatalysts Ltd. sponsors CASE awards at some universities on more speculative areas of enzyme research.

Appendix 9.

BIOCATALYSTS LIMITED
A manufacturer of speciality enzymes and formulator of enzyme complexes

BAKING

BREWING

FRUIT AND VEGETABLE PROCESSING

FLAVOUR

PROTEINS

DIETETICS

TEXTILES (GARMENT WASHING)

DIAGNOSTICS

PHARMACEUTICALS

ENVIRONMENTALS

Biocatalysts Ltd is unique amongst the world's enzyme companies. Our willingness to supply custom-tailored products for our clients means that the whole company focus is directed towards our customers and towards giving total customer satisfaction. This customer focus has resulted in Biocatalysts Ltd growing at more than twice the industry average over the past 10 years.

Biocatalysts Ltd is an independent company, located just outside Cardiff, the capital city of Wales. Biocatalysts, as our company name suggests, only makes and sells enzymes. We are not a division of a larger chemical, food ingredients or pharmaceutical company.

Biocatalysts Ltd has many exclusive agreements with blue chip companies around the world, who value the products and technical services we supply. But we are also happy to deal with both small and medium sized companies and our customer base has a full spectrum of company sizes.

Biocatalysts Ltd does not make or sell high volume commodity enzymes, such as those used in the detergent or starch processing industries. We operate in selected parts of the enzyme market where our technical support and willingness to work with customers on a one-to-one basis is highly valued. These enzyme sectors usually require not single enzyme entities but enzyme complexes where the ratios of each of the components are crucial to the efficacy of the whole enzyme product and our customer's process. We do not believe in our customers making do with compromise enzyme products just because that is the way they come off the fermenter! Our own fermentation for the manufacture of our enzyme products is sub-contracted out. This, we believe, allows us to be more flexible, our focus is on investing in enzyme technology – not stainless steel!

Our R&D programme is focused on the development of new enzymes and enzyme complexes mainly identified to us by our customers. We have many allegiances with leading British Universities where most of our basic research into new enzymes is carried out. This allows us to focus our in-house scientists onto the needs of our customers, whilst keeping fully up to date with the latest developments in bio-research.

If you are not sure that you are getting optimum performance from your current enzymes, or if you think your process could benefit by the use of enzymes, why not give Biocatalysts a try and find out what makes us unique amongst the world's enzyme companies.

BIOCATALYSTS

BPP PROFESSIONAL EDUCATION

ENZYMES FOR THE FOOD INDUSTRY

PRODUCT	CODE	PRINCIPAL ACTIVITIES	APPLICATION NOTES
BAKING			
AMYLASE	A011P	Amylase	Fungal alpha amylase, protease free, full range of activities to 100,000 SKB.
CATAMYL PLUS	C380P	Mixed amylases, Pentosanase	Anti-staling for bread.
COMBIZYME 261P	C261P	Alpha amylase, Proteinase, Pentosanase	For improving loaf volume, crumb texture & retarding staling in bread.
COMBIZYME 275P	C275P	Proteinase, Alpha amylase, Pentosanase	Protein modifier for biscuits & crackers.
COMBIZYME 359P	C359P	Pentosanase	Bromate replacer.
COMBIZYME 365P	C365P	Xylanase, Proteinase	Viscosity control in batters.
COMBIZYME 366P	C366P	Proteinase, Pentosanase	Metabisulphite replacer in biscuits & crackers.
→ COMBIZYME 485P	C485P	Amylase, hemicellulase & protease	Metabisulphite replacer in biscuit manufacture.
DEPOL 112P	D112P	Glucanase, Xylanase	Viscosity control in batters.
DEPOL 222P	D222P	Pentosanase	Amylase free pentosanase.
DEPOL 267P	D267P	Alpha amylase, Pentosanase	Amylase/pentosanase formulated at working strength for direct incorporation into baking flour.
DEPOL 333P	D333P	Xylanase	High activity, amylase free hemicellulase.
DEPOL 364P	D364P	Xylanase, Cellulase	For viscosity control in batters & use in doughnut manufacture.
DEPOL 414P	D414P	Alpha amylases	Speciality amylase for French type bread.
→ DEPOL 453P	D453P	Hemicellulase	Aspergillus hemicellulase without amylase for bread improvers.
→ DEPOL 454P	D454P	Hemicellulase (xylanase)	Endo-xylanase for bread improvers.
PROMOD 223P	P223P	Proteinase	Bacterial protease for biscuits & crackers.
PROMOD 388P	P388P	Proteinase	Fungal proteinase for improving dough handling & bread texture.
PROMOD 451P	P451P	Proteinase	Fungal proteinase/peptidase for improving dough handling & crumb texture.
BREWING			
→ AMG BC300	D339L	Glucoamylase	Production of lite beers.
→ COMBIZYME 108L	C108L	Protease, Alpha amylase, Beta glucanase	High activity formulation for yield improvements in brewing.
→ GLUCANASE 1XL	G011L	Beta glucanase	Improved mash & fermentation performance (run off & solubles) in brewing applications.
→ GLUCANASE 5XL	G015L	Beta glucanase	Concentrated (5X) glucanase for improved mash & fermentation performance in brewing applications.
→ PROMOD 144L	P144L	Papain	Beer clarification, removal of chill haze.
FRUIT AND VEGETABLE PROCESSING			
→ CELLULASE 13L	C013L	Cellulase	Cellulose hydrolysis.
DEPOL 40L	D040L	Cellulase, Pectinases, Beta glucosidase	Versatile formulation for maceration, viscosity reduction & extraction of a wide range of fruits & vegetables including mangoes.
DEPOL 220L	D220L	Alpha amylase, Glucoamylase	Hydrolysis of starches during fruit processing.
→ GLUCOSE OXIDASE	G168L	Glucose oxidase	Oxygen removal from fruit flavoured drinks.
MACERS FJ	M263L	Pectinases	Improved performance in a wide range of fruit juice extraction applications (high pectin lyase, low pectin esterase).
MACERS O	M265L	Pectinases	Significantly improved yield of olive oil & easier to handle waste.
MACERS W	M264L	Pectinases	Improved extraction performance & flavour enhancement for white wine.
PECTINASE 62L	P062L	Pectinases	General depectinising applications & broad spectrum depolymerisation activity, particularly in fruit.
PECTINASE 444L	P444L	Pectinases	Highly active formulation for general depectinising applications.
CITRUS FRUIT PEELER PECTINASE 162L	P162L	Pectinases	Cost effective peeling of citrus fruits (automation aid).
→ TANNASE	T510P	Tannase	Removal of tannins.

BIOCATALYSTS

New Products are Shown with →

ENZYMES FOR THE FOOD INDUSTRY

PRODUCT	CODE	PRINCIPAL ACTIVITIES	APPLICATION NOTES
FLAVOUR			
DEPOL 40L	D040L	Cellulase, Pectinase, Beta glucosidase	Versatile formulation for maceration & extraction in a wide range of vegetables including vanilla, carrots, tea etc.
DEPOL 112L	D112L	Glucanase, Xylanase, Beta glucosidase	Flavour extraction from fibrous botanicals.
FLAVORPRO 192P	F192P	Peptidases	Debittering of protein hydrolysates.
FLAVORPRO 373P	F373P	Glutaminase (Bacillus)	Conversion of glutamine into glutamate in protein hydrolysates.
LIPOMOD 187P	L187P	Esterase	Protease free microbial lipase for enzyme modified cheese (EMC) production. Cheddar type flavours. Kosher certification available.
LIPOMOD 224P	L224P	Esterase (protease)	Enzyme modified cheese (EMC) production. Cheddar type flavours.
LIPOMOD 299P	L299P	Esterase (protease)	Enzyme modified cheese (EMC) production. Cheddar type flavours.
LIPOMOD 29P	L029P	Esterase, Lipase (protease)	General fat hydrolysis & enzyme modified cheese (EMC) production.
LIPOMOD 338P	L338P	Esterase	Protease free microbial lipase for enzyme modified cheese (EMC) production. Blue cheese type flavours. Kosher certification available.
LIPOMOD 34P	L034P	Lipase, Esterase	Protease free, high activity lipase for hydrolysis of oils, tallow & fats including butter fat. Kosher certification available.
PEPTIDASE 436P	P436P	Aminopeptidase, Carboxypeptidase	Debittering of protein hydrolysates. Contains proline peptidase activity. Kosher certification available.
PEPTIDASE 433/4P	P433/4P	Aminopeptidase, Carboxypeptidase	Broad spectrum peptidases for debittering of protein hydrolysates.
PROMOD 215P	P215P	Endo-proteinase, Peptidase	For use with protease free lipases in enzyme modified cheese (EMC) production. Introduces protein notes. Kosher certification available.
PROMOD 446P	P446P	Endo-proteinase, Peptidase	For use with protease free lipases in enzyme modified cheese (EMC) production. Introduces protein notes. Kosher certification available.
PROTEINS			
→ BC PEPSIN 1:3000	P389P	Acid protease	Protein hydrolysis at acid pH values.
DEPOL 20L	D020L	Pectinase	For viscosity reduction of soya polysaccharides.
PROMOD 144L	P144L	Proteinase	Papain liquid 100 TU.
PROMOD 144P	P144P	Proteinase	Papain powder 100 TU.
PROMOD 184P	P184P	Proteinase	Bromelain powder.
PROMOD 192P	P192P	Endo-proteinase	Acid fungal protease with exo-peptidases.
PROMOD 194P	P194P	Proteinase	Neutral fungal protease with exo-peptidases.
PROMOD 24L	P024L	Proteinase	Neutral bacterial, general purpose liquid proteinase.
PROMOD 278P	P278P	Proteinase	Mixed fungal & bacterial proteinases for Stage 1 in the Biocatalysts eHVP (enzyme hydrolysed vegetable protein) Cascade: the bulk hydrolysis stage.
PROMOD 279P	P279P	Proteinase, Peptidase	Fungal proteases & peptidases for Stage 2 in the Biocatalysts eHVP Cascade: the debittering stage.
PROMOD 280P	P280P	Proteinase, Amylase	Mixed fungal & bacterial enzyme activities for Stage 3 in the Biocatalysts eHVP Cascade: the filtration aid stage.
PROMOD 298L	P298L	Proteinase	Broad spectrum bacterial proteinase, will rapidly reduce viscosity of soya protein pastes.
PROMOD 31L	P031L	Proteinase	Neutral bacterial, broad spectrum liquid proteinase.
DIETETICS			
AMYLASE	AD11P	Amylase	Aid for digestion of dietary starch. Ready for tableting.
→ BC PEPSIN 1:3000	P389P	Pepsin	Animal derived acid enzyme to aid protein digestion.
→ BROMELAIN 1200GDU	P523P	Bromelain	Broad spectrum plant protease to aid protein digestion.
CELLULASE CP	C013P	Cellulase	Aid for digestion of dietary cellulose. Ready for tableting.
DEPOL 333P	D333P	Xylanase	Aid for digestion of dietary hemicellulose. Ready for tableting.
HEMICELLULASE 334P	H334P	Glucanase, Cellulase, Xylanase	Aid for the digestion of dietary fibre. Ready for tableting.
LACTASE	L017P	Lactase	Aid for digestion of dietary lactose. Ready for tableting.
LIPASE, Rhizopus sp.	L036P	Lipase, Esterase	Aid for digestion of dietary fats & lipids. Ready for tableting.
PANCREATIN 4XNF	P211P	Amylase, Lipase, Protease	General aid for digestion. Ready for tableting.
PROMOD D24P	PD024P	Protease	Broad spectrum proteases for aiding the digestion of dietary proteins. Ready for tableting.

BIOCATALYSTS

New Products are Shown with →

Page 36 of Biocatalysts

N O N - F O O D   G R A D E   E N Z Y M E S

PRODUCT	CODE	PRINCIPAL ACTIVITIES	APPLICATION NOTES
TEXTILES (GARMENT WASHING)			
→ CATALASE	C495L	Catalase	Inactivation and removal of hydrogen peroxide.
DESIZE 277L	D277L	Amylase	Very high activity bacterial amylase for cost effective garment & textile desizing applications. Can be diluted.
→ DESIZE 569P	D569P	Amylase	Very strong desizing amylase powder.
→ DESIZE (NON-ENZYMATIC)	D574L	Non-enzyme product	Desizing fabrics with difficult sizes or where minimal backstaining is required.
INDIFADE 7.5L	I07.5L	Cellulase	Range of liquid acid cellulase activities from medium to high activity. Ready to use,
INDIFADE 9L	I009L	Cellulase	cost effective formulations for bio-washing applications.
INDIFADE 11L	I011L	Cellulase	
INDIFADE 13L	I013L	Cellulase	
→ INDIFADE 9 LAS	I480L	Cellulase	Acid cellulase with anti-redeposition chemistry.
INDIFADE 426P	I426P	Cellulase	High activity, buffered mixed acid & neutral cellulase powder.
INDIFADE 501P	I501P	Cellulase	High activity, buffered acid cellulase powder with added anti-redeposition chemistry for an economical, near neutral type of stone wash effect.
→ INDIFADE 555P	I555P	Cellulase	Boosted cost effective neutral cellulase.
→ INDIFADE AGER	I478L	Non-enzyme product	Gives antique look to denims.
→ INDIFADE BRIGHT	I476P	Non-enzyme product	Optical brightener.
→ INDIFADE COLD	I539L	Cellulase	Cellulase for use in cool water (40 - 45°C).
INDIFADE LAS	I014L	Cellulase	High activity, liquid acid cellulase with added anti-redeposition chemistry for an economical, near neutral type of stone wash effect.
INDIFADE NC-1G	I001G	Cellulase	High activity, unbuffered neutral cellulase granules.
→ INDIFADE SOFT	I477L	Non-enzyme product	Specially formulated softener for denims.
INDIFADE SUPER	I474P	Cellulase	Highly cost effective, buffered neutral cellulase powder.
INDIFADE SUPER PLUS	I475P	Cellulase	Cost effective, buffered neutral cellulase powder with added anti-redeposition chemistry.
SOFTZYME	S425L	Cellulase	Bio-softening, anti-pilling formulation for cellulosic fibres (Tencel®).
DIAGNOSTICS			
ALKALINE PHOSPHATASE	A500L	Alkaline phosphatase	High stability reagent for immunodiagnostics.
GALACTOSE DEHYDROGENASE	G471P	Galactose dehydrogenase	For determination of galactose in blood of neonatals.
MANNITOL DEHYDROGENASE	M093P	Mannitol dehydrogenase	For determination of mannitol in sugar permeability test in human gastric disorders.
MYROSINASE	M044P	Myrosinase	Determination of glucosinolates in rape seed meal.
PHENYLALANINE DEHYDROGENASE	P098P	Phenylalanine dehydrogenase	For determination of phenylalanine in blood of neonatals.
→ GLUCOSE OXIDASE	TP 574P	Glucose oxidase - catalase free	Determination of glucose - available summer 1998.
→ GLUTAMINASE	G420P	Glutaminase	Determination of glutamine.
→ PEROXIDASE	P558P	Peroxidase	Immuno-diagnostics.
PHARMACEUTICALS			
LIPASE, Candida sp.	L034P	Lipase	Stereoselective hydrolysis of esters.
LIPASE, Pseudomonas sp.	L056P	Lipase	Stereoselective hydrolysis of esters.
LIPASE, Pancreatic	L115P	Lipase Esterase	Stereoselective hydrolysis of esters.
SEC ADH 300	S300P	Alcohol dehydrogenase	Synthesis of chiral alcohols.
TRYPSIN 250	T069P	Proteinase	Standard formulation for mammalian cell culture.
TRYPSIN IRRAD.	T070P	Proteinase	Irradiated formulation for mammalian cell culture.
TRYSIN SVF	T071P	Proteinase	Certified specific virus-free trypsin for cell culture.
ENVIRONMENTALS			
GREASE BIOSOLVE (COMBIZYME 209P)	C209P	Broad spectrum lipases & carbohydrases	High activity enzyme formulation for reduced fouling of grease traps & drain maintenance.
LATRINE DEODOURISER (COMBIZYME 253L)	C253L	Broad spectrum enzymes	High activity product for significant odour reduction in many waste treatment applications.
ODOURWAY 10X	OO73L10	Mixed, broad spectrum	10X concentrated version. Available with a choice of perfumes.
ODOURWAY 20X	OO73L20	Mixed, broad spectrum	20X concentrated version. Available with a choice of perfumes.

New Products are Shown with →

CUSTOM TAILORED PRODUCTS:

This catalogue contains our standard products that are sold regularly to our customers. In addition we have many other products that have been developed exclusively for individual customers. If you do not think your current enzyme product is optimised for your process or would like an exclusive enzyme product (not available to your competitors) then contact the Sales department at Biocatalysts to find out how we can develop new enzyme products exclusively for your company.

If there are any enzyme activities that you are interested in that are not mentioned in our standard listing then please enquire; we have many new enzymes under development for release in the near future.

WORLD-WIDE SALES AGENTS:

Biocatalysts has an extensive network of agents and distributors in over 40 countries right around the world. Our most recent list is given in our company newsletter 'IN BRIEF'. This is sent out routinely to all clients on our database. If you would like to be added to our mailing list then please fill out a reader reply card included with this catalogue.

PACKAGING:

Biocatalysts products are packaged by weight (not volume) according to the following:

Powders (designated 'P' in product code)
Standard packaging   25 kg in fibre kegs or Lesac² lined square boxes.
Liquids (designated 'L' in product code)
Standard packaging   25, 215 and 1000 kg
Granules (designated 'G' in product code)
Standard packaging   25 kg
Other pack sizes are available including 1 and 5 kg on request.

DATA ACCURACY:

Whilst Biocatalysts makes all practicable efforts to ensure the accuracy of the information it gives, the data might be subject to change without notice. Biocatalysts cannot guarantee performance in any end application. Prior to carrying out any commercial application, clients should ensure that they are not infringing third party patent rights.

SAMPLES:

Product samples for trials are generally available on request. Please fill out and return an enquiry card included with this catalogue or contact the sales department at Biocatalysts.

PRODUCT DATA SHEETS:

Further information is available for each of the products listed in this catalogue. Please contact Biocatalysts for individual Product Data Sheets.

HEALTH AND SAFETY:

Always read and retain the Health and Safety data sheets supplied with each product, before use. If you are in any doubt about recommended product handling and safety, please contact Biocatalysts before use. Generally, when handling enzymes avoid contact with the skin and eyes and do not breathe dusts or aerosols containing them.

TECHNICAL SUPPORT:

Biocatalysts offers a Technical Support Service for all its products.

Page 38 of Biocatalysts

KOSHER STATUS:

Most Biocatalysts products are available with Kosher or Kosher Parve certification in accordance with current Orthodox Union requirements. Kosher certification requirements must be specified with order as retrospective certification cannot be issued.

TRADE MARKS:

COMBIZYME, DEPOL, INDIFADE, LIPOMOD, MACER8, PROMOD and the Biocatalysts logo including the cat symbol are trademarks of Biocatalysts Ltd.

ENZYMES FROM GENETICALLY MODIFIED ORGANISMS (GMOs):

Genetically modified organisms (commonly called GMOs) are being increasingly used by many companies for enzyme production. There are many reasons for this, but some of them include:

- the production of purer enzyme products
- shorter development times for new enzymes
- reduced usage of energy and raw materials for production giving reduced production costs

At the moment none of our products listed in this catalogue is derived from a GMO. We expect to launch our first enzyme produced from a GMO in 1999. All literature regarding these new enzymes will clearly state that they have been produced from GMOs. This is now the norm for the enzyme industry. It is our belief that the use of GMOs for enzyme production offers many benefits and that they are safe and efficient to use, and that they pose no threat to the environment or the end consumer.

ANIMAL DERIVED ENZYMES:

None of the enzymes listed in this catalogue is derived from a bovine (cow) source. One of our specialisations is to offer microbial derived alternatives to commonly available animal enzymes (e.g. our alkaline phosphatase). By not processing or dealing with bovine derived products we can ensure that there is no risk whatsoever of any of our products being contaminated with BSE.

The only animal derived enzymes included in this catalogue are from porcine (pig) sources. No primary processing of animal glands is carried out at Biocatalysts Ltd. All partially processed animal derived material comes from animal certified as healthy at the time of slaughter. Our premises are inspected annually by an Officer of the British Ministry of Agriculture, Fisheries and Food (MAFF) and an Approval certificate issued (copy available on request).

HACCP (HAZARD ANALYSIS AND CRITICAL CONTROL POINT SYSTEM):

As well as operating under ISO 9001 Biocatalysts Ltd also has additional operating procedures which conform to HACCP.

If you would like product datasheets, quotations or samples of any of the products in this catalogue or would like to be added to our database, please fill in the reply card and post or fax it back to Biocatalysts.

BIOCATALYSTS

Step 1: Overview of Biocatalysts

4

Chapter Topic List	
1	What are we trying to achieve at the overview?
2	Bringing order to the case material
3	Adding context to turn information into intelligence
4	The pitfalls
5	The practice: completing the overview for Biocatalysts

Introduction

☑ This chapter shows how to get started on a case study and how to establish the **context** of a case study. By the end of this stage you will be able to describe and explain the implications of:

- Your role and what you have been asked to do
- The company, its size, sector and key capabilities
- The main environmental challenges
- The customers
- The competitors

Skills and knowledge reminder: techniques and tools at overview

The analysis tools you have already studied will help you to organise and assimilate information quickly. You can identify those you will be able to use during the overview stage and apply them at the inview stages. During this chapter you will see two techniques applied to this case study:

- A mind map used to help sort out the data about enzymes (see 2.9)

- A schematic pulls together a picture of the stakeholders and their needs and interests (5.5)

If you are unfamiliar with any of the basic tools and techniques we use here, take time to review your Analysis and Evaluation notes.

BPP
PROFESSIONAL EDUCATION

1 What are we trying to achieve at the overview?

1.1 The **overview** begins the process of bringing order and method to the case study.

1.2 The mistake at this stage is to keep reading the case without picking up a pen and actually doing something with the data it contains. Simply rereading the case will only give you a superficial picture: you need to really understand the business and the implications of what you are being told. You should **first** sort and **then** analyse the clues and data provided, turning it in the process into relevant information which will eventually help you to make and justify a credible strategy. So, what needs to be done?

1.3 You have already read Biocatalysts and thought about the business: now you are going to start work on it.

1.4 What did you find out?

Action Programme 1

Even after one read of the narrative, you can probably answer these questions. Try and do this without referring back to the case.

(a) Is this a B2B or B2C case study and what are the implications of that?
(b) What is the product Biocatalysts are producing and why is it a challenging business?
(c) Who are you and what is your role in the case?
(d) What is the role of agents in Biocatalyst's market?

Turn to the end of this chapter to check your answers with ours.

1.5 Before you start getting down to any more detailed work on the overview, just take a few minutes to **familiarise yourself with the appendices**. What do they contain? Again do not try to do anything with this data, but simply assess what sort of information might be available to you once you analyse and cross analyse the various appendices. For example, Appendix 6 on page 29 gives you some headline financial information and, considered against some of the competitor information in Appendix 1 (from page 17), you can see how small the Biocatalysts operation is and that you will be able to assess its financial strength. Clearly Biocatalysts is a very small fish in a big and turbulent global pond.

2 Bringing order to the case material

2.1 You won't understand the case study yet and shouldn't expect to but you are at least beginning to get a sense of the **scenario and scale**. There is no shortage of information but at this stage it is scattered throughout the narrative and appendices. In your overview you need to sort out:

■ Information about the industry and its fortunes
■ Information about Biocatalysts and its business
■ Information about products and markets (sorting the general from the Biocatalysts specific)

2.2 Do not be surprised if the material seems muddled at first. As you work with it and sort it into relevant groups it will start to make more sense. Do avoid rushing into ad hoc analysis: it pays to work through the case thoroughly and logically, so that you can be sure that you have stripped out all the relevant data.

2.3 This next step in the overview process could take you two to six hours, depending on the complexity of the case. Take this task in two or three short bursts and don't worry at this stage about what you are going to do next.

2.4 **Note. You must not do any research outside the Case Study as this will be penalised by the Examiner.** Additional information would only confuse the issues, so just use you own knowledge and the information given. Certainly you must not bring 'facts' from any external search to bear on your answer in the exam. The world is as described by the examiner for the duration of the case.

2.5 **Reminder**

As you work through the case, keep an **information shopping list** so that you can use it later if you need to prepare for a research question.

2.6 **Head up pages** with key areas for analysis to help you sort through the case.

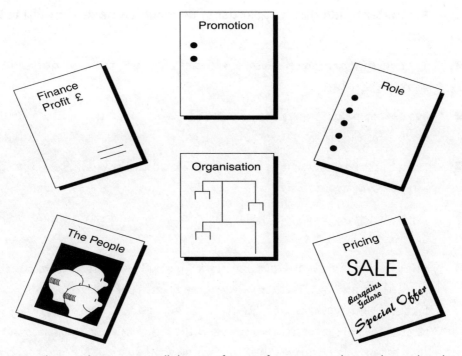

Examine every line and categorise all the significant information under a relevant heading.

- People
- Products
- Current performance, profitability etc
- Organisational structure
- Competitors
- Customers/audiences
- Potential environmental change, eg legislation or customer attitudes to GM products
- Brand and competitive position

The aim of the overview is to familiarise yourself thoroughly with Biocatalysts.

Take a further sheet of paper and use this to record information about the **consultancy role you have and make key notes about your client Stewart North**, his needs and interests and the expectation of the Board.

2.7 Note that with different cases you will need different headings. You will choose these based on what seem to be the key issues in the case. For example, if there was a lot of information on the brand or the sales force, you would pull that information together.

2.8 The idea is that at the end of this process you have, for example, all the financial information or macro environmental information together on one sheet.

Tutor Tip

■ Do not be tempted at this stage to make decisions and/or jump to conclusions. Collect all the information and analyse it carefully before you start changing things.

■ Try not to work in a mechanistic way as though this were an academic exercise; play your part. What questions do you think Stewart and the Board will want to ask? What extra information would you want if you were the consultant? **Remember to add these to your list of information needs – it may be invaluable later.**

■ Take care with the appendices: currencies change – some are quoted in dollars, others in sterling.

■ We are apparently geared up to work in Euros. Does that imply a strategy is needed for Europe?

■ Do not just rely on what is written. Think about the business; try and picture it in your own mind.

■ What do you know about the characteristics of marketing in an international business to business sector?

■ Enzymes are raw material products, consumables used in the production process and they play a role in determining the quality of the customer's finished product. Their value is potentially high, and price is relatively insignificant as a percentage of total costs. Customers will tend to be relatively price insensitive (inelastic), but ensuring they understand the basis of comparison between different offerings is, it seems, a key issue.

■ Channel management, promotion, particularly in relation to presenting GM products and pricing, all seem to be issues which could be on the Examiner's agenda: certainly the service element of the marketing mix is key to differentiating Biocatalysts's offering.

2.9   As you pull the materials together at this overview stage, you will find that the business becomes clearer. When you are faced with detailed and complex narrative in a case study, as we are in this case about enzymes, you might find that a mind map helps to bring various strands together in a way that helps build the bigger picture.

A Mind Map of Enzymes and their Market

Catalysts of the Living World

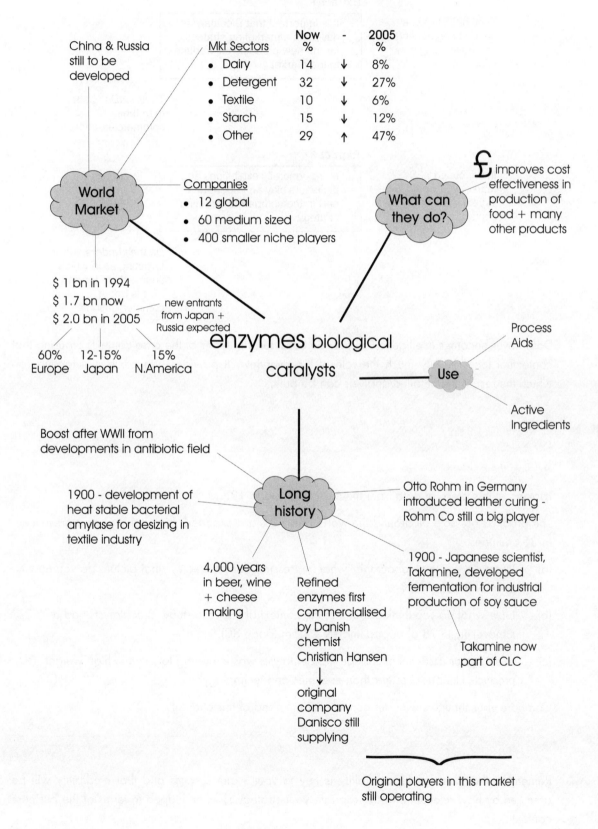

BPP PROFESSIONAL EDUCATION

3 Adding context to turn information into intelligence

3.1 Being a consultant or a case study student is a little like being a detective. You can't take the evidence at face value but need to read between the lines to really appreciate what is being said. Let's look at two extracts from the paragraph on page 14 under **targeting.**

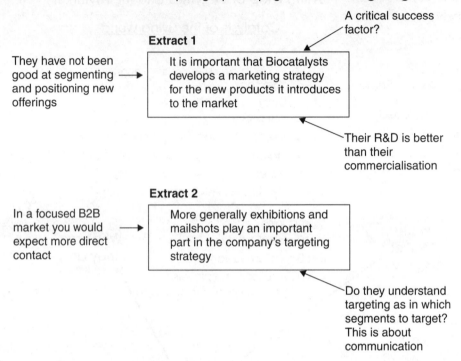

They have not been good at segmenting and positioning new offerings

Extract 1

It is important that Biocatalysts develops a marketing strategy for the new products it introduces to the market

A critical success factor?

Their R&D is better than their commercialisation

Extract 2

In a focused B2B market you would expect more direct contact

More generally exhibitions and mailshots play an important part in the company's targeting strategy

Do they understand targeting as in which segments to target? This is about communication

3.2 Data never becomes intelligence unless you consider it in terms of the case context, ensuring that contextual focus is very much the role of the overview. It provides firm contextual footings on which the rest of the detailed analysis can be built.

Action Programme 2

Adding the context

Looking at this piece of data from the case study page 13:

The products are sold all around the world and 70% are exported. Biocatalysts has a presence in 35 countries.

(a) What do you think about this, what impression does it create, what picture do you now have of Biocatalysts?

(b) Now what do you think about it in the context of the case study. Biocatalysts had a turnover in 1998 of approximately £2.5m (page 30).

(c) Would your assessment change if Biocatalysts was exporting low value/high weight products like bricks rather than enzymes and technology?

Compare your thoughts with our comments at the end of this chapter.

3.3 Remember that commercial credibility is key to your exam success and that credibility will be assessed by how relevant and appropriate your strategy is when judged in terms of the business context.

4 The pitfalls

Not too deep, not too shallow

4.1 One of the hardest things about case study is getting the analysis, both overview and inview, right. Analysis can be very reassuring, particularly when the alternative is to move on to the much more challenging and scary decision making!

4.2 You need to avoid analysis for its own sake. Ask yourself **why** am I analysing this – what kind of information will it generate and what will I do with it? Look for example at Appendix 9. You can use it to show a number of things:

- It provides some clues about the company's communication skills
- It shows how many new products they have as a proportion of the portfolio
- It identifies their key markets
- It provides clues about their potential differential advantages

Which of these pieces of information are important to you? In this case they probably all are, so you can analyse the information accordingly, but **be discerning**.

5 The practice: completing the overview for Biocatalysts

5.1 It is very difficult to undertake the case overview for you – it **must** be done by each individual to give you a meaningful view of the case. Below we have pulled some observations and comments together to help your overview analysis. You may like to have a go at this yourself before moving on.

5.2 **About the company**

(a) **Biocatalysts** is well established in this industry, formed in 1986 and located in Wales. However, it has already had two transformations, starting life as a wholly owned subsidiary of Grand Metropolitan and, in 1991, becoming an independent company following a management buyout from Shell Ventures. (Page 2)

(b) A leading developer and producer of specialist enzymes, the question seems to be **whether it has got the same ability to commercialise these innovative solutions**. We are told (page 2 paragraph 3) that the wide geographic sales and broad spread of sectors served gives a balanced portfolio with steady profitable, income streams. The question is do we believe this? With only £2.5 million turnover, this is a **small** company. You need to stay aware of this scale context as you work through the case, because the narrative reads as a much bigger global player operating in 35 countries and with pages of product offerings and a customising service for big and small companies.

(c) It is certainly an interesting and topical sector; if you live in Europe, the ongoing controversy about genetically modified (GM) foods seems to roll on and on. There are some clear indications that, in your role as consultant to Biocatalysts, you may need to advise on how to handle the communication and PR challenges currently faced by biotechnology companies wanting to use GMOs in their production (Case Study page 24 paragraph 4). The organisation chart on page 28 shows a functionally organised business with no reflection of the international aspects of the business. R&D, design and production all seem to be involved in doing their own thing.

5.3 Your role

(a) **Your role is clear**. You are an **independent consultant**, Joseph Mendes, apparently of some repute. (You must strive not to damage that hard earned reputation with your response to Biocatalysts' problems!)

(b) You have been invited to develop a marketing report, to be presented to the Managing Director, Stewart North, prior to a piece of strategic work. Unfortunately, this brief (page 1) is not presented with as much clarity as we would like. It seems the Case Study itself represents this first stage in this process, the report, which has been sent in advance of the Board Meeting to Stewart North. It seems likely that in response to this you will get some additional information from Stewart and be asked your views on the strategic issues which will frame the next stages of presentation to the Board and preparation for the strategic exercise.

(c) What you might be asked to report on is less clear than it has been in other CIM exams but you can assume the emphasis will be strategic not tactical. You **need to be able to discuss corporate positioning and competitive strategy as well as market segmentation,** short and longer term marketing plans, developing international markets, managing channels as well as the communication issues facing GM products.

5.4 Performance

(a) At first read of the case, Biocatalysts comes over as successful (20% growth, achieving double the industry average over the last 10 years: page 16) and seemingly very customer oriented. **However, for such a small business they seem very over-stretched.** Operating in 35 countries might mean they are trying to be all things to all people. They seem to be reactive to customers' needs, customising their offerings, but less successful at proactively developing a segment of the market as in the case of the olive farmers. Positioning maps can help plot current approaches or culture.

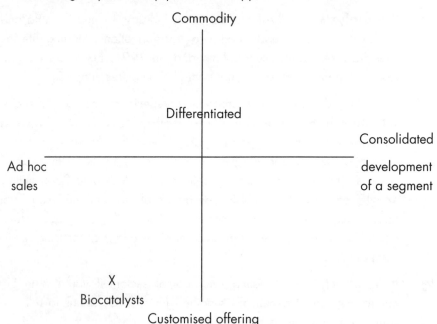

Stakeholder concerns

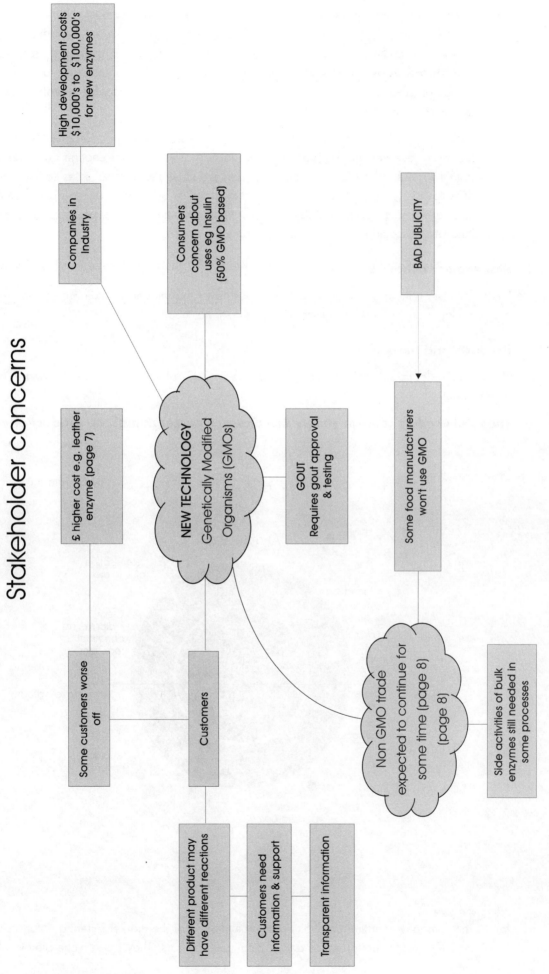

(b)   It seems the company is mainly involved in a **niche of the market**, offering customised services, and it is said that this is a unique service, providing an important basis for sustainable competitive advantage. However, this is an **expensive process if additional demand is not generated**. In the last pages of the case you will see the listings of products offered by this company and there are a **large number of new products** in the list.

(c)   The question of the product portfolio's balance is an obvious one to consider. Are there too many question marks/problem children and stars and not enough cash generated from the cows to fully exploit them? Certainly we know that 80% of sales come from 20% of customers (page 30), so an analysis of profitability by product and customer would I'm sure reveal some poor contributors. And the challenges of successfully commercialising innovations should be a framework for some of your planning.

5.5 Stakeholder concerns

The schematic on the previous page demonstrates how using models and diagrams can help you capture a lot of related data in a simple to review format.

5.6 Products and markets

The company launched 26 new products last year. 30% of sales are domestic and 70% are international.

The total product concept shows Biocatalyst's perception of the product offering.

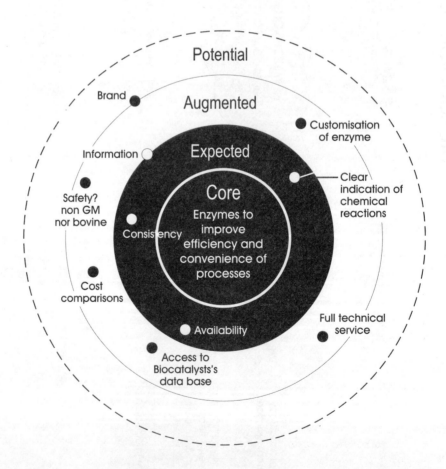

(a)   The company is at the high value, low volume end of the market, offering catalysts which improve process performance across a range of sectors. They are a niche player, able to offer a customised solution to their clients and a full technical service, which should help them avoid price battles and commoditisation as the industry shakes down, with medium-sized players expanding or specialising.

(b) The niche sectors could get crowded, but it is a growing market. Potential is different in the various segments and you will need to sort this out. For example, the Diagnostics Market offers good margins and repeat business (as there are high switching costs) but Biocatalysts is one of three UK suppliers. Some segments like textiles are more price sensitive and protecting these customers from competitive action may be more challenging.

(c) This seems like a company well positioned for future success, with all the essential requirements:

- A unique service offering
- Excellent network of innovators and researchers
- A 'customer focused' culture
- Presence in markets across the world

5.7 The Marketing Mix

There are issues about all elements of the marketing mix which will need sorting out.

(a) **Promotion**

- Dealing with publicity issues relating to use of GMOs
- Developing the 'brand' values and positioning as an expert in the field
- Finding a solution to keeping agents overseas up to date, perhaps the internet and the new website offer an opportunity here

(b) **Pricing**

- Establishing a value/price positioning and avoiding the slide towards commoditisation

(c) **Place**

- Selecting and organising overseas sales

(d) **Product**

- Managing the innovation and NPD process
- Commercialisation of new products

(e) **The service mix**

- Likely to be critical in this knowledge based and customised market: processes and people are going to be key

5.8 The Challenges

The challenges are:

- Turning stars into cash cows
- Establishing a clear focus for activities, not trying to be all things to all people
- A strategic plan: prioritising products and markets, and segmenting those markets is needed
- International distribution needs reviewing and options evaluating

■ A clearer positioning is essential: whilst Biocatalysts have the opportunity to carve out a clear niche with customised services, their promotion comes across as an 'off the shelf' product catalogue.

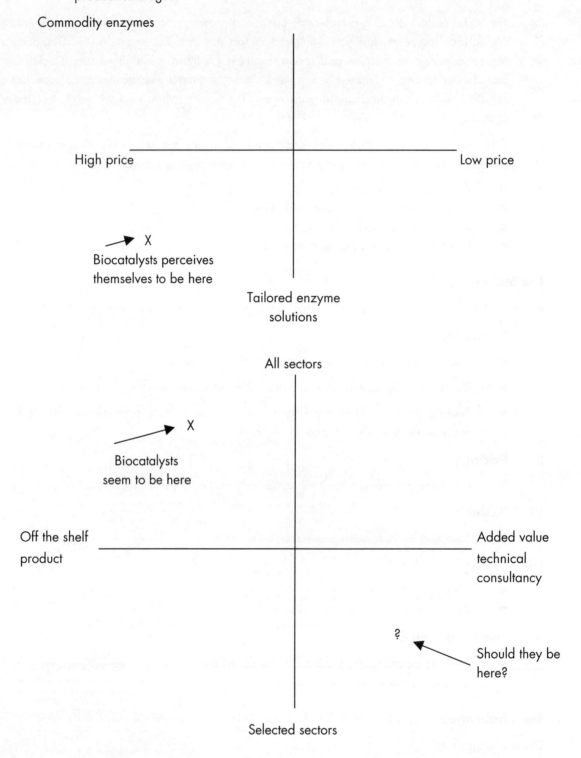

Commodity enzymes

High price   Low price

→ X
Biocatalysts perceives
themselves to be here

Tailored enzyme
solutions

All sectors

→ X

Biocatalysts
seem to be here

Off the shelf   Added value
product   technical
          consultancy

?
          Should they be
          here?

Selected sectors

Where are you now?

5.9 By now you should have a much clearer picture of:

■ Biocatalysts – the company and their business in terms of products and markets

■ Current performance – financial, operational etc

BPP
PROFESSIONAL EDUCATION

- The company's competitive position and competitive advantage, actual and potential – focusing on the marketing mix

- The current organisation and the environment it is in

- The enzymes market, developments and challenges

- The market place for these products – now and in the future

- New product development at Biocatalysts

- Who the customers are and what matters to them

- The international markets

You should now feel much more ready to tackle the more detailed inview analysis but before you do, test your current understanding of the case.

Action Programme 3

SO YOU THINK YOU KNOW THE CASE..?

QUESTIONS

1   Who are you? What is your role?

2   How would you describe Biocatalysts Ltd?

3   What is the extent and current state of Biocatalysts's international business?

4   How is the product development work managed and paid for at Biocatalysts?

5   What is the value forecast for the structure of the world enzyme industry?

6   What sector of the market is Biocatalysts active in and what is happening to it?

7   What makes Biocatalysts unique?

8   What are the limitations to growth for Biocatalysts?

9   What is the customer's view of price in this market?

10   What is the PR dimension of communication which the company needs to face?

Action programme review

1   (a)   This is a business to business market (page 2); this means communication strategies are likely to be sales led and key account management and relationship marketing could be key aspects of Biocatalysts's approach to the market. As you might expect from a B2B firm Biocatalysts has a smaller number of higher value clients and corporate reputation rather than emotional brand values will be important.

(b)   Biocatalysts develops and produces speciality enzymes for industry. It is a challenging global business because it is growing and developing rapidly, but the advent of new genetic engineering techniques and new applications have created their own marketing problems (page 16).

(c)   You are Joseph Mendes, a marketing consultant who (like you) has no experience of this sector. This report is the output of Joseph's initial analysis into the firm and the market – you can expect to be asked to use this to help recommend future strategies.

(d)   Agents are largely involved in export markets.

2 *Adding the context*

(a) It creates the picture of a large successful global player with a number of international markets. Its ethnocentric strategy could be explained by the high knowledge content of its services and the need to customise its services.

(b) Instead of its global expansion being a strength, suddenly it seems more of a weakness. Here we have a business that has stretched itself too thin when it comes to its geographic markets at least. Only an average of 2% of its income, some £50,000, is generated from each country. Clearly there has been little market penetration strategy operating. You start to get a picture of a reactive and opportunist company more like the one we described in a) and the challenge would be to improve penetration and performance in their chosen markets.

(c) An exporting strategy would probably be better replaced with local production, close to eventual markets, thus lowering distribution costs and either improving profitability or local price performance.

SO YOU THINK YOU KNOW THE CASE..?

ANSWERS

1 You are Joseph Mendes, you are a marketing consultant working with Biocatalysts Ltd.

2 A small Welsh-based independent company producing speciality enzymes for a range of industrial clients. They are in the low volume/high value end of the market.

3 70% of sales are exported currently to over 35 countries. Business is managed by agents, who are difficult to control and mainly motivated by finances. The agents earn a 5% commission.

4 Most of the basic research is handled by UK universities where they have many contacts. In-house scientists can focus on customer needs. Funding for higher margin products in diagnostics and pharmaceuticals comes from profits and from European and UK grants.

5 A rapidly growing market:

1994	$1 billion
1997	$1.3 billion
1998	$1.7 billion
2005	$2.0 billion

A polarising market: 12 big global payers with clear positioning/distinct ranges; 60 medium-sized companies and 400 smaller players being forced out because of economies of scale. New competitors from Russia and China forecast.

6 The 'other sector' – likely to be worth over $500m by 2005 (representing 70% of the total market growth).

7 It provides custom-tailored products for its clients.

8 Current capacity would allow output to double. Further growth requires investment funds.

9 We are told price is always an issue, yet enzymes represent a small part of costs (so should be price inelastic) and liability and service is more important. Price comparisons are difficult and Biocatalysts offers a unique customisation service.

10 Genetically modified organisms are increasing by being used for enzyme products (page 24) and Biocatalysts has several under development. A clear communication plan and policy on communications is needed.

Step 2: The Inview – internal analysis

Chapter Topic List	
1	Introduction to planning route maps
2	What needs to be done
3	Biocatalysts: product analysis
4	Biocatalysts: situation analysis
5	The pitfalls

Introduction

☑ In this chapter we will:

- Review the knowledge and skills you will use in the internal analysis
- Identify the strengths and weaknesses of the Biocatalyst marketing audit
- Identify the strengths and weaknesses of the Biocatalyst business
- Consider the pitfalls at this stage of the process

1 Introduction to planning route maps

1.1 Throughout the file we will be guiding you through the process of analysis and decision with the use of the planning route maps. These maps enable you to quickly assess where you are now in the process and what the next stage is.

Purpose

1.2 At these second and third case steps we will be working on further but deeper case analysis. We need to really get to grips with the information available to us. Because our overview provided us with a real sense of the case context, we will be much better able to make sense of and appreciate the implications of our evaluations and assessments.

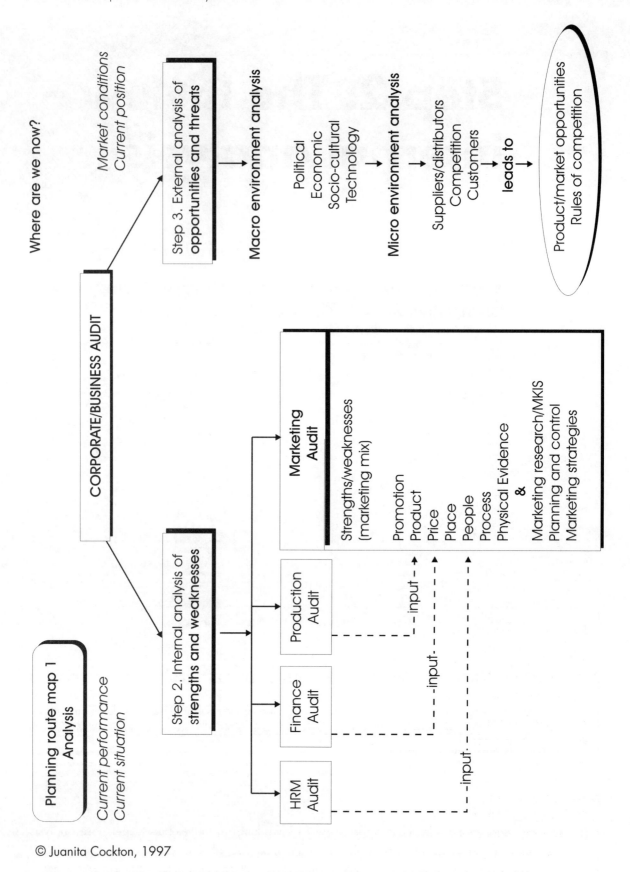

Where are we now?

Market conditions
Current position

Step 3. External analysis of **opportunities and threats**

Macro environment analysis

Political
Economic
Socio-cultural
Technology

Micro environment analysis

Suppliers/distributors
Competition
Customers

leads to

Product/market opportunities
Rules of competition

CORPORATE/BUSINESS AUDIT

Planning route map 1
Analysis

Current performance
Current situation

Step 2. Internal analysis of **strengths and weaknesses**

HRM Audit

Finance Audit

Production Audit

Marketing Audit

Strengths/weaknesses
(marketing mix)

Promotion
Product
Price
Place
People
Process
Physical Evidence
&
Marketing research/MKIS
Planning and control
Marketing strategies

-- input --

-- input --

-- input --

© Juanita Cockton, 1997

Tutor Tip

As we said in Chapter 3, in practice, analysis steps are likely to be undertaken **simultaneously**. Amongst academics there is some debate as to whether it is most appropriate to undertake an internal analysis before or after the external one. Our overview alleviates that issue to some extent but in reality this audit stage can be sequenced however you like, as long as the internal position is then considered in the **context** of the external and *vice versa*. For example, at the end of our internal analysis, we would expect to be able to summarise our findings in a weighted and rated table of strengths and weaknesses. To do this, the external perspective must be taken into account because the assessment of strengths and weaknesses must be made against competitor's performance ie bench marked.

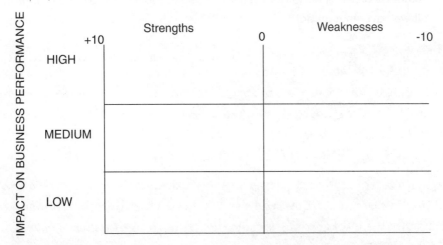

Point 0 indicates equal to the competitor(s). In this way we can review internal assessments in an external context. We will only be able to interpret our analysis in this way after both internal and external audits are complete, so we will do this in Chapter 7 as a stepping stone to establishing the critical success factors.

Skills and knowledge reminder

It is at the analysis stage where the tools and techniques really come into their own. Different cases will lend themselves to different tools and you need to learn to be selective and not to worry if you have incomplete information:

- Use what you have
- Make assumptions if you need to, to fill gaps
- Remember to note the gaps on your information shopping list

Typically the tools and techniques you might need to use at this stage of a case study will include the following. (Again you will need to take time out to refresh your memory on how each of them is used if you have any doubts or knowledge gaps.)

- Ratio Analysis
- Benchmarking
- Product Life Cycle
- Boston Matrix
- GE Matrix
- Strength and Weaknesses Analysis

2 What needs to be done

2.1 What needs to be done and how much work is involved at this stage very much depends on the case study. You may have a lot or a little information on the products, marketing or resources of the business. You may have already done quite a bit of work at the overview stage which now needs incorporating or building upon. In this case study though, you can see the distinction between the **overview** and **inview** quite clearly.

(a) At **overview,** we looked at the generic enzyme products and tried to understand what they were and did

(b) We also had an **overview** of the Biocatalysts range – recognising its size, the proportion of new products and its sector focus

(c) At **inview** we need to get even more depth, looking for example at product profitability, if we have enough data

Tutor Tip

You may have already begun to appreciate how much paper can be generated when working on a case study and why management material is such a key skill for the successful student. To help keep your stress levels down by minimising lost pages and work, you should really take positive steps to organise your analysis now.

Steps 2 and 3 are the most paper-intensive, particularly if you are working with a syndicate. You can start by organising your overview into internal and external factors and then working under specific headings like Product, Finance.

2.3 By the end of this step we will be able to assess:

(a) Strengths and weaknesses of Biocatalysts's marketing activities
(b) Strengths and weaknesses of Biocatalysts's business situation

2.4 Remember internal analysis assesses the current situation, warts and all!. If staff morale is low, that is what needs to be identified. The fact a new incentive scheme is planned for next year or next month is not relevant. Our task is to evaluate the situation as it is **today**.

2.5 **The distinction between internal and external analysis is decided by controllability.** Low morale, profitability or brand perceptions are all internal controllable factors. Changing them may be difficult, take time and require investment but they can all be tackled. Factors like a declining birth rate, economic recession or introduction of a new technology are external and outside the control of the business.

3   Biocatalysts: product analysis

3.1   We will begin by looking in detail at the Biocatalysts's product portfolio.

We are working in a relatively new technology-driven and global market. We can use a Boston Matrix to help us assess the various Biocatalysts's products/markets within the whole sector.

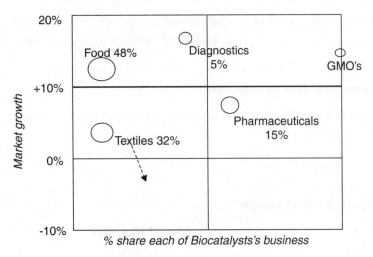

A MODIFIED BCG MATRIX

You can see why the tools are so valuable, when you look at this grid and think about what it tells you.

Action Programme 1

Take five minutes to review this indicative BCG Matrix of Biocatalysts's portfolio and identify what this information is telling you. Turn to the end of this chapter to compare your interpretation with ours. You may be wondering where we got the information to apply to our modified Boston Matrix.

Tutor Tip

It is quite acceptable to modify the various tools and models but do make it clear with your labelling. In this case we have used the extended grid which adds warhorses and dodoes to indicate products where the total market is in decline rather than growth. Here you might try to do the analysis based on relative market share. Remember it is the served market, so even a niche player can be leader in that niche. The data defining the served market is not clear, so the model has been adapted: we have used the relative share of their own market rather than relative market share of the total market.

To build this matrix we needed information about:

- Biocatalysts's products
- The product/market sectors

Take a few minutes to look at where we found this and check it against the case study. You can see from this illustration how you need to cross relate data to turn it effectively into information, and then the intelligence we gleaned earlier.

Tutor Tip

You will remember we indicated that internal analysis could only be considered when viewed in an external context. The market information is just that in this example. We will also show how competitor information helps to give us some insight into Biocatalysts's position.

Biocatalysts's Product Information

Information on pages 34-36 in Appendix 9 is most helpful when you try to sort out the Biocatalysts's portfolio.

Biocatalysts product range

1	Baking Brewing Fruit and veg Flavour Proteins Dietetics	**Food industry** **48%**
2	Textiles (garment washing)	**Textile Industry** **32%**
3	Own specialist enzymes No npd	**Pharmaceutical industry** **15%**
4	Phen Dehyd Glactose Peroxidase etc	**Diagnostics industry** **5%**

Market information

3.3 Food Industry (from page 34)

(a) 12.5% of all new Biocatalyst's products/investments are in the food sector.

(b) In total, they have 71 old and 14 new products in this area.

(c) 48% of revenue means it represents the largest percentage of sales and Biocatalyst appear to get high margins in this sector.

(d) Their competitive advantage lies in:

- Niche production of specialist enzymes
- Kosher
- Tailored offering
- Safety

(e) This is where GMOs are currently causing concerns and in the UK and Europe the backlash of BSE etc is having a considerable impact.

(f) On average, each product in this part of Biocatalyst's portfolio represents 0.5% of total revenue.

(g) In the UK the closest competitor is Amano (Appendix 1).

Optimum performing

Biocatalysts*

*Amano

High value ⎯⎯⎯⎯⎯⎯⎯⎯⎯⎯⎯⎯ Low value

Multiple bulk process

3.4 (a) The Textile industry

(i) 21 products in total, and 9 are new (ie 43%). It is clear that Biocatalyst are investing heavily in this sector, with cost implications.

(ii) Yet this is a declining market.

Sales review

←Textile sector

0 ⎯⎯⎯ Time

(iii) Gaining a share in a declining market is not an obviously strong strategy. The market, once mature, will commoditise and differentiation will be increasingly difficult and expensive. Biocatalysts will need to decide whether the level of investment needed to stay in this market is worthwhile.

(iv) Textiles represent almost one third (31%) of Biocatalysts' business

(b) Competitors

(i) Genzyme and Biozyme do not appear to offer many (if any) textile products.

(ii) What about Rhone-Poulenc: does it have textile products? More information is needed here.

(iii) There appears to be no major competitor in this sector, perhaps this is why Biocatalysts has commanded such a high share of sales from this market.

3.5 **(a)** **Pharmaceuticals**

    (i)   No new products out of a total of 7 offered – so no new investment. Why?

    (ii)   These represent 15% of total sales.

    (iii)   We have no real information on positioning or share in this sector.

    (iv)   Pharmaceuticals are not featured in the world market (page 4). Why not?

    (v)   Biocatalysts could be a niche player in a small market with high potential profitability.

    (vi)   Its competitive advantage would be unique enzymes which could command higher prices.

(b) **Competitors**

    (i)   Genzyme: what does 'healthcare' cover?

    (ii)   Biozyme: more information is needed

    (iii)   Amano: 51% of their sales are from pharmaceuticals. How does that translate to market share?

    (iv)   Gist Brocades: largest antibiotics producer in the world

3.6 **(a)** **Diagnostics**

    (i)   8 products in total – 3 of them are new

    (ii)   They represent just 5% of revenue

    (iii)   Biocatalyst is a monopolist in PD enzyme (page 10)

    (iv)   In this sector customers become a captive audience with high switching costs that essentially tie them into a deal.

    (v)   This is another niche market which again does not feature in world figures.

    (vi)   There are new US customers which might lead to growth but also stimulate new competitors.

    (vii)   There are high margins to be made here and it is a profitable product range.

    (viii)   Biocatalyst is investing here and operates in several diagnostic areas and so can offer some depth of product range and experience.

(b) **Competitors**

    (i)   Amano: 10% of their sales in Diagnostics which amounts to $9.2m a very large player in a small market

    (ii)   Biozyme: more information needed

    (iii)   Genzyme: more information needed

3.7 **GMOs**

Biocatalysts has two genetically modified organisms in development which they are due to launch next year.

Tutor Tip

As you pull your analysis together you will see how the picture builds and those information gaps close up.

3.8 Consolidating information

There are no short cuts to working through case information but you will find it easier if you find ways to summarise and consolidate it.

Product group	Sub Group	Number of products	Number of new products
Food	Baking	18	3
	Brewing	5	5
	Fruit & Veg Processing	11	3
	Flavour	14	0
	Protein	13	1
	Dietetics	9	2
Non Food	Textiles	21	9
	Diagnostics	8	3
	Pharmaceuticals	7	1
	Environmentals	4	0
		110	27

(a) A simple table shows the company's spread of activity – 110 products (plus 2 GMOs in development) offered to 10 sectors across food and non food based clients.

(b) Of the 110 products, 27 are new. Five of these are within brewing, a market the company has had no previous experience of. You do need to ask the question **why**?

(c) Has this come about because a researcher wants to work in this sector? If so, we would be worried about the product orientation this demonstrates.

or

Is this development in response to customer requests which shows the company as reactive? In this case we would want to look at the **screening process** for such requests. Does the company simply respond to the scientific challenge rather than assess the commercial feasibility of the new products being developed?

Tutor Tip

The analysis alone is not enough, you must think about what it is telling you. What are the implications?

(d)   Again mind maps and charts can help you to summarise and consolidate information.

Biocatalysts's product portfolio

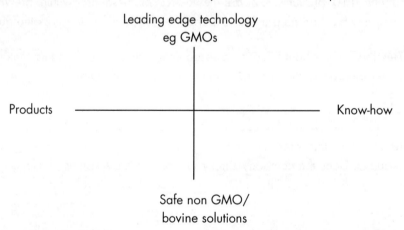

Biocatalysts:
- High value, low volume end of market
- Exports to 35/40 countries (70% of sales)
- Mainly working in 'other sector' serving 10 groups
- Produce for food speciality
- For diagnostic/pharmaceutical unique
- Technical expertise, customer relationships

Environmental:
paper/pulp, waste treatment

Unique enzymes

Speciality enzymes:
complexes, additional chemicals, moderate margins

Pharmaceuticals

Diagnostics
- test kits
- high tech
- good margins
- high R&D

Textiles
- fading jeans
- almost commodity 'cash cow'

Food: 50% sales
Banking, brewing, fruit and veg processing, flavour, proteins, dietetics

3.9   We often find positioning maps useful for clarifying information as well as communicating options and you can see in the one provided here how, in terms of its product, Biocatalyst appears to be uncertain about 'what business they are in' and how to position themselves.

Leading edge technology
eg GMOs

Products ——————————— Know-how

Safe non GMO/
bovine solutions

3.10 Any position could be tenable but for a very small business, such a big portfolio has them stuck in the middle of the road.

Action Programme 2

Auditing the rest of the marketing mix

Having looked in some detail at the 'product', take no more than 30 minutes to review your case materials and complete a summary strengths and weaknesses analysis for the remaining 6 'P's of the mix.

Tutor Tip

Remember: case studies are never complete, so do not be surprised to find gaps or limited information under certain headings.

Strengths	Weaknesses
Place	
Price	
Promotion	
People	
Physical evidence	
Processes	
Turn to the end of this chapter to compare your analysis with ours.	

4 Biocatalysts: situation analysis

4.1 To tackle a case study effectively, you need to address yourself to the whole business **not** simply the marketing activities. This requires that our internal audit is broadened to include:

(a)   Financial perspective

(b)   Operational overview

(c)   People overview

(d)   Pan-company issues, including culture, management skills, management information planning processes and new product development

BPP PROFESSIONAL EDUCATION

4.2 When added to the marketing analysis, you then have a complete situational analysis which will enable us to:

- Assess available resources

- Consider issues of capacity

- Identify any limiting factors

- Establish corporate capabilities which could be used as a basis for establishing a competitive advantage

Tutor Tip

If you are working with a syndicate, you may rely on others to complete parts of your audit analysis for you. That is quite acceptable but you must take the responsibility of owning and understanding the output of that process.

Action Programme 3

Before moving forward in this chapter, you might like to practise your analysis skills by pulling together an analysis of these other business areas.

Financial perspective

4.3 Biocatalyst's chosen market is one which requires **high investment** but **delivers high returns** as a result. New products are currently funded from profits and grants from the government and Europe. (The impact of losing grants is a pressing issue.)

4.4 The industry as a whole is growing steadily with sales raising from $1bn in 1994 to $1.3bn in 1997. This is expected to top $2bn in 2005.

4.5 With 70% of sales revenue coming from exports, the company is used to handling different currencies (although it usually only handles $s, £s, and Euros).

Creditors increased in 1997 over 1996 (up 27% or £109k); however debtors have increased by 51% (266k) in the same period.

4.6 Cash flow does not appear to be a problem at the present time. This is assisted by the company policy against stockpiling of finished goods: only raw materials and work in progress is generally held as stock.

- Current ratio > 2:1
- Acid test > 1:1

4.7 The business is growing by 20-30% pa but profitability (page 30) is not improving. There is a danger Biocatalysts is working harder rather than smarter.

Analysing financial information

During your studies of strategic marketing management, you will have covered financial ratios. There has been criticism of marketers' lack of financial skills and the Senior Examiners have made it clear that this area will be tested. We have seen an increase in the financial data and need to be able to work the numbers and interpret financial information. There are many financial ratios but here is a reminder of the key ratios you are most likely to use.

Liquidity and working capital ratios

- Current ratio

$$\frac{\text{Current assets}}{\text{Current liabilities}}$$

- Quick ratio (acid test ratio)

$$\frac{\text{Current assets} - \text{inventory}}{\text{Current liabilities}}$$

Efficiency and turnover ratios

- Asset turnover ratio

$$\frac{\text{Sales}}{\text{Average total sales}}$$

- Debtor days (average debt collection period)

$$\frac{\text{Sales}}{\text{Debtors}}$$

- Average stock turnover period (days)

$$\frac{\text{Sales}}{\text{Inventory}}$$

Profitability ratios

- Return on capital employed (ROCE)

$$\frac{\text{Earnings before interest and tax}}{\text{Capital employed}}$$

- Return on investment (ROI)

$$\frac{\text{Net operating income}}{\text{Operating assets}}$$

- Return on sales (ROS) (net profit as a percentage of sales – net margin)

$$\frac{\text{Earnings before interest and tax}}{\text{Sales revenue}}$$

- Gross profit as a percentage of sales (gross margin)

$$\frac{\text{Gross profit}}{\text{Sales}}$$

- Return on net assets (RONA)

$$\frac{\text{PBIT}}{\text{Sales revenue}} \times \frac{\text{Sales revenue}}{\text{Net assets}}$$

Debt and gearing ratios

- Debt ratio

$$\frac{\text{Total debt}}{\text{Total assets}} \; or \; \frac{\text{Long term debt}}{\text{Shareholder equity}}$$

- Gearing ratio

$$\frac{\text{Total debt}}{\text{Total assets}}$$

- Cash flow ratio

$$\frac{\text{Earnings before interest and tax} + \text{depreciation}}{\text{Interest} + [\text{payment}/(1 - \text{tax rate})]}$$

Tutor Tip

Knowledge check: how many of these ratios are familiar to you? Skills check: can you use these ratios? You will need to be able to for the case study.

4.8 There are nearly always discrepancies in the numbers, for example, Biocatalysts's claim to have achieved growth of 20% to 30%. Is it 20%, 30% or somewhere in between? This is one of those occasions when we have to make an assumption before we can start working the figures. Anything from 20% to 30% is acceptable but once you decide what figure you are going to work with, you must remain consistent.

4.9 On page 30 there is reference to the company turnover being approximately £2.5 million. It does not tell us in what year. Again we must make an assumption and, at the time of working the case study, we assumed 1998. We can then work this figure backwards, using whichever figure we have assumed as growth, to give us a turnover figure for 5 years.

4.10 This page also has what is called a profitability index. It is not, in fact, a profitability index but a profit chart.

Action Programme 4

Using appropriate financial ratios, analyse Biocatalysts's financial data. Remember, information is scattered around the case study material, so make sure you collate all the information before you start.

Biocatalysts – working the numbers/key numbers sheet (pages 29/30)

4.11 Remember your figures might be different depending on what growth rate, and therefore turnover, you identified.

Liquidity/working capital

		1994	1995	1996	1997
Current ratio	$\dfrac{\text{Current assets}}{\text{Current liabilities}}$			$\dfrac{736,915}{399,078}$	$\dfrac{953,622}{508,073}$
		2.3	**2.2**	**1.8**	**1.8**

(Good, 1.8 to 2.3 so fairly sound)

Acid test	$\dfrac{\text{Current assets, less inventory}}{\text{Current liabilities}}$			$\dfrac{548,449}{399,078}$	$\dfrac{795,745}{508,073}$
		1.4	**1.5**	**1.4**	**1.6**

(Good, greater than 1 so fairly sound)

Efficiency (productivity) and turnover

		1994	1995	1996	1997
Assets/T/O $\dfrac{\text{Sales}}{\text{Average total assets}}$				$\dfrac{1,601,562}{910,589}$	$\dfrac{2,002,952}{1,131,291}$
				1.8	**1.8**
Debtor days $\dfrac{\text{Sales}}{\text{Debtors}}$				$\dfrac{1,601,562}{517,462}$	$\dfrac{2,002,952}{783,623}$
	(days)	75	72	**118**	**143**

(Poor risk bad debt/cash flow)

Stock turnover $\dfrac{\text{Sales}}{\text{Inventory}} =$				$\dfrac{1,601,562}{188,466}$	$\dfrac{2,002,952}{157,877}$
	(days)	**4.9**	**4.8**	**8.5**	**12.6**

(Depends on 6 week lead time)

Creditor days	(days)	**75**	**75**	**91**	**93**

4.12 This enables you to use very specific case material and therefore provides you with the opportunity to added value and offer insights into financial performance.

Tutor Tip

Have a look at the figures on page 30 of the case data. This is a good example of how you need to take care with years and comparisons. The table makes you think profit margins are improving significantly: from 4.9% in 1994 to 8.2% in 1995.

There are two issues with this:

(a)   Is 8.2% a reasonable return on investment in a high risk, high tech sector? Would the shareholders be better off putting their money in a bank?

(b)   It isn't 1995, it is 1998. If you now look at the profitability index you can see the improved performances in 1994 – 1996, but profitability in 1997 and 1998 has levelled off or only increased marginally over the last twelve months.

The available financial analysis is weak. We have no profit analysis by:

■   Country
■   Product
■   Sector
■   Agents
■   Sales people

We do know that 80% of business comes from 20% of the customers but we do not know whether this also represents 80% of the **profits**.

4.13 Remember the marketer's impact on gross profit

Marketing decisions impact directly on the gross profit margins of the business. Appreciating the implications of your decisions is critical to your ability to share responsibility for the financial health of the business.

(a) **Changing the customer mix**

Different market segments will have different gross profit potential. Large customers may be more or less profitable than small ones. There are no hard and fast rules, just the margins are likely to be different. Before deciding which segments to target, marketers must know which segments are most profitable.

(b) **Changing the product mix**

Different products will have different profit margins. Knowing which are your most profitable offerings is fundamental to decisions at a strategic and tactical level.

(c) **Changing the marketing mix**

Discounts or increased advertising might increase sales revenue and total profit but will depress gross profit margins. Decisions to change any element of the marketing mix will have financial consequences: marketers need to be aware of these and budget for them.

Tutor Tip

Improving Profitability

Biocatalysts is unlikely to be the last case where we are faced with a need to improve profitability and it would be useful for you to ensure you are familiar not only with how marketing can impact on profitability, but on how it can be improved by actions across the business.

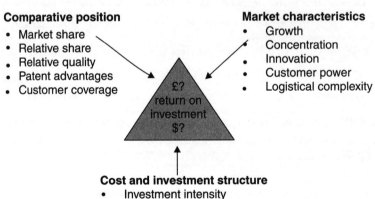

Comparative position
- Market share
- Relative share
- Relative quality
- Patent advantages
- Customer coverage

Market characteristics
- Growth
- Concentration
- Innovation
- Customer power
- Logistical complexity

£?
return on investment
$?

Cost and investment structure
- Investment intensity
- Investment mix
- Capacity utilisation
- Productivity
- Vertical integration

Porter's value chain can be a useful model to help identify and communicate profit drivers from across the business.

Operational overview

4.14 Biocatalysts Ltd have only one site: this is in Wales and is an 8,000 square feet modern factory unit. Facilities include:

- Liquid and powder blending facilities
- Small scale fermentation/filtration equipment
- Pilot chromatographic purification and drying units

4.15 Batch sizes for all in-house production is flexible and the company is ISO 9000 compliant, enforcing the highest levels of quality control. All of the above machinery is fully depreciated but envisaged to be capable of another five years' output before replacement is necessary.

4.16 Customer requirements are established and the appropriate enzyme solution is researched by the Biocatalyst Ltd scientists (and researchers at various universities).

4.17 Large scale production/fermentation is contracted out. This has both good and bad aspects – good from the point of view of flexibility for the place/country of production and removal of the need for capital expenditure (for purchase and maintenance of facilities) but bad from the point of view of control. Quality control amongst other things can fall short of the required standards, facilities may not be available when needed and so on.

4.18 A £1m investment would enable all fermentation processing to take place in-house for the next five years (taking into account the sales growth we can expect). It should be noted that this could produce logistical problems in the transport of the finished product that would add to the costs of production and delivery of the final product.

4.19 Currently facilities already in place are not fully utilised. It has been calculated that in-house production could double with limited investment and only one or two more production staff.

4.20 Heavy investment after five years will be needed.

4.21 No fermentation takes place on site.

People overview

4.22 Currently there is a very simple structure in place with small teams for Sales, Administration, Purchasing, Production, Design and R&D projects. The structure is not marketing oriented at present which will need addressing.

4.23 Marketing/Sales is made up of five people including the MD (Stewart North). They look after new product development and long-term strategy. Of these five, there are three dedicated sales staff who spend 80% of their time directly involved with sales. This team of three is responsible for the relationship with the agents who conduct Biocatalyst's business to business sales.

4.24 Nearly all overseas sales are generated by agents and distributors. This has inherent problems such as that agents are not solely representing Biocatalyst Ltd and may sell competitor products in preference to Biocatalysts's; they need constant review, the quality of individuals varies. They are hard to monitor and they are not always motivated to educate the customers as they should.

4.25 Scientists are not full time employees and so their availability and commitment could be an issue.

4.26 There may be an element of 'pet project syndrome' when it comes to evaluating new opportunities.

4.27 High staff costs are minimised by using a project approach.

4.28 Contact with overseas sales teams is inadequate. A newsletter is sent out every six months to all distributors and customers. This details R&D advances and other changes in current products. Training sessions are held every year to bring agents up to speed with the current portfolio. Unfortunately many agents are absent from these meetings, drastically reducing their impact.

4.29 More and more, specialised/narrow niches are emerging and pressure is rising to provide dedicated sales teams who work only for Biocatalyst. Although it would be a challenge to replace all agents with dedicated staff in all countries, there are certain areas where potential volumes demand them, eg the Olive Oil sector and the PKU diagnostics enzyme recently approved for use in the USA.

5 The pitfalls

5.1 For the marketing student, the inview analysis can cause problems and there are a number of pitfalls you need to avoid:

(a) Focusing only on the **marketing aspects** and ignoring other **business issues and factors**.

(b) **Ignoring the numbers**: yes we know it's tempting but the numbers will provide you with the keys to setting objectives and controls so work with them **not** around them.

(c) Failing to consolidate and summarise your analysis so that there are pages of information but you fail to use it as intelligence because it cannot be easily assimilated.

Action Programme 5

Having worked through the internal analysis you should now be in a position to share your understanding of Biocatalyst with others.

Take no more than 20 minutes to prepare some brief notes in answer to a colleague's questions about Biocatalyst. Try and do this without referring back.

1 What are the key points you would make about the company's products?

Key Points

■

■

■

2 How would you summarise the strengths and weaknesses of Biocatalysts in relation to its current markets?

Strengths   *Weaknesses*

3   How would you summarise the company's overall weaknesses?

Check your answers with ours at the end of this chapter.

Action Programme Review

1   (a)   Over half of Biocatalysts' product/markets are high growth – net cash users not generators.

     (b)   The company is operating in four main sectors – so it begs the question, 'are they spread too thinly?'

     (c)   The main cash cow, textiles, is a market going into decline.

     (d)   GMOs are a classic. They could be highly profitable or, if rejected by customers, immediately become a dog. They should be concerned about future cash flow and funding the effective commercialisation of new products.

2   *Auditing the rest of the marketing mix*

Strengths

Place

- Network of agents and direct sales covering 35 countries
- Direct sales team, but it's very small

> **Implications**: Little control over agents or access to the customer in international markets.

Price

- Euro may resolve our exchange problems for Europe in the future
- Some new sectors and markets are attracting premium prices

> **Implications**: A one-size fits all pricing strategy will not maximise returns for this business.

Promotion

- Key account handling exists in principle if not always in practice
- They feel mailshots and exhibitions are important

> **Implications**: There is more of a B2C feel to the communications thinking. Networking and relationship marketing need to be cornerstones for this sector.

People

- High calibre scientific staff
- Flexibility in staffing should enable the right people for the right task and keep costs down
- Links with University staff

BPP
PROFESSIONAL EDUCATION

- 80% of five sales and marketing people's time dedicated to sales

Physical evidence

> **Implications**: In a service business physical evidence can add tangibility and value. It needs to be included in our thinking.

Processes

> **Implications**: Another black hole with no real insights but would be critical in ensuring customer satisfaction

Weaknesses

Place

- Inconsistent ability of agents to add value
- Training and updating: Biocatalysts' business has limited commission value to agents
- Shipping costs
- Agents will be driven by commission
- No website

Price

- Pricing strategy is not delivering profits expected
- Some sectors are commoditising and prices are low
- Pricing strategy doesn't support the company's positioning
- How are exchange rates impacting on prices – benefits or takes the hit?

Promotion

- Personal sales coverage is weak due to limited resources
- Brand values are undefined and positioning is confused
- Communication with agents is patchy and unfocused
- No website for communication
- The literature is product led, offering few benefits and not focused on the various sectors with very different needs!
- Bad PR related to GM products

People

- No obvious marketing experiences
- There are question marks over the agents' motivation and capability
- Training not taken seriously
- High technical support promised but is it given?

> **Implications.** Selling know-how is dependent on the people. There is a question as to the commitment and availability of this academic community

Physical Evidence

- No mention of any tangible aspects of the brand eg packaging, product literature, van livery, etc

3   Compare your activities with ours.

4   *The answer is given in the text.*

5

1 Key points about the Biocatalysts' products

- Positioned at high value, low volume end of market, need to build strong positioning to counteract threats from changes in the market

- Have unique products: however need to protect them – intellectual property

- Diagnostics = good margins: however low percentage of current sales

- New product development led by customers – lack of focus

- Research part funded by grants – what if these were withdrawn

- Over represented in declining product sectors, many new products being produced in these

- GMO's could present both opportunity and threat: need to consider implications in terms of PR and marcomms

- Threats from competitors: they are producing products in a very attractive niche of the market

- Technical ability – but product led

2 Biocatalysts' markets: strengths and weaknesses

Strengths	Weaknesses
Experience in many markets	Overstretched serving too many sectors and countries
Diagnostic high margin	
Food sector expertise and high growth area	Never fully exploit sector/product potential
Pharma high margin	Textiles in decline
Seeks niches	Fragmented
Monopoly of PKU testing	Three players have 75% of market
	No market analysis
	No environmental screening
	Very competitive – many players
	Commoditisation of some markets
	8% profitability very low – some markets very unprofitable
	Little in-house overseas knowledge

3 Overall weaknesses

- Reliance on other parties for sales and for R&D

- Resources spread thinly in over 35 countries

- Lack of production facilities leaving Biocatalysts at the mercy of other companies (time frames etc)

- Independent sales advisers are used who do not have it in their main interests to promote Biocatalysts's products all of the time(extended portfolios etc). These staff have no one to answer to.

- Lack of sales channels

- Communication channels to existing sales channels are unacceptably poor

Step 3: External analysis

6

Chapter Topic List	
1	Mapping the context: skills and knowledge
2	Building a market map for Biocatalysts

Introduction

In this chapter we will cover:

☑ The micro analysis for Biocatalysts covering market analysis, competitor audit and customer analysis

☑ The macro analysis for Biocatalysts

1 Mapping the context: skills and knowledge

1.1 Organisations **do not exist in a vacuum and so therefore they cannot plan in one.** It is the **changes** in their external macro and micro environments which create the **opportunities and threats** which drive their fortunes. Those who only look inwardly will be caught out by the environmental threats and will fail to respond to the opportunities. In today's fast moving and dynamic markets, the environmental impact can be swift and significant. Only those really aware of their markets and environments can effectively capitalise on emerging opportunities or minimise the impact of the threats. The smaller the business, like Biocatalysts, the fewer resources they have to weather an environmental storm, and the enzyme market is one where change is a fact of life.

1.2 You need to look **outside** the business to establish the **external context** and conditions facing the case company.

1.3 In the situation analysis, you needed to assess the current position but in the **environmental audit you need to address the future.** Planning is about tomorrow, not today, so we need to look forward and prepare the business for the markets of one, three, five or even ten years time. **This planning horizon will often be clear from the case.** A business struggling to survive might expect to be concerned with short term strategy, whereas a capital intensive industry may be planning for a longer term future.

Tutor Tip

*This immediately gives us a problem in case study. The CIM tells you **not** to look outside the case study, yet you are unlikely to have been furnished with environmental forecasts. You may be able to establish environmental trends from case information but you can also use your common sense and experience to make reasonable assumptions about the future.*

1.4 By the end of this chapter you will have:

(a) Created a market map for Biocatalysts

(b) Recognised the value of Porter's Five Forces and competitive strategies models in evaluating the micro environment

(c) Undertaken an environmental audit

(d) Considered the international aspects and the implications of different external environments on planning and strategy for a business such as Biocatalysts

---

Skills and knowledge reminders

There are a number of tools and models which are helpful when completing the external audit. You may need to familiarise yourself with the following before approaching this chapter.

- Ratio analysis
- Benchmarking
- Product life cycle
- Boston Matrix
- SE matrix
- Strengths and weaknesses

- Market maps
- Perceptual maps
- Porter's Five Forces
- Porter's generic strategies
- Diffusion of innovation

What needs to be done

1.6 What and how much needs to be done depends on the actual case you are working on. In some, we have a lot of external information and in others very little. However, the principles will stay very much the same. And the sequence might look like this:

1. Build a **Market Map**. You may need two or three if the company is active in different sectors facing different market conditions. If you have already used this framework at the inview stage, you could add detail now.

2. Market dynamics are important in understanding the business. Try to extend the market map into a Porter's **Five Forces Analysis** and assess the implications.

3. A **competitor analysis** is essential to any future strategy. Sort out who is active in what markets and what strategies they are adopting. (We began to collect some of that information when we were looking at the key Biocatalyst product markets in the last chapter.)

4. As customers are key, we need to assess who they are, how the market is segmented and who is in the DMU. We will need to think of channels as customers in this process. We want to assess how customers are changing: what are the emerging needs or concerns?

5. We need to consider the external macro environment, PEST or SLEPT or PESTLE analysis. Your terminology is not important so long as you have considered all the key factors and influences facing the business:

- Political and legal
- Social and cultural
- Economic and demographic
- Technological and environmental

6. **Market structure analysis – a check list**

Every market will differ in its characteristics. However, the following general analytical framework can be applied to most markets or segments. You should identify:

- What are the **market parameters**? In other words, what are its boundaries? The UK domestic market's parameters are the borders of the UK.
- The size of the market within these parameters
- Whether the market is **growing,** stable or declining
- How the market is **segmented**?
- To what extent **each segment** is growing, stable or declining
- The **key players** in the market/segments (eg manufacturers, distributors, others).
- The **key success factors** in this market or segment
- The **buying behaviour characteristics** of this market/segment
- The **major market/segment competitors**, their distinctive competences
- **Future environmental factors** affecting this market/segment
- How **easy** or **difficult** is the market and/or segment to **enter** or **exit**

2 Building a market map for Biocatalysts

Suppliers

Microbial
Industrial processing fermentation micro organisms Use GMOs in production Companies buy increasingly microbial or GEP

Contract Fermentation

Speciality chemicals

Research universities

Crop farmer
Proteases (cereals, soya, fruit) Affected by growth cycles, climate etc GMO developments

Cattle farmer
Provided as ultra refined entities or in bulk. Affected by agricultural policies etc

Biotech Co.s competitors

Biocatalysts turnover $3.99m

Nova Nordisk turnover $2.053m bulk heath (3K employees)

Gist Brocades (7k E) Bulk - 25 countries Antibiotics, food animal feed

Genecor largest 1,200P Bulk - international industrial biotech

Nagasi - Turnover $4.6bn so not just enzymes! Dyes chemicals, plaster H?

Amano - turnover $92m Spec pharm - international 420 employees

Rohm (food)

Danisco (food and dairy)

Biozyme diagnostics

Genzyme turnover $490m speciality Health care

Rhone Poulenc

Intermediaries

Agents

Regu-lations

Manufacturers/ producers

Food

Diagnostics

Pharmaceutical

Textiles

Paper/pulp

Waste treatment

Environmental maintenance

Retailers/ users

Supermarkets

Drinks industry

Hospitals Health

Chemists

Clothing industry

Industry

Government environmental agencies

End users

US

Pressure groups

Scientists

Journalists

2.1 In practice, you are unlikely to just sit down and complete a perfect market map for the case: you build it up and evolve it as you collect more information. This one is simple; it lists competitors but does not show how each of them is operating in terms of suppliers or access to customers. As we build our knowledge of competitors and customers through this step, you will be able to add more detail to the map.

Understanding market dynamics

2.2 Here is a table summarising the dynamics of the Biocatalysts market as produced by a student group working the case. It gives an idea of how you might synthesise this information, but compare it with the visual communication of the same material using the model. You can see how this gets information across quickly and can be a real asset in the exam room when time is at a premium.

Market analysis

Porter's model

Category	Remarks	Rating
Competitive activity	**General**: ■ Biocatalysts Ltd is a small company turnover just £2.5m – 70% export sales. ■ Biocatalysts Ltd provides full technical support, exclusive agreements and 1 to 1 relationship this high dependency relationship makes **switching** less likely ■ Biocatalysts Ltd operates in food 48%, textiles 31%, diagnostics 5%, pharmaceuticals 15% and other 1% ■ 12 major global producers all with relatively distinct offerings ■ 60 smaller range global producers ■ 400 very limited industrial quantity global producers ■ Geographically – 60% production in Europe, 15% in North America and 12-15% in Japan ■ Russian market large but undeveloped ■ Chinese market large (especially for food enzymes) but relatively 'closed' **Medical/diagnostic** (used for testing for abnormalities in humans) **sector**: ■ Japan weak in bulk enzymes but strong in speciality, especially medical diagnostics ■ Growth market ■ High margins **Textiles** (used for fading jeans) **sector**: ■ A near commodity business with little or no R&D required: this appears totally alien to Bio's offering ■ Moderate margins ■ Declining market **Food** (used to increase yields and quality) **sector**: ■ Moderate margins	Textiles: HIGH Other: MEDIUM
Buyers	**General:** ■ Price as a % of customers' production costs will be very low so price likely to be inelastic ■ A lot of product ignorance leading to some buyers focusing on price ■ Business to business market ■ Customers will often be very large and powerful ■ The needs of the deferred customer, the public, need to be considered ie fears in Europe leading to supermarkets not stocking ■ Agents selling many company products	Textiles: HIGH Other: MEDIUM
Suppliers	**General:** ■ Other enzyme producers (patents often in place) ■ University knowledge base ■ Fermenters (as this is outsourced)	MEDIUM

Category	Remarks	Rating
New entrants	**General:** ■ Growth market which is likely to attract others but high technical expertise may well act as a discouragement ■ Due to GMO option, R&D is lower, so ease of entry is higher ■ In-house option ■ Under-developed countries ie China and Russia	MEDIUM
Substitute products	**General:** ■ Traditional/natural production methods – but these are inefficient and of poor quality ■ Remember the GMO (lower R&D)/non-GO (higher R&D) option	LOW

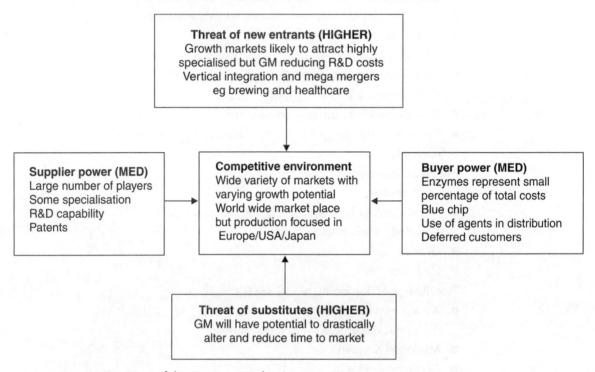

A Five Forces Map of the Enzyme Market (version 1)

Tutor Tip

You should also be aware that in case study there is no single correct answer. The examiners are looking for rigorous process and justification which is credible but not some pre-determined standard approach. Sample answers and our approach should therefore be viewed as indicative rather than prescriptive. You can see this by looking at this alternative version of Porter's Five Forces developed by a different group – equally valid and accurate but perhaps you can see how you might choose the modified content in a model you were presenting if the questions or additional information were different.

If the focus was on international markets and developments, then the first version might be most useful but if the extra information was about a merger between key competitors, the second would have more impact.

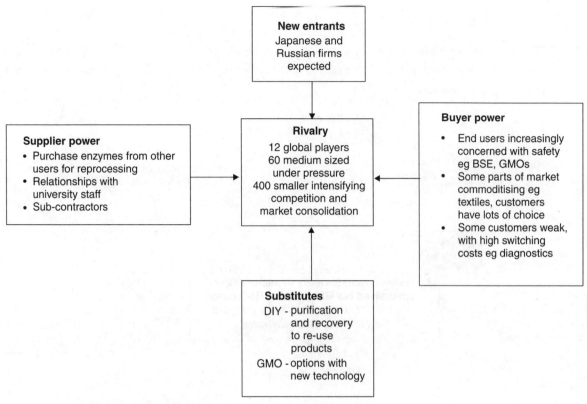

Porter's Five Forces (version 2)

Add the competitor dimension

2.3 Business would be a lot easier without competitors.

Action Programme 1

Assessing Competitor Responses

Take a few minutes to think about what you already know about competitors and how this knowledge could help you get a more detailed insight into how competitors in a case context might behave.

1   Who are likely to be the most aggressive competitors – those operating in a growing or mature market place and why?

2   If a new entrant, moving into a market which was itself in late growth or early maturity, wanted to avoid head to head competition with the existing players in that market, what strategy should they adopt?

3   Who would you expect to be the most aggressive competitor in an established market place: the market leader, market challenger or one of the other players?

4   Are there any circumstances when a smaller firm might respond more aggressively to a competitive threat?

5   In the Biocatalyst case, how do you expect competitors like Amano and Rhom to respond to changes in Biocatalysts's strategies?

Check your answers with ours at the end of the chapter.

BPP))) PROFESSIONAL EDUCATION

Who are the real competitors?

2.4 In a large marketplace, not every competitor is a major threat (although it will probably mean they could be a potential one). You need to identify the closest competitors: positioning maps are an easy framework to use for this.

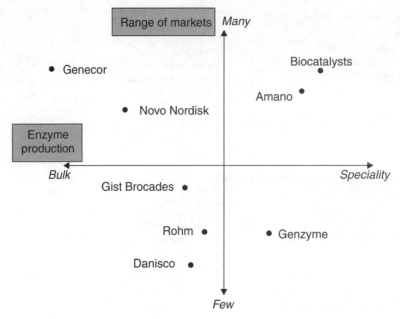

Positioning Enzymes

2.5 Of these players, Amano is the closest competitor (hence their potential interest in acquiring Biocatalysts' expertise). Companies like Genencor and Novo Nordisk are really in a quite different part of the market with expertise in volume production.

Understanding competitor strategy

2.6 Having identified the competitors, you want to understand their competitive strategies. Porter's Generic Strategies model provides a simple framework for this. The analysis below is too kind to Biocatalysts: although a niche player, their lack of product or market focus leaves them vulnerable and 'stuck in the middle'.

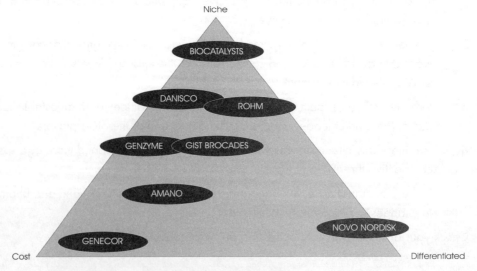

Porter's generic competitive strategies applied to enzymes

Adding the customers

2.7 As marketers, it is fundamental that we remember to add the customer dimension. Changes in buyer behaviour can have significant impact on business success and we need to bring our understanding and knowledge of the customer to any strategic assessment or decision-making.

2.8 This is the work which will eventually provide the basis for effective **segmentation**. At a macro level, we will need to define the markets and understand their needs and, at a micro level the decision making unit. You can see here how a student group tackled this part of the analysis for Biocatalysts.

Understanding the Markets

The world market for enzymes is growing, doubling in the 10 years from 1994.

World market for industrial enzymes:

1994	$1 billion
1997	$1.3 billion
1998	$1.7 billion
2005	$2 billion

The Biocatalysts customers come from a number of industries.

Distribution of enzyme sales by product sector:

Year	Other	Detergents	Diary	Textiles	Starch
1994	29%	32%	14%	10%	15%
2005	47%	27%	8%	6%	12%

The 'Other' market is growing. The rest are in decline.

Breakdown of 'other' market:

- Alcohol
- Animal feed
- Baking
- Chemical biotransformations
- Diagnostics
- Fats and oils
- Flavour
- Fruit and wine
- Leather
- Protein (for milk coagulation, flavour and detergents)
- Pulp and water
- Water

The 'other' sector is becoming increasingly significant to Biocatalysts. so this is worth some further review and analysis

---

Action Programme 2

Mind mapping 'other'

Take 20 minutes and produce a mind map or schematic which consolidates the information and analysis we have available about 'other' customers.

Compare your analysis with ours at the end of this chapter.

2.9 Analysis of customers by industry

(a)   Biocatalyst's customers are in 35 countries including:

- UK   29%
- Spain   17%
- South America   7%
- Asia Pacific   7%
- Japan   2%
- Europe   9%
- USA   7%
- Other   22%   (28 countries)
                     100%

- Sales in Food   48%
- Textiles   31%
- Diagnostics   5% (now 10%)
- Pharmaceuticals   15% (all figures from 1997)

These customers include blue chip, medium and small accounts, buying products and services. The **pareto** rule applies with 80% of the sales going to 20% of the customers.

(b)   **Food**. Biocatalysts' products are used as a processing aid. Competitive advantage is function, security and cost in use. This includes baking (bread, biscuits, crackers, batters), brewing, protein modification, fruit and flavouring.

(i)   **Decision Making Unit (DMU)**: mainly industrial businesses involved in food and beverage processing of ingredients to produce branded consumer goods. Examples are Hovis, Premier biscuits, Ryvita, Tetley, Robinson's. Also flavourings for snack food and cheese manufacture with Enzyme Modified Cheese (EMC).

People involved are food technologists, industrial buyers, process production and quality staff.

(ii)   **Critical issues**

- Consistent quality for customers' production efficiency
- Cost in use is competitive
- Complies with legislation and consumer trends (GM and bovine safety)
- Communication between technical service, agents and customers

(c)   **Textile**. Products are used as washing agent that causes the stone-washed effect on jeans. The competitive advantage is low with a declining fashion based market buying on price as a commodity.

(i)   DMU: industrial buyers and production staff

(ii)   Critical issues
- Correct product specification as set
- Competitive pricing at time of purchase

Action Programme 3

Analysing diagnostics

Take 15 minutes to complete the same analysis of the diagnostic sector. Compare your answer with ours at the end of this chapter.

(d) **Pharmaceuticals**. Cell cultures and hydrolysis of esters. Competitive advantage unknown.

   (i) Critical issues ■ Technical service support
                        ■ Consistency and quality of product

   (ii) DMU: similar to diagnostics market with less due diligence

(e) **Environmental**. Waste water treatment for odour reduction and lower drain maintenance. Competitive advantage unknown.

   DMU: the customer, the local drainage and sewerage authorities (these civil servants include maintenance managers and procurement officers). The workers will feed back the performance and ease of use of the product and packaging.

(f) **Other markets**

Alcohol	World wide demand; near-commodity business
Animal feed	BSE and safety issues, high volume low margins
Chemical	Green issues for industry, opportunity for environmentally friendly products
Biotransformers Fats and Oils Leather Protein	} information gaps
Paper and Pulp	Environmental issues and packaging waste regulations.

Combining product/market information

2.10 From this next chart, you can see how a student has linked product information with end use to give us a further perspective on the variety of customers the company is trying to satisfy.

Biocatalyst's current products by sector

Sector	No. of Products	New Product	End use
Baking	19	3	Bread, biscuits, crackers, batters
Brewing	5	5	Beer
Fruit and Veg	12	3	Fruit juice, wine, citrus fruits
Flavourings	14	0	Vegetables, fibrous botanicals, ECM
Proteins	13	1	Bacterial proteinase Soya
Dietetics	10	2	Aid for digestion ready for tableting
Textile	21	9	Stone-wash, cost effective development
Diagnostics	8	3	Immuno-diagnostics, food testing
Pharmaceuticals	7	0	Cell cultures, hydrolysis of esters
Environment	4	0	Waste odour reduction, drain maintenance

Table 1 Products by sector

Competitor	Geographic focus	Target markets/ product range	Market share (of $1.7bn	Supplier to Biocatalysts	GMO	Summary
Novo Nordisk	Worldwide (RBCDs)	Industrial and technical enzymes including textiles	[50%]	✓	?	RBDCs allow flexibility to adapt to local conditions Also in healthcare Cost cutting and productivity improvements
Genencor	Worldwide	1,200 patents	[12.5%]	✓	✓	Largest company devoted exclusively to industrial biotechnology State of the art production capability
Genzyme		Medical-diagnostics, therapeutics and surgical			?	Mainly healthcare $490m turnover
Amano	Production in Japan/ USA/UK	Pharmaceutical/food/ diagnostic 50 patents	[7%]	✓	?	'World No 1 speciality enzyme producer' Surface fermentation?
Gist Brocades	Worldwide especially in growth areas of Asia and South America – 70 sites	Food and agriculture Very active with patents	[12.5%]	✓	?	
Nagase					?	Part of $4.6bn turnover company
Biozome		Baking/food		✓	?	
Rohm		Food/sweeteners		✓	?	
Danisco					?	
					?	FDA approval for PKU test in USA

Table 2 Competitor summary

Adding the macro dimensions

2.11 Finally, to complete your external audit, you will need to build up the picture of the changing external environment for the enzyme market. Here you can see such an environmental audit completed and prioritised helping you to summarise and consolidate the many clues provided within the case study.

Political/legal	Economic	Social/demographic	Technological
■ Food sector – politicians increasingly responding to public's concerns ■ Food and medical sectors – tight legislation controlling release of new products ■ Food sector – packaging disclosure laws ■ All sectors – employment laws ■ All sectors – worldwide trade agreements/ barriers/ embargoes	■ Food sector – higher yields could lead to an over-capacity and an agricultural recession in the medium term ■ All sectors – large parts of Wales classed as Economic Development Areas inc grant assistance ■ All sectors – strong pressure on industry from analysts/city to improve productivity ⇒ performance enhancing technology (ie enzymes) will be in demand. ■ All sectors – worldwide trade so UK's involvement in EMU could be important ■ Exchange rate risk from trading across 3 currencies – $, £ and the euro ■ Worldwide recessions eg instability in Asia ■ Merging of large Blue Chip companies ■ China and Russia	■ Food sector – expected population growth will require higher food yields. ■ Food sector – widespread anti-GM feeling in European society building on BSE scare. This includes well organised pressure groups. Far less the case in other continents. ■ All sectors – increasingly 'green' sensitive society in developed countries ■ Food sector – developing countries however want reliable food sources and are not 'green' ■ Textile sector – some linkage to fad and fashion through involvement in textile industry ie faded jeans ■ Medical sector – people becoming more health conscious so medical and diagnostic trade will become more important ■ Increasing demand for global brand foods ■ Global warming ⇒ medicines required and reliable crops	■ All sectors – high new product R&D costs but reducing where GMOs are used. ■ Food sector – strong growth area ⇒ an agricultural revolution is taking place as important as that in electronics ■ Food sector – GM food is actually already widespread ■ All sectors – reliance on universities for research ■ All sectors – Internet makes them more accessible, including deferred customers' products

Table 3 PEST analysis

Moving on

2.12 You have now completed the detailed inview and overview analysis essential to providing the detailed understanding of the case context. In the next chapter we will look in more detail at how you take the next steps to action by sorting and refining the internal and external analysis and identifying the critical success factors.

Before moving on, take a few minutes to reflect on what you have learnt about the process of analysis and how it can best be completed. Look at the pitfalls we have identified and take the time to tackle this end of chapter activity.

Pitfalls

2.13 **The most common pitfalls when completing the external audit**

(a)   Focus on PEST analysis and forget to really work on the micro analysis of competitors and customers

(b)   Try to do **two steps** at once during the macro analysis so instead of

■   threat of recession

the student says

■   falling sales because of recession

This is going from the **external factor** to the **product/market implication**. This is a mistake because an environmental change could generate **both** product market opportunities and threats.

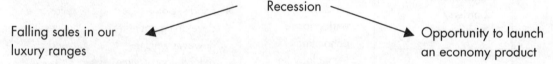

Make sure at this step you stick to the uncontrollable and external PEST factors, and leave the translation into product/market implications until Step 5.

2.14 **Failure to think ahead**. The external analysis requires that we try to think ahead even though forecasting is **not** a very precise art. Keep it reasonable and realistic but use your own knowledge and look ahead.

Action Programme 4

We have handled a lot of data and information in this step of the case process. Are you using this to build a clearer picture of Biocatalyst and its challenges?

Take a few minutes to work through the following questions which might help you consolidate your thoughts.

1   Why would a change in Government policy regarding the funding and support of biotechnology be significant to Biocatalyst?

2   Competitor Amano has 400 products and an income of £92m. How might this information help us set an objective for Biocatalyst?

3   Is a differentiated strategy an option for Biocatalyst?

4   Why are GMOs an important issue for Biocatalyst and what impact might decisions about them have on strategy?

5   Why is the 'other' sector of the enzyme market potentially attractive to Biocatalyst?

6   Take 10 minutes to produce a checklist of questions to pose about competitors which you could use in future cases.

Compare your answers with ours before moving on.

Action Programme review

1   *Assessing Competitor Responses*

1   Those working in a mature market because winning new business means taking customers away from someone else.

2   They should target the 'laggards' who will be the only new customers still entering the market place. In this way they can win market share without taking customers from someone else.

3   The market challenger normally who will be focused on winning market share and can often best do this by taking on smaller players rather than the market leader.

4   Yes, if this was its core market and more important to it or if the challenge being made was a direct head to head one.

5   Probably hardly at all. They are significantly bigger and Biocatalyst is a small niche player. Amano may, however, be interested in acquiring them for their expertise and patents but that would probably be the extent of things.

2   *Mind mapping 'other'*

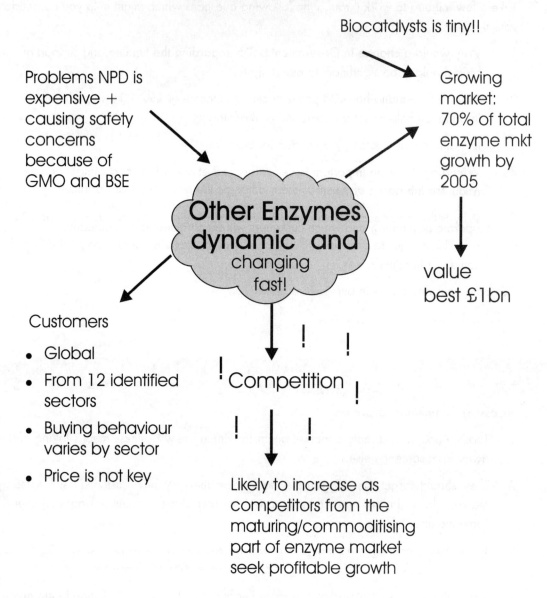

The 'other' sector of the Enzyme Business

Biocatalysts is tiny!!

Problems NPD is expensive + causing safety concerns because of GMO and BSE

Growing market: 70% of total enzyme mkt growth by 2005

value best £1bn

Other Enzymes dynamic and changing fast!

Customers

- Global
- From 12 identified sectors
- Buying behaviour varies by sector
- Price is not key

Competition

Likely to increase as competitors from the maturing/commoditising part of enzyme market seek profitable growth

3   *Analysing Diagnostics*

Diagnostics. Medical applications for determination of presence and immuno-diagnostics. The competitive advantage is technology-based with partnership agreements.

Testing for genetic disorder, blood tests, gastric disorders, determination of glocosinates in rape seed meal.

DMU. This is a highly scientific environment with leading edge technology transformed into commercial reality. The DM is protracted with extensive independent testing and field trials before approval; these include medical bodies, associations and FDA approval. This work would be championed by the drug companies looking to supply the diagnostic kits via the medical profession. Dealing with scientists, doctors, professional supply chain managers, process engineers and marketing.

Critical Issues
- Unique formulation and confidentiality agreements
- Quality and consistency of product and process performance
- Medical approval for targeted markets
- Technical support and partnership approach

4   1   Much of Biocatalysts's work attracts grants which could be reduced or stopped. The Government could also influence the extent of support provided by university research if their priorities changed.

2   This means Amano (based in the same sector of the market place) earns some £230k per product compared with approx. £22k per Biocatalyst product. This is a useful benchmark indicating how product rationlisation and improved marketing of say 30 instead of 112 products could increase revenues to say £7m.

3   Not really – it is too small a player, a niche or multi-niche approach feels more credible.

4   GMOs are the cause of much concern amongst the general public, particularly in Europe. The decision to include or reject them from the portfolio will strongly influence both the corporate positioning and which customers will be attracted to the company.

5   Because this sector is growing and profitable, whereas others like textiles are increasingly mature and commoditised. Biocatalyst has the skills, competence and experience to focus very effectively on this £1bn part of the market.

6   A competitors checklist

A great deal can be accomplished in understanding competitors by relatively simple numerical analysis and financial and market review. Here is a checklist of questions about competitors you should find answers to.

Question	Answer
(a) How many?	
(b) Size?	
(c) Growing or declining?	
(d) Market shares and/or rank orders?	
(e) Likely objectives and strategies?	
(f) Changes in management personnel?	
(g) Past reaction to:	
(i) price changes	
(ii) promotional campaigns	
(iii) new product launches	
(iv) distribution drives?	
(h) Analysis of marketing mix strengths and weaknesses	
(i) Leaders or followers?	
(j) National or international?	
(k) Analysis of published accounts?	

Step 4: Prioritisation and critical success factors and analysis summary

Chapter Topic List	
1	Prioritising analysis
2	Prioritising strengths and weaknesses
3	Prioritising opportunities and threats
4	Critical Success Factors (CSFs)
5	Analysis summary

1 Prioritising analysis

1.1 Professional marketers have a duty to present analysis in a way that is of value to senior management and the organisation. This requires going further than just establishing SWOT; it requires making connections and inferences, drawing conclusions and, ultimately, providing insights that ensure decision making is based on valued information.

1.2 During analysis, the SWOT and other auditing techniques help to determine the current situation. For the results of the audit to be of any value, SWOTs etc must be **prioritised to ensure the organisation is focused on those issues that matter most**, for example the weaknesses and threats that will impact on organisational success.

1.3 A long list of SWOT might provide an improved understanding of the current situation but it can be a daunting step to move from this list to decisions. There are also always constraints on resources, money, time, processes and people, and so priorities must be established to determine what is important and must be invested in, and what can wait.

1.4 There are some helpful techniques for prioritising analysis. We will now describe others.

2   Prioritising strengths and weaknesses

2.1   It is of course helpful for employees to comment on the organisation's strengths and weaknesses. However, much more important are the **external** perceptions and opinions on the organisation's performance.

2.2   Customers, suppliers, distribution channels and other stakeholders should be canvassed for their opinions. For example, a technique that can help identify what is important to customers and prioritise its importance is the **semantic differential**.

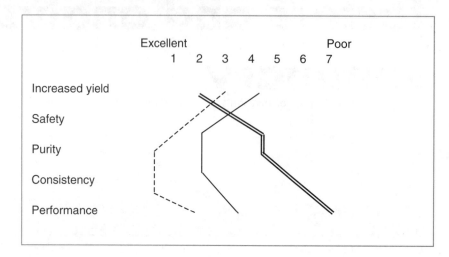

Biocatalysts ————
Competitor A ════
Competitor B --------

2.3   Please note, this is not meant to suggest that this is how Biocatalysts's results would look. We do not have the information to enable us to do this. It is an example of how we might be able to identify performance if we did have the information.

2.4   Management can then use this information to rank activities as strengths and weaknesses and to establish some understanding of the importance of each activity to customers. There is no point in an organisation identifying a weakness and allocating resources to improving performance if it is of no importance to the customer. Resources must be used where they will do the most good, or where there is an opportunity to maintain or develop competitive advantage.

2.5   Activities can be weighted and rated to enable marketers to determine whether a strength is major, medium or low.

Activities	Prioritising strengths and weaknesses								
	Strength			Weakness			Importance		
	Major	Medium	Low	Minor	Medium	Serious	High	Medium	Low
Promotions reach									

People
   technical skills
   service skills									

Process simple									

2.6 When prioritising weaknesses, consider the effort involved in dealing with the weakness. Is it a simple matter of investing more money, (eg a computer)? Or will a major change be required in processes, people skills, organisation structure and so on?

| | | **Performance** | | |
		Excellent	Average	Poor
Importance (to customer)	High	Maintain	Improve	Urgent attention
	Average			Improve
	Low	Over investing	Monitor	Monitor

2.7 Speed may also be a factor. How quickly can the organisation solve the problem? Can it be solved within the planning period and in time to make a positive difference to the organisation?

3 Prioritising opportunities and threats

3.1 Prioritising **threats** forces us to consider the **likelihood** of something happening and how **serious** the threat is. Constraints on resources prevent us from developing contingency plans for every likely threat: it would be impractical. To avoid or at least reduced a 'crisis management' syndrome, we do need to establish threats which are most likely to occur, during the planning period.

(a)   **Threats matrix**

| | | **Likelihood of occurrence** | | |
		High	Likely	Unlikely
Seriousness	Very			
	Average			
	Low			

(b)   The aim is to make sure we are focused on threats that could damage our prospects and jeopardise business performance. This technique forces us to consider the likelihood of something occurring and how serious it is. We can then decide whether resources should be allocated to develop contingency plans or whether we simply monitor the situation.

3.2 In the same way, we cannot pursue every opportunity that presents itself, and often it is not appropriate for us to do so if it does not fit with our strategic objectives and goals.

Opportunities matrix

		Probability of success		
		High	Medium	Low
	High			
Attractiveness	Medium			
	Low			

Action Programme 1

Try to complete both threats and opportunities matrix for Biocatalysts. Compare your answer with ours at the end of the chapter.

3.3 Realities of the case study analysis

(a) Usually we do not have the right, or enough, information to enable us to prioritise analysis, and in the case study we cannot go out and obtain the information we want. Therefore we must make some **intelligent and reasonable assumptions**. A professional job on analysis will generate information for us to make reasonable assumptions, and to justify them with evidence.

(b) One of your objectives is to pass the examination. **If we get the Critical Success Factors right, we will identify, broadly, the question areas**.

4 Critical Success Factors (CSFs)

4.1 The terminology varies from company to company (eg Significant Performance Indicators (SPIs), Key Results Areas (KRAs)), but Critical Success Factors is widely used.

4.2 The stepping stone from analysis to decision is agreeing **critical success factors** which can only be determined from the results of analysis. These are the factors that will impact on the organisation's ability to pursue the opportunities it has identified and intends to implement.

4.3 Critical success factors are any factors essential to the success of organisation and strategy.

- Profitability and cash flow
- Market development and market position
- Productivity
- Identifying/developing competitive advantage and new product development
- Marketing orientation, employee attitudes and public responsibility
- Marketing management skills and personnel leadership
- Competitive positioning and product leadership

Underpinning each CSF are some key issues. Examples are given below.

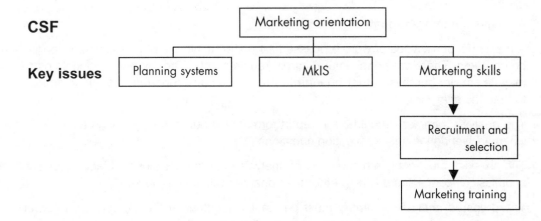

CSF

Key issues

4.4 Identifying and agreeing CSFs ensures corporate decisions are focused on the issues that will produce the desired results. Major problems/obstacles to success must be dealt with. Resources must be allocated to support **critical success factor outcomes**.

Action Programme 2

From your analysis, identify the Critical Success Factors you believe Biocatalysts face, and compare them with ours at the end of the chapter.

5 Analysis summary

The following is the guidance notes sent out by CIM.

Introduction

The overall purpose of the analysis summary is to allow for marks to be awarded for preparatory analysis undertaken prior to the Strategic Marketing in Practice examination.

The analysis summary allows students to demonstrate their ability to:

■   Apply the appropriate models and techniques to analyse information on an organisation/sector in particular circumstances

■   Interpret the results of this analysis, to provide insights into the current situation and the conclusions they are able to draw

■   Utilise their own ideas and create their own models for interpreting the data

Students are expected to bring some individuality to their analysis and submit their own work. No group submissions are accepted.

Marks will be awarded as follows:

■   Up to 10% is awarded for originality and appropriateness of analysis in the context given

■   Up to 15% is awarded for appropriate application of analysis within the questions set on the examination paper

Students must not repeat or copy the analysis summary when answering exam questions. It is important for the student to refer the examiner to the analysis summary, where and when

---

appropriate. Repetition or direct copying from the analysis summary will not achieve any extra marks.

Analysis summary format

A maximum of six sides of word processed A4 paper, minimum of 11 (eleven) size font should be prepared. There are no minimum margin requirements. The content of models or diagrams may be smaller but these **must be legible**. Remember it is important that the examiner is able to read the analysis.

The analysis summary should be in report format with numbered headings and sub-headings when answering the set examination questions.

The six sides must contain a summary of analysis **only**, no decisions, objectives or plans. Any submissions containing anything other than analysis will not be marked.

The prepared analysis summary must be stapled together at the top left hand corner and a single hole punched into the paper just below the staple. This must be done before taking the analysis summary into the examination.

TWO items can be taken into the examination:

1.   The analysis summary (remember a maximum of **six sides** *only*)
2.   Student's own copy of the case study that has been provided by CIM

The case study may be annotated. The student is *not allowed* to bring any other type of material into the examination room, eg papers, files or books.

Students may not attach any other additional information in any format.

Any attempt to introduce such additional material will result in the student's paper being declared null and void.

The examination invigilators will be ensuring compliance with these examination regulations and will report any irregularities to CIM.

NOTE: students with defined special needs should have contacted CIM or their course director concerning their individual requirements before enrolling for this examination.

CIM reserves the right not to mark any submission that does not comply with these guidances.

Before the examination

Students must have stapled their analysis summary together at the top left hand corner and have punched a single hole punched into the paper just below the staple.

Students should have written their student membership number and examination centre name clearly on the top right hand corner of the analysis summary.

At the close of the examination

At the close of the examination the student must secure their analysis summary   to the examination booklet with a treasury tag.   This will be provided by the examination centre invigilator.

5.2   Summarising analysis is the most difficult task you will undertake. If you have worked the case properly and done a good job on your analysis you will have a lot of information, the details of the current situation. You cannot present all of this in the exam. Your task now is to translate the analysis, add value and provide insight. Long lists of SWOT do not provide insight. Take the following example:

Stating what we already know

"Biocatalysts' internal perception is that they are positioned as high value. However their financial performance does not necessarily reflect this."

Or providing insight and winning marks

"Biocatalysts produce tailor made products with levels of service that are valued by customers. There are two problems.

1.   Their new product development reveals a lack of focus on high value with nine new products in the low value textile range, the market for which is decreasing. The only real competitive advantage they have in the product range is diagnostics and only three new products where produced here.

2.   Their financial performance does not indicate they are pricing as premium priced products with profitability running at approximately 6%. While their turnover and profits have increased their profitability is decreasing. It would be reasonable to expect more from high value products."

The analysis summary should be a balance of narrative where your comments provide insight through inference and conclusion and models and techniques in use. The models **used** should provide further insight. Aim for at least two to three models per page.

An analysis summary template

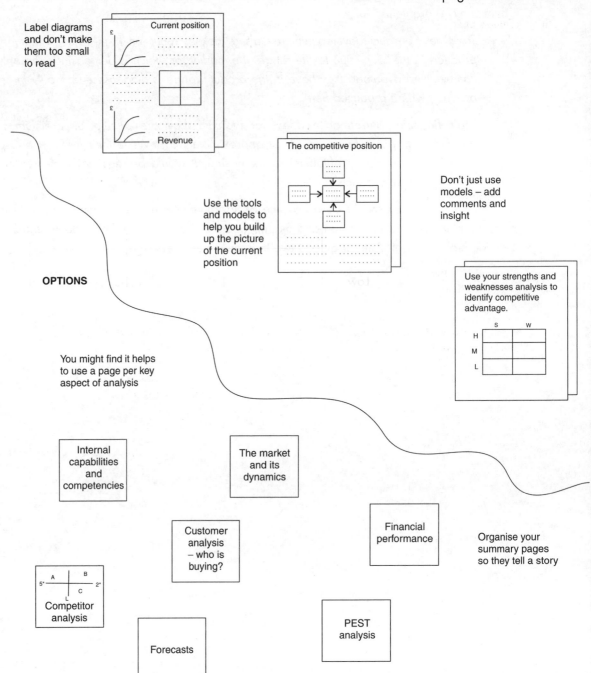

5.3 Six page analysis

You will see an example of a student analysis summary for the Signifo case study, December 2005 in Chapter 17.

Action Programme review

1   *Threats matrix*

Likelihood of occurrence

	High	Likely	Unlikely
Very	Growing anti GMOs	Government withdraw funding	
Seriousness **Average**	Competitors merge Legislation	Russia or China enter market	
Low			

Some of the issues that emerge can be both opportunities and threats depending on the organisation's ability to identify and address the opportunity or threat.

Opportunities matrix

Probability of success

	High	Medium	Low
High	Diagnostics Food		
Attractiveness **Medium**		Environmental products	
Low		Changing fashions eg faded jeans	

2   *Biocatalysts' CSFs*

CSFs	*and*	Key issues
■ Competitive positioning		Competitive strategy Brand/values Marketing skills
■ Distribution		Agency skills/expertise/knowledge New channels/Web
■ New Product Development		Processes Marketing information Marketing skills
■ Communications		Strategic and integrated Marketing skills Brand Changing perceptions
■ Marketing information		International problems
■ Relationship marketing		Stakeholders/nurture relationships
■ International market entry		Level of involvement
■ Funding/cash flow		Cost efficiency, profitability, growth

The business implications here are covered in:

- ■   NPD
- ■   Marketing information
- ■   Relationship marketing
- ■   Funding/cash flow

Step 5: Establishing strategic direction. Corporate/business decisions

Introduction

In this chapter we will:

☑ Turn our environmental analysis into a forecast, set quantified objectives and so establish a planning gap for Biocatalysts

☑ Assess the role of vision and mission, and develop them for Biocatalysts

☑ Use the Ansoff matrix and others to identify strategic options for the business

☑ Develop and use criteria for evaluating and selecting strategies to fill the planning gap

☑ Consider the potential pitfalls for students working at this critical case stage

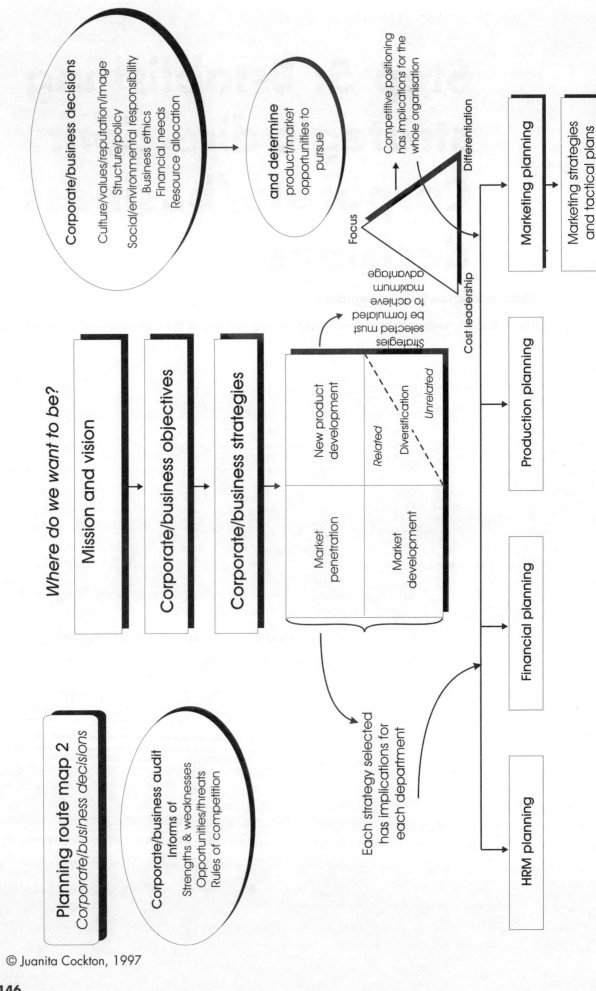

Planning route map 2
Corporate/business decisions

Corporate/business audit
Informs of
Strengths & weaknesses
Opportunities/threats
Rules of competition

Corporate/business decisions

Culture/values/reputation/image
Structure/policy
Social/environmental responsibility
Business ethics
Financial needs
Resource allocation

and determine product/market opportunities to pursue

Where do we want to be?

Mission and vision

Corporate/business objectives

Corporate/business strategies

Market penetration

Market development

New product development

Diversification
Related
Unrelated

Strategies selected must be formulated to achieve maximum advantage

Focus

Differentiation

Cost leadership

Competitive positioning has implications for the whole organisation

Each strategy selected has implications for each department

Marketing planning

Marketing strategies and tactical plans

Production planning

Financial planning

HRM planning

© Juanita Cockton, 1997

1 Establishing strategic direction

1.1 So far we have been working to establish the current position of Biocatalysts' business. You have seen a number of tools, techniques and models employed to help us really get to grips with the 'where are we now' question for this business. Case step 5 is the one which will allow us to answer 'where are we going?'. It is the first real step down the path of decision making. Many students (and, in fairness, managers) find this a difficult step to take. Analysis is comforting and reassuring. It keeps you busy and productive but at some point you must move forward. This is that point, and from now on you will be faced with uncertainty and assumptions which have to be addressed if decisions are to be made. Try not to worry too much about this; it reflects the real world but remember that assumptions can be monitored by your control systems and that we are only working through the planning process. The planning process is iterative, and decisions made now can still be modified or addressed later if they prove unworkable at the operational planning level.

Skills and knowledge reminders

You will see a number of tools and models during this step of the case process. You need to be familiar with:

- Gap analysis
- Multifactor matrix
- Ansoff matrix
- The structure of visions and missions

Revisit our analysis to help us quantify our planning gap

1.2 **Auditing the present and forecasting the future**

(a) It is only when we have a clear picture of where we are now (and how we've come to arrive here) that we can decide, realistically, where we want to be in the future. This relationship between auditing and forecasting can be seen in the following diagram.

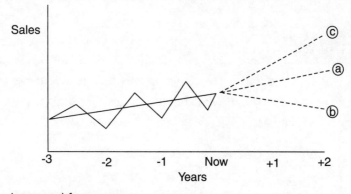

Auditing and forecasting

(b) Here you can see how sales for the last three years have been plotted and a line of 'best fit' added. One approach is to simply extend this line indicating where (all things being equal) the business could expect to be in two years (a).

However all things are not equal. Some people might argue that the more recent past is a more reliable indicator of the future than the more distant past and so weight the last year accordingly. Furthermore one or more of the external environmental factors may be on the verge of radical change.

- The collapse of Amano or a sudden surge in consumer support for enzyme based products could boost Biocatalyst sales to (c).

- A backlash of opinion about GMOs or a sudden economic recession could make (b) a more likely scenario.

(c)   Your external analysis (completed at Step 3 and reviewed in the opportunities and threats matrices in the last chapter) will inform this bottom line forecast of your planning gap. In essence, you are trying to add the forecast of how profitable the business **would be** if we stuck with the current products in the current markets.

(d)   Having established the bottom line, we now need to add the **top line**, created once you have set a realistic objective.

Again this decision should not be made until the external analysis is complete. You may want to double your profits this year but is that realistic given the market and environmental conditions?

In the following diagram, the economy may be booming (leading to a 'high' objective for sales) but competitive activity may be intense, leading to poorer forecast results.

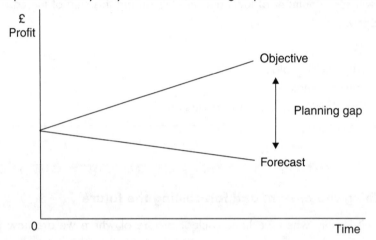

(e)   We will now have established a planning gap which is realistic and credible because it was informed from analysis rather than wishful thinking.

Tutor Tip

In practice, the objective will often be a trade off between what the stakeholders aspire to achieve and the assessment of what is realistic or reasonable. There are two things you should bear in mind when writing up a case answer:

(a)   Acknowledge the stakeholder's expectation

(b)   Justify your objective

It is conservative because ....

It is bullish because ....

Complete your Ansoff matrix

1.3 The opportunities identified in your environmental audit should now provide us with the context for identifying product market opportunity:

(a) Technology breakthrough creates the opportunity for new diagnostic products
(b) Political change provides funding for new development of GMO products
(c) Business growth increases demand for textile and food based products

Completing the Ansoff matrix requires you to look at your environmental analysis and say 'so what'? If this changes, what are the product market implications?

Selecting strategies

1.4 This is the heart of decision making and examiners will be looking hard at how you do this. Decisions made need to be:

■ Objective
■ Customer focused
■ Justified

The multifactor matrix criteria will be scrutinised and it **must** be **case specific**:

Not detailed enough	But
Increase revenue	The potential to generate at least £220k per opportunity; this is 10 times more than currently achieved but reflects the 'best of breed' competitor Amano

Notice in this example the criterion is not only **quantified** and **case specific** but **justified**. You leave the examiner in no doubt that you understand what you need to do and how to do it.

Filling the planning gaps

1.5 Once the criterion is determined, the various strategic options can be applied. You do **not** need to show **the calculation** of **weighting** and **rating,** just acknowledge it has been done.

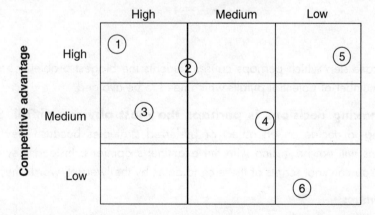

BPP
PROFESSIONAL EDUCATION

1.6 The strategic options in the **high** and **high/med** boxes are those you will implement in order to fill the planning gap.

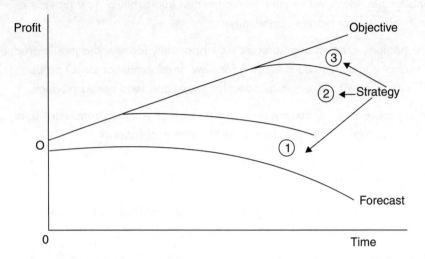

1.7 All the business has to do now is:

(a) **Assess the business implications** of selecting these strategies (see step 6)

(b) Develop the **operational plans** to implement the selected strategies (Step 7)

Action Programme 1

A knowledge review

Before we complete this step for Biocatalysts take a few minutes to check that you are completely happy with the process and tools which underpin this stage.

1 How will you decide on a reasonable objective for the case company?

2 Where will the criteria for assessing the strength of competitive advantage come from?

3 What do you do if the potential contribution of the strategies in the high/med cells of the matrix are insufficient to fill the planning gap?

4 What characteristics would you expect the examiner to be looking for in a 'good' mission statement?

The pitfalls

1.8 This is the case step which perhaps causes students the biggest problems and not surprisingly there are a number of potential pitfalls which need to be avoided.

1 **Not making decisions is perhaps the most obvious pitfall**. Students are often unwilling to decide on an object or preferred strategies because they are worried their decisions will not be in line with the examiner's opinions. Instead they try and sit on the fence. You can spot scripts of these candidates by the 'weasel' words they employ:

■ Perhaps
■ On the one hand
■ On balance
■ Maybe

As we have said before, there are no single correct answers to a case study, so the examiner will not have fixed ideas about the right strategy. What he or she will be looking for is evidence that you have worked through a logical process resulting in:

- Clear decision making
- Justified decisions
- Convincing arguments in favour of those decisions

Tutor Tip

If you are not confident about the recommendations you are making, it is unlikely you would convince the case organisation or the examiner. The successful selling of strategy in business is being directly tested in how you present your case proposals.

2   **Failing to add the numbers.** We appreciate most marketers hate the thought of numbers, but trust us, it is essential. Objectives and decisions criteria need quantification and those numbers must be drawn from the case study. You must understand them and be able to work with them.

3   **Failing to use the analysis to inform decision making**. Too many candidates fall into the trap of treating each case step in isolation and the result is commercial nonsense.

There is no point in recommending a strategy of expansion through acquisition if a business has no cash.

Neither is a long-term product development strategy sensible if there is a short-term survival strategy required.

2   Biocatalysts: what needs to be done

Tutor Tip

You are now ready to start making decisions and you will need to 'own' these in the exam room. If you are working in a syndicate group, it has been quite appropriate for you to share your work up to now but take care from here on in. If the examiner gets twenty scripts from the same centre with a word perfect mission statement, he or she is likely to assume a group answer, which will result in an automatic fail. Discuss and review together by all means but the words need to be yours.

A vision

2.1 Remember the vision is an aspiration. It needs to be realistic and something which will inspire the organisation to strive for its achievement. A good vision can act as something of a *crie de coeur* for the business.

Action Programme 2

Establishing a Vision

Take a few minutes to look at the following possible visions for Biocatalysts. Which would you reject and why? Which would you choose?

1   It is our vision to be the global leader in the development and production of enzyme solutions for industry.

2   We are in the business of providing enzyme solutions to our clients.

3   We want to be the first choice provider for organisations who have 'other sector' clients who have enzyme problems or opportunities.

4   We want to be the biggest producer of bulk enzymes in the food and textile industries of Europe.

5   We want to be the acknowledged technical leader in UK based enzyme research.

Turn to the end of the chapter for our comments.

2.2 Take another 10 minutes to craft your own vision for Biocatalysts.

> A Vision for Biocatalysts

Check it for:

■ Relevance
■ Realism

What business is Biocatalysts in?

Mission

2.3 We must now tackle the mission statement. What do you think of this for Biocatalysts?

> We are in the business of helping our globally-based customers improve the efficiency and effectiveness of their processes through the provision of tailor made enzyme solutions, employing leading edge technology, combined with over 13 years of experience and expertise.

Comments

....

....

....

It is a little longwinded but it incorporates the **customer benefits** of 'efficiency and effectiveness'; it has focus; it is for processes and there is a hint of differentiation built around the technology in safe hands.

An alternative mission

2.4 We will be the leading global supplier of specialised enzymes to diagnostic, food processing and GMO sectors within five years.

2.5 Again take 10 minutes to craft your own mission

A Mission for Biocatalysts

Check it for:

■ Distinctiveness
■ Focus on customer benefits

Tutor Tip

When using a vision or mission in the exam, do first check it makes sense in the light of questions set.

Action Programme 3

Establishing the Planning Gap

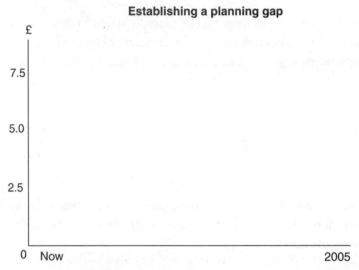

Before you turn to the end of this chapter to look at our thoughts on a possible planning gap, have a go at producing one for yourself:

1   Check out current revenue and profit

2   What do you think will happen to both if Biocatalyst continues to operate as it has with the same products and markets?

3   Next, think about the future environment and what the shareholders might expect, and try and set a realistic objective

4   Can you justify your decisions?

Do not agonise about these decisions: be brave and a little bold. Remember you are in essence quantifying the added value marketing might give to this business.

Now turn to the end of the chapter to see our planning gap but remember there will be many variations equally acceptable. Ours is only a sample developed to show you the process.

The strategic options

2.6   The only problem now we have established the planning gap, is to decide how to fill it.

2.7   The first step is to identify the options. The company can only expand its business with combinations of products and markets. Its strategic options are based around four strategies:

- Market penetration
- Product development
- Market development
- Diversification

Action Programme 4

Ansoff options

We have begun to populate the Ansoff Matrix for Biocatalysts – what can you add?

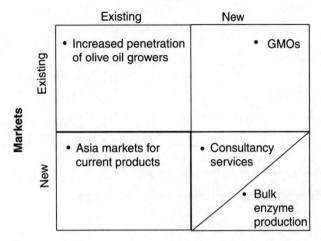

2.8 Having identified the strategic **alternatives open to a business**, the next step is to decide which are **most attractive** for the business. Remember there may be an excellent opportunity in the market, but your firm may **not** be suited to exploiting it.

2.9 You are looking for opportunities which are both attractive to the business and where the business has the propensity to deliver a competitive advantage.

Making strategic decisions

2.10 The **multifactor matrix** is an excellent framework to ensure you have taken account of both the attractiveness of the opportunity and the potential competitive advantage.

2.11 Examiners will be looking for evidence that you can adapt the theory to meet the specific context of the case. That means case specific criteria are needed. What you do **not** need to do is add the weighting and rating to calculate each strategic option. It is highly unlikely you would have the data to do this in a meaningful way anyway.

2.12 What you **do** need to do is explain that you would, or indeed have, weighted and rated the alternatives and then demonstrate the assumed or potential outcome on a multifactor framework.

Action Programme 5

Biocatalysts Decision Criteria

Take ten minutes to think about the criteria you could use for assessing Biocatalysts' options.

You only need 5-6 in each list, but make them as case specific as possible.

Strategy attractiveness	*Competitive position*
1...	1...
2...	2...
3...	3...
4...	4...
5...	5...
6...	6...

Our example is provided for you at the end of this chapter.

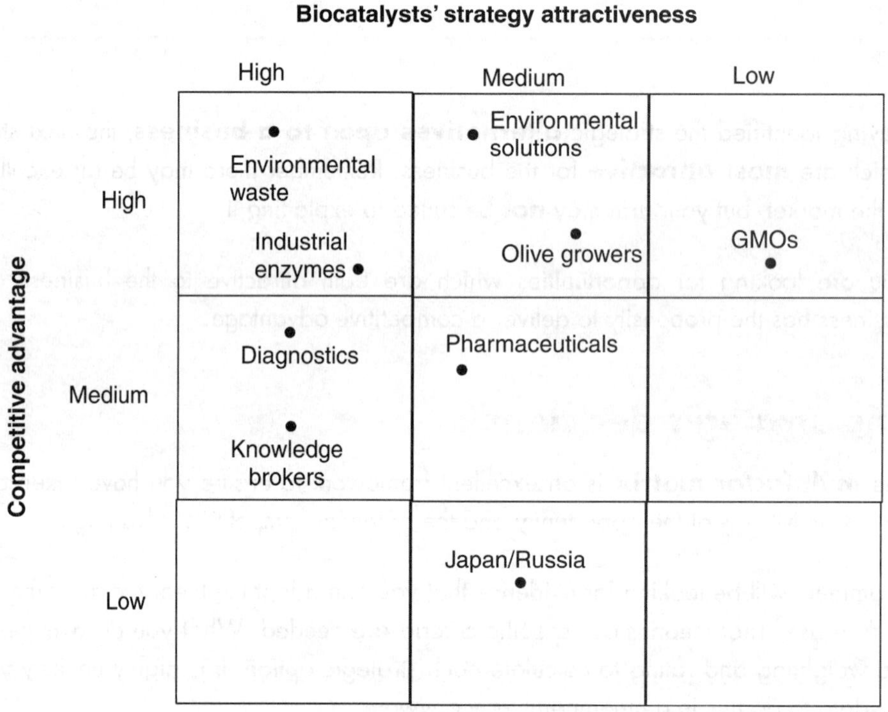

Biocatalysts' strategy attractiveness

	High	Medium	Low
High	Environmental waste • Industrial enzymes •	• Environmental solutions • Olive growers	GMOs •
Medium	• Diagnostics • Knowledge brokers	• Pharmaceuticals	
Low		Japan/Russia •	

(vertical axis label: **Competitive advantage**)

2.13 Note that there is **no single right or wrong answer as to where to log opportunities on this matrix**. The examiners will be looking for your thought process and in the exam you would want to highlight the selected strategies and comment on their justification. You may like to conclude your strategy section with a completed planning gap, showing how your selected strategies will fill it.

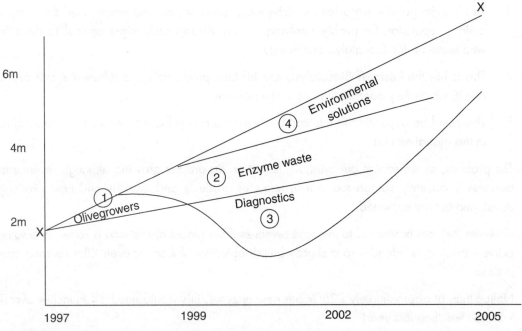

Filling Biocatalysts's planning gap

Action Programme review

1   *A knowledge review*

1   By considering likely stakeholder expectations, current and past performance and what competitors seem to be achieving. These to be considered against the general state of the market but there can be many different views. The important thing is to be specific and able to justify the objective set.

2   It should come from the customers buying criteria so always an aspect of the marketing mix. So for Biocatalysts:

■   Safety
■   Customisation
■   Technical support

may all be more important than price

3   There are two options:

■   Either the objective needs to be reviewed downwards

■   Less attractive med/low strategies can be reconsidered and a decision made about their potential to review or re-engineer to make them more attractive. For example, if this strategy was unattractive to the firm because of the high levels of investment needed, perhaps a partner could be found.

4   Simple, distinctive and based on customer benefits **not** product features

2   *Establishing a vision*

1   Simply unrealistic – Biocatalyst is a tiny global player.

2   No, this is a mission statement, not a good one as it has no source of differentiation incorporated in it.

BPP
PROFESSIONAL EDUCATION

3 This is quite good – it provides a niche focus 'other sector' and would need the company to build a reputation for problem solving. It is a vision which might appeal to the scientists who make up the Biocatalyst community.

4 This is not the business Biocatalysts are in; bulk production is a different sector and is not one in which they operate with core competence.

5 This could be appealing to the staff but is too narrow a focus to provide commercial returns in this global market.

The problem, as we saw in our analysis, is that profits are not growing although revenue is. The business is currently spread too thin in terms of products and markets and new products are developed but not exploited.

However they are positioned to increase revenues if the global distribution is sorted and some pro-active marketing is added – so a slightly bullish objective of £6m or even £8m revenue could be justified.

Notice that, at approximately £250k per new enzyme, this would need 14 launches over 1998 – 2005: less than last year!

The real key though is the profit. If you assume a 15% gross profit margin this needs to be increased from its current low level to £1.5m by 2005.

Rationalisation of products and markets will be needed to get rid of unprofitable activity. Such a strategy would make the planning gap look like this:

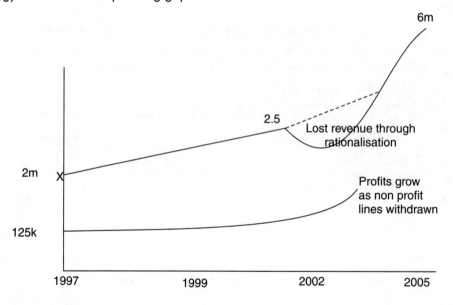

Tutor Tip

Look at how adding legends to your diagrams helps with the process of justification and explanation

3   *Establishing the Planning Gap*

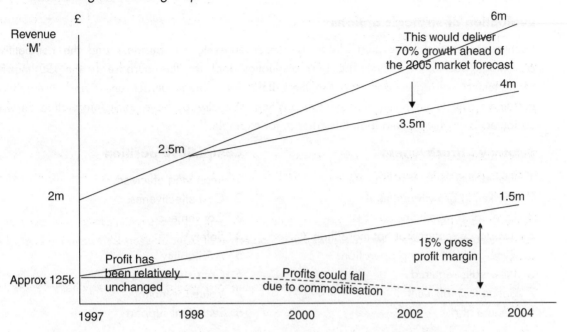

You can see we have included both the profit and revenue picture on one graph. You may prefer to do it on two.

4   *Ansoff options*

A number of options emerged during analysis.

Products

		Existing	New
Markets	Existing	Environmental maintenance Waste treatment Textiles Health care Unique speciality foods Alcohol, baking, fats/oils Fruit/wine, flavour, protein Animal foods, leather Paper/pulp Chemical biotransformation	More testing kits GMOs By-products High tech diagnostic New Tech foods Full consultancy service Technical backup service

	New	Geographic - eg Russia
		         China
		         USA
		         Japan
		New industries/sectors
		Oil spillage
		Pharmaceutical
		Licensing
			Knowledge brokers
			
			Backward
			Forward
			integration

BPP
PROFESSIONAL EDUCATION

5   *Biocatalysts' decision criteria*

Evaluation of strategic options

Each strategy must be evaluated for its attractiveness to the business and the competitive advantage/position it offers. The best evaluation tool for this purpose is the GE matrix. Management will agree and prioritise the criteria for strategy attractiveness and research on customers can determine the competitive position. We already have some information on why customers buy which would form this criteria, for example:

Strategy attractiveness	**Competitive position**
1 Profitability of net less than X%	1 Improving efficiency
2 Marketing growth potential	2 Cost effectiveness
3 Levels of competition	3 Convenience
4 Investment required of not more than X%	4 Safety
5 Synergy with existing operations	5 Availability
6 New skills required	6 Consistency and quality
7 Speed to implement	7 Value for money
8 Degree of risk	8 Technical support

Weighting and rating the criteria enables us to plot the strategies on the matrix to reveal which strategies are worth pursuing and should be rejected.

Biocatalysts need to plan for the short- and medium-term. In this fast changing, dynamic market longer term strategies can be difficult to identify. Strategy selection will need to provide immediate profits given our financial position, followed by medium-term strategies that will grow the business and establish a competitive position.

Step 6: Marketing management and business implications

Chapter Topic List	
1	Business implications of marketing plans
2	Market orientation
3	Structure
4	Strategic role of the brand
5	Strategic and Integrated Marketing Communications (IMC)
6	International marketing strategy
7	Pitfalls

 Tutor's comments

To date no case study has really tested this area. There has been an expectation by the Senior Examiner with all case studies that students pay some attention to the implications of strategic marketing decisions on the organisation, for example changes in structure, requirement for new information systems, training and development needs and possible sources of funding. Students would only be expected to make the briefest of reference.

However with the inclusion of these issues in Managing Marketing Performance we can expect to see this in future case studies. We cannot give you real case examples as non exist so we present here a reminder of what some of those issues might be that you could expect to use, if and where appropriate in recommendations or explanations on implications.

BPP PROFESSIONAL EDUCATION

1 Business implications of marketing plans

1.1 Marketers developing marketing strategies and plans to meet the challenges and demands of the business environment must think of the **implications to the business of developing and implementing their plans.** These implications will usually be to the business as a whole as well as to marketing. Marketers who fail to consider these issues are not thinking or acting strategically and jeopardise the chances of success. **Business implications include:**

- Culture of the organisation (eg marketing orientation)
- Structure
- Financial and funding

- Processes
- People
- Communications and information systems

1.2 **Marketing implications** are inevitably interlinked with business implications and are those strategic issues associated with marketing activities which include:

(a) **Customer focus** (implicit in a marketing orientation and dependent on good marketing intelligence, marketing information systems and the ability to segment markets)

(b) **Product/services** offered and the quality, benefits and value they represent to the customer (including e.g. accessibility – place, value for money – price)

(c) **Customer service** (implicit in the people, processes and physical evidence policies)

(d) **Communications**, positioning and the brand

2 Market orientation

2.1 A marketing orientation ensures that management's key tasks are to determine the needs and wants of selected target markets, and to adopt appropriate structures and design activities to meet those needs. Marketing research is a key activity and marketing intelligence forms the basis of decision making. Marketing programmes are tailored to meet the needs of specific, selected groups of people with similar needs and characteristics.

Clues to market orientation

People

2.2 **Board level/senior management**

Marketing is represented at board level by qualified marketing professionals. The Chief Executive, from whatever background, has a marketing qualification or training.

2.3 **Staff**

People are valued and trusted by the organisation and this is reflected in internal policies and procedures, and in management attitudes to employees.

Culture and structure

2.4 The values of the organisation are reflected in the way staff are treated, how responsive the organisation is to the local community and the responsibility assumed for social and environmental issues.

2.5 Customers are not considered the sole responsibility of marketing and sales, but the responsibility of everyone in the organisation. All employees understand their role and contribution in delivering benefits to customers; they know who their customers are and what is important to them.

2.6 Organisational structure is designed to meet the challenges of external demands rather than internal convenience. Continuous improvement is a corporate goal that is assimilated into departmental, team and individual objectives.

Tasks and processes

2.7 Strategies

Senior management are concerned with the long-term future and direction of the organisation and developing strategies that reflect the reality of the market place. Marketing plays a pivotal role in determining what product market opportunities the organisation pursues. Financial resources for marketing are determined by objectives to be achieved, not spare cash left over.

2.8 Marketing information

(a) There is a **formalised** Marketing Information System (MKIS) feeding into a Management Information System (MIS) and **primary marketing research is regarded as an essential activity**. Management decisions are based on the results of marketing research activities and reflect business strengths and competitive positioning.

(b) The business understands its business environment, the likelihood and nature of opportunities and threats and how well it is performing compared with competitors. It understands customer behaviour and the values customers attribute to the organisation's brand(s).

2.9 Co-ordination and integration

(a) Planning and control is recognised as the most efficient and effective way to use limited resources and organise activities. Activities across the organisation are co-ordinated and integrated by senior management to ensure consistency of delivery and take advantage of maximising value-added opportunities.

(b) Departments understand each others' problems and needs, and work in partnership to solve problems and accomplish overall departmental and corporate objectives.

(c) This partnership philosophy extends to suppliers, distribution channels and other stakeholders who are included in the planning process and whose activities are assimilated into the organisation's plans.

2.10 Communications

Communications, internal and external, with employees, customers and all stakeholders, incorporate values and positioning, and reflect the needs of different target groups. Two-way communications are encouraged, with mechanisms for listening as well as talking.

2.11 New product/service development

New product development involves the customer either directly or through marketing intelligence and customer contribution to this process is considered fundamental. Customer service is designed in at the start, developed with the product or service and is seen as key to competitive advantage and customer retention. Different customer needs are reflected in different products, and services are designed to meet those needs.

2.12 Measuring effectiveness

Setting targets and standards is regarded as pivotal to successful outcomes and measuring effectiveness as an integral part of planning. Employees have customer satisfaction performance targets as well as the usual easily quantified targets. Evaluation of successes and failures determines the nature of future plans.

2.13 Training and development

Training and development of employees is recognised as key to ensuring business success, and marketing and customer service training is **not confined to marketing personnel.** Appraisals form part of continual improvement, and the development and motivation of employees is seen as a significant management task. Training and development is also seen as the most effective way of ensuring employees are prepared and able to accept and implement change in response to market conditions.

2.14 Peters and Waterman suggest that eight basic attributes of excellence appear to account for success. These include a bias for action, closeness to the customer, autonomy and entrepreneurship, productivity through people, a hands on value-driven approach to management, stick with the 'knitting', simple form, lean staff numbers and finally simultaneous centralised control and decentralised operations. They developed the McKinsey seven Ss to describe influences on strategy and structure.

Shared values – beliefs, values, attitudes held by people reflected in organisation culture

Strategy – the organisation's planned and organised response to delivering internal goals and ambitions in the light of external market forces.

Structure – coordination of functions with the organisation

Systems – formal and informal procedures that support operations

Style – dominant patterns of behaviour and action by managers

Staff – human resources developed and managed effectively

Skills – attributes and capabilities of the organisation

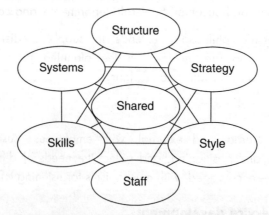

2.15 You will have studied organisation cultures in Managing Marketing Performance and explored their impact on organisation performance. Models include Handy's power culture, task culture, person culture and role culture.

Johnson's **cultural web** represents the "taken-for-granted" assumptions (or paradigm) of an organisation and its physical manifestations in organisation culture.

Routines – the behaviour of members of organisation towards each other and external stakeholders.

Rituals – special events that confirm and reinforce values

Stories –link the past to the present, confer "status" on individuals (positive or negative)

Symbols – physical evidence eg logos and buildings, language, titles

Power structures – based on seniority and/or expertise

Control systems – the design and focus of reward systems and measurement

Organisational structure – establishes relationships, reporting lines, communication process

The paradigm – is the sum of the other elements of the cultural web, the concept and principles of the culture.

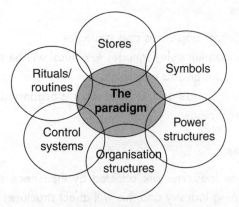

Innovation and organisation culture

2.16 An important aspect of marketing orientation is innovation. This is the only way businesses can stay ahead. Central to innovation is an **environment that allows creativity**. Control therefore, must be flexible and is able to adapt when circumstances demand a different approach.

2.17 A key driver of innovation is **attitude**.

(a) People in the organisation are not interested in following but in leading, wanting to be first. This attitude will also affect the type of innovation.

(b) Incremental innovation is less risky, costly and more likely to succeed due to its nature. The business learns as it evolves and, because the innovation is usually built on something the customers already know and understand, they are likely to appreciate the 'new' benefits.

(c) Innovation can be revolutionary and involve 'megaprojects' or 'do everything'. This requires heavy investment, the 'unknowns' are greater including the market's response and the learning curves are far steeper. It is only usually an option if it is a matter of business survival (due to falling so far behind the competition) or the innovation is known to meet a significant identified need and has guaranteed commercial viability.

Continuous improvement

2.18 An attitude of, and systems for, continuous improvement is also essential in developing an innovative culture and environment. Change can be very disruptive and threatening.

2.19 Change can be gentle and continuous, a part of everyday life, so people are used to it and work with it. This requires flexibility in structures, systems and processes so that events can evolve gradually, but continuously, where appropriate. An attitude of wanting to improve on what is done now is encouraged through rewards and recognition. Continuous improvement is included in personal and team targets.

3   Structure

Key factors affecting organisation design/structure

3.1   Internal influences

- **Mission**: corporate objectives and strategies
- **Culture**: management style/attitudes to control will be reflected in design
- **People**: skills requirements and levels
- **Task**: the product made and the way work is organised
- **Processes**: technology

3.2   External influences

(a)   **Location**: some industries are affected by their necessity to be in a certain geographic location eg mining industry and this will affect structure

(b)   **Customers**: organising around customers can be driven by necessity or a desire to differentiate

(c)   **Legal/political**: eg organisations producing dangerous or toxic products.

Centralised versus decentralised operations

3.3   The extent of centralisation and decentralisation depends on a number of factors including size of organisation, number of markets it operates in, industry type, products and processes. Usually the more complex and competitive the environment the greater the need for decentralisation.

Advantages of centralisation	Advantages of decentralisation
■ Facilitates the co-ordination of marketing	■ Allows local responses
■ Can dilute low management expertise in some areas	■ Improves effective local performance
■ Should result in better control	■ Improves management development
■ Ensures transfer of ideas across teams	
■ Avoids duplication of effort and therefore reduces costs	

3.4 Structural options

- Functional eg finance, marketing, product
- Territory eg north, home countries
- Product
- Market
- Process/technology
- Knowledge/skills eg paediatrics, radiology
- Matrix

4 Strategic role of the brand

4.1 The brand plays a more significant role than ever before. Its value to the organisation as a source of competitive advantage and means of securing customer loyalty has been recognised and the nature of brand management has changed as a result.

Brands and their strategic role

4.2 Managing brands at a **tactical** level has always been easier than at strategic level. It did not require co-ordination across the organisation or consideration of integrating business activities.

4.3 The role of the brand has become much more 'strategic' in the last decade. This has been driven by brands appearing on balance sheets as assets. Suddenly organisations realised the financial value of brands. To build and maintain financial value requires a strategic approach which, in turn, requires long-term commitment to the brand, investment and innovation.

4.4 All business activities must be co-ordinated to represent the desired meaning and values of the brand.

Objectives and benefits

4.5 Objectives and benefits of brand management include:

- Building demand and building/holding margins
- Protection (eg reputation and quality)
- Added value
- Competitive advantage
- Customer loyalty and repeat purchase

Brands and corporate image/reputation

4.6 Image and reputation come from a number of sources. How the business performs in its markets can help build a positive image and reputation (or not). Customers' views and perceptions, and competitor actions, will also affect image and reputation.

4.7 A key factor in building a positive image and reputation will be the **effectiveness** of the organisation's **communication activities**. Fundamental to this will be the brand and what it has come to represent. The brand can be (and increasingly is) the company name or product names.

4.8 The communications effort, amongst other things, should be concerned with promoting **positive associations** with the brand that are meaningful and valued by customers. Sony is a good example of a brand that is perceived as trustworthy and reliable, with high quality performance. This reduces the customer's need to take time deciding between brands: the Sony brand is trusted and so the **perceived risk** is lessened.

Brands, corporate culture and customer service

4.9   Corporate culture can affect perceptions of the brand either positively or negatively. An organisation that receives bad publicity for the way it treats its staff is likely to damage its image in the eyes of its publics. An organisation that values its staff and is perceived as a good place to work will add value to the brand. This also extends to its role in the local community, society and environmental responsibility.

4.10   Customer service, increasingly a source of competitive advantage, is one of the most difficult elements of the marketing mix to manage. Variability in service affects customers' perceptions of the value of the brand.

4.11   To ensure consistent and desired customer service levels, the right people need to be recruited, employees need to feel valued and receive the appropriate customer service training if the desired levels of service are to be achieved and maintained.

Action Programme 1

What brand values would you recommend Biocatalysts consider? Think about what they do well and how they need to build a niche position in the future.

There is no feedback for this Action Programme.

5   Strategic and Integrated Marketing Communications (IMC)

5.1   Key to achieving a unique position in the market place, and managing the strategic role of the brand, is ensuring that all the ways in which the organisation communicates with its publics, both directly and indirectly, are consistent. Everything the organisation does and the way it does it reinforces the positioning values. There should be no confusing or conflicting messages.

5.2   This requires a strategic approach and planning and the rewards include:

■   Improved effectiveness of communications with selected targets
■   Improved efficiency in use of resources
■   Improved profits as a result of above two
■   Improved competitiveness

5.3   The organisation does not simply communicate through its marketing mix promotional activities. There are four main levels at which the organisation communicates, spanning strategic and tactical levels.

5.4   **Strategic communication levels** are the industry (or institutional) and company levels and include:

■   Corporate actions (eg social responsibilities, influencing industry and government)
■   Corporate identity – brand values
■   Management style and behaviour
■   Corporate strategies
■   Positioning

5.5   Integrated communications require vertical and horizontal co-ordination of activities.

Corporate vision, mission and communications

5.6 **The company's mission statement defines the purpose of the business**. The role of strategic marketing communications is to **signal that purpose** to the market and reinforce the message through regular, planned promotional activities. The company's aspirations are defined in the vision and this also is communicated to the market. The messages signal future intentions and aspirations to the market.

5.7 Fundamental to the success of these messages is that the **market believes** what is communicated. Developing credibility is core to messages of business purpose and vision: therefore the organisation's know how and capabilities are given prominence.

Corporate culture and communications

5.8 The **culture of the organisation** is expressed through the **behaviour of the people** within the organisation, both management and staff. The culture is the personality of the business and increasingly culture is playing an important role in adding value to the corporate brand. The organisation's reputation may be built through quality, reliability, innovation and so on, and these become part of what the company is known and respected for. Positive attributes become core communication messages.

5.9 The values and attitudes held by people in the organisation are reflected in the way people are treated, both internally and externally. They also reflect attitudes to risk, and influence strategic choices. These values and attitudes communicate the sort of 'personality' the organisation has, and will have a positive or negative impact.

Management style and communications

5.10 **The culture of the organisation significantly affects the style of management**. The extent to which management trusts and respects employees is demonstrated in the extent of supervision and control. Rules, regulations and procedures all reflect attitudes towards employees perceived capabilities and how they are valued (or not). This trust and respect is passed on to customers through employee attitudes to service. Customers will either feel they have been processed or that they have been served. The result of this communication with the customer is either an impersonal experience that resulted in the customer feeling uncomfortable, unhappy and/or unsatisfied or a personal experience where the customer felt valued and expectations were at the very least met or exceeded.

Corporate image/identity and communications

5.11 Corporate image is achieved through the combination of:

- Culture: its personality, values and attitudes

- Visual cues: the physical evidence e.g. buildings, logos, colours

- Behaviour: performance (eg competitive and reliable) and integrity (conducting business, eg with awareness of, social and environmental responsibilities, ethics)

All these organisational issues are interwoven.

Corporate strategy, positioning and communications

5.12 **Competitive positioning** and growth strategies depend on effective marketing communications to achieve the overall goal. Customers may position a company in their minds but it is up to the organisation to influence that position positively and in line with their strategic goals. This position follows on from the mission and vision, and is reinforced through the company's performance in the market.

5.13 Growth strategies depend on identification of specific market segments to target with specific products. The success of these strategies depends on the effectiveness of the marketing mix including communication messages targeted at those existing and new segments. Different strategies will require different messages; for example, market penetration messages are targeted at existing customers with whom a relationship has already been built. This will differ from market development where messages are targeted at new customers who will not be so familiar with the organisation.

6 International marketing strategy

6.1 The same processes and frameworks are used in international marketing. The difference is the complexity and increased need for co-ordination and integration of strategies, particularly if global strategies are to be pursued.

6.2 As well as vertical planning systems, there is a need for horizontal planning systems, a framework for senior management to co-ordinate and harmonise Strategic Business Unit plans. The goal is to maximise competitive advantage through sharing best practice and skills and develop coherent global strategies.

International business operations

6.3 Structure and control present problems for international companies, and structuring and re-structuring has become part of normal life for the multi-national in a bid to find the 'best' structure for managing international activities. Organisations have centralised control and decentralised control and back again.

6.4 There are no easy answers or perfect solutions. The international market place is changing rapidly, not least because of the impact of technology. Organisations must therefore remain flexible and ensure that continuous improvement and adaptation is part of day to day operations.

Managing across borders

6.5 Organisation culture and the influences of national culture affect both management style and communications. Marketing is responsible for responding to the needs of external customers and stakeholders. Marketing management must therefore respond to the needs of internal employees to ensure those external customers and stakeholders receive what they want.

   (a) **Staffing policy**. Decisions include whether to recruit locally, post home country staff to overseas appointments or a combination of both. There are advantages and disadvantages to recruiting local people (see your international notes). Staff should receive support and training for overseas assignments and communications systems should ensure employee/s feel as in touch as they did before moving abroad. This requires extra effort from the organisation, not the same effort. Motivation must take account of differences for example, while Maslow's hierarchy of needs is still valid, the order of the needs changes depending on the culture.

(b) **Training programmes**. Factors to consider include and learning styles and expectations, training methods available, training skills available and attitudes to training. If training is not common practice in a culture, it may be seen as threatening, a criticism of performance. It is important to communicate the purpose and benefits of training and ensure people perceive training positively.

(c) **Communication programmes**. Factors to consider include language and interpretation, style and tone, expected forms of communications, technology availability, symbolism and cultural influences e.g. meaning of colour and use of humour. In high power distance cultures employees will expect to be 'told' what to do and communications are one-way. If the manager wishes to encourage two-way communications and involve employees, plans will be needed to change employee expectations and perceptions of their role in decision making. In low power distance cultures, two-way communications will be the norm. Employees expect to be allowed to clarify instructions and challenge actions.

Action Programme 2

Consider the implications of Biocatalysts' business and strategic marketing. What might affect their ability to implement strategic marketing plans and what changes may they have to make?

6.6 All of these issues impact directly or indirectly on marketing planning. Marketers need to ensure they have taken account of the impact and incorporated, where appropriate, actions to address the business and marketing implications of the mission, vision, corporate objectives and strategies selected.

6.7 In this chapter we have discussed the business implications that may arise as a result of developing strategic marketing plans. In fact, for Biocatalysts, all of these issues are relevant. For example they need to adopt a **marketing orientation** if they are going to achieve their goal of being a respected **niche player**. This cannot be achieved with their current business and marketing planning skills.

6.8 Strategic and integrated marketing communications will also be essential to success. Particularly as Biocatalysts do not have much cash to fund communications activities and so must ensure that everything they do will maximise results.

6.9 Their international development has been unmanaged and appears to be ad hoc. There is no clear strategy and, given their financial performance, they cannot afford to operate in this way any longer. Again, to produced successful results they need to develop coherent international plans and this may require re-structuring the business.

7 Pitfalls

7.1 Sometimes the exam questions do not ask specifically for you to identify implications for the business of the recommendations you have made. The danger is of failing to incorporate these vital issues within your answers even if they have not been specifically asked for. We do not suggest that you spend much time discussing them but, for example, if adopting a marketing orientation or customer focus is essential to the success of building a brand or integrated communications strategy, you should briefly refer to the need to change the culture to a marketing orientation.

Action Programme review

2   There are many factors you might include here:

- The lack of customer orientation
- Shortage of funding and uncertainty of funding
- Lack of marketing skills
- The product focus of technology staff
- The product focused business structure
- Lack of information

Changes which would be needed:

- To restructure around customer groups
- To establish an effective marketing information system
- To establish internal marketing skills

Step 7: Marketing strategy and marketing mix plans

10

Chapter Topic List
1   Marketing planning
2   Marketing objectives
3   Marketing strategy: segmentation
4   Marketing strategy: positioning
5   Marketing strategy: targeting
6   Marketing strategy: international issues
7   Marketing strategy
8   Implementing marketing strategy
9   The marketing mix for Biocatalysts

173 BPP
PROFESSIONAL EDUCATION

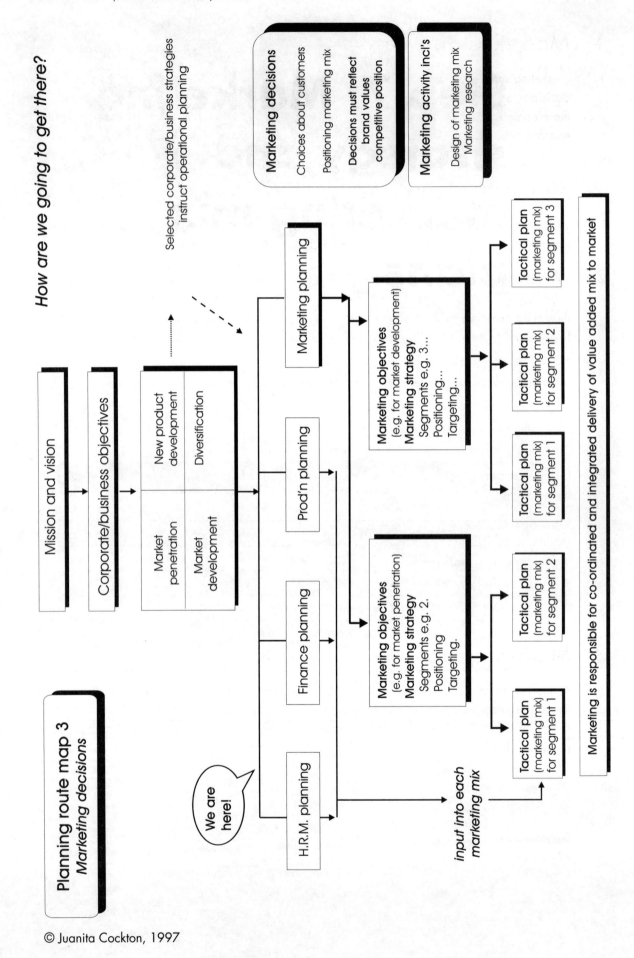

How are we going to get there?

Selected corporate/business strategies instruct operational planning

Marketing decisions
- Choices about customers
- Positioning marketing mix
- Decisions must reflect brand values competitive position

Marketing activity incl's
- Design of marketing mix
- Marketing research

Planning route map 3
Marketing decisions

© Juanita Cockton, 1997

Mission and vision

Corporate/business objectives

New product development	Diversification
Market penetration	Market development

Marketing planning

Prod'n planning

Finance planning

H.R.M. planning

We are here!

Marketing objectives (e.g. for market development)
Marketing strategy
Segments e.g. 3...
Positioning...
Targeting...

Marketing objectives (e.g. for market penetration)
Marketing strategy
Segments e.g. 2.
Positioning
Targeting.

Tactical plan (marketing mix) for segment 1
Tactical plan (marketing mix) for segment 2
Tactical plan (marketing mix) for segment 3

Tactical plan (marketing mix) for segment 1
Tactical plan (marketing mix) for segment 2

input into each marketing mix

Marketing is responsible for co-ordinated and integrated delivery of value added mix to market

1 Marketing planning

1.1 Marketing objectives and marketing plans cannot be developed until the organisation has made decisions on which broad product market opportunities it intends to pursue. You will see from the planning route map that marketing plans need to be developed for each business strategy selected and, for each segment identified, tactical plans will be developed and implemented.

2 Marketing objectives

2.1 When senior management have communicated their decisions, marketing can set marketing objectives for each business strategy selected by the business.

2.2 The marketing objective is translated from the business objective. So for example a business objective of £1.2 million profit and forecast gross profit margin of 10% can be translated into a marketing objective of £12 million revenue. If we are able to value customers and/or markets in financial terms then marketing objectives can also be interpreted in these terms.

This will be cascaded further when we get to tactical plans. For example products sold, brand awareness, and customer numbers can all be calculated from your revenue objective.

Action Programme 1

Using your analysis and business objectives, set a marketing objective for each strategy you have selected.

Check that the figures work and that it is an interpretation of the business objective. Also is it realistic given Biocatalysts' strengths and market conditions? Please note we do not give feedback for this.

3 Marketing strategy: segmentation

3.1 As markets become more competitive, there are increasing constraints on **budgets**. At the same time, consumers having more choice. How can resources be used more efficiently and effectively to ensure consumers make the 'right' choices? Segmentation achieves this by identifying target groups for marketing purposes.

Key Concept

Segmentation is the process of splitting customers into different groups, or segments, within which customers with similar characteristics have similar needs. By doing this, each one can be targeted and reached with a distinct marketing mix.

3.2 Successful segmentation can be a key source of competitive advantage. Unfortunately, of those businesses that do bother to segment their markets, few consciously adopt an approach that maximises their competitive advantage, opting instead for traditional methods of segmentation.

Knowledge brought forward

Here is a brief reminder of segmentation techniques

Traditional methods of segmentation

Geographic

- Postcode, city, town, village, rural, coastal, county, region, country, climate

Demographic

- Age, sex, family life cycle, family size, religion, income, occupation, ethnic origin, socio-economic group

Psychographic

- (AIO) Personality traits, attitude, family life cycle, lifestyle, VALS, product specific

Behavioural

- Benefits sought, purchase behaviour, purchase occasion, usage

Geodemographic

- Combines geographic and demographic **plus** overlay of psychographic **and** patterns of purchasing behaviour; most well known are ACORN and MOSAIC

Business to business

- SIC codes, process or product, geographic, size of company, operating variables, circumstances, purchase methods

Increasingly organisations are developing segmentation models combining the above, the DMU and personality characteristics (eg loyalty, attitudes to risk, beliefs and values).

3.3 Decision Making Unit – (DMU)

Users - those who will use product

Influencers - often help define specifications, provide information

Buyers - formal authority for selecting supplier, arranging terms of purchase

Decision Making Unit DMU

Deciders - have power to decide on product requirements and/or suppliers

Gatekeepers - have power to prevent sellers or information reaching members of buying centre

Approvers - authorise proposed actions of deciders

Action Programme 2

Who is the customer?

How many of the roles in the DMU above can you identify for Biocatalysts?

Decision making units are also valid in consumer markets.

The company's own segmentation techniques

3.4 As well as using some of the more traditional methods of classifying the information, organisations should be gathering more precise information about their customers, tailored to the exact needs of the organisation. This information should provide answers to needs and motives. It can then inform product and promotion development and insights into achieving competitive advantage. It requires systematic gathering of information on their motives/needs from customers over time.

Action Programme 3

Segmental analysis

Choose one or two of Biocatalysts' markets and think about:

- Who buys
- What is bought
- Where
- When/how
- Why

You may have gaps or have to make assumptions but complete what you can and turn to the end of the chapter for a Biocatalysts Segmental Analysis.

Tutor Tip

We often do not have as much information as we would like to segment markets effectively. We will have broad industry sectors and sometimes we will have some information about business to business customers or consumers. We can make realistic assumptions about segments and identify any information gaps that would help us improve segmentation.

We should be able to make recommendations on **how** we can improve segmentation. This is when the segmental analysis process and the identification of information gaps can help us.

4 Marketing strategy: positioning

4.1 **Positioning takes place in the minds of customers**. They evaluate and compare companies, products and services, and position them according to the values they attribute to them based on their experience. Companies have influence over positioning, through communications, product quality and customer service. Positioning is critical to competitive advantage. The more value customers perceive, the greater the competitive advantage.

4.2 **Positioning is based on rational and emotional evaluations**. The functional benefits of a product are easily copied by competitors and provide little opportunity to differentiate. Emotional evaluation, often intangible values attributed to the product such as status, can offer much more opportunity to differentiate the product offering to appeal to customers.

4.3 **Successful positioning requires a realistic approach**. To aim for a 'world leader' position when there is no chance of this happening, particularly if resources and marketing skills are lacking, is unproductive. However realism should be balanced with vision. It is realistic to aim for a 'lead' position, for example, a leader in a segment/s, in industry or a particular process or technology.

4.4 **Successful positioning requires commitment, investment and sustained effort.** Leave it up to the customers and they may not bother. Worse, the competition may decide to position you, for example, Qualcast very successfully re-positioned Hover mowers.

Positioning and the competition

4.5 Know your position. Are you a market **leader, follower, challenger or a nicher?** These positions will affect the strategies adopted. Decisions influence the position and resources will be allocated and strategies designed to build and maintain actual position. Know where you are going. There may be a need or desire to change position. This will require a change in strategy.

Firms A, C, F

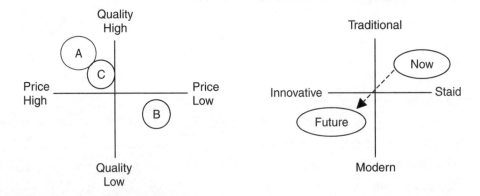

Action Programme 4

Decide how you would position Biocatalysts for the Diagnostic sector. Remember the buying criteria identified during analysis: what matters to customers, on what basis do they make decisions on which product/services to buy? Compare your answer with ours at the end of the chapter.

Blank positioning maps for you to use

5 Marketing strategy: targeting

5.1 The word **'targeting'** is too often confused with **'targets'** (segments). Targeting makes the connection between the segments identified, the positioning strategy and the design of the marketing mix. The targeting strategy is simply a statement on how the marketing mix is used eg undifferentiated to the whole market or differentiated to identified segments.

5.2 Information acquired during analysis will determine which targeting options are viable both in terms of business operations and marketing effectiveness.

5.3 The choices are these.

Undifferentiated strategy (one marketing mix unchanged for entire market)

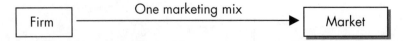

Differentiated strategy (tailored to meet needs of selected segments)

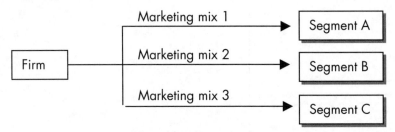

Concentrated strategy (undifferentiated for a niche)

Tailoring the mix

5.4 To maximise effectiveness, the marketing mix is tailored to meet the specific needs of selected customers. To maximise efficiency, marketing mixes should be standardised and so provide opportunities to achieve economies of scale.

5.5 To be efficient in business operations **and** effective in the market place there must be a balance between standardisation and adaptation: only change elements of the marketing mix that will have impact. Sometimes this can be achieved by promotional messages alone or small changes to the product.

Action Programme 5

Assessing target options

Take 10 minutes to assess the suitability and implications of these targeting alternatives for Biocatalysts.

Turn to the end of the chapter for our feedback.

6 Marketing strategy: international issues

Marketing planning: planning for differences

6.1 In some instances, differences will have to be accepted and planned for: in fact these differences, from a marketing perspective, may be essential to success.

(a) Customer service is significantly influenced by culture. What is expected in one culture is not necessarily expected in another. For example, self-service has become part of Western life. In other parts of the world, customers do not expect to serve themselves in any exchange with a business.

(b) When selling, in some cultures the price is publicised and that is the price people expect to pay. In other cultures the expectations is that you will always bargain over price. In some parts of the world fast and direct negotiations are the norm; in others, time is taken over building a relationship before any negotiations can begin.

6.2 The same frameworks and tools can be used to develop marketing plans. There are, however, some extra considerations.

(a) **Country selection** should be an objective process (Harrell and Kiefer matrix).

(b) **Methods of entry** must also be evaluated for their suitability in terms of levels of involvement as well as managing control. An increasingly important trend is SAs, JVs, M&As as a means of developing international markets. It is also significantly affecting the nature of competition.

(c) **Segmentation**: standard techniques can be used in many markets such as identifying strategically equivalent segments (SES) and acknowledging similarities and differences across rather than within markets. Segmentation can be based on consumers not countries. In some markets, however, it cannot be assumed that the same customer characteristics apply. Geodemographic Euromosaic, VALS 2 (Europe) and Euro-styles, RISC Euro type.

(d) **Positioning**: changing markets can mean having to change position. For example product use might change (Japanese using strimmers to cut lawns) and benefits may be sought for different reasons (eg four wheel drive in most European countries and part of the USA is often about adventure; in other parts of the world durability and reliability really do matter if you are driving through difficult terrain. Decisions on global, regional, country, market or segment positioning.

7 Marketing strategy

Tutor Tip

Reference has been, and will be made to the need for communications in the examination to be persuasive. When developing outline notes for the exam, as with the real world, we must **explain** and *justify* our decisions and recommendations. Recommendations usually require senior management to allocate resources, people, time and money and they will only be prepared to do this if we can justify that what we proposed will result in successful outcomes. The Examiner will be looking for justification.

7.1   The outcomes of the marketing planning process are decisions recorded in the plan; your activities in this chapter have been reaching those decisions. So you will now have:

- Marketing objectives
- Segments identified to target
- Positioning of the marketing mix
- Targeting strategy adopted

The marketing plan must reflect the competitive position of the business strategy.

Marketing strategy: statements (decisions) for marketing plan document

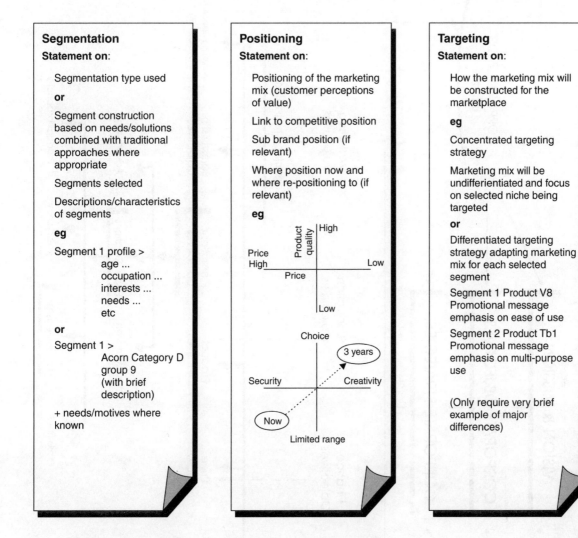

Segmentation

Statement on:

Segmentation type used

or

Segment construction based on needs/solutions combined with traditional approaches where appropriate

Segments selected

Descriptions/characteristics of segments

eg

Segment 1 profile >
    age ...
    occupation ...
    interests ...
    needs ...
    etc

or

Segment 1 >
    Acorn Category D
    group 9
    (with brief
    description)

+ needs/motives where known

Positioning

Statement on:

Positioning of the marketing mix (customer perceptions of value)

Link to competitive position

Sub brand position (if relevant)

Where position now and where re-positioning to (if relevant)

eg

Targeting

Statement on:

How the marketing mix will be constructed for the marketplace

eg

Concentrated targeting strategy

Marketing mix will be undifferientiated and focus on selected niche being targeted

or

Differentiated targeting strategy adapting marketing mix for each selected segment

Segment 1 Product V8 Promotional message emphasis on ease of use

Segment 2 Product Tb1 Promotional message emphasis on multi-purpose use

(Only require very brief example of major differences)

8   Implementing marketing strategy

8.1 Implementation is an area that is too often undertaken as an unrelated activity to the business and marketing strategies. The marketing mix tactical plans implement the marketing and business strategies.

8.2 It is assumed you are knowledgeable about developing tactical plans. There are also strategic issues associated with each element of the marketing mix, for example new product development requires a strategic and integrated approach, the type of product or service will affect communications plan at a strategic level, and these will be discussed briefly.

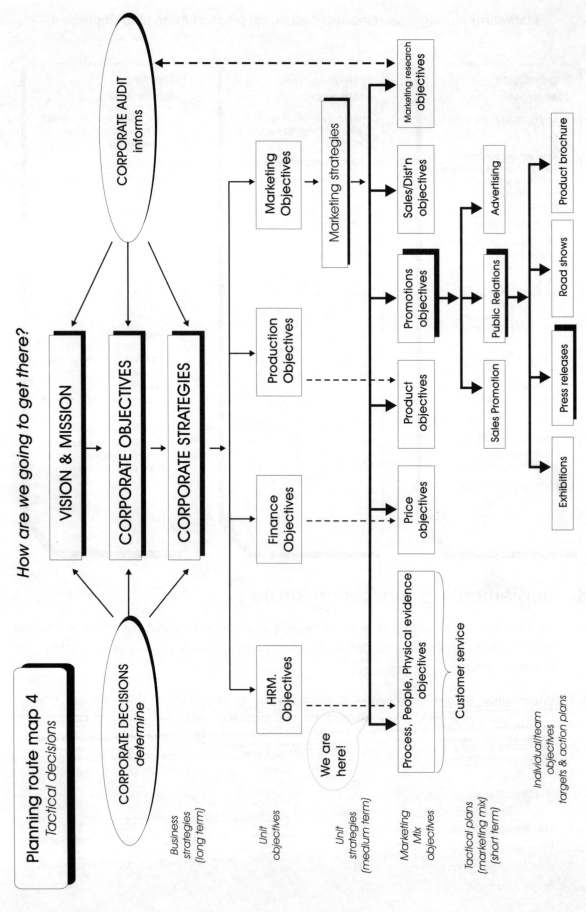

Planning route map 4
Tactical decisions

How are we going to get there?

© Juanita Cockton, 1997

9 The marketing mix for Biocatalysts

'Product' for Biocatalysts

9.1 With Biocatalysts we know that important issues in product development include to increase yield, to improve efficiency, cost effectiveness, safety (track record), expertise, consistent quality and activity, to be kept informed (openness, transparency), guidance on developments, availability, reliability, strength, purity, value for money reflects quality and similar analytical techniques.

Other issues that also need to be planned for include, for example, where Biocatalysts' products are in the product life cycle.

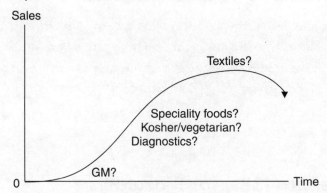

NPD. Another issue for Biocatalysts was that of developing new products **reactively in response to any customer** instead of **proactively in response to selected customers** in the context of **business goals and market conditions**.

Price for Biocatalysts

9.2 For Biocatalysts, a significant strategic issue is that they have been customising products using their expertise and high technical skills but their **financial performance suggests they are not charging premium prices for premium products**. Decisions will need to be made on pricing in relation to their desired position.

Place for Biocatalysts

9.3 **Biocatalysts have not been managing their channels**. There is clearly evidence in the analysis, of poor revenue generation in some markets, particularly overseas markets. Evaluation of existing channels and of new channels is critical, as will be their need to manage channels more effectively in future. Channel management must also improve international development.

Promotion for Biocatalysts

9.4 (a) Biocatalysts's promotional activities need to become more strategic and focused. Their major problem is cash so any recommendations must be realistic in terms of budgets and the context of the industry they are in. Business to business promotions need not be expensive activities and most certainly should not be extravagant campaigns.

(b) Building and maintaining a strong brand over time will be important. Maintaining and building their reputation for quality and expertise are potentially powerful brand values and any promotional activities should be designed to build the brand. Remember that in different countries there are different attitudes to GMOs, for example, and this needs to be considered when building brand values.

(c) Biocatalysts promotional activities require a strategic and integrated approach to marketing communications including international ones.

Tutor note

International marketing mix issues: some reminders

The international marketing mix must be designed appropriate to market conditions, particularly cultural. Decisions on the extent of standardisation v adaptation should be balanced with the need for economies of scale, profitability and consistency, and meeting the diverse needs of different markets.

Customer service (3Ps) for Biocatalysts

9.5 Customer service in this case study is pivotal in transforming their technical capability into an offer that adds value. Biocatalysts's expertise and ability to advise and guide customers in a way that enhances the customer's performance is central to business success.

Tutor note

It becomes even more difficult to standardise service when businesses start to operate in international markets. The organisation has to establish whether it is appropriate to standardise customer service. People have different attitudes to customer service in different cultures. For example, attitudes to waiting for service include these issues.

(a) Time. Is waiting for service viewed as wasting time or is it seen positively as an opportunity to socialise? In Europe, time spent in a restaurant is not only for eating but also for conversation and relaxing over a meal. Japanese people waiting for service in a restaurant would view this as poor service.

(b) Rules. It is traditional in some countries to 'wait your turn'; in other words queuing for service is typical and this can range from expectations of short queues and time to long queues and time. In other cultures, queuing is not a cultural norm and people expect to fight for what they want.

(c) Power. In cultures where power distance is strong, it is seen as acceptable for 'superiors' to bypass the queue. Less powerful people expect to wait longer.

Action Programme review

2   *Who is the customer?*

Example: food

At company level	Known	Assumed
Approvers		Finance
Buyers		Purchasing managers
Gatekeepers	{ Industry technicians	Standard setters
Deciders		Food technologists
Influencers		{ Industry analysts Consumer watchdogs
Users		Production staff

Note. Beyond this industry DMU, there would be the end-consumer and the people influencing their decision to buy GM products or not.

3 Segmental analysis

Biocatalysts – segmental analysis

Who buys	What is bought	Where	When? How	Why
Food and drink industries	Enzymes	Direct	Seasonality foods/drugs	**Buyers** have common needs: Increase yield, improve efficiency, cost effectiveness, safety (track record), expertise, consistent quality and activity, to be kept informed (Openness, transparency), guidance on developments, availability, reliability, strength, purity, value for money reflects quality
Mass and niche markets Diagnostics*	Enzymes	or through	Initially sample trials Small batches	**Food**: information on animal derived enzymes, safety, guidelines allergenic potential, kosher certified enzymes, reassurance additional chemicals are safe for human consumption, improve/alter texture, extend life of food products, improve processing eg faster fermentation, flavour enhancement, depectinising, peeling, easier to handle waste products
Textiles		agents	Bulk	**Diagnostic**: high specificity, high sensitivity, stable products, ideally product that can be versatile, stable in small scale and bulk production (for R&D trailing then commercial production). Information on financial stability of firm as one kit been approved Diag Co loath to change a component therefore purchase is quite a large commitment to the supplier
Pharmaceutical Pulp/paper Water Animal feed Environment			Currency issues	**Textile**: product that will maintain its stability in bulk production, wide ranging heat stability

---

Investigators and industry analysts: open and transparent information and procedures reputation	**Trade bodies/associations/professional societies**: access to company documentation, is endorsement sought?, encourage ethical practices, conduct research, represent industry effectively, keep up to date

Other stakeholder needs and objectives

FDA. Needs: ensure product produced safe for consumer, health and safety procedures met, clearly documented procedures
Objectives: protect consumers and promote public health, alert of potential danger, work with government to promote uniform activity in food/drug related matters, assist manufacturer in understanding how to comply with good practice standards, remove unsafe/ unlawful products, work with international harmonisation committees to develop accepted standards, monitor companies with regulations

Many have characteristics in common including buying criteria. Some reasonable assumptions can be made on specific criteria.

4   *Positioning Biocatalysts*

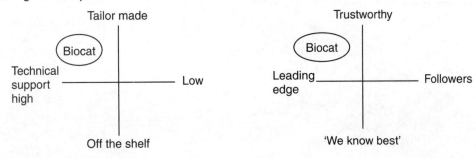

5   *Assessing targeting options*

Undifferentiated

Biocatalysts already offer customised solutions: their strength is their expertise and ability to customise so undifferentiated not a realistic option. Also offers no competitive advantage opportunities.

Differentiated

This requires ability to deliver a broad range to variety of customers. Medium to large size players have strength and resource to do this. Biocatalysts do not.

Niche

Requires expertise and customisation and to work effectively on a global scale can also adopt multi-niche strategies. Works well in highly specialised or narrow markets. This fits well with Biocatalysts's position.

Step 8: Contemporary issues and marketing plans

11

Chapter Topic List	
1	Contemporary issues
2	What is a brand?
3	Ethical, social and environmental responsibilities
4	Customer relationship management
5	Customer service
6	Collaborative partnerships
7	Supply chain management
8	E-commerce and Internet strategies
9	Contemporary issues for Biocatalysts

1 Contemporary issues

1.1 Business practice and academic theory continually evolves to reflect our changing environment. The way we solved problems yesterday will not be the same way we solve problems today or tomorrow. Different business models, environmental conditions, competitive behaviour etc. means we need to respond with new ideas and solutions.

What they are

1.2 The case study syllabus is a **strategic** approach to business analysis, decision making and implementation. We can therefore always expect these core elements to be reflected in one way or another in the case study and the examination. What changes are the latest **developments** in these areas? **Contemporary issues** in the case reflect the latest thinking on how businesses operate – how they manage people, produce goods, develop strategies and so on. We do not intend to take an exhaustive look at contemporary issues, as they are many and varied, and are continually evolving.

BPP PROFESSIONAL EDUCATION

1.3 The contemporary issues we will look at briefly here are:

- Brand strategy and management
- Customer relationship management
- Collaborative partnerships
- Supply chain management
- E-commerce and internet strategies
- Ethical, social and environmental responsibilities

How you identify contemporary issues in the case

1.4 The contemporary issues are usually fairly easily identified and flagged in the case studies. For example, with Biocatalysts we look at **partnerships** with stakeholders, **customer relationship management** and **environmental** issues which we identify with clear headings and text and/or models.

1.5 Contemporary issues have never been difficult to identify. Ignoring them, however is possible, particularly if a tick box approach to developing plans is adopted.

How you use contemporary issues in the case

1.6 Sometimes there is a specific question on a contemporary issue raised in the case study but often not. This does not mean that the issues should be ignored, far from it, the expectation is that you understand these often strategic issues and incorporate into your plans and solutions as and where appropriate.

1.7 For example if we had developed an Internet strategy and it did not come up as a question then you would look for opportunities to include elements of your internet strategy in the appropriate and relevant answers to questions.

2 What is a brand?

2.1 A brand is more than just a physical product or service, it can help build relationships with customers. This is particularly important in markets where the organisation has no face to face contact with customers eg fmcg. A brand is also more than just the component parts that make up a product, it has additional values attributed to it **by customers**.

2.2 A brand adds value to the product. Added value often has more potential to differentiate one product from another than the **core** and **expected** functional **benefits** sought by customers.

Where is value added?

Total brand concept – adding value

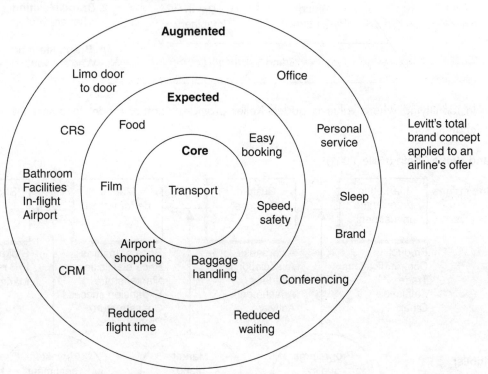

Brands, positioning and the marketing mix

2.3 The marketing department does not have control over all of the marketing mix; the whole organisation is involved. The marketing department should, however have significant influence over the marketing mix, particularly if the brand is to perform effectively and provide a source of competitive advantage.

2.4 The entire marketing mix must represent and reflect the brand values. Any inconsistencies confuse customers and damages the brand's reputation and performance. The marketing task is to ensure that, in the first place it understands the brand values as perceived by customers and, secondly, manages the mix to build positive brand values effectively position the mix in the market.

2.5 We have seen reference to brand building, image and strategies in many of the case studies. Many case studies, as you will learn, make specific reference to brand models and concepts.

Kevin Keller (2003) believes there are four key steps of brand building.

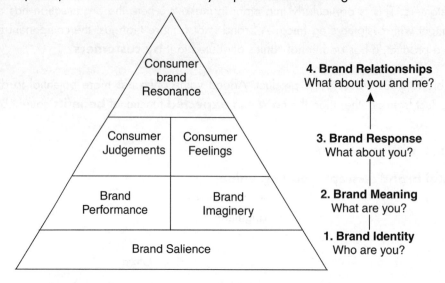

2.6 In identifying where value is added Keller provides another model to assess the brand value chain.

Brand Value Chain (Keller 2001)

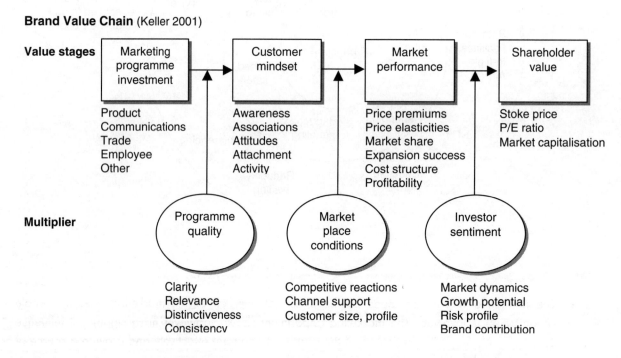

Criteria for choosing brand elements

2.7 Keller identifies six brand elements that are essential in building a brand. These are:

1	Memorability	4	Transferability
2	Meaningfulness	5	Adaptability
3	Likeability	6	Protectability

These elements provide an excellent checklist of what we need to take into account when identifying values, names, symbols, slogans etc. We can then develop our brand and ensure it meets these requirements.

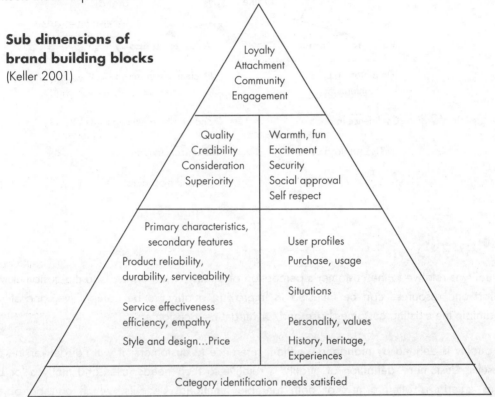

Sub dimensions of brand building blocks (Keller 2001)

Loyalty
Attachment
Community
Engagement

Quality
Credibility
Consideration
Superiority

Warmth, fun
Excitement
Security
Social approval
Self respect

Primary characteristics, secondary features

Product reliability, durability, serviceability

Service effectiveness efficiency, empathy

Style and design...Price

User profiles

Purchase, usage

Situations

Personality, values

History, heritage, Experiences

Category identification needs satisfied

Brand equity

2.8 The equity of a brand lies in the name, symbol, slogan, the meaning of the brand and, ultimately its perceived value to the customer. The resources and effort, invested in the product and/or service delivered to the customer, all contribute to brand equity. Representative of this investment is:

- Brand loyalty
- Brand quality
- Brand association
- Brand awareness
- Brand properties (patents, trademarks etc.)

2.9 Brand equity is derived from the value it represents to both customers and the organisation.

Brand equity (Aaker 1991)

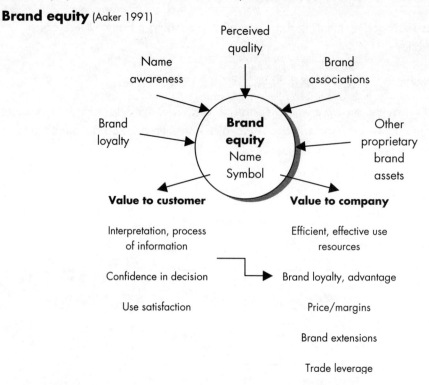

Brand quality

2.10 Quality is relative to the customer's perception of quality, what it means to the customer. A lot of effort and resources can be invested in improving quality, to be competitive, and still fail to maintain the existing customer base and/or attract new customers.

2.11 If quality is defined by managers, without reference to customers, it will not deliver the desired results. Customers' definition of quality is relative to their needs, uses and motives for buying. This criteria is often a mix of both tangible functional benefits, which can be objectively measured, and of intangible emotional benefits which are far more difficult to measure objectively. Even the rational evaluation is susceptible to subjective evaluation.

2.12 Quality is derived from a number of sources

- Component quality (the ingredients of the product)
- Process quality (the way in which the product or service is made or delivered)
- Service quality (how the product or service is delivery through personal service)

2.13 Perceptions of quality can be influenced by a number of factors, some of which are a result of deliberate strategies by the organisation and some of which are not. Those that are not can be both positive and negative eg good or bad press coverage or accidents. Brand associations also influence to perceptions of quality.

Brand association

2.14 **Brand association** comes from the connections people make between names, symbols and slogans. McDonald's are associated with golden arches, Cadbury's chocolate with the colour purple, the 'Orange' mobile phone company with the colour orange and so on. The brand image is a set of associations derived from a number of sources.

2.15 The value of the brand is represented in these associations and provides meaning to the values attributed to the brand. Associations can contribute to the success of the brand by:

- Speeding up evaluation through easy retrieval processing and of information
- Provoking positive attitudes towards the brand
- Broadening definitions of the brand's know how and ability
- Aiding and enlightening interpretation of name, symbol and slogan
- Providing a context for positioning (with whom does the brand mix)

2.16 Associations are not confined to the activities of the organisation such as the marketing mix but also of the circle within which the brand moves. High tech, celebrity status, adventurous, all say something about the brand to the customers. Aaker provides a model for brand associations as follows.

Brand associations (Aaker 1991)

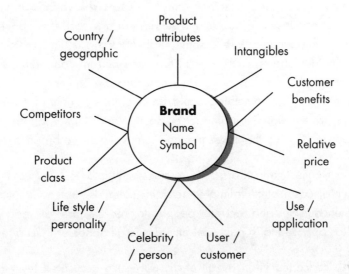

Building the brand

2.17 Building the brand requires **vision**. Where is the brand going, what is its future? A long-term vision should be established and then strategies and plans designed to build the brand to achieve the vision. This will take time and there will be distinct stages and tasks during the building of the brand, with possibly, a different emphasis at each stage.

Brand awareness

2.18 In building the brand, developing credibility and raising visibility are important tasks. Brand awareness objectives will depend on the industry, the company's position in that industry and its markets. **'Top of mind'** awareness requires establishing the brand as one people know without reference to an industry or a prompt. **'Brand recall'** awareness requires a context prompt (eg industry, product category). **Brand recognition** awareness requires the brand being named, among others, and people will recognise the brand name. Each objective has implications for investment and resources. Top of mind will require heavy investment and effort and may not be worth the return. The objective must be realistic and practical.

Brand awareness pyramid
(Aaker 1991)

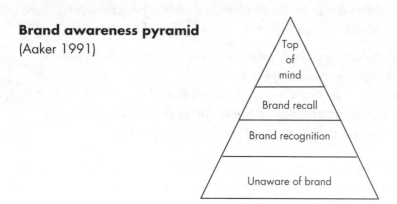

3 Ethical, social and environmental responsibilities

3.1 A central theme of marketing orientation must be **ethical behaviour** and social responsibility. Marketing is not about selling goods and services at any cost, it is about conducting business in a way that is irreproachable. While some might think this is uneconomic or impractical, it does not take a very demanding review of history and current conditions to recognise that cutting corners, ignoring ethical codes of conduct and focusing on short term bottom line will eventual damage something. That something could be people, our natural environment or our society. Organisations have a significant impact on society and cannot ignore their responsibilities. An intelligent approach is one that takes the long term view and a broad perspective.

3.2 Evidence of our collective lack of social responsibility is all around us. Packaging, the materials used and our disposal of it, failing to recycle materials and goods and lack of provision of facilities to encourage and enable people to recycle are all part of the problem. Our 'disposable' as apposed to 'repairable' attitudes to all goods are just a few examples.

3.3 It does take a concerted effort by all of us, not just a dedicated few, if we are to be socially responsibility. **Collectively** people need to believe in our social responsibilities, adopting green or environmental principles and practices. **Collaboratively** organisations need to provide the enablers that allow people to be socially responsible. It is all very well insisting we recycle waste, but unless there are relatively easy methods for us to do this we are unlikely to engage in action and rarely get beyond engaging in the debate.

A marketing orientation can encourage ethical practices internally and externally. Ethical behaviour does not just confine itself to social and environmental responsibilities. Unfortunately it is not a simple question of defining ethical codes of conduct and making sure everyone abides by them. How we conduct business also raises questions about what is acceptable behaviour. Bribery or 'softeners' are not uncommon in business practice in different parts of the world and in fact expected as part of business and seen as acceptable. On such occasions organisations are faced with the challenge of whether or not their code of ethical conduct is reasonable in the context of the culture the business might be operating in.

3.4 There are a growing number of models and techniques for developing CSR practices and many of these are still evolving. For example:

Pyramid of CSR
(Carroll 1991)

Philanthropic responsibilities
'Be a good corporate citizen'
Contribute resources to the community;
improve quality of life

Ethical responsibilities
'Be ethical'
Obligation to do what is right, just and
fair. Avoid harm

Legal responsibilities
'Obey the law'
Law is society's codification of right and
wrong. Play by the rules of the game

Economic responsibilities
'Be profitable'
The foundation upon which all others rest

4 Customer relationship management

4.1 Building customer relationships in business to business markets has been long understood and practised. The difference now is that there is a focus on the **formality** and **process** for building relationships with customers. Objectives are set and strategies developed to ensure the efforts succeed. Building relationships in consumer markets can be more complex, particularly where the organisation never comes into direct contact with consumers. The relationship here is built with the brand. Reasons for building relationships in business to business markets are usually the result of a need one or more of the **Five Relationship Needs**:

	Comment
Need for trust	If the product or service involved saving, maintaining or improving life, for example, the caring professions
Need for security	If secrecy, privacy or sensitivity were issues the customer had to believe their interests would be protected, for example financial services
Need for time	If projects had long time scales e.g. 5, 10 even 15 years businesses had to be patient, think and act in the time scales typical of the industry, for example, the military
Need for co-operation	Products required the input of customers in development, working partnerships with customers are a feature of business operations
Need to reduce risk	If large sums of money were involved the investment had to be worthwhile, solve problems and prove beneficial, for example aerospace

Source: *Five Relationship Needs*, J. Cockton 1998

4.2 In markets where demand exceeds supply, there is little or no incentive to focus on building relationships. As markets became increasingly competitive and customers have a choice, businesses have to find ways to improve customer retention and the concept of 'relationship marketing' held the answers.

Relationship marketing

4.3 Relationship marketing is about building long term customer relationships with profitable customers. Another term is customer relationship management (CRM). In some organisations that means changing behaviour from short term transactions to long term relationships.

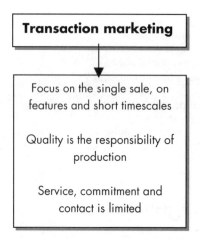

Transaction marketing

Focus on the single sale, on features and short timescales

Quality is the responsibility of production

Service, commitment and contact is limited

Relationship marketing

Focus on retention, on benefits and long timescales

Quality is the responsibility of everyone

Service, commitment and contact is prominent

4.4 Relationship marketing requires that within marketing strategy development there is a focus on:

- **Genuinely valuing people** both internally and externally and this is evident in working practices

- **Quality** as central to all operations and evident in the belief that it is the responsibility of each and every person in the business

- A prevailing culture that facilitates **continuous improvement** evident in the organisation's responsiveness to change and the employees willingness to do so

- **Marketing orientation** as a feature of the culture and evident in professional marketing practices and activities focused on customer benefits and retention

- **Customer service** designed and developed with the product

It involves the bringing together of quality, customer service and continuous improvement, managed through marketing activities.

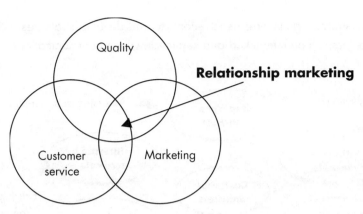

Christopher, Payne, Ballentyne

4.5 The principles of managing the three Ps of customer service and broader integration and coordination of the marketing mix ensure the customer receives value. The objective of relationship marketing is to build the loyalty of **valuable customers**, not **all or any customers** and therefore use the limited resources of the organisation effectively.

4.6 Relationship-building requires a sustained effort over time and one of the most effective tools an organisation has to do this is communication. If we take the difficulty of building relationships with consumers, communications and promotional activities will be the major method for doing this. Developing a strong brand that customers recognise, respect and connect with establishes a bond and can be used to build customer loyalty over the long term. If we want customers to be loyal we need strategies that move them from occasional customers to devoted advocates of the brand.

The loyalty ladder

4.7 Through customer service **and communications** the aim is to move customers up the loyalty ladder.

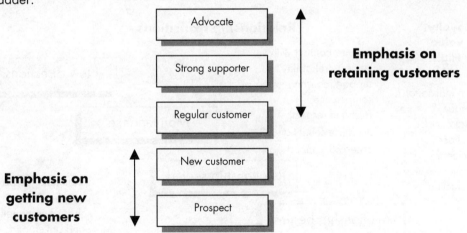

Adapted from Christopher, Payne, Ballentyne

4.8 Advocates of the organisation and/or brand are both valuable and loyal customers. They will actively and willingly refer others to the organisation, promoting, through word of mouth, the organisation and what it offers. The power of word of mouth communications has already been discussed and the advantages it offers should not be underestimated. It has credibility, far and above that of other promotional activities. Advocates bring new customers to the organisation reducing the effort and expense usually associated with acquiring customers.

4.9 Relationship marketing requires us to recognise and develop strategies with all key stakeholders. These strategies will be interlinked and key to all will be communications.

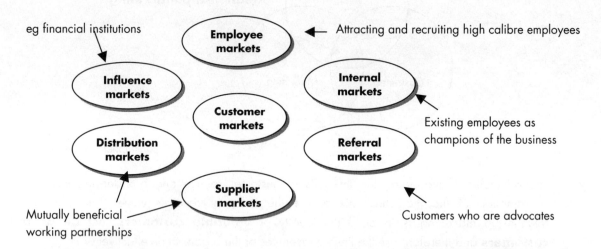

Adapted from Christopher, Payne, Ballentyne

4.10 **Key contacts** between employees within the organisation and the stakeholders of the organisation are identified, and strategies developed to communicate and build long term relationships. These relationship strategies will focus on stakeholder needs and motives, so that communication tools and messages will be tailored to the stakeholder group. The great advantage of relationship strategies is the emphasis on collaboration and partnerships and encouraging two way communications.

4.11 Relationship strategies are designed to manage the different phases of a **customer's life cycle** and communications used to manage the transitions in the relationship. Needs change over time as does the relationship and these phases and transitions need to be understood and strategies designed to reflect the changing needs and the transitions.

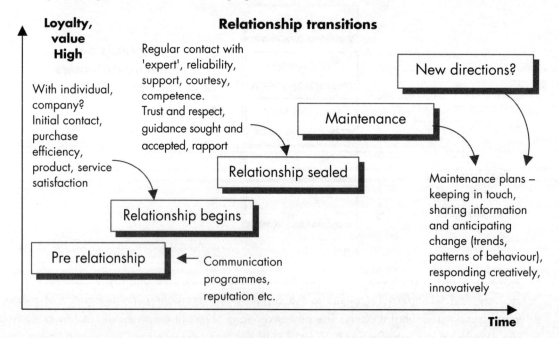

J Cockton © 1996

There are many examples of customers being lost during organisational change or a customer's transition. This happens because no thought is given to communicating with customers during these developments.

5 Customer service

5.2 Organisations are turning to customer service as a way of achieving and sustaining competitive advantage. Customer service, for companies faced with increasing competition and more demanding customers, is no longer a choice but a necessity if they are to survive. Consumer protection is increasing and tolerance of poor service has never been lower.

What is service?

5.2 Service involves two key elements.

(a) **The actual product or service** the customer receives, and benefits and solutions to problems. Businesses have steadily improved in this area through efficiency and quality drives.

(b) **The personal service:** way in which the product or service is delivered and the interaction between companies and customers. This is probably the most visible aspect and often the one on which the company is judged. This has been neglected through lack of training the right people with the right skills.

Developing customer service

5.3 Culture has been referred to throughout the file but note in particular that if management distrust employees and believe in high levels of supervision and control, are poor at communicating, giving little understanding to staff of the purpose of the business or of the customers served, then employees will feel de-motivated and undervalued. In these circumstances, establishing a customer care culture will be difficult.

5.4 There may be an atmosphere of trust and respect between management and employees, where the company believes in its social and environmental responsibilities, and staff understand the purpose of the business and customers served, are motivated and feel valued. In these circumstances the company is in a strong position to develop a customer care culture.

5.5 Until the appropriate culture and values have been established, efforts to implement customer care programmes are futile and will result in limited short-term success. They may even do more damage than good if customer and staff expectations are raised only to be disappointed.

The customer's chain of experience (moments of truth)

5.6 Customers come into contact with a company in a number of different ways, at different points and with a number of different people during any transaction. These pre-transaction, transaction and post-transaction activities are the **customer's chain of experience**, and whether or not this experience is good or bad depends on the organisation's efforts to understand the customer and manage the experience.

5.7 The customer will come in contact with both **processes** and **people** and both have the potential to **add value** to what the customer receives, thereby providing opportunities for competitive advantage.

5.8 A review should be undertaken to determine:

- The customer's chain of experience
- The customer's expectations and buying criteria
- Opportunities to improve the experience

5.9 The design of future processes and training of staff should reflect the goal of at least matching experience with expectations or, better, exceeding expectations if any competitive advantage is to be secured.

6 Collaborative partnerships

6.1 Recent years have seen an increase in collaborative partnerships, for example competitors collaborating on research and development and market development. Reasons for collaborating include reducing risk and cost, and increasing revenue.

Collaborating with the customer/consumer

6.2 Prahalad and Ramaswamy (*Harvard Business Review* Jan-Feb 2000) comment that the changes in our business environment have resulted in the breaking down of clearly defined roles in corporate relationships, deregulation, globalisation, technological convergence and the evolution of the Internet. This therefore requires a new approach to the way businesses operate, that we now need to co-opt customer competence. They make the following observations.

> 'Consider the relationship between Ford and its main suppliers. Far from being passive providers of materials and parts, Ford's suppliers have become close collaborators in the development of new vehicles. At the same time, however, they compete for value by negotiating the prices for the parts and the materials they supply.
>
> The story's the same for distributors. For example, Wal-Mart does more than just distribute Procter & Gamble's goods. It shares daily sales information and works with P&G in product warehousing and replenishment to ensure that consumers can always find the goods they want at low prices. In some categories Wal-Mart competes head to head with P&G.
>
> The talk now is of companies competing as a family. They talk about alliances, networks and collaboration among companies. But managers and researchers have largely ignored the consumer, the agent that is most dramatically transforming the industrial system as we know it.'

6.3 Customers in many business-to-business markets have been involved in product and service development with companies for decades. The organisation's stakeholders, including B2B customers, can now participate in the organisations innovative processes using technology such as 3-D CAD online. This allows organisations to set up global innovation teams that go beyond direct employees.

6.4 The involvement of consumers in the development process is now possible thanks to the Internet. They can comment, make suggestions, share ideas with each other and with companies. They become co-creators of value, and so they are a source of organisational competence. Even in business to business markets, while they might have played a significant role in co-creation, many companies may not have recognised or formally identified this as a source of competence or even of competitive advantage.

6.5 This source of competence and competitive advantage is only a reality if it has firstly been identified and recognised by the organisation and secondly harnessed to the organisation's advantage. We need to collaborate with people to ensure we maximise the positive outcomes of our creative and innovative process.

6.6 Key collaborators in the creativity and innovation process include the following.

Collaborator	Comment
Actual customers	The ultimate consumers of whatever an organisation produces; will decide whether or not what is on offer meets their needs
Employees	The people who are responsible for developing, designing and delivering what customers want. They have unique insights into the process of getting products and services through the value adding process to the customer.
Employers	We should not exclude those who own and run the organisation. In small to medium-sized businesses they are often the entrepreneurs who originally developed an idea that was marketable, they tend to be creative and innovative.
Intermediaries	If we are reliant on our channels to get to our customers our distribution chain is critical to our success. They may be the only contact with our customers and therefore have knowledge that informs creative and innovation ideas.
Suppliers	Part of the value adding supply chain. Their knowledge of supplies and developments in the supply chain can enable them to provide useful insights and ideas from a different perspective
Potential customers or non users	There may be a reason why these people do not buy or use the product or service other than they do not need it. It maybe that the product or service in its current form does not solve their problem, meet their need. These people can provide unique insights into new and quite different ideas.
Innovation incubators	Or innovation/idea companies such as IDEO, Idealab etc.
Academics	People who research and think about environment and business provoke and challenge old ways of thinking and doing and present ideas on new ways of thinking and doing.
Industry experts and analysts	Could be the captains of industry who challenge traditional business practices and evangelise their ideas or experts in a particular technology or craft.
Authors, journalists	These people, as well as coming up with their own ideas, will be well read and, as part of their job, collectors of ideas and thoughts from a wide variety of sources. They can make connections between diverse ideas and thoughts, industries and organisations that can lead to creativity and innovation.

Collaborator	Comment
Anthropologists	Who study societies and customs, make connections between different civilisations. Some companies have started to recruit anthropologists and they literally go out and mingle with the crowds. They observe behaviour, what people are doing, with what, where, how etc. and come back to the organisation with their observations. Anthropologists, in the telecommunications industry, recognised the growing importance of text messaging long before organisations believed this would become the main form of communicating between the young.
Inventors	You may know some! A neighbour, someone in the local community or be able to access inventors through writings in journals etc.

6.7 Collaboration requires a strategy and management and good communications skills. Some of the marketing communications processes can help in managing collaborative partnerships as can customer relationship management strategies.

7 Supply chain management

7.1 Supply chain management has become increasing important for a number of reasons including:

- Distribution of goods and services becoming more complex
- Distribution of goods and services becoming more expensive
- Increasing need for speed and timeliness in movement of goods
- The need to build competitive advantage through the value chain

7.2 Supply chain management is a comprehensive activity that involves the movement of materials from source of supply through to the finished product being delivered to the customer. Material management concerns the procurement of supplies, movement of materials and components and assembly of products or services into the business and during production. Physical distribution concerns the movement of finished products to customers. It includes all financial aspects and costs involved and information requirements and flow. Logistics management embraces all movements of goods, including storage and inventory management, to achieve the most efficient and effective outcomes for both the business and the customer. Central to supply chain management is identifying added value opportunities and developing appropriate solutions.

7.3 Companies in the grocery trade have benefited from supply chain management in terms of significant savings (Wal-Mart reduced inventories by 90% saving the company hundreds of millions of dollars) and in terms of customer satisfaction (GE's Trading Process Network allows all parts of the business around the world involved in buying to find and purchase products from approved suppliers electronically at far greater speed and more efficiently than before).

7.4 Supply chain management is essential in industries where companies need to operate JIT inventory systems.

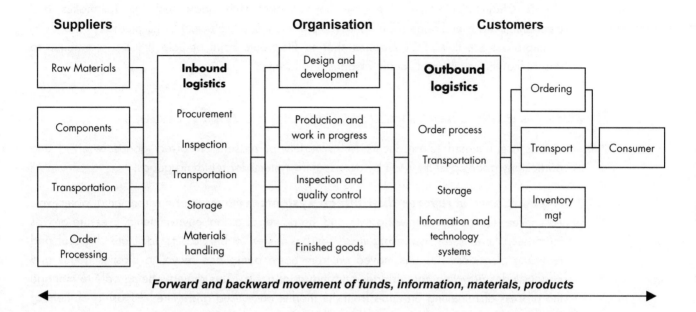

Suppliers **Organisation** **Customers**

Forward and backward movement of funds, information, materials, products

7.5 Another driving force behind supply chain management is the trend of **strategic alliances**. Decisions to form an alliance with one company or more are usually the result of the need to improve profits and reduce costs and risk. Alliances based on research and development, technological expertise, access to distribution outlets etc. can all potentially improve competitive and business performance. Once the decision has been made management should be developing a strategy to make the alliance work including attention to organisation cultural and operation differences. It will also be important to manage the supply chain as this will now become more complex and the potential for more to go wrong increases, damaging any gains the alliance was designed achieve. For the same reasons **outsourced** activities also requires Supply Chain Management.

The role of the Internet and supply chain management

7.6 The Internet is putting new demands on companies that make supply chain management an even more important issue. 24 hour service, 7 days a week and the customer's need for information and progress reports mean companies must be able to offer service at all times and provide information, almost instantly, on the current situation of any order. To be able to do this companies have no choice but to manage the supply chain through electronic links.

7.7 The Internet can also provide benefits in adding value for customers by improving opportunities to customise. Electronic links that integrate supply through to demand mean that customisation becomes easier and more cost effective. Comprehensive information on what a customer wants and comprehensive information on what a supplier can provide can quickly (and relatively cheaply) be collected and accessed. This does require sharing and exchanging information.

(a) Well designed and effective intranets and extranets linking employees internally, particularly in global businesses, and linking suppliers and distributors with employees can ensure that information on customer orders and responses to queries can be accessed and dealt with immediately.

(b) Tesco have a system called Tesco Information Exchange (TIE) based on extranet technology. This system links Tesco to a number of suppliers so suppliers can access information on sales of their products and promotional activities in store.

7.8   Supply Chain Management requires sophisticated technology such as Telematics and Electronic Data Interchange (EDI). For example retailers use Efficient Consumer Response (ECR) to improve stock flow. ECR requires sharing Electronic Point of Sale (EPOS) information to ensure that the retail supply chain responses efficiently.

Reverse distribution systems/reverse supply chains

7.9   Goods are returned to producers for a variety of reasons. Incorrect goods received and particularly goods past their sell by date require systems for returning goods.

7.10   A growing trend in **reverse distribution systems** is the result of environmental objectives. As concern for the environment grows and the power of global environmental pressure groups increases, there is an increasing need for businesses to be able to facilitate disposal and recycling of goods. This has moved on from bottle banks and recycling plastics goods and now includes recycling cars, fridges and industrial goods. This requires being able to manage the process of retrieving products from the market once used and either disposing of them or recycling them. Again sophisticated supply chain management processes will make this task easier and keep the costs down making it more acceptable and attractive to businesses.

7.11   Environmental regulations may force companies to develop reverse supply chains, for example the ISO 14000 standard assesses a company's environmental performance at two levels, the organisation (management and operations) and the product (quality, standards, packaging etc.). In 2003 EU legislation required tyre manufacturers operating in Europe to arrange for recycling of one used tyre for every new tyre they sell.

7.12   Some companies are seeing the benefits, reducing operating costs by reusing products or components and taking the initiative. Kodak remanufactures its single use cameras after the film has been developed. Over the past decade the company has recycled more than 310 million cameras in more than 20 countries.

7.13   Tracking product life cycles becomes an important part of proactively managing reverse distribution. The chain needs to be analysed for options, costs and benefits of the following.

- Product acquisition – retrieving the used product – quality (is it reusable), quantity (are they manageable), timing (not being overwhelmed by returns)

- Reverse logistics – collection, transported to facilities for inspection, sorting, disposable – depends on bulk, volumes etc.

- Inspection and disposition – testing, sorting and grading of products is labour intensive and time consuming. Quality standards, sensors, bar codes all improve this process

- Reconditioning – depends on product condition on return and processes needed as to whether or not to recondition or reuse parts

- Distribution and sales – is there a demand for recycled products? Requires communications – education, persuasion to end users and distribution channels

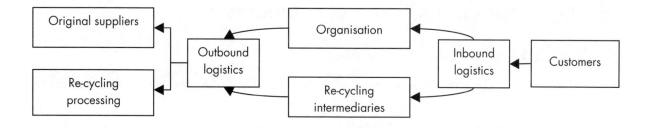

The role of marketing and supply chain management

7.14   Improvements in technology and the use of the internet in supply chain management can result in organisations becoming obsessed with the technology and how clever it is and fail to remember supply chain management involves the customer. The marketing manager's task is to ensure supply chain management is customer focused. Key aspects to ensure customer focus include:

■   Identifying key issues in the supply chain of importance to customers

■   Customer access to information (accurate, relevant and timely)

■   Proactive sharing of information (do not wait until the customer asks if all is not going according to plan)

■   Sourcing materials ('the best' from the customers' point of view not just the business)

■   Journeys (ensuring transportation and routing of journeys is also in the best interests of the customer not just the business)

■   Anticipating customer supply needs – particularly in business to business markets

7.15   Many processes are implemented to improve business performance through increased efficiency and reduced costs. It is important that processes affecting customers in any way are evaluated for their impact on the customer and how 'user friendly' they are. This is no less important with supply chain management and the use of the Internet.

7.16   While many involved in the management of the supply chain will be focused on efficiency (improving processes for speed, cost reduction etc.) it is marketing that should be focused on effectiveness. This requires attention to where value can be added and how. For example JIT inventory management may be attractive in business to business markets where significant savings can be made but in consumer markets availability often means providing a product or service when the customer wants it – now – and that may require holding stocks.

7.17   In business to business markets supply chain management provides real opportunities to offer valued added services for business customers. Companies who have invested in the technology can offer the service of managing the supply chain for business customers.

7.18   Supply chain management should not just be managed as a business objective but also as a customer satisfaction objective.

8 E-commerce and Internet strategies

Role of the Internet in business

8.1 Businesses should establish what the role of the Internet is to be. The Internet has four broad functions:

- **Communications** – dynamic two-way interactions
- **Information** – gathering, sharing, retrieval, transmission
- **Distribution** – physical direct and intermediary
- **Transactions** – ordering, negotiating, invoicing, paying

The Internet offers an organisation many benefits, particularly as diffusion globally increases.

8.2 Benefits of the Internet

(a) *Now (potential)*

- Speed – transactions, communications, innovation, products received
- Quantity
- Quality – improved consistency, better control, easier standardisation
- Cost efficient (operations, packaging, promotions)
- Operation efficient
- Communication – interaction – two way – engaging customers
- Flexibility
- Information – searching, distributing and sharing, retrieval
- Stakeholder partnerships and collaboration
- Entry barriers
- Market penetration (depending on markets)
- Innovation
- Trial options

(b) *In the future* (All of the above will improve but as the diffusion of technology spreads, the size of memories improve and speed increases also)

- Increased visibility
- Market development
- Global niches

These benefits will only be realised if valid strategies are developed and implemented. One of the issues marketers need to keep in mind is customers' attitudes to the internet.

(c) *Resistance to the Internet*

- Security
- Impersonal, remote, faceless
- Credibility of on line companies
- Predominance of features not benefits
- Relationship with personnel – intermediary or company

Customer behaviour

8.3 One area that can easily be overlooked as attention is focused on building Websites and Internet architecture is that of customer behaviour. The increasing ease of the internet as a search tool is likely to change buyer behaviour from a tendency to be reactive to promotion/sales to being proactive and searching for information and engaging with sellers who can provide what is wanted.

8.4 As customers become more familiar and comfortable with the internet they will begin to play an increasing role in driving the development and character of the internet. Companies who ignore changes in behaviour and identifying real benefits of the internet from a customer's perspective do so at their peril.

Developing Internet strategies

8.5 There is a subtle difference between (a) taking a leap into the unknown with the clear objective of learning all you can, translating this into a strategy for future development, and (b) following the latest craze. The first former (a) accepts the unknown but has a vision, if hazy, for the future and ensures there are systems and processes in place to facilitate **learning** and incorporate continuous improvement. The latter (b) will waste a lot of resources on tactical activities that might deliver very short-term gains and fail to learn or improve for the future.

8.6 Unfortunately there are too many companies who fall into the latter category and are dazzled by the features of the internet. They have yet to interpret the benefits of the internet from the customer's perspective and as a strategic goal. However, some companies are now addressing internet strategies which will change the dynamics of competition and customer service.

8.7 The key to success, of implementing internet strategies, is ensuring that designed into the strategy are mechanisms to ensure learning takes place and is transferred across the organisation and into new strategies. This requires **continuous improvement links** that are designed to build on each learning experience and improve practice before moving on to the next stage.

8.8 Organisations need to establish their own needs and the needs of other stakeholders and then they can design their strategy.

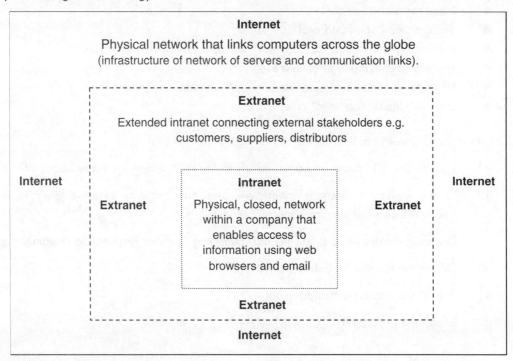

It may be worth considering the Internet in a number of contexts.

8.9 Internet as a direct distribution channel

The Internet provides an ideal channel for digital product categories (software, text, image, sound). Examples of industries/businesses that can benefit include publishing, information, services, technology companies (computers, software, entertainment games), multi media (films, music etc) and financial services.

The increasing ease of the Internet as a search tool is likely to change buyer behaviour from a tendency to be reactive to promotion/sales to being proactive and searching for information and engaging with sellers who can provide what is wanted.

8.10 Internet as an indirect distribution channel: intermediaries

Many products and services cannot be distributed down the line and therefore intermediaries are still needed. The role of the Internet in these circumstances can be:

- Communications and information channel
- Transactions
- Extranet link with intermediaries who distribute goods
- Co-ordinating/monitoring physical logistics

As with any intermediary strategy, a business must have clear objectives of what it expects from its intermediaries. Internet distribution strategies may require the role of the intermediary to be redefined. Is the Internet just extending the chain or adding value? Traditional intermediaries may eventually disappear if they do not redefine the value they add and the role they can play in e-commerce.

Internet communication strategy

8.11 Many of same processes and rules apply for Internet communications as for more traditional media.

- Need for objectives
- Strategy: push, pull and profile
- Positioning and messages: consistent with brand values and targets
- Targets: identifying who talking to
- Promotional techniques: can use on-line brochures
- Controls: measuring effectiveness

8.12 Differences between the Internet and other media are as follows.

(a) Targets are still limited and often poorly defined: assumptions made about who is online

(b) Online communications is interactive and can engage target audiences in a way traditional communications cannot

(c) Dynamic, instantly updating, moving, changing in direct response to customer demands

(d) Different measures for online activities

(e) Role of the database management

(f) Information overload

8.13 Factors to consider

(a)   How are (or can) brand values (be) interpreted? Will the Internet affect perceptions in anyway and if so how?

(b)   Ensuring it is a two way process: capturing customer information

(c)   Matching experience with expectations: ensuring communications are clear, unambiguous, helpful, avoid 'click help' syndrome (ie no help at all)

(d)   Because it is dynamic, must engage, interact

(e)   Do not use as an alternative to all other forms of communication, in particular if a telephone call will do the job better, make the call.

9   Contemporary issues for Biocatalysts

9.1   We prepared students for a strategic marketing plan question and an international marketing strategy, particularly as Biocatalysts operate in many countries, but is performing poorly and has little resource to support an international presence.

9.2   "The contemporary issues we identified in the biocatalyst case study were as follows

1.   **Corporate branding.** Biocatalysts, as with many firms operating in business-to-business firms had not recognised, and had certainly not exploited, potential brand strengths. Given the context at this time, consumer hostility to GMOs and media delight in exploiting it, the brand could do much to signal clearly to the market where Biocatalysts stood. If Biocatalysts **did** go down the GMO route, the firm should provide information so consumers made informed decisions. At this time, the lack of trust in biotechnology companies was growing rapidly. Their poor profit record added more problems. We paid attention to what the Biocatalyst brand values might be.

2.   **Integrated Marketing Communications.** We knew this might be part of the same question as a branding strategy but encouraged students to develop IMC plans taking on board the current climate. The theme of ethical and social responsibility ran through decisions. It was not particularly strong as we did not feel it would be an exam question but it affected our thinking and was reflected in our decisions. There were differences of opinion among students and it was a good example of how opposing views could be argued successfully. Neither view was right or wrong. What mattered was how convincingly and credibly it was argued and supported.

9.3   It was particularly interesting for us when, in 2002, Biocatalysts appeared again as a case study (called Enzymes UK). It was a wonderful example of how a company moves on and how the context changed, and we will use it here to illustrate how the contemporary issues changed.

9.4   Biocatalysts had taken on board some of the recommendations made at the time (by CIM students?) but now they were facing new challenges. Strategic alliances and partnerships were a feature of the external environment. The debate on GMOs was still reverberating, except now consumers were better informed and more demanding.

9.5 They still had not rationalised their international market spread or dealt with the problems with agents. For Biocatalysts revisited, we the contemporary issues were:

1. **Customer Relationship Management.** Biocatalysts had good relationships with customers on a personal level. They did not engage in customer relationship management and were not customer focused. Customer focus means a company is targeting specific customers with specific products. Biocatalyst was quite happy to produce any product for any customer. This was impacting seriously on their profitability, not to mention confusing their position in the market.

   Biocatalysts firstly needed to clarify their position in the market and then start thinking about which customers they should target and with what products. This established they could then develop CRM strategies with customers and with other stakeholders who impacted on their business significantly, for example regularity bodies, universities and most importantly agents.

2. **Collaborative strategies.** This could form part of the CRM strategy or might be focused on partnerships with competitors or up or down stream organisations. It was becoming increasingly difficult to be competitive in this market without partnerships. Students explored the options for **Biocatalysts** including who might improve their competitive advantage and who they might potential be attractive to and how they could make themselves attractive.

3. Again, **an integrated communications strategy** was developed and this time the theme of ethical and social responsibility was stronger.

4. **E-strategy.** popular at the time and clearly, for a small business to business company like Biocatalysts an essential efficient and effective way to communicate, share information and ideas and to conduct communication activities. Ideas on improving what they were doing with their website and e-strategy were explored and developed.

9.6 Questions on the December 2002 paper

1. Develop a three year strategic marketing plan taking the international markets and green issues into consideration

2. Develop a customer relationship strategy, taking into account the company's presence on the web

3. Develop a communications plan taking into account the different stakeholders that it needs to address.

9.7 The contemporary issues are easy to weave into the mainstream strategies of an organisation and they should not be thought of as distinct and separate but rather part of the same marketing activity. It is about developing or improving a source of competitive advantage in the current context.

Summary of contemporary issues

9.8 "These are only a few examples of contemporary issues and they impact at all levels either changing the way things are done or what is done. New contemporary issues emerged, for example we have been experiencing outsourcing as an issue, and they develop or improve. Our job is to recognise them, identify their relevance and use them to the organisation's advantage."

Step 9: Control

12

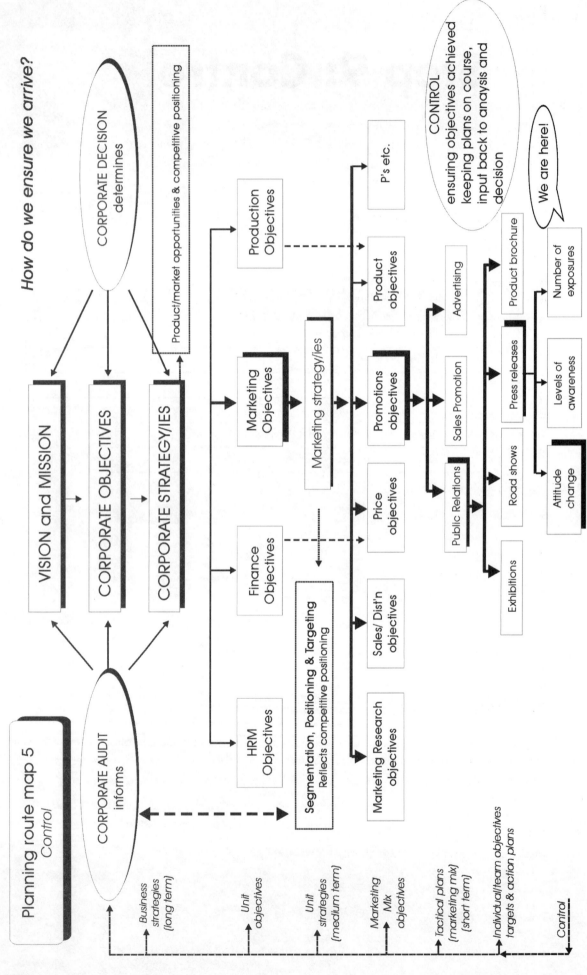

How do we ensure we arrive?

Planning route map 5
Control

VISION and MISSION

CORPORATE OBJECTIVES

CORPORATE STRATEGY/IES

CORPORATE DECISION
determines

CORPORATE AUDIT
informs

Product/market opportunities & competitive positioning

Production Objectives

Marketing Objectives

Finance Objectives

HRM Objectives

Marketing strategy/ies

Segmentation, Positioning & Targeting
Reflects competitive positioning

P's etc.

Product objectives

Price objectives

Sales/ Dist'n objectives

Marketing Research objectives

Promotions objectives

Advertising

Sales Promotion

Public Relations

Product brochure

Press releases

Road shows

Exhibitions

Number of exposures

Levels of awareness

Attitude change

CONTROL
ensuring objectives achieved
keeping plans on course,
input back to anaysis and
decision

We are here!

Business strategies (long term)

Unit objectives

Unit strategies (medium term)

Marketing Mix objectives

Tactical plans [marketing mix] (short term)

Individual/team objectives targets & action plans

Control

1 Financial and human resource implications

1.1 Any recommendations and plans will have both financial and people implications. Marketers have, in the past, been criticised for ignoring these critical issues when developing plans.

1.2 A review of each recommendation made for its implications on business operations is required. In practice the **justification** for each course of action would play an important role in persuading senior management to accept the proposals made and the same applies to the exam case. Any proposal will cost money and require other resources and senior management have to be convinced the expenditure will see worthwhile returns.

1.3 Financial implications (example)

- Capital investment
- Risk
- Revenue
- Profit, profitability
- Working capital
- ROI/ROCE — Also consider major or new projects
- Creditors/debtors — eg re-organisation/structuring
- Stock — new markets (exporting)
- Liquidity — new product development
- Depreciation — additional costs (patents, legal etc)
- Budgets
- Financial control

1.4 Human resource implications (example)

- Known/expected staff losses due to normal wastage
- Transfers in/out
- New appointments
- Promotion plans
- Current staffing requirements
- Future staffing requirements
- Surplus/shortfall in staffing requirements
- Current skills needs
- Future skills needs
- Training requirements (costs/timing)
- Changes (eg conditions of employment, health and safety)

1.5 A good marketer will make the link between the resource implications and benefits of using these resources, and the consequences of not using them. The task is to use these benefits and expected outcomes to persuade management of the value of the strategies and plans you have developed.

1.6 In the case study, you are using the same process to persuade the examiner that, based on your analysis, you have developed credible plans to ensure the organisation achieves its goals.

2 Budgets

2.1 Budgets are required for the planning horizon to determine the cost of implementing the plan against expected revenues. Problems lie in the difficulties of accurately forecasting demand for products and services, so monitoring revenues is vital to ensure the financial stability of the business.

2.2 The availability of resources can sometimes be difficult to predict and managers can be reluctant to commit to a budget.

2.3 **Purposes of budgets**

- Co-ordinate activities across organisation
- Communicate financial performance
- Monitor effectiveness of performance

2.4 **Setting marketing budgets**

The most common methods are:

- % of previous year's sales
- % of budgeted annual sales
- % of previous year's profit

2.5 This safeguards the risk of spending more than can be afforded but does not take into account the objectives set.

2.6 **Objective and task method** requires that once the objective is set, investigation on how much it will cost to achieve the objective is undertaken. This then has to be balanced against what can be afforded but if achieving the objective in the long term is vital to business survival and success, profits may have to suffer in the short term.

3 Scheduling

3.1 All plans have a planning horizon, a time within which the plan must be executed and objectives achieved. Activities are also often dependent on each other: one activity must be completed before another can commence, so scheduling activities to make the best use of time is necessary.

3.2 Gantt charts, and for planning that involves hundreds of activities, critical path analysis, are useful techniques for ensuring activities have deadlines and are scheduled according to sequence.

Simple Gantt Chart

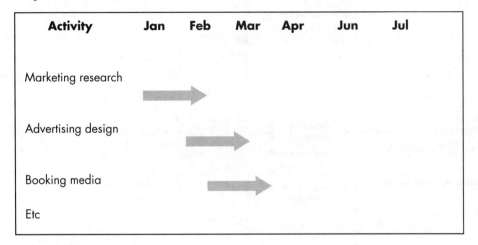

Simple Critical Path Analysis

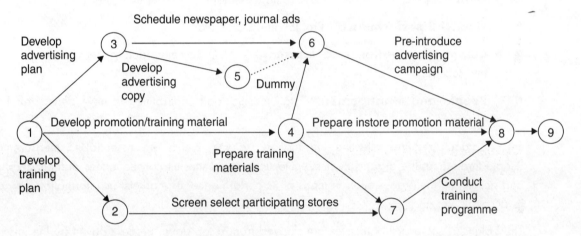

4 Measuring performance

"Control has become more sophisticated as organisation's recognise measuring the single bottom line and quantitative sales and financial targets is short sighted and damaging.

4.1 One concept that has become popular is that of the balanced scorecard.

The balanced scorecard takes a far broader and more comprehensive approach to measurement and informing strategic development and embraces strategic as well as tactical performance.

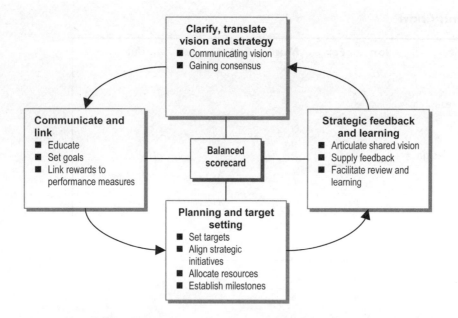

- **Customer** – satisfaction, loyalty, value, complaints, repeat purchases

- **Financial performance** – Profitability, ROCE etc.

- **Culture (innovation and learning)** – NPD success, idea generation/transference into success

- **People and management** – staff morale, staff contribution to new ideas, staff T/O, absence,

This approach requires effective information systems, which are essential to measurement. People throughout the organisation need to understand the full consequences of their decisions and actions on the organisation in terms of its performance, its markets, its information flow and its access.

The balanced scorecard objectives are derived from a top down process driven by the mission, vision, corporate objectives and strategies, which are translated into tangible objectives and measures. The measures represent a balance between external measures for shareholders and customers, and internal measures of critical business processes, innovation, learning and growth. The measures are balanced between the outcome measures (past performance) and measures that drive future performance. The scorecard is balanced between objective easily quantified outcome measures and subjective, somewhat judgemental performance drivers of the outcome measures.

4.2 **Triple bottom Line** can provide a framework for CSR performance analysis, measuring performance against the "Triple Bottom Line" the simultaneous pursuit of economic/financial prosperity, environmental quality and social equity, not just a single financial bottom line.

Triple bottom

Economic/financial	Environmental	Social equity
Shareholder value, profitability, cash flow, ROCE, ROI etc.	Renewable, sustainable materials and resources balanced against cost	Health, safety, well being, sustainability balanced against cost

4.3 Increasingly, businesses are looking at the competition to determine how well their own performance compares. Competitive benchmarking requires that a business identifies key performance indicators to benchmark against the competition and against best practice which may be a company outside the company's own industry. This benchmarking forces an external focus on performance and provides opportunities for the company to establish a base with the intention of out-performing the competition in the eyes of its customers.

How easy it is to benchmark the competition will depend on the industry. If it is intense, competitive information will not be easily accessed: in other industries where technology is 'newsworthy', information flows freely. If there are few competitors and they are concentrated in one area it is usually easier to acquire information. Benchmarking partners can be established which requires trust, open communications and mutual exchange of information.

It may be unrealistic to attempt to be 'the best' but improvement targets are important.

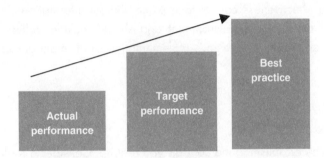

Warning: competitive benchmarking is not about copying the competition, it is about out-performing them, doing things well but differently.

5 Measuring marketing effectiveness

5.1 Quantitative and qualitative measures must be used to establish the effectiveness of marketing.

	Comment
Product	Contribution to sales revenues and volumes, contribution to profit, increasing market share, accessibility to new markets, reliability and durability, adaptability
Price	Impact on profits, impact on sales volumes, perception of value for money, attraction of new sales, customer loyalty
Place	Support and service to us and customer, reliability and consistency, added value (specify), accessibility, claims procedures, condition of goods
Personal selling	Sales by customer and by product, customer call frequency, average sales value per call, average cost per call, number of new customers obtained, customer retention
Promotions	Advertising (queries generated and conversion rates, attitude change – pre, during and post testing), PR (column inches), sales promotion (sales volume and sustainability)
People	Attainment of targets set, productivity, efficiency measures eg order turnaround, problem solving, delivery of training (content, presentation, visuals etc)

	Comment
Processes	Reliability, speed, simplicity
Physical evidence	Perception of material evidence e.g. atmosphere/impressions created by offices, reception, training support materials, exhibition stands, impact on awareness, recall
Customer service	Measure customer complaints (numbers, types), analyse levels of repeat business, analysis of chain of experience (customer contact points)
Marketing research	Methodologies used, accuracy of information, utilisation of information, accuracy in determining future information needs, analysis of usefulness in decision making

Measuring marketing effectiveness cannot take place without information. Measurement should be in the context of the business environment and should include indications of competitive performance. This requires the design, implementation and management of an effective marketing information systems.

Action Programme 1

Complete your plans by establishing the controls you require. Consider a realistic budget, establish a timetable and confirm what you are going to measure and how. This does not need to be a lengthy activity, keep it brief.

Compare your answers with ours at the end of this chapter.

6 Marketing Information Systems

6.1 Pivotal to control is the establishment of information systems. The monitoring, gathering, analysis and reporting of information allow the business to control its internal operations and be prepared for external opportunities and threats. Most businesses are gathering in information in various forms all the time but the difference between a successful business and the less successful will often be the formality of that information gathering process. Making connections between pieces of information makes the difference.

An MkIS ensures an ongoing information flow that enables the business to be prepared for events as they unfold. It accesses information from numerous sources in a variety of ways to build a complete picture of external opportunities and threats, market characteristics and dynamics.

Action Programme 2

A more strategic control issue is that of management and marketing information systems. Briefly consider the information system needs and how you would tackle them.

Compare your answer with ours at the end of the chapter.

Action Programme review

1   Budget – Obviously Biocatalysts's financial constraints are a real problem. You need to think creatively, for example marketing research costs can be significantly reduced by working with customers who will be willing to share information and through participating where appropriate in omnibus research and of course partnerships with universities.

They are already spending some money on marketing – we could use this to far greater effect with more focused strategies and, as Biocatalysts's financial situation improves, increase marketing spend.

Schedule – remember Biocatalysts has some short-term survival needs as well as the longer-term vision.

Measurement – key issues include financial performance and critical cash flow, market position and share, product performance and communication.

2   **Introduction**

■   Importance of marketing information (and fast developments in biotechnology)

■   Consequences of not knowing/understanding market dynamics (eg changing nature of competition with competitors adopting more strategic positions)

■   Biocatalysts current situation re marketing information

Internal information needs

Biocatalysts performance S/W
■   Financial performance
■   Marketing skills levels
■   Management skills levels
■   Planning and control systems and processes (product/market selection etc)
■   Competitive position and strategy
■   Market share and performance by country, industry, segment (value customers)
■   Distribution channel performance

Market information needs

■   Market characteristics – PEST, life cycles etc growth, sectors
■   Competition – who, strategies (response profiles), size, location/market coverage
■   Customers – who, demand forecasts, buying criteria, DMUs
■   Channels – poor performance and market implications

Potential problems

■   Our skills – current information held, lack resources, experience
■   International markets – comparability, accessibility, reliability, accuracy
■   Cost and time scales – short term little money, increase investment longer term
■   Security, sensitivity particularly given nature of industry
■   Conflicts of interest – who owns the information e.g. university, Biocatalysts?

Overcoming problems

- Senior management commitment (allocation of resources, responsibilities, set objectives)
- Audit current information and effectiveness how gathered/used etc
- Establish formalised system MKIS – funding
- Role/selection of agents/distributors
- Sources of information – governments, embassies, trade associations etc
- Contacts – formalise network of stakeholders (global) e.g. universities
- Role of interactive website
- Planning process for

Formalised gathering and analysis of information for planning and control purposes

Marketing Information System MkIS

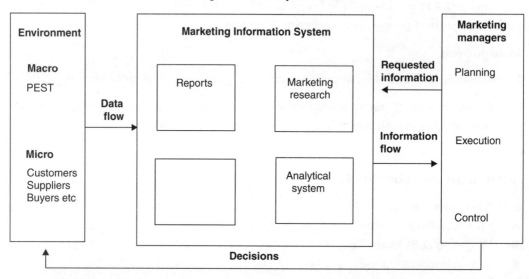

Step 1. Design

- Evaluate current information, flows, sources etc. S/W and processes
- Review requirements e.g. use in decision making, identifying, collecting, recording, analysing, reporting, storing, retrieval, removing outdated, use for control
- Involve staff in design – project teams

Step 2. Technology

- Evaluate systems – meet needs of everyone, flexibility, networking

Step 3. Implementation

- Project teams develop implementation plan
- Staff training
- Test run
- Monitoring and evaluating

Step 10: Managing your materials and preparing for the exam

Chapter Topic List	
1	Preparing for the exam
2	Annotating your case

1 Preparing for the exam

A reminder

1.1 The semi closed book examination means you:

   (a)   Cannot take a case file into the exam room

   (b)   Can develop a six page appendix to attach to your exam answer

   (c)   Can take your annotated copy of the case study into the exam

What you should NOT do

1.2 You should not:

   (a)   Try to incorporate all your analysis squashed into six sides

   (b)   Try to produce any solutions in advance of the questions and any additional information

   (c)   Try to second guess the questions

   (d)   Present analysis without added value

What you should do

1.3 You should:

   (a)   Think about how best to use your A4 sheets in the context of the case

   (b)   Ensure you add the commentary, business implications or links so the examiner understands 'why' this analysis is valuable or relevant and how it might inform strategy

   (c)   Use models and frameworks: it will save you time in the exam

   (d)   Label them and number them for easy reference in your answer script

(e) Make your figures and illustrations big enough to be read by an ageing and tired examiner!

(f) Remember the value of colour and white space

(g) Go for quality rather than quantity

2 Annotating your case

There is not much room to add notes in the case study so you need to be disciplined and organised. Here are some hints and tips to help you in annotating your case. Please note these examples are not intended to fit with or reflect the practice cases, they are just examples of annotation notes.

Write a contents list on the front page so you know on what pages to access your notes.

The purpose of your notes is to act as prompts and help to provide **possible** structures to answers. For example if asked for a strategic marketing plan your structure would be:

1. Background
2. Vision and mission
3. Country objectives (one quantified and possible 2 or 3 aims)
4. Country strategies
5. Competitive strategies and positioning
6. Marketing objectives
7. Marketing strategy
8. Marketing mix
9. Control

Under each of the above headings you would have the briefest of notes on case specific issues you want to ensure you include and a reminder of the models you would use. You will have no trouble remembering most of what you want to say. You will only need one of these outlines. If you think you might need different solutions/structures for different opportunities you only need a few brief notes on the other issues.

Corporate Social Responsibility

1. CSR Vision and objectives
   Emphasise move to fair trade

2. Changing the business model
   Change in processes to reduce emissions and waste, use of new energy sources and improve recycling

3. Stakeholder policy and practice
   New employee policies and training. New management practices. Change in partnership selection and management. (use stakeholder influence and impact matrix)

4. Marketing activities
   Building ethical brand values (use brand pyramid). Cause related marketing activities

5. New forms of control
   Triple bottom line – now measure social and environmental factors as well as economic. Learning as part of targets and measures (use BSC model)

You would probably have more specific notes and may have more notes but not much more. Remember you do not know the question so these notes will only be a reminder of some of the things you could do.

Some people prefer mind maps, for example (a very simple example)

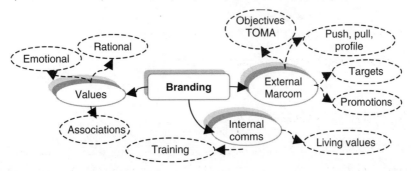

Think about where in the case book you are going to write your notes. For example you may feel it is logical to write notes around a model if one has been included in the case and the space allows eg:

Brand equity: increase customer brand awareness from X% to X%, change customer brand attitudes through brand associations and customer perceptions of brand ethics through a programme of cause related marketing.

Drivers of customer equity

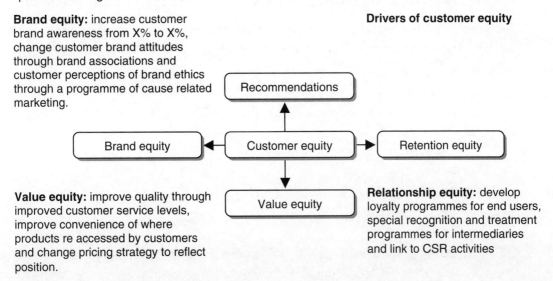

Value equity: improve quality through improved customer service levels, improve convenience of where products re accessed by customers and change pricing strategy to reflect position.

Relationship equity: develop loyalty programmes for end users, special recognition and treatment programmes for intermediaries and link to CSR activities

The purpose of these notes is to provide ideas on how you might tackle a question. You must modify and adapt structures and frameworks to answer the specifics of the question asked. You may draw on one particular set of notes to answer a question but are more likely to draw on a number of different ideas and pull them together to answer a particular question. Do not allow your notes to constrain you or your creativity.

Biocatalysts Ltd: The examination 14

Chapter Topic List	
1	Exam hints
2	Additional information
3	The examination paper
4	Reading the exam paper
5	A sample answer

BIOCATALYSTS LTD

DO NOT LOOK UNTIL YOU ARE READY TO SPEND

THREE HOURS DOING THESE AS A MOCK EXAM

---

1 Exam hints

1.1 Equipment, aids and exam centre. Make sure you have all the equipment you need.

(a) Good quality pens – **not** highlighter or felt tips: use colour for models, underlining etc but **not red**: use a ruler where appropriate when drawing models

(b) Calculator (in the past this has not been needed but take one just in case)

(c) Tipp-Ex fluid or similar (in good condition)

(d) Stencils for drawing charts, boxes, models

(e) Watch/clock

(f) Six pages of pre-prepared analysis

(g) Copy of case - annotated

1.2 Make sure you know where the exam centre is and where you can park (do you need permission, change etc). If travelling by public transport, where is the nearest station etc and how long does it take to walk from the station to the centre, train/bus times and so on.

1.3 Allow plenty of time on the day: you will not be allowed into the exam room 15 minutes after the start. Check with the exam centre when they intend to start the examination and be prepared for there to be other people in the room taking other exams. Their exams may be shorter and they may leave earlier.

1.4 Examination and presentation techniques

(a) **Always** plan all your answers. Even if you have prepared well and anticipated questions successfully, you will still need to plan your answers, particularly to take on board the specifics of questions. You must be selective in the material you draw on and it will require modification to meet the specifics, emphasis and slant of the question.

(b) One area where the well prepared student often fails is **poor time management**. Time and again this comes back as a problem. Manage your time and be disciplined about moving on to the next question. If you have run out of time on a question, leave space to go back to it later, if you have time.

(c) Structure your answer to keep you focused on the question **and** make it easier for the examiner to mark your script. Where appropriate, use headings from the question to help keep you focused. Always use report format, unless otherwise stated.

(d) **Use good communication skills**. Get your points across succinctly: explain and justify where appropriate (never make a recommendation without some explanation and justification). Be persuasive: you would have to use this skill if you were trying to convince senior management of the validity of your recommendations and the same is true for the examiner. Do not allow the examiner to get lost (or worse bored!) in a wall of words that wanders around the point.

(e) **Demonstrate both knowledge and experience**. Do not leave the examiner to fill in gaps and guess whether or not you know the theory or how to apply it: they will not do that, it is not their job. Make the connection and links: the point of the case study examination, in particular, is for you to demonstrate your skills as a marketing professional.

(f) **Do not deliver what you want to as opposed to what the question has asked for**. Unless the question specifically asks for analysis, you are expected to deliver decisions. The quality of your analysis is tested in the 6 page analysis summary and through the quality of your decisions. If a 'current situation' type question is asked for, do not deliver SWOTs. You are expected to give an overview of the current situation that adds value, an interpretation of the current situation that provides insights. A SWOT cannot do this.

(g) **Always** check your answer: particularly important when you have had to adjust your pre-thinking to the specific questions. Check for integration and consistency.

2 Additional information

2.1 **Additional information** has in the past been featured in the exam paper. CIM have informed us it is unlikely to be included in future papers but they reserve the right to include additional information if they wish to. It was never more than a small paragraph or two and it was always reasonably easy to anticipate. Examples of additional information include:

■ Some change in the external environment e.g. a marketing opening up or new competitors into the market

■ Some internal change or decision that would impact on marketing e.g. intention to develop new products or markets or to change competitive position

2.2 During our decision process we will have considered all these issues and possible outcomes and solutions so they are easy to deal with.

All you have to remember is to ensure you take on board the additional information if presented and highlight you have done so. It may change your thinking or possibly the speed with which you might implement decisions.

3 The examination paper

Additional information to be taken into account when answering the questions set.

Owing to the problems in the South Asian and South American economies, Biocatalysts is likely to face an erosion of margins within its textiles business. Clients are demanding cheaper enzymes for jeans and other textiles production. The agents in the key offices in Hong Kong and Singapore are also finding that they need more time and support from the Head Office in Wales. They are, however, finding that some of the specialist food enzyme demand is growing, although many of the potential customers require high levels of technical support.

Examination questions

Based on your analysis of Biocatalysts' competitive position, and after further discussion with the Managing Director, as the appointed marketing consultant to the Managing Director, you are to prepare a report which should address the following.

Question 1

Produce a strategic marketing plan for Biocatalysts Ltd for the next five years, justifying your recommendations. **(30 marks)**

Question 2

Biocatalysts Ltd sells a diverse range of products into many geographical areas. Critically assess the best possible international marketing strategy that the company should follow, taking into account the generally poor performance of its agents and distributors. **(20 marks)**

Question 3

Given the long-term prospects of the development of genetically modified organisms (GMOs) for the production of enzymes, develop a marketing communications strategy for Biocatalysts Ltd. **(20 marks)**

25 marks allocated for the 6 page analysis summary. **(100 marks in total)**

4 Reading the exam paper

4.1 Remember exam technique is vital to your success and the first action you need to take is to note the marks for each question and allocate the appropriate time to each question.

4.2 Next you need to read the entire paper, additional information and all questions. Then you need to look for clues on what is being asked for.

Additional information

> 'Owing to the **problems** in the **South Asian** and **South American** economies, Biocatalysts is likely to face an **erosion of margins** within its **textiles** business'

Already you have clues on how you should develop your answer.

We now know there are problems with some economies which will affect Biocatalysts's margins and that textiles is not an attractive option.

> **'Clients are demanding cheaper enzymes** for jeans and other **textiles** production.'

How does this fit with your analysis and decisions, particularly on Biocatalysts' position? Were you intending to stay in textiles? Does staying in textiles fit with Biocatalysts' potential position? How does it fit with their strengths?

> 'The **agents** in the **key offices** in **Hong Kong** and **Singapore** are also finding that they **need more time and support from the Head Office** in Wales. They are however finding that some of the **specialist food enzyme demand is growing** although many of the **potential customers require high levels of technical support**.'

So specialty food enzymes are looking attractive and Biocatalysts's expertise and technical skills can be used to help position them as a premium priced service.

The questions

Question 1 is asking for the strategic marketing plan, question 2 for an international strategy (with specific reference to agents) and question 3 for a communications plan (with specific reference to GMOs).

Question 2 and 3 mean we do not have to spend much time on international issues, 'Place' or 'Promotions' in question 1. We can refer the examiner to questions 2 and 3. It does mean that in question 1 our strategic marketing plan must refer to and reflect an international focus.

5 A sample answer

Planning your answer

Now you have examined the examination paper to determine precisely what you have been asked for, you can start to plan your answer.

Tutor comments on example answers

Please note this is an example only. You may have tackled the question differently. Providing you answered the specifics of the questions and within a marketing framework, there is no reason why your answer is not as good or better.

The most important lesson to learn from this is, how much could you write in three hours (broken down into 90 minutes and 45 minutes × 2)? This is what you need to know before you go into the exam.

Remember you need to make reference to your analysis as you work through the questions.

Contents

Leave the first page blank, go back when you have finished and complete this page. Normally you would include subheadings but this may be too time consuming in the exam

4.1 Question 1

1. Five year strategic marketing plan

1.1 Current situation

1.1.1 Market conditions

The biotechnology industry is young and very dynamic and technology is a key driver of developments and change, both of which occur with increasing frequency. Governments in many countries have supported developments in biotechnology through funding and a reluctance to over-regulate the market. Pressure from consumers may change this.

Economic conditions have been relatively stable in Europe and North America, but as highlighted in the additional information, this stability is not reflected across the globe, with South Asia and South America suffering from economic downturn.

Predicted future market growth in enzymes is from $1.7 billion to $2 billion by 2005. The greatest opportunity is the growth in 'other' eg animal feed, baking, fruit and wine, speciality applications and is predicted to be very rapid and collectively likely to be the largest section of the enzyme market exceeding £500 million sales by 2005. Bulk enzymes will increasingly be produced from GMOs. Some of Biocatalysts' markets are predicted to decline, for example textiles, while value will increase with total growth. Markets need to be examined for future viability.

Market/industry life cycle

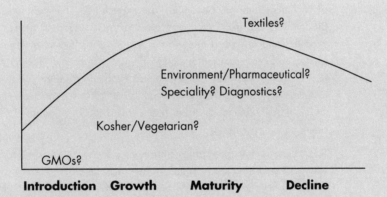

1.1.2 Competition

The nature of competition is changing. In this young industry, competitive 'positions' have not been an issue until now. Competitors are now clearly thinking about future positions. This would indicate a move to a more strategic marketing approach and you can expect clear competitive positions to emerge.

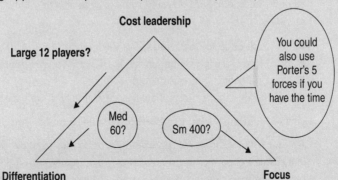

With the competitive information we have, it is difficult to be precise about competitors as we are not always comparing like with like but some assumptions can be made. Novo is a major player with 50% of the market. Gist and Genecor share 25% of the market. These players are most likely to have the potential to develop cost leadership positions. The remaining 25% of the market is shared by the rest of the biotechnology companies so the competition amongst these players is likely to become increasingly intense.

The 60 medium-sized companies are most likely to have enough market share to enable them to segment their markets and adopt differentiated positions. The remaining 400 small players will not have the strength to take on the medium and large players and are likely to look for opportunities to develop niche markets.

1.1.3 Customers

The end consumer significantly influences your customers who are typically manufacturers, producers and retailers and their future decisions will be based on what is acceptable to the consumer.

The industry has a complex network of many stakeholders that influence, directly and indirectly, what the industry does. For example MAFF, universities, industry analysts, FDA, HACCP etc.

1.1.4 Biocatalyst's current position

If adding pre-prepared analysis remember to refer to it here. The business has highly qualified experts providing strong technical competence. With high levels of technical support becoming an expectation, this will be a key strength. Biocatalysts are innovative and have a track record of developing customised products and are good at customer relationships. However the customer focus is tactical not strategic or marketing orientated and new product development has not included business screening or marketing input suggesting a product orientation. This is evident from their poor financial performance. No segmentation seems to take place resulting in Biocatalysts tending to do anything for anyone.

A concern is that three sales people appear to be looking after 35 countries. The poor performance in some of the overseas markets, for example as little as £40,000 from Japan in 1997 and £140,000 from the USA, suggests this is not working. There does not appear to be an international strategy. There does not appear to have been a rigorous process for appointing, managing and evaluating agents and distributors. There is a lack of clear strategy, and competitive position.

Broader issues of market conditions, trends and competitive activities do not seem to be considered. Overall there is a lack of planning and control, evident in:

- Lack of up to date marketing intelligence. (lack of analysis)
- No monitoring of the market (performance, developments)
- Competitor information is patchy
- information is not gathered systematically or analysed methodically

This will inevitably lead to missed opportunities and threats.

An analysis of financial performance indicates a lack of control and is of immediate concern. The business has grown faster than the industry average but profits are low, running at around 6%. At the moment they are fairly liquid and able to cover liabilities. However increased debtors days (75 in 1994 to 143 in 1997), together with paying creditors faster than receiving debts suggests availability of funds and cash flow could become critical. The cash balance has come down to £12,000, down 61% ('96 on '97).

In conclusion the market is changing rapidly, competitors are becoming more strategic in their approach, customers are more demanding and Biocatalysts have some critical issues facing the business.

1.2 Mission, vision and business objective

Biocatalysts need to clarify the purpose of the business and their aspirations. Decisions will include whether or not Biocatalysts intend to pursue GMO production and, if so, the time scales involved. Biocatalysts are not in a strong position to launch a GMO product into the current hostile market without a clear strategy.

1.2.1 Mission statement

Biocatalysts are in the business of providing...

Add your mission and vision here

1.2.2 Vision

To be...

1.2.3 Business objective

A profit objective is recommended to keep the business focused on what it must achieve and to provide a measure.

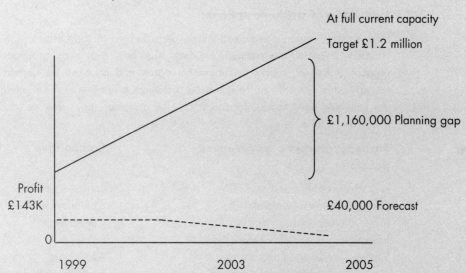

This profit objective requires an increased margin to 10%.

A company can grow when a market is growing substantially. However, given the rapidly changing nature of the market and increasing competition, to carry on as Biocatalyst is now, the forecast is likely to be a decline. With such low profits, unless a clear strategy and direction is implemented, there is a danger Biocatalysts will not be around in 2005.

Strategies now need to be identified to fill the planning gap.

1.3 Business strategy and competitive positioning

A number of options emerged during analysis.

PRODUCTS

	Existing	New
Existing	Environmental Waste treatment Textiles Health care Unique speciality foods Alcohol, baking, fats/oils Fruit/wine, flavour, protein Animal foods, leather Paper/pulp Chemical biotransformation	More testing kits GMOs By products High tech foods Full consultancy service Technical backup service
New	Geographic - eg Russia, China, USA, Japan New industries Oil spillage Pharmaceutical Licensing	Knowledge brokers Backward forward integration

MARKETS (row label)

1.3.1 Evaluation of strategic options

Each strategy must be evaluated for its attractiveness to the business and the competitive advantage/position it offers. The best evaluation tool for this purpose is the GE matrix. Management agree and prioritise the criteria for strategy attractiveness and research on customers to determine the competitive position. We have some information on why customers buy. This would form one of the criteria.

Strategy/market attractiveness position

Profitability of not less than 10%
Marketing growth potential
Levels of competition
Investment required of not more than X%
Synergy with existing operations
New skills required
Speed to implement
Degree of risk

Competitive

Improving efficiency
Cost effectiveness
Convenience
Safety
Availability
Consistency and quality
Value for money
Technical support

Weighting and rating the criteria enables us to plot the strategies on the matrix to reveal which strategies are worth pursuing and which should be rejected.

Biocatalysts need to plan for the short and medium term. In this fast, changing, dynamic market, longer term strategies can be difficult to identify. Strategy selection will need to provide immediate profits given your financial position, followed by medium term strategies that will grow the business and establish a competitive position.

The information we do have suggests the most attractive strategies are:

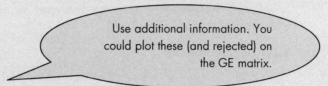

Use additional information. You could plot these (and rejected) on the GE matrix.

- Short term market penetration strategy diagnostics

- Short to medium term market development strategy – Speciality foods

- Medium term new product development strategy – Technical support with selected products and as stand alone service

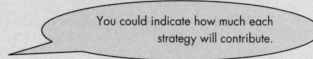

You could indicate how much each strategy will contribute.

More accurate and up to date marketing research will confirm validity of this selection and profitability.

1.3.2 Competitive position

Strategy selection must be more focused than has been the case to date. The mission and vision will guide strategy selection and formulation. Biocatalysts cannot be all things to all people so product rationalisation and customer segmentation is going to be important. When formulating strategy, a clear competitive position should emerge and this can only be established through a co-ordinated effort by the business.

Analysis shows there are 12 major players in this market. Their size makes a cost leadership position possible. This is not an option for Biocatalysts given their size. The investment is too great. Increasingly even large companies are moving towards a differentiation strategy to improve their competitive position. 12 major players and 60 medium sized companies will be vying for positions using a differentiation strategy.

This leaves some 400 small companies, including Biocatalysts, to decide how they are going to compete. Analysis of the market and trends and Biocatalysts's strengths would indicate that a niche strategy would be the best option.

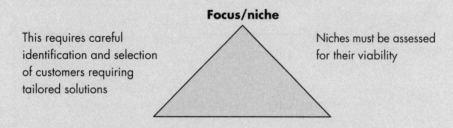

Focus/niche

This requires careful identification and selection of customers requiring tailored solutions

Niches must be assessed for their viability

Cost leadership   **Differentiation**

1.4   Marketing objectives

An overall marketing objective is recommended to generate £12 million revenue by 2005 to deliver a £1.2 million profit.

Marketing objectives must then be further broken down by industry/market and for each strategy eg:

Diagnostics 35%   £4.2m (from £100K 1997) at 12% = £504K
Pharmaceuticals 35%   £4.2m (from £300K 1997) at 12% = £504K
Food 30%   £3.6m (from £960K 1997) at 5.3% = £192K

1.5 Marketing strategy

A marketing strategy will need to be developed for each business strategy selected. The following plan is for speciality foods.

1.5.1 Segmentation

More information is required to segment the market effectively. However we do have some information, which will enable us to make a start.

Options for segmentation include initial segment bases determined by industry sectors, so for speciality foods, Kosher and vegetarian producers. Product, process and size of company may provide some opportunities for segmentation but none for competitive advantage. We must identify decision making units and needs and motives for buying. Many of these emerged during analysis. For example:

NEEDS	Users	Influencers	Deciders	Buyers	Approvers	Gatekeepers
Purity	X					
Cost efficiency				X		
Increase yield			X			

Research will improve information on precise needs and motives for Kosher and vegetarian foods. The technical support required may also affect segmentation. You may find customers from different sectors have commonalities by which we can segment. The advantage of this type of segmentation is that it can be used again, with small modifications and improvements, across national and industry boundaries.

1.5.2 Positioning

The positioning of the marketing mix should reflect the desired competitive position and customer needs. For example:

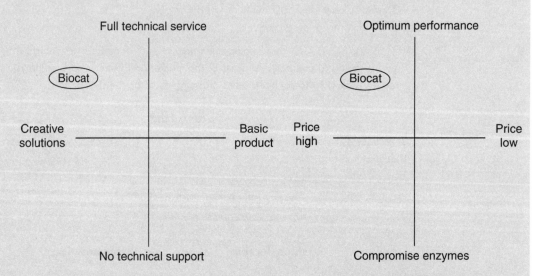

It is important to establish current competitor positions and to monitor this activity and ensure Biocatalysts maintain a position that differentiates itself from the rest.

The role of the brand will be crucial in communicating and establishing desired position.

1.5.3 Targeting

It is recommended that Biocatalyst pursue a multi-niche strategy. It would be risky to pursue only one niche for two reasons. The speed of change might result in a new entrant taking an interest in the niche and a single niche might not support the desired growth objectives.

The targeting strategy will therefore be differentiation. Specific needs of niches will be identified and marketing mixes designed to meet those needs.

1.6 Marketing mix plans

A distinct marketing mix plan will need to be developed for each niche targeted. By way of illustration, this plan is for speciality vegetarian foods.

1.6.1 Product

Objectives: to be determined: number of products sales by sector/market should be established

Actions: To rationalise the product range and ensure focus on profitable niches
To identify precise needs and possible future needs of vegetarian enzymes

1.6.2 Price

Aims: To reflect value for money and added value technical service: to achieve profit objective through premium price that reflects technical service

Actions: Research on price in the market and clarify price sensitive areas, complexities
Review sources of supply
Review impact of currency and exchange rate

1.6.3 Place

See answer 2

1.6.4 Promotion

See answer 3

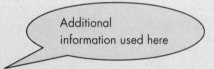

Additional information used here

1.6.5 Customer service and technical support (service 3Ps)

Aims: To provide full technical support that will add value and differentiate the company to establish clear competitive position

Actions: Research customers, existing and potential, to establish nature of technical support needed

Evaluate current skills levels, both technical and customer care, and identify training needs

Design training programmes and review recruitment policy to meet above

1.7 Control

1.7.1 Budget

Cash flow is a problem and the reality is this will affect the marketing budget. However with a more strategic, efficient and focused plan, the current budget can be used much more effectively. Biocatalysts should consider alliances with customers on some activities e.g. research to help finance plans. Omnibus research might be of use.

If Biocatalysts are to survive and succeed, money will need to be spent on marketing and a recommended budget of X%.

You would need to specify

1.7.2 Scheduling

It is not the intention to detail every activity, these will be included in each plan, but rather to cover broadly key tasks.

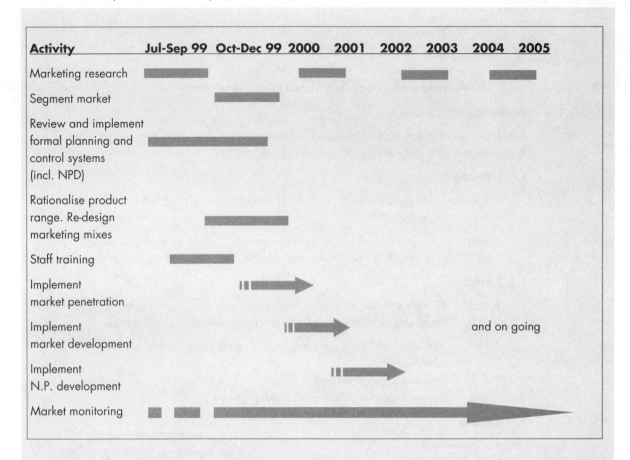

Activity	Jul-Sep 99	Oct-Dec 99	2000	2001	2002	2003	2004	2005

Marketing research

Segment market

Review and implement formal planning and control systems (incl. NPD)

Rationalise product range. Re-design marketing mixes

Staff training

Implement market penetration

Implement market development   and on going

Implement N.P. development

Market monitoring

1.7.3 Measurement

Biocatalysts must track performance and ensure they are on course. Performance measures will include:

- Profits and profitability

- Product sales by sector

- Effectiveness of competitive positioning (customer, supplier, distributor surveys to track attitudes and perceptions)

- Customer satisfaction and loyalty

- Technical support performance

4.2 Question 2

2. International marketing strategy

The strategic marketing plan developed above has outlined vision, mission, business objectives, competitive position and issues on product and some market selection.

The intention in this plan is to recommend how Biocatalysts's international efforts can be very much more effective than they currently are.

2.1 Country/market selection

Not all markets are performing well and decisions need to be made on which markets to develop, particularly in view of Biocatalysts's limited resources.

A useful model for evaluating which countries or regions to operate in is the Harrell and Kiefer model. It works on the same principles as the GE matrix but the dimensions and criteria are different.

Criteria to enable the business to evaluate the attractiveness of the market eg:

Country attractiveness

Political stability, risks and legal requirements
Economic conditions/growth
Infrastructure
Local technical skills and knowledge
Levels of competition

Biocatalyst's capabilities

Experience of market
Investment required
Management skills
Existing channel performance
Control issues

We know from the additional information that the South Asian and South American economies have problems. Added to this, these markets have been significant textile markets, a market that appears to be commoditising, possibly in decline.

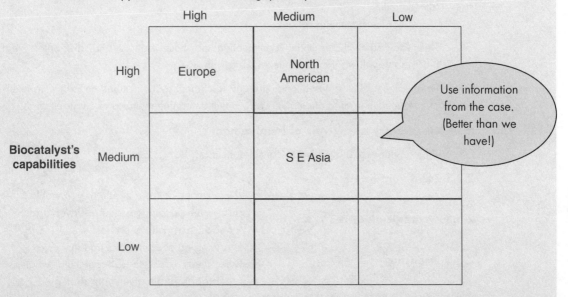

Europe and North American are stable markets where food, particularly specialist food, is a rapidly growing market. North America is very competitive and would be difficult, initially, for Biocatalysts to manage, given their financial situation. Europe, however, is closer to home and showing significant growth.

2.2 Agents and distributors

We must evaluate and rationalise the current network. The results of the analysis suggest performance is mixed. In some markets, Biocatalysts are hardly making enough money to make it worthwhile. The additional information suggests that agents in Hong Kong and Singapore are performing well as they are described as **'key offices'** so both these markets and agents are likely to be part of Biocatalysts's future developments in the medium-term when the economic situation improves. What we must establish for the short- and medium-term is the strength of distribution channels in Europe.

2.2.1 Evaluating current situations

As mentioned in the additional information, market conditions vary and will also need to be taken into account.

The GE matrix is again a very useful tool for evaluating distribution channels. The criteria will be different for evaluating distributors. Criteria will include for example:

Distribution attractiveness/performance

Order quantities/value
Profitability
Delivery performance
Technical know-how, experience, knowledge
Customer technical support capabilities (including problem handling)

Marketing performance (activities)

Market performance (penetration, development)

The customers' view of the effectiveness of distribution channels is important. They should be surveyed and their criteria will be similar to that discussed in part 1.

The evaluation process is two way. Biocatalysts need to establish their performance from the channels' point of view. Their criteria will include:

Reliability

Support – both technical and marketing

Profitability

Consistency

Compatibility

Motivation and communications

This exercise will result in identification of those agents and distributors that Biocatalysts will want to continue working with.

Development of an international strategy for Biocatalysts includes decisions on levels of involvement in different markets as this will determine methods of entry selected.

2.3 Methods of entry and levels of involvement

Other viable options for Biocatalyst to consider include:

2.3.1 Joint ventures

2.3.2 Strategic alliances

Under each of these headings you would discuss the advantages and disadvantages of each, **not** as a theoretical exercise but drawing on case material and in view of Biocatalysts' aspirations. In particular what is appropriate given your strategy selection?

2.3.3 Licensing

2.3.4 Wholly owned subsidiary

2.4 Marketing objectives

Once countries/regions have been selected and methods of entry identified, marketing objectives by market can be established. Marketing research will clarify market value and therefore what Biocatalysts can realistically aim for. However there will be a minimum acceptable level for the market to be viable.

Illustrate your quantified marketing objectives by market. Make sure they link back to the business objective

2.5 Marketing strategy

The marketing strategy will be developed along the lines illustrated in the five year plan. Specifically, segmentation will identify similar niches across Europe initially, other regions later, that can be targeted. Positioning should have a broad theme for all niches and each niche will have specific needs and values. Research will identify any market-specific issues.

2.6 Tactical plans

Marketing mix design must reflect the constraints of the country including laws, standards and cultural issues.

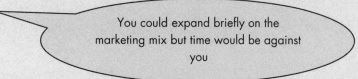

You could expand briefly on the marketing mix but time would be against you

2.7 Control

Span of control increases with market development. Control issues include the extent of centralisation and decentralisation, and managing and motivating channels of distribution.

An important strategic issue will be the structure of the organisation as this impacts on control.

Budgets need to be set by market and measures of control would be similar to those outlined in the five year plan with performance measures for market and channel performance.

4.3 Question 3

3. Marketing communications strategy

Our communications strategy should focus on our customers and key stakeholders. However, as mentioned, in the current situation, there is increasing hostility in the market about GMOs in particular and, more generally, the biotechnology industry is beginning to suffer from some of the backlash. We therefore cannot ignore what is happening in our customers' markets. The responsibility for this hostility lies partly with governments and particularly with biotechnology companies, so we must be part of the solution.

Consumers in developed countries are usually better educated and informed and are more sophisticated and demanding. Governments and large companies have, in the past, presumed they know best and made decisions about goods and services with little, if any, consultation with consumers. Consumers want to be informed and will make decisions about purchases based on that information.

Biocatalysts has the opportunity to build a brand that represents quality, safety and ethical practice so is of value to our customers who in turn have to address the needs of their consumers.

3.1 Communications objectives

Broad aims can include the intention to inform, reassure and if necessary persuade and change attitudes towards biotechnology and GMOs. However it is important to be clear about what is to be achieved. Aims can include the need to raise awareness or attention, generate interest, create a desire and encourage action.

It is difficult to quantify objectives until we have some indication of number of customers and stakeholders we need to influence. Once this has been established we can set quantified objectives. For example:

To raise awareness from X% to X% within three years of the benefits of GMOs

To change attitudes towards GMOs from a negative view of X% to a positive view of X% within five years

3.2 Communications strategy

Because of Biocatalysts' limited financial and marketing resources, some realistic decisions will have to be made about the development of communications strategy.

Biocatalysts should have a push and profile strategy. It is essential to ensure effective use of all resources and maximum impact on the marketplace.

A pull strategy is unrealistic and must be left to your customers. Biocatalyst's role could be to provide evidence and information to help customers communicate more effectively with consumers. This support might encourage customers to return the support and help with the funding of some communication activities.

Biocatalysts customers' pull strategies will play a significant role in dealing with negative perceptions and cannot be ignored.

3.2.1 Push

This strategy will be designed to encourage and persuade existing and new distribution channels and business to business customers to purchase Biocatalysts's enzymes and services.

3.2.2 Profile

This strategy is intended to promote broader issues to a wider audience, the complex and very influential stakeholders involved in this industry.

The communications strategy will build the brand and competitive position over time.

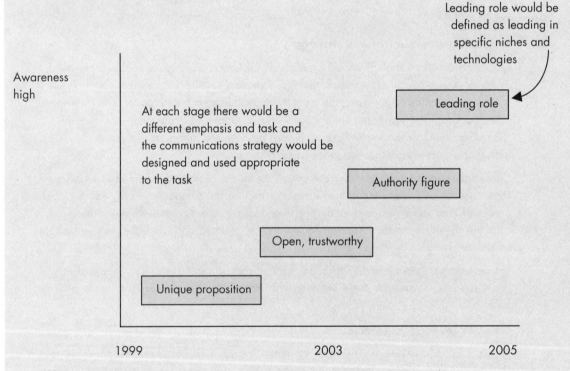

3.3 Targets

The targets for communications will be broader than the marketing strategy. The reason for this is the need to influence the significant number of stakeholders involved that in turn influence, directly or indirectly, developments in the biotechnology industry. These stakeholders include:

Performance network - stakeholders directly influencing include:

■ Suppliers, MAFF, FDA, universities, agents/distributors, industry producers, consumers, competitors, employees

Support network - Stakeholders that indirectly influence include

■ Pressure groups, industry analysts, investigators, scientists, journalists, trade bodies, religious groups, slaughterhouses, environment agencies, food and drug agencies, governments

All stakeholders need to be targeted with clear, tailored messages and promotional mixes to ensure effective communications.

3.4 Promotional activities

3.4.1 Positioning and messages

The key issue to address in this business is that of trust. Consumers have lost faith with businesses and governments and no longer trust them to make decisions that are in the best interests of consumers.

This is an opportunity for Biocatalysts to position themselves as trustworthy and as the biotechnology company that puts safety first. Testing procedures would take account of consumer concerns, not just the profit motive. Creativity is going to be vital and Biocatalysts, while able to provide the information, do not have the creative communications skills. An agency will need to be considered.

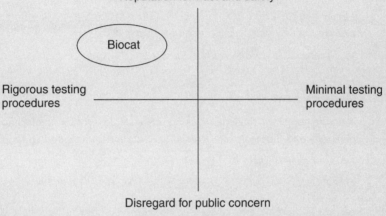

3.4.2 Promotional mix

Because of limited financial resources, the promotional budget will have to be used creatively. PR will be a main feature, which is in Biocatalysts favour because of its credibility and the current interest. Identifying newsworthy items will be crucial.

There has never been a better opportunity to tap into the 'human interest' story and encourage media to print.

Push strategy – sales force, technical support team, brochures, exhibitions, trade press

Profile strategy – PR, papers at seminars and conferences, explore opportunities for sponsorship

3.5 Control

3.5.1 Budget

> You would need to specify

Biocatalysts's cash flow problems means that, until improved market penetration leads to improved profits, the communications strategy, though crucial, will have a slow start. However until research is completed the design of the campaign cannot start in earnest.

Other sources of funds should be reviewed and allocation of existing marketing budgets examined for more effective use. This can be used in the short term with more funds allocated as profits improve.

A budget of £X is recommended for the first year, increasing to £X for years 2 – 4. By year 5 the success of the campaign should lead a lower volume of funds being required. However the communications effort will remain vital and should be sustained.

3.5.2 Schedule

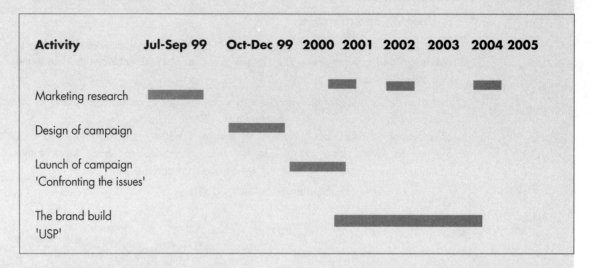

Activity	Jul-Sep 99	Oct-Dec 99	2000	2001	2002	2003	2004	2005
Marketing research	▬			▬	▬		▬	
Design of campaign		▬						
Launch of campaign 'Confronting the issues'			▬					
The brand build 'USP'				▬▬▬▬▬▬▬▬▬▬▬				

3.5.3 Measurement

Measurements will include tracking attitudes to GMOs, biotechnology companies generally and Biocatalysts in particular, awareness levels and so on.

Appendices

Six pages of appendices will be added here. Remember the more you have related these to your report the more marks you will get.

We haven't replicated the analysis here but you have seen how the models are populated and insight is added. This will be a personal perspective and under no circumstances should be tackled as a group.

You will find an actual student example in the next case, Mauritius.

Part C

Practice Cases

Tackling a practice case: Signifo Expenses

Chapter Topic List

1	Introduction
2	Signifo Expenses: December 2005 case
3	Step 1: Initial overview

By the end of this chapter, you will have:

(a) Read the Signifo Expenses case
(b) Completed your overview analysis
(c) Compared your analysis with our tutor comments and feedback
(d) Tested your understanding of the case

1 Introduction

Tackling a Practice Case: Signifo Expenses

1.1 You have already been practising your case study skills by working the Biocatalysts case study, as we demonstrated the approach in Section B. This second case is one you really should work through yourself, using the materials we have provided as samples against which you can monitor and benchmark your own output. Simply reading the material is really not good enough. Case study analysis, as you have seen, is made up of a series of techniques which you need to develop and practise for yourself so that by the time the exam case is issued, you are confident about tackling it, whatever the business or sector.

1.2 In the second half of this manual, you will find two more cases. We have included the next, Signifo Expenses, with analysis and decision material developed for the case study. The final case study, the June 2006 case, which focused on a retailer, is to give you a final rehearsal case and is supported only with general guidance and some tutor comments.

1.3 For Signifo Expenses, we will remind you of the process at each stage and then present and guide you with sample material and tutor comments. We will not be reminding you of 'how' to tackle each step, so if you are in doubt, you will need to refer back to Section B.

1.4 It is now time to begin your overview. If you are unsure of the process consult Chapter 4 for detailed 'how to' guidance. Broadly the process is:

(a)　Read the case study

(b)　Stop and think about the case context

(c)　Sort out the case narrative into topic areas eg finance, marketing environment and so on

(d)　Identify what is included in the Appendices and what information their analysis might generate

(e)　Remember to start your information shopping list

2   Signifo Expenses: December 2005 case

Page 1 of Signifo Expenses

The Chartered
Institute of Marketing

Professional Postgraduate Diploma in Marketing

64 – Strategic Marketing in Practice

Case Study
December 2005

Signifo Expenses

Page 2 of Signifo Expenses

Case Study December 2005

Strategic Marketing in Practice

Important Notes for Candidates

The examiners will be marking your scripts on the basis of questions put to you in the examination room. Candidates are advised to pay particular attention to the mark allocation on the examination paper and budget their time accordingly.

Your role is outlined in the Candidate's Brief and you will be required to recommend clear courses of action.

Candidates are advised not to waste valuable time collecting unnecessary data. The cases are based upon real-world situations. No useful purpose will therefore be served by contacting companies in the industry and candidates are **strictly instructed not to do as it may cause unnecessary confusion**.

As in real life, anomalies will be found in the information provided within this Case Study. Please simply state your assumptions, where necessary, when answering questions. The Chartered Institute of Marketing is not in a position to answer queries on case data. Candidates are tested on their overall understanding of the case and its key issue, not on minor details. There are no catch questions or hidden agendas.

Additional information may be introduced in the examination paper itself, which candidates must take into account when answering the questions set.

Acquaint yourself thoroughly with the Case Study and be prepared to follow closely the instructions given to you on the examination day. To answer examination questions effectively candidates must adopt a report format.

As part of your preparation for the examination, you need to carry out a detailed analysis of this Case. You will then need to condense your analysis into a 6-page summary (a maximum of 6 sides of A4, no smaller than font size 11). This summary, and how you use it to answer the questions set, will be awarded marks and should be attached, with a treasury tag, to your answer booklet at the end of the examination. Your tutor should provide you with guidance on how to compile your summary 6-page analysis.

The copying of pre-prepared 'group' answers, including those written by consultants/tutors, is strictly forbidden and will be penalised by failure. The questions will demand analysis in the examination itself and individually composed answers are required to pass.

254

Candidate's Brief

You are Ed Walker, a marketing consultant with considerable amount of e-commerce experience in the business-to-consumer market. You have been appointed by Signifo Expenses to consider, amongst other issues, positioning and branding of the company. In order to do this you have been asked to profile the company and look at as many aspects of this specialised business as possible.

Signifo is a successful niche company in the business-to-business market that deals with business applications through the Web. It has many well-known clients within its portfolio. You have already spent considerable time gathering useful information for a meeting that is to take place on 9th December 2005, where you will be asked specific questions by the Signifo Board of Directors.

Important Notice

The following data has been based on a real-life organisation, but details have been changed for assessment purposes and no not reflect current management practices.

Candidates are strictly instructed **NOT TO CONTACT** Signifo Expenses or any other companies in the industry. Additional information may be provided at the time of the examination. Further copies may be obtained from: The Chartered Institute of Marketing, Moor Hall, Cookham, Berkshire SL6 9QH, UK or may be downloaded from the CIM student website www.cimlearningzone.com

---

Signifo Expenses

Introduction

Signifo Expenses is a small software and services company that was formed by James Brewis, Richard Dewar and Sanjay Parekh in March 2000. It has been managed by the founders since its inception. As the Internet and mobile telephony have evolved over the years, the founders felt that there was a real gap in the market for streamlining expenses that employees incur during the course of their work.

Companies often struggle with paper, messy receipts and a range of sources to work out each individual's out-of-pocket expenses incurred on behalf of the company. It is common for manual processes to cost a company as much as £30-£50 per expense report, and to take a month or longer for reimbursement. For most companies this means that considerable time is wasted in tracking, filing and formatting claims.

Expense solutions dramatically cut the cost of processing an expense report by reducing inaccuracies in the expense management process, processing claims rapidly, and controlling travel and entertainment costs. An easy and cost-effective implementation system means that neither the employees nor the companies utilising the system are unnecessarily burdened. This makes Signifo Expenses a leading provider of expense claim solutions for medium-sized and small organisations. Implementations range from organisations with only a single employee submitting claims, to those with as many as a thousand.

Signifo Expenses minimises implementation costs as follows:

- The applications allow for immediate implementation by the customer with a flexible configuration handled remotely by an experienced team at Signifo. There is no requirement for implementation staff to visit a customer's location.

- The user interface allows employees to create and submit claims with a minimum of formal training. In fact, the Signifo Expenses user manual has been condensed to a single postcard-sized document. As a result, the customers achieve rapid implementation, immediate cost savings and a very high return on investment.

The expense claims solutions are differentiated because:

a) They can be speedily implemented at a low cost

b) The system is very easy to use

c) The configuration is very flexible and can be completed immediately and implemented across any organisation quickly and efficiently. The cost savings are considerable, with time saved in data capture, expense approval and accounts processing.

The Market

In terms of supply chain management, employee travel and entertainment expenses are not often thought of as significant costs of doing business. However, these expenses can be as much as 20 per cent of indirect expenses, sometimes even higher where companies are service oriented. As Web applications have become more and more sophisticated, most companies have concentrated on Web-based automation that is directly related to e-commerce and revenue-generating information technology on the Internet. Recently, more companies have been looking for technologies that can help to improve efficiency within business processes. This has forced them to examine their expenses. In doing this, a new niche area for process automation and cost savings has emerged for most organisations, large or small.

Many large companies that undertake business on a global basis find it quite difficult to work out how much employees spend on hotels, where these hotels are located, etc, without considerable time and effort. Generally, they rely on travel agents, and even individual hotels, to get the information, even if they have millions of pounds at stake. Often manual audits are undertaken. By utilising complex forms and systems, employees are usually caught up in spending an hour each week, filling out paper forms with receipts. They also then have to deal with internal accounts managers for approval and scrutiny, leaving highly paid employees chasing refunds via meetings or telephone conversations, and waiting several weeks for reimbursement. At the same time, accounts clerks who look after the expenses can ignore claims that have been put forward as credit card receipts without VAT (Value Added Tax) receipts. Normally credit card receipts are not regarded as claimable by HM Revenue and Customs (the department of the British government responsible for tax). This makes expense claims perfect for automation.

Expense claims solutions are suited to any organisation that utilises paper-based processes. These are used for various reasons:

- Distributed workforce

- Field-based sales staff or engineers

- Multiple offices

- Home workers

- Frequent domestic or overseas travel

- A need to recharge expense items to clients or projects

- Large volume of expense claims

Companies with multiple subsidiaries, divisions or cost centres can configure each of these separately with separate base currencies, account codes, credit card feeds and approval structures for each entity. The market for Application Service Providers (ASPs) has grown substantially over the last five years, after the dotcom bubble had written off many Internet-based ventures.

Page 6 of Signifo Expenses

IT Services Industry

The worldwide IT services sector is highly fragmented, with few companies other than the 'Big 4' possessing important market shares. The largest concentration (49.8%) of IT Service firms has between 2 and 4 employees and a turnover of less than $200,000. Medium-sized firms, with more than 25 employees, are doing the largest proportion of the IT Services work in the global marketplace. Figure 1 illustrates the key groupings on a global scale.

Figure 1: IT Service Firms Groups
(Source: Deutsche banc, Alex Brown, IT Services Sourcebook, 1 July 1999)

IT Service Firms Groupings

TIER 1
IBM Global Services, EDS, Anderson Consulting, CSC

TIER 2
Ernst and Young, KPMG, Deloitte and Touche, PricewaterhouseCoopers, Hewlett Packard, Compaq, SAP, Perot Systems, Lockheed Martin, Xerox, Fujitsu, Oracle, Keane, AMS, Metamor

TIER 3
Cambridge Technology Partners, Modis Professional Services, GTSI, Bantec, Ciber, WCI and thousands of medium and small sized firms scattered throughout the world

According to the research firm Forrester, the IT spending appetite of European small and medium-sized enterprises (SMEs) will continue to be strong throughout 2005. To understand these firms' plans for software and services adoption, Forrester surveyed 308 SMEs across 19 European countries. Compared with the slowdown in the large enterprise segment, SMEs show a healthy 4.6% IT spending increase during 2005, with certain sectors, such as financial services and manufacturing, driving the buying activity. But where will SMEs spend their software and services budgets? IT security and customer service tools top the platform software and application lists, respectively. Vendors hoping to offer application hosting services, however, will have to strengthen areas like data security or pricing models to get SME buy-in. When it comes to IT services, consulting demand will focus on security assessment projects and application implementation, with new and growing demand on the outsourcing side.

Gartner Dataquest forecasts that the $536 billion worldwide IT services industry will grow through 2007 to reach $707 billion, with a compound annual growth rate of 5.7%. According to the Meta Group, when the market for expenses software is fully mature, it is likely to be worth around $5bn. Currently, 97% of transactions are on paper or spreadsheets, leaving plenty of scope for market penetration. According to AMR Research, the expense management market is expected to reach $1.8bn by 2006 (from $700m in 2002). The software has matured and become more robust, says Monica Barron, AMR research analyst. As vendors in the field have merged with and acquired each other, it has also made the evaluation process quicker. The two obvious camps are specialist software vendors and larger software companies offering expense management as a module of their enterprise suites. In the 'added functionality' space, procurement specialists and enterprise resource planning (ERP) vendors, among others, have tried to extend existing deployments. IBM, for one, treats expense management as part of its overall approach to employee productivity. Many of the vendors have begun offering digital imaging services, to scan and store receipts and invoices required by the IRS (USA's Internal Revenue Service) for auditing purposes. Itemised corporate credit-card account data (American Express, Diners' Club, Bank One) feed directly into the system, as does up-to-the-minute exchange rate information.

Signifo's Market Positioning

As indicated above, Signifo Expenses has pioneered the market for expense claim solutions for mid-sized and small organisations since launching its first product in 2000. The company has reached profitability through organic growth and a keen focus on cost control. Until the company launched its first product, the market for expenses solutions was characterised by well-established, primarily US-based participants selling to corporate (i.e. large company) customers, with few alternatives to the paper-based expense claim process for smaller organisations.

Accordingly, Signifo established the business to target the **SME market**, where there was little competition. This strategy proved to be sensible, indicating that the product benefits are as relevant to smaller organisations as to large ones. The company has successfully implemented solutions in industries as varied as television broadcasting, computer chip manufacture, consumer goods marketing, data storage, engineering consulting, hardware sales, organic food distribution, pharmaceuticals, recruitment consultancy, security systems and the public sector.

The company now has customers around the globe, although the majority are based in the UK. While it has been successful in working with **small customers**, the majority of revenues have resulted from sales to **mid-sized customers** such as Chivas, EMI Music, E*TRADE, Heineken, Hitachi, Pernod Ricard, Teletext and Woolmark. The company is well positioned to take advantage of relationship marketing strategies. Signifo is also giving serious thought to its branding. (Ranchhod and Marandi, 2005; Ranchhod, 2003; Little and Marandi, 2003.)

Page 8 of Signifo Expenses

There is a subtle but crucial difference in selling to each of these two groups. Specifically, mid-sized customers typically require face-to-face meetings and a degree of bespoke product functionality, whereas small customers can be accessed with a phone/Web-based sales effort. When the company sells to mid-sized customers, it is typically engaging head-to-head with the competition, while for small customers, it faces no competition. The company therefore:

- Is the UK market leader in SME markets

- Has a global customer base

- Has products differentiated by

    - rapid implementation

    - ease of use

    - robust and relevant functionality

- Has applications that are robust and secure

- Is represented by mid-market customers as shown below:

    - E Trade

    - Chivas Regal

    - EMI

    - Woolmark

    - Realplayer

    - Teletext

    - Hitachi

    - Heineken

- Has almost 400 customers and 20,000 active users

- Has been awarded the DTI (UK Department of Trade and Industry) SMART award, and a loan under the DTI Small Firm Loan Guarantee scheme

- Was shortlisted for the 2004 Accountancy Age Awards mid-range software solution of the year.

Product overview

- The core product is a **Web-based application** that replaces the paper-based expense claim process and provides significant reports and administration functionality. See Figure 2.

- The **offline version**, developed using .NET, allows expense claims to be created and submitted when not connected to the Internet. This product is important to users based on the road, such as field-based sales people and engineers. See Figure 3.

Figure 2

Figure 3

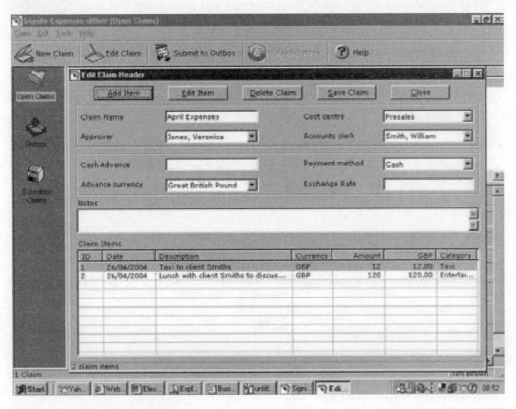

Page 10 of Signifo Expenses

- The **credit card interface** allows expense claims to be populated with data from American Express, Barclaycard, HSBC and RBS Natwest.

  This product resolves a significant failing of corporate credit cards; namely that an organisation still needs to deal with paper-based card statements, and card data must be manually typed into the company's accounting software, line item by line item.

  Credit card interface allows data to be processed seamlessly from merchant through the approval process to the consolidated upload of card data to the accounting software. See Figure 4.

- **Interfaces into accounting software products** allow consolidated expense claim data to be posted to the relevant purchase and nominal ledgers at the click of a button or selection of a menu item from within Line 50, Line 100 and Multimedia Messaging Service (MMS). See Figure 5.

Recently completed product development work:
- The **Short Messaging Service (SMS) mobile version**, which allows claimants to submit claims by sending a simple SMS text message. This functionality allows users to record expense items as they are incurred, and following a November 2004 launch it is now being used by 30 companies around the world, including USA, Hong Kong and Australia. (November 2004 release)

- **Multicompany/multicurrency functionality**, which allow for separate configurations (e.g. base currency, expense categories, reporting hierarchies etc) for each business unit. Individual users can, however, be active in different units (e.g. as a claimant in one unit and an approver in another), while the configuration can be administered (e.g. joiners/leavers maintained) both centrally and at business unit level. (December 2004 release)

- **Category limits**, which allow items that exceed a defined threshold to be flagged or blocked. (January 2005 release)

- **VAT rules**, which allow default VAT rates to be set per category and region. (February 2005 release)

- **Re-engineering project** to consolidate all product work to date and leverage latest technologies. This will improve scalability, introduce additional functionality, allow for **white-labelling** and provide platform for all future product development work. (Development commenced May 2005; for pricing and benefits see Appendix 1)

Signifo Expenses user survey results (Feb/March 2005, 455 respondents):

Please rate your overall view of Signifo Expenses

Very good	45.5%
Good	43.5%
Average	8.4%
Poor	2.6 %

Figure 4

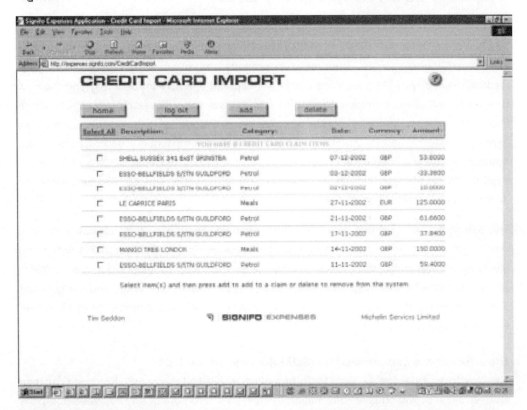

Figure 5

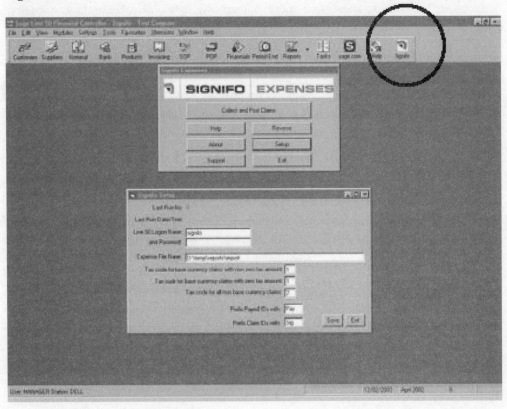

Corporate Social Responsibility Issues

A new era of corporate governance began in the USA the moment President Bush signed the Sarbanes-Oxley Act (SOX) in 2002, with Chief Executive Officers (CEOs) and Chief Financial Officers (CFOs) becoming personally responsible for their companies' disclosures. Many of the provisions of the Act became effective immediately and the new rulemaking initiatives combine to lay the foundations for a developing New Corporate Order of required internal procedures, checks, oversight, and standards, as well as expanded external liability when companies are not in compliance. The corporate board structure is now a combination of both federal and state law, in which CEOs and CFOs are exposed to significantly increased personal liability, including long prison sentences for intentional non-compliance.

The Sarbanes-Oxley Act has been called the most significant securities legislation in more than a generation, with one of its stated objectives being to provide markets with more timely and transparent information, in addition to increasing protection for shareholders. The first tranche of new rules became effective on 5th September 2002, and many senior executives recognised this as an opportunity to raise shareholder confidence by filing their statements early.

The effect of the Sarbanes-Oxley (SOX) Act beyond the USA

The directors of the former Worldcom organisation are to face criminal charges for their alleged role in providing false information to investors. Directors of any overseas company listed in the United States are already exposed to this area of potential liability, including, indirectly, directors of overseas subsidiaries of American companies. However, the new Act extends to these companies, and more particularly, to individual directors, imposing criminal liability and financial penalties on those in breach of the new regime.

Directors will be required to certify, personally, the accuracy of the company's financial statements, in addition to certifying that the company has established and maintained internal financial and disclosure controls, which they have evaluated within 90 days of giving that certification. Failure to give a true certification will be a criminal offence under US law. Leaving US jurisdiction will not protect the director of a foreign company, as the Sarbanes-Oxley Act provides for extradition proceedings, if certain criteria are fulfilled.

The Act also extends the restrictions on company loans to directors and senior executive officers, with no exception for loans of low value. Officers and directors could also face penalties for financial misstatements, including forfeiture of bonuses or other rewards. In addition, the US Stock Exchange Commission has new powers to require a company to disclose its code of ethics for its senior financial officers.

Many of the US regulations differ from, and in some respects conflict with, UK corporate governance and audit codes, but directors need to be aware of these differences, as it may soon be a requirement for them to explain how the British rules differ from those in the US. Directors of UK-based subsidiaries of US Corporations need to introduce more rigorous internal procedures, and to sign internal audit certificates in order to assist their main Board in the US to comply with their new obligations. This may have an effect on plans for listings on the New York Stock Exchange. Porsche abandoned such plans last year, on the grounds that the liability imposed on individual directors was incompatible with the German concept of the collective responsibility of the Board.

The Sarbanes-Oxley Act of 2002 was developed to protect investors by improving the accuracy and reliability of corporate disclosure. This Act makes reporting on internal controls mandatory for companies registered with the SEC (US Securities and Exchange Commission) and their independent auditors. Section 404 of the Act directs the SEC to adopt rules requiring annual reports to include an assessment, as of the end of the fiscal year, of the effectiveness of internal controls and procedures for financial reporting. Section 404 also requires the company's independent auditors to attest to and report on that management assessment. The Act covers Analyst Conflict of Interest, Auditor Independence & Reporting, and Corporate Responsibility, as well as the creation of a Public Company Accounting Oversight Board.

In essence, this Act was passed in order to protect various stakeholders from being exploited by company directors who mismanage companies and do not run them ethically. The lack of strict monitoring over financial reporting in enterprises had created major losses and investor distrust. As a result, enterprises today have to comply with stricter regulations and standards. For any business enterprise, compliance with regulations and standards has become a necessity.

Signifo Expenses is currently undertaking a major product development project that will not only deliver advanced functionality, but will also make the products compliant with the requirements of the US Internal Revenue Service. In the long run, the Sarbanes-Oxley Act will cascade down to the SME market from the large corporate sector listed on the stock markets. SOX is likely to drive takeup of expenses solutions amongst larger corporates, in particular in the USA, with considerably less effect in the SME market.

The Sarbanes-Oxley Act calls for three main areas of compliance:

- Legal and regulatory requirements

- Accounting standards and guidance

- Internal operations and management

In this respect, Signifo is well placed to work with companies, and complies with all the legal requirements. Signifo is also strictly audited by the banks who are their clients, so CSR issues are incorporated within the company. The company is ISO 9001 compliant.

Forward Plans

The company produces monthly and quarterly marketing updates on how the business is progressing. The main objectives concern gaining and retaining customers, and understanding what the Customer Lifetime Value is to the organisation.

- Customer Lifetime Value (CLV) indicates the profits that flow from customer transactions. These transactions are a result of marketing investments. As transactions grow, this will have a positive impact on the ROI. This measure also helps with allocation of resources for target marketing and the development of retention and new customer procurement strategies. The use of technology and customer relationship management (CRM) software helps to determine the value of each customer, currently and in the future.

Figure 6: Seven Step Process to Measure Customer Lifetime Value
(Source: ©Booz Allen Hamilton, 2001)

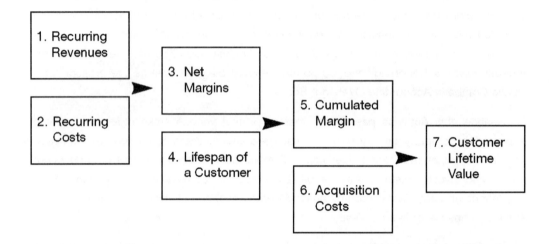

- The total number of customers generated through marketing investments. The ROI will continue to improve, unless the cost of generating new customers exceeds the cost of retaining old ones.

- The marketing expense undertaken, in order to generate returns. As profits grow and the expenditure ratio lessens, the ROI will improve. (Ranchhod, 2003)

Examples of how Signifo deals with different sets of customers are highlighted in Appendices 2 and 4.

On a monthly basis, Signifo follows these strategies:

- **Lead generation**: In the last quarter, the number of leads has increased while the cost of leads has decreased significantly. The number of leads is increasing and the conversion rate from trial to sales is in excess of 50%.

- **Pay-per-click advertising**: Utilising Google Ads effectively reduces the cost per lead and increases volume without compromising quality.

- **Working closely with providers of accounting software (e.g. Sage)**: Increasingly, this is providing the company with greater opportunities to reach the end user, such as advertising opportunities in their publications and events targeted at end users.

- **Mid-sized customers**: Sales to mid-sized customers are constrained at the moment by insufficient functionality, typically in one of three areas:

–   detail of entertainment events (attendees etc)

–   splitting of hotel bills

–   recording of mileage

These are being addressed by the re-engineering project, and sales to mid-sized customers will increase once these are delivered.

• **Email marketing**

Email marketing to cold leads proved effective in 2004, and in 2005 the company is extending this to include all of the following:

–   existing users (loyalty)

–   Sage resellers (referrals)

–   cold leads (sales leads)

–   opt-in list (sales leads)

The Competitive Landscape

The company has based itself as THE provider of Expenses Software to SMEs. However, it is clear that the corporate market, where the market leader is Concur, is by far the largest segment to aim for. Signifo is now moving into the USA market and will be competing in the mid-sized market sector. It is also trying to build strategic alliances with other foreign suppliers so that the company becomes more internationally based than it is now. The DTI (UK Department of Trade and Industry) will offer help with this. See Appendix 3 for Sales and Marketing Information and Competitor Profiles.

Branding

Branding in B2B markets tends to be different from developing consumer brands, as many issues need to be taken into account. Various strategies are possible:

Brand Architecture
Effective business-to-business branding establishes a strong corporate or competency platform that supports multiple products and audiences, and links to the organisation's business strategies.

Co-Branding
When developing business-to-business marketing strategies, many organisations join with others to leverage the value of their brands. This is often undertaken via joint marketing alliances, market development partnerships, or co-branding relationships. Co-branding can be achieved through:

• Licensing

• Ingredient branding

Page 16 of Signifo Expenses

- Composite branding

- Sponsorship

As Signifo develops its markets internationally, branding becomes increasingly important for it. The company has started to advertise on taxi receipts in London, as most users are likely to claim expenses.

Summary

The company is at an interesting position within the marketplace. There are resource issues in pursuing both small and mid-sized markets. The mid-sized market needs face-to-face meetings, necessitating a growth in the salesforce, with accompanying expenses. At the same time the international market is wide open. Currently, the international customer base has largely been built through UK customers expanding their use of the product to their overseas affiliates, or through customers contacting the company. The product will soon be US IRS compliant, which will allow the company to take a more proactive approach to increasing the international business, in particular in the USA. This will require extra resources and possibly the re-launch and re-branding of the products. Sector-specific marketing strategies could also be incorporated. For instance, the pharmaceutical industry has a very large salesforce, but the methodology for expense reporting can be quite complex, as the salesforce deals with doctors, retailers and the NHS (UK National Health Service), amongst others.

APPENDIX 1

Signifo Product Information

A simple upload once a month allows an organisation to populate its employees' claims with corporate credit card data, and for out-of-pocket expenses, a user can input claims online using an internet browser, the offline version, or by sending an SMS message from any mobile phone.

Pricing and return on investment
Pricing is based on a fee per user per month. Because Signifo Expenses provides both simple and rapid implementation and a very compelling pricing model, the return on investment is very high and the payback period is typically less than three months. You can calculate a return on investment and payback period for your organisation using the ROI calculator.

Benefits

Signifo Expenses delivers significant benefits in terms of cost savings through direct processing efficiency gains and increased control over travel and entertainment spending. In addition, there are substantial benefits in terms of employee goodwill.

Benefits at all levels of the organisation
Web-based expense claim automation solutions allow expense claims to be submitted, approved and processed electronically:

- Employees' claims can be populated with corporate credit card spending and out-of-pocket expense items can be submitted using any internet browser, the offline version or any mobile phone by sending an SMS text.

- Managers can approve claims electronically and are able to view a detailed analysis of where resources are being consumed, for which activities, on which clients and by whom.

- Comprehensive reports allow for upload to the general ledger, client recharging of expenses, VAT returns and Revenue and Customs reviews.

- The user-friendly interface and simplified user instructions ensure that minimal training is required.

Cost Savings and ROI Analysis
Signifo Expenses delivers cost savings in many ways:

- Travel and Entertainment Costs

  Travel and Entertainment spend typically falls by between 5% and 15% as a result of automating the expense claim process, according to US studies.

  Signifo Expenses allows a company to easily enforce compliance with its expense policy, resulting in lower travel and entertainment spend. Because the system provides transparency over the claims submitted, self-policing is more rigorous than with a paper-based process.

Page 18 of Signifo Expenses

APPENDIX 1

As consolidated claim data is available to the accounts department at the click of a button, trends in spending can be readily identified and addressed.

• Processing Costs

Expense claim automation delivers cost savings that allow finance-decision makers to calculate cost reductions and justify an investment from an ROI perspective.

Here are some independent statistics that show what you can expect to achieve with an automated expense claims process:

– average time to complete an expense claim falls by 60%

– average cost to process an expense claim falls by 80%

– average time to settle an expense claim falls by up to 90%

(Source: Aberdeen Group)

By capturing data at source, Signifo Expenses reduces the time taken to compile, submit, approve and account for expense claims.

A return on investment (ROI) calculation, based on studies by American Express and Ernst & Young, suggests that the reduction in total processing costs can be as much as 50%.

To calculate the processing efficiency gains for your organisation, use the ROI calculator.

VAT Reclaim

Companies registered for VAT in one country in the European Union are entitled to reclaim much of the travel and entertainment spend in other member countries. However, many companies do not claim such VAT refunds because of the difficulties in collating the necessary data.

Signifo Expenses allows for more complete VAT reclaims by giving country-by-country data at the click of a button.

To automate the recovery of foreign VAT, Signifo Expenses has formed a partnership with a leading provider of automated VAT recovery and reporting services. You can read more about this service on the VAT reclaim page.

Client/Project Recharging

Signifo Expenses allows claim data associated with a particular client or project to be viewed on a consolidated basis. This allows for easy recharging of expenses as appropriate.

Vendor Negotiation

A vendor list captures spending to key vendors (e.g. hotel chains, rental car companies, taxi companies). This consolidated data allows for the negotiation of lower prices from such vendors. Companies that use an expense claim automation solution can expect to pay 10% less for goods and services through improved purchase negotiations

(Source: Aberdeen Group).

APPENDIX 2

Internet Application Service Providers (ASPs)

Defining an Internet ASP

In most cases, the term ASP has come to denote companies that supply software applications and/or software-related services over the Internet.

Here are the most common features of an ASP:

* The ASP owns and operates a software application.

* The ASP owns, operates and maintains the servers that run the application. The ASP also employs the people needed to maintain the application.

* The ASP makes the application available to customers everywhere via the Internet, either in a browser or through some sort of 'thin client'.

The ASP bills for the application either on a per-use basis or on a monthly/annual fee basis. In many cases, however, the ASP can provide the service for free or will even pay the customer. This is the case with Signifo.

Advantages of ASPs

The ASP model has evolved because it offers some significant advantages over traditional approaches. Here are some of the most important advantages:

* Especially for small businesses and startups, the biggest advantage is low cost of entry and, in most cases, an extremely short setup time.

* The pay-as-you-go model is often significantly less expensive for all but the most frequent users of the service.

* The ASP model, as with any outsourcing arrangement, eliminates head count. IT headcount tends to be very expensive and very specialised, so this is frequently advantageous.

* The ASP model also eliminates specialised IT infrastructure for the application as well as supporting applications. For example, if the application you want to use requires an Oracle or MS-SQL database, you would have to support both the application and the database.

* The ASP model can shift Internet bandwidth to the ASP, who can often provide it at lower cost.

One thing that led to the growth of ASPs is the high cost of specialised software. As the costs grow, it becomes nearly impossible for a small business to afford to purchase the software, so the ASP makes using the software possible.

Another important factor leading to the development of ASPs has been the growing complexity of software and software upgrades. Distributing huge, complex applications to the end user has become extremely expensive from a customer service standpoint, and upgrades make the problem worse. In a large company where there may be thousands of desktops, distributing software (even something as simple as a new release of Microsoft Word) can cost millions of dollars. The ASP model eliminates most of these headaches.

(Source: http://computer.howstuffworks.com/asp4.htm)

APPENDIX 2

The Guardian, Thursday 28 April 2005

BUSINESS SOLUTIONS
Web trading: How to fish for business on the web
by Guy Clapperton

If you have followed e-commerce since the dawn of the web, you'll know – perhaps to your cost – that fashions have changed over the years. Once it was all about 'virtual malls' and portal placement. Then content was king. And then many businesses discovered that, in fact, a straightforward site, properly set up to appeal to search engines, would do their businesses just fine.

Of course, many businesses have no website at all, and may still be nervously eyeing the prospect. But the good news is that while the rules may have changed, it's not too late to catch up. First, they're not alone: according to PayPal, 51% of small retailers don't actually have a website at all. Of those that do, 35% have them simply to match the competition.

If you have a website, or want to set one up, there are a number of ground rules and even a couple of obligations to bear in mind. David Needham, consultant for business internet company Datanet, is clear: "The first step for an SME is to ensure that its site meets with the Disability Discrimination Act 1995. It's also imperative that the site has been written to standards approved by the World Wide Web Consortium, and has good grammar so that it can be translated without a problem, whether into a foreign language or by a reading aid for the blind."

Why? Because most of your visitors will likely come via a search engine – and they will usually look for sites that have been coded in line with these guidelines, too, he says. To check a site, log on to validator.w3.org/ and type the full web address you want to check into the address field.

This kind of compliance, done properly, is not cheap – either it costs a lot of money to do, or you end up spending a lot of time on it yourself. Once you've done so and your site is legal and standard, assuming it's clear enough and the design is relatively easy to look at, many companies would consider their site a prime asset.

It's surprising, then, to talk to people who have their own website with full e-commerce catered for (meaning a shopping cart, encryption for credit cards and an automated payment into a bank account) who are also using eBay as part of their online presence. Some use it to sell end-of-line stock and cut their losses, for instance.

Alex Bosch, however, owns tropicalfish4u.co.uk – fully specced up with a web 'shop' from Actinic – but sells 80% of his goods, including live fish, through the auction route. "Basically a lot of people trust eBay more than they'd trust a site they haven't heard of," he says. "And a lot of people go to eBay – the sheer volume of traffic of people looking for a particular item works in your favour."

Once he had his own site established, that served as much to validate the eBay sales as to generate sales in its own right, he says. "Obviously once people saw that they could bid

APPENDIX 2

for the same goods on eBay and get them more cheaply, they did so. The cost of selling on eBay is greater than selling direct but the volumes and the trust are good – and people often have a PayPal account with money in it, so it's like having spare money they wouldn't otherwise spend."

Using a service such as eBay in this way is perhaps a surprising thing to do as many people would expect a 'serious' business not to go through a consumer site, but it clearly works wonders in this case.

There are other new technical tricks that can help your business look bigger than it actually is, if that matters particularly to your customers. Alison Baron, director of custom uniform manufacturer Lookfly, regards the blogging site at lookflynews.com as an excellent source of customer goodwill. The business sells specialist sports equipment in the Ultimate Frisbee line, and the news site reports on what's happening in the sport. It gives the same sort of effect as a major sponsorship, she reckons. And, moreover, customers come back to your site not just to buy things but also for information – the site becomes 'sticky', to use a net retail cliche.

But just as there are lots of tools to use on or around your site, there are lots of ways to come unstuck. This is why companies such as WebTrends offer analytical tools to show you exactly what's happening on your site. They stress the basics; your site should feel as though it's come from your company and nowhere else. "The idea that it can be changed by someone else is like logging on to the Guardian and finding news from the Daily Mail and The Sun," says Conrad Bennett, technical services manager for EMEA at WebTrends.

His company urges people to use tools such as Web Analytics and usability testing – you may not have any partially sighted customers at the moment, for example, but you won't want to exclude them inadvertently if they arrive. As much as anything, it's illegal.

Bennett warns against third parties designing and updating sites without a good brief. Everything a good analytical tool can do has to be backed up by the in-depth knowledge of the site's owner, he says.

> "The danger with third-party or end-user customisation of the experience is that site owners may find themselves unable to answer questions using just their knowledge of the site," he says. "For example, bottlenecks in a purchasing process can be resolved by examining the page concerned then designing and testing alternatives. However, if you don't know what the customer actually experienced, this becomes significantly more difficult."

Essentially the best advice on websites is to start by disregarding many of the thoughts that were around when the web first became popular, at which point many of the 'dotcom boom' companies assumed that standard business rules didn't apply to the internet. They do, and the kiss principle – Keep It Simple and Straightforward – applies to even the biggest sites. Just look at Amazon, where you can buy whatever you want in whichever category and the checkout page will look the same in whichever country you're buying from.

Page 22 of Signifo Expenses

APPENDIX 2

Other useful rules include staying in control, complying with the regulations and maintaining a look that is in line with the rest of your business. And don't discount ideas because some people think they won't look professional – selling through eBay, for instance, brackets you alongside home-based sellers of old clothes and furry collectables, but it's doing a lot of businesses a lot of good too.

"You've got to be clear about what you want the customer to do to make you lots of money"

Mark Chapman is managing director of Photobox, which sells prints at a low cost (10p each) of files sent from your digital camera. It started as a classic small business working from someone's bedroom, which was possible because Chapman had a technical background in the first place. "We figured out what the service should offer and what it should look like, designed it on the back of an envelope and contracted out. We were funded by 25 individuals we knew and to whom we'd put the proposition, so we were in the fortunate position of being able to contract some of the work out."

He says there are two key elements to a successful website. "There's the customer proposition – you've got to be clear about what you want the customer to do to make you lots of money, and what's going to bring them back, and the next thing is about choosing an appropriate toolset. It's a matter of working out which bits of it are cost-effective to implement and which aren't."

Cost-effectiveness works in any business area, but a lot of people forget it when it comes to the internet. The other element they often overlook is the flexibility the internet offers. "Be prepared to change things," he says. "The great thing about the internet is that you get feedback in buckets, much more than any other retailer could hope for."

The other thing to look at is timing. Chapman started in 2000 but it took two years to pull into profit because the business relies on broadband, which took its time to get implemented fully in the UK.

© Copyright Guardian Newspapers Ltd 2005

APPENDIX 2

Thought Leadership

On Demand Software:
From Revolution to Evolution
by K.B. 'Chandra' Chandrasekhar, CEO Jamcracker Inc.

New market demands create opportunities and challenges for software companies

'On Demand Software Delivery' describes software delivered to the customer via a network (like the internet) as a service. This was originally a revolutionary concept in the late 1990's. The software market is now in an evolutionary stage as businesses and the software vendors serving them become serious about On Demand Software Delivery. The current market has proven that On Demand Delivery is in demand now and demand will grow substantially in the coming years. Research firm IDC predicts that by 2008, subscription license revenues will hit $43 billion worldwide, or 34% of the total software market.

Jamcracker Inc. was a pioneer during the initial revolution with a clear and simple vision: allow business to consume applications like a utility via the On Demand model. The vision was clear and simple, but as the first major player in this new model, Jamcracker found the implementation complex and difficult.

Jamcracker has taken all it has learned about delivering software On Demand – from a business, operational, and engineering perspective – and developed an On Demand Enablement Kit to assist software vendors and in developing their own On Demand solutions.

While On Demand software delivery prevents many of the headaches that installed packages create for the customer, it presents new headaches for software vendors as they try to figure out how to deliver cost effective On Demand Solutions.

With only a few 'established' On Demand vendors, this is uncharted territory for most software companies, but market demands will require all of them to venture into this model. What follows are some of the best practices Jamcracker established for successfully deploying On Demand Software delivery.

Business Model Challenges

Software companies must create a plan for successful introduction of On Demand solutions through new channels without distracting existing channels or cannibalizing existing license sales opportunities. They must also have a good grasp of how the new model will increase top line revenue.

Developing new distribution channels for On Demand solutions is key to increasing top line revenue. To develop new On Demand channels Jamcracker advises software companies to:

- Minimise capital required for partners to begin selling the solution

- Maximise partner's ability to independently demonstrate and extend the product

Page 24 of Signifo Expenses

APPENDIX 2

- Ensure partners can manage the implementation process and own the move-add-change (MAC) requirements not handled by the customer

- Allow partners to build value-added services on top of your solution by bundling their own services or by adding business process/vertical expertise

To avoid distracting existing channels or hurting existing license sales, Jamcracker recommends targeting new markets like small business by creating a lower entry price point and a pay-as-you-go model. You can also simplify the product to better serve limited IT staffs. Simplifying the product and restricting the functionality will also prevent overlap with existing and future licensed products.

To help software companies simulate the delivery of a set of offerings in the On Demand delivery model, Jamcracker has developed a business-modeling tool as part of its On Demand Enablement Kit. The business-modeling tool includes ways to analyze projected adoption rates in conjunction with pricing, product mix, and channel mix variables.

The model also aids in estimating the cost infrastructure as the business begins to scale and user counts rise. The model includes a P&L statement, a channel partner P&L statement, and key metrics including breakeven point and cash out requirements. Software vendors developing an on demand solution must consider all of these business factors as part of their planning if they wish to be successful with this evolving delivery method.

Operation's Challenges

An effective and flexible Operations Infrastructure is critical. The operational infrastructure and associated management are the greatest contributors to cost of goods sold and the most difficult to manage. For an effective infrastructure, you must have standardization of processes, increased automation, improved accuracy and lower component costs:

- Standardize key administrative workflow processes at the onset and refine them over time; Jamcracker doesn't recommend a phased approach requiring new tools and process as you begin to achieve volume – a crucial time to be efficient and not burdened with managing change

- Build automation into as many tasks as possible to speed task completion, reduce personnel costs and minimise costly human errors in the order-to-bill processes

- Improve the accuracy of common processes; errors are expensive and lead to customer dissatisfaction; for processes not easily automated, strive to simplify the workflow and implement better process checks; review all of your non-standard cases where high error rates are common

- Deploy your infrastructure on 'commercial off the shelf' products wherever possible to help keep costs down; research solutions that support Linux and other open source components, as they are now mature and reliable and can be deployed at much lower costs than comparable Unix and Windows systems

On Demand Software delivery will continue to evolve faster than the rest of the IT market. You must be able to adjust your offering quickly. Whether you are adding new

APPENDIX 2

distribution channels or new On Demand solutions, flexibility will separate the best providers from the rest.

Most software vendors want On Demand solutions to expand their available market, often through new channels. Your infrastructure must be flexible enough to allow channel partners to resell and re-brand your On Demand offering. In addition to creating an infrastructure that can support your channels, it should integrate with the customer's own infrastructure (especially for the large-enterprise sale) and it should have the ability to delegate user management and application administration:

- Design your infrastructure to deploy new services and add new providers easily allowing you to broaden your portfolio and allowing downstream partners to sell their own solutions in addition to your On Demand offering – all from a single instance of the infrastructure

- Ensure integration with the customer's existing infrastructure if you want to sell to larger enterprises; you must support connectivity to a customer or partner's directory, HRIS system or other user profile data source as a standard process

- Build in the ability to activate new users and manage MAC work through multiple methods to lower costs and increase customer satisfaction; the ability to delegate administration of MAC functions is a key to customer satisfaction

For its own managed services business, Jamcracker built an integrated platform, designed to maximise efficiency and flexibility in the operational aspects of delivering On Demand solutions. Jamcracker now sells the platform, called Pivot Path, as a commercial software product designed to assist software vendors to easily transition to an On Demand Software Delivery model. With Pivot Path Jamcracker reduced operating expenses for its managed service business by 65%.

Pivot Path fuses the key operational processes of user management, provisioning, and service management with a flexible integration framework. This On Demand Delivery Platform is capable of automating many or all of the administrative tasks associated with the order-to-bill business processes required to support the On Demand business model.

Application Architecture Challenges

Software vendors must develop versions of existing and future products that support multi-tenancy at the business logic, data, and administrative levels. As with any new complicated infrastructure and architecture designs, Jamcracker recommends seeking consulting services from companies with domain expertise and to keep the following in mind when developing your application architecture:

- Build a reusable set of administrative components for on boarding users and managing MAC, this is critical even before your application is business logic and data multi-tenant.

- Leverage a common set of services for user access management across each software instance in your managed service environment; this is critical for your On Demand solution, but less important for software installed within the enterprise

Page 26 of Signifo Expenses

APPENDIX 2

- Architect your solution so channel partners can 'own' their own customer implementation and MAC work; this is vital for cost containment and enables channel partners to maintain a close relationship with their customer

- Address both application data levels and business process levels of integration within your design; the application data level is where customers will integrate your solution with other applications in their environment; the business process level is where customers will integrate your user add and delete business processes with their existing directory or HRIS system

- It is important to keep the above in mind as you develop your On Demand solution. As with any IT infrastructure architecture design it is best to seek the services of a consultant like Jamcracker with a solid foundation in On Demand Software Delivery that can help you design a near – and long-term, scalable architecture for your On Demand strategy.

Who Will Lead The Evolution?

On Demand Software Delivery is here and it will grow substantially in the coming years. Recent announcements by nearly all of the biggest software vendors about On Demand Software Delivery shows that the success of companies like SalesForce.com and RightNow Technologies has caught everyone's attention – customers and software vendors alike. You know who started the revolution, which software companies will evolve to be the leaders?

(Source: http://www.softwaremag.com/L.cfm?doc=1204-ThoughtLeadership-k_Chandrasekhar)

About the Author:

K.B. Chandrasekhar ('Chandra') is co-founder, CEO and Chairman of the Board of Jamcracker. His career as a high technology entrepreneur has spanned Exodus Communications, Fouress Inc., Rolta India, Ltd and Wipro. He is also the co-founder and Chairman of the Board of e4e, Inc., a global technology holding company. For more information, go to: www.jamcracker.com

APPENDIX 2

Thought Leadership

The Business Case for Wireless Software Applications in the Enterprise
by Iain Gillott

Wireless and mobile solutions have moved up in priority for CIOs, who see financial benefit and opportunity to gain a competitive edge.

Over the last 20 years of the wireless industry, little attention has been paid to the return on investment (ROI) offered by wireless and mobile solutions. Justifying wireless voice, messaging or data services has not been a priority for a variety of reasons: the employee was responsible for procuring the services and expensed the cost back to the company; the employee traveled extensively and wireless communications were considered a basic necessity; or the assumption was made that the wireless solution would provide a competitive advantage and was therefore justified.

In the last couple of years, wireless and mobile solutions have moved nearer to the top of the CIO's 'to do' list. Naturally, more attention is being given to cost issues that have become complicated in direct proportion to the variety and number of products, services, devices, and software offered to support efforts within enterprises to provide wireless access to corporate data and applications. CIOs are now starting to ask more difficult questions and they want more detailed information before signing off on a wireless project. The recent global economic slowdown has intensified this situation.

Throughout late summer and fall of 2001, iGillottResearch prepared 35 case studies of major companies and corporations that were using wireless and mobile applications as part of their business. Using data from these studies, we then prepared a detailed ROI model to show the financial costs and benefits of various mobile applications. This research has continued into 2002 with additional case studies. The results show that given the right circumstances, wireless and mobile applications can be very productive and efficient, even today when the market is in an early stage.

While skeptics may say that implementing a wireless and mobile application is not worthwhile, the results show that there are some very real financial benefits, and that many companies are realizing increased competitive advantage through the use of mobile applications.

Many companies today are making use of wireless and mobile solutions – they are just not talking about it. Given the very real financial benefits, with the resulting competitive advantage, many companies we approached were reluctant to talk about their solutions and the benefits they were seeing. They simply did not want their competitors to see what they were doing, call up the same vendors, and say "Do for me what you did for them!" For this reason, some companies we profiled wished to remain anonymous.

All of the 35 companies we interviewed deployed wireless with a clear vision of the benefits. All of the companies have incorporated wireless into the total business planning process whether the implementation is for SFA, CRM or work force automation. Not all

Page 28 of Signifo Expenses

APPENDIX 2

companies know exactly where their wireless strategy will take them, but the need to get wireless and mobile capabilities into the business processes and to be ahead of the technology curve is judged critical to future planning. This is an important point – for these companies, their mobile solutions have become as indispensable as their LAN or PCs, and for this reason they have made wireless a part of their everyday planning session. Wireless is not an adjunct or an extra to these companies – wireless is part of the solution from the start.

Benefits Are Being Defined

The naysayers will say there are no real quantifiable benefits to wireless and mobile applications – they are wrong. One hundred percent wrong. All of the companies interviewed for the study identified some benefits with their solution and the majority had quantified the benefits, either in terms of payback period, dollars saved, or increased revenues.

Benefits can be divided into direct (or hard), where the benefits can be identified and quantified, and indirect (or soft), where the benefits are more tangential or harder to quantify.

Direct benefits we identified included

- Wireless LAN installation: $6,000 per doctor. Expected return: $90,000 per doctor.

- Two to three percent cost savings on first-fill prescriptions.

- Increased sales 10 to 20 percent

- 32 percent increase in service calls per day

- Service call responsiveness increased from 88 to 95 percent.

It is important to understand that these companies had moved beyond the trial phase and had 'production' systems. Thus these benefits were real, not just those that were imagined or anticipated for a future application.

Indirect or soft benefits were also identified – these varied widely, from "improved corporate brand image" to "increased customer credibility" and "spending less time to close deals, means more time for new deals."

Payback Periods

The longest payback period was 30 months. Most, especially for e-mail and calendaring, were in just a few months – payback periods between four and six months were typical. Sales force application implementations expected additional revenue from the sales force – several companies commented that a single additional sale would justify the implementation. Thus, in general, the payback periods are more attractive when additional revenues can be incorporated into the analysis.

Factors that affect the payback period, in addition to the obvious costs and benefits, are:

- If users are able to use their existing mobile device without change or just by adding a wireless modem.

APPENDIX 2

- If the application can be effectively used with a mobile handset compared to the need for a Personal Digital Assistant (PDA)

- If the mobile system is an extension of an existing corporate or enterprise application.

It was specifically stated by several companies, particularly large ones with a high number of transactions, high value transactions, or time critical services, that any system that can increase the flow of information and reduce costs, even by a few cents or minutes per transaction, makes a large difference in the bottom line.

Multiple Vendors in a Single Solution

Excluding mentions of mobile operators and devices, a total of 48 vendors were mentioned that are being used to implement wireless initiatives – just for the 35 companies in the study. It is evident that successful wireless implementations require a significant amount of research to select the technologies that are most appropriate to the business and consumer environments in which they will be used. And multiple vendors are usually required to complete the task – few companies can do it all.

Likewise, the most suitable vendors must also be selected. Given that each implementation involves multiple vendors, it is important that the vendors are able to effectively work together, sometimes through a systems integrator. Our research therefore supports the premise that the strength of a single vendor is assessed by the strength of its partnerships.

Wireless and mobile solutions are made more complex by the fact that a service provider and device manufacturer must be involved. For companies that chose to be their own systems integrator, they had to deal with at least three vendors (service provider, device manufacturer, and application/solution provider), usually more. Some vendors offer turnkey solutions but may not have relationships with service providers – this simplifies the task for the enterprise somewhat.

Trials and Testing

Testing of new systems and applications is necessary and time consuming but it has to be done. Some of the IT professionals interviewed felt that more resources could have been used in testing the wireless and mobile implementation. For the most part, the process was completed with only a few, overextended IT professionals.

Several month-long user trials of the mobile application were also a common tactic. Some companies chose to trial among a small segment of users. Several companies, particularly those with national sales force automation and e-commerce strategies, have chosen to effect a geographic rollout of the application to track effectiveness, demands on the system, content relevance, and costs.

Many companies also realized that wireless and mobile applications required more, or different, testing. For example, if the enterprise were deploying a wireless solution in a warehouse with a metal roof, it would be a good idea to test inside and outside – everywhere the application would be used. Radio frequency signals do not like metal buildings!

APPENDIX 2
_____

Devices should also be tested with a full, partial and low battery charge. Does the modem actually work when the battery charge is very low? Or does it require a certain charge to connect? All of these eventualities should be tested.

IP and Internet Strategies

Major corporations have invested heavily in Internet Protocol (IP), Internet and intranet technologies in the last five years – the rise of companies like BEA, Sun Microsystems, Oracle, and many others demonstrates the power of this spending. The wireless industry is now benefiting from that investment. From the case studies we completed, it was clear that companies had less difficulty and lower initial costs when successful, existing Internet-based strategies were leveraged into the mobile solution.

Several companies commented that they expected the wireless and mobile application to use industry open standards and not use proprietary interfaces or protocols. In the past, the wireless data industry has relied on closed, proprietary systems, but this no longer needs to be the case. By using open standards for networking and programming, the ROI of the solutions is increased since the implementation and ongoing maintenance costs for IT will be lower – the corporation will by and large be able to use its own IT department to maintain the application.

Wireless Services and Devices

Bad news for fans of the Palm OS – the evidence from the case studies is that the Pocket PC platform is becoming a more popular platform. Older implementations supported Palm but most new applications support Pocket PC – companies commented on the processing power, display and browser as strengths of the platform. This does not mean that Palm devices are not used extensively in the business environment (they are of course) but rather that many of the new wireless and mobile applications being deployed require more horsepower and the Pocket PC platform provides this.

The most common mobile operators mentioned were Sprint PCS and Palm.net (for the Palm VII). But many companies also made the comment that the wireless networks are disjointed, with multiple standards and operators needed to cover a region.

Many implementations used wireless LANs – this is likely to grow in interest in the next few years, especially for applications that can use synchronization throughout the day, rather than a real-time connection. With the growth of wireless LAN deployments in "hotspots," such as hotels, conference centers and airports, we can expect that many more examples of enterprise wireless LAN implementations will emerge in the next couple of years.

Mobile Versus Wireless

One final point worth noting: mobile does not necessarily mean "wireless connection" as well. Some good examples used simple desktop synchronization to take information into the field, reference the information throughout the day, and then resynchronize in the evening. These types of solutions can be very simple and very powerful – the question then becomes how much better can these solutions be when wirelessly enabled?

The ability to work off-line, when not connected to the wireless network is critical. Several companies commented that their choice of vendor was dependent on this capability.

APPENDIX 2

Implementation Issues

Each of the profiles includes some details of problems faced during the wireless and mobile implementation. While some good points were raised, it should be remembered that these companies were successful with their implementations – we did not profile companies who had failed. These issues need to be addressed by the vendors or wireless industry – while they did not prevent implementation in these cases, no doubt concerns of this type have contributed to other projects being delayed or cancelled.

Business Drivers: Before the physical implementation actually starts, it is important that the technologies be carefully researched and that there is a good answer to the questions: "Why are we doing this? Does it benefit the customer, the business or both?" If those responsible for the implementation are unable to answer these questions, then the implementation is unlikely to be a success. The project must have a clear business goal and benefits – if the implementation is just to test new technology or to prove a concept, then it will not be successful commercially.

Another issue raised was to ensure that the project requirements are completely fulfilled so the benefits can be made available to the whole organization, rather than just a few select users. This, of course, applies to any large-scale IT implementation.

Wireless Services: There were several comments made by the profiled companies about the need for better wireless data services, both for bandwidth and for coverage. This point addresses the very real need to set realistic expectations for the application. Education by the industry for the decision-makers and users should therefore be a priority.

Comments were also made about the need to control wireless communications costs. If the company is using rate plans with a usage component, then this could be an issue.

One company mentioned the need for common interfaces into all of the operators' networks – it seems that some operators have non-standard interfaces, which caused problems.

Devices: While there were few comments on the devices being supported, there were a couple of key points:

- The need to support mobile applications from any mobile device is very real.

- To get the best returns out of some mobile applications, some companies realized that they would have to deploy PDAs with additional features and processing power. This would raise the cost of the implementation but may be required to realize some of the additional benefits.

Architecture: Most of the issues raised during implementation were around the architecture. Since the mobile architecture must interface with the enterprise IT systems, it is a critical element (at least until wireless and mobile capabilities are built into the core of every IT system). Issues raised include:

- The need to control the volume of mobile transactions, so as not to overload the mobile system.

APPENDIX 2

- The need for open standards was stressed several times, so that the enterprise can leverage existing investments in e-business and e-CRM.

- The need to focus on systems that can provide much of the applications in the form of canned or software-based tools to reduce the need for custom programming and maintenance.

- The need to implement core infrastructure that can be easily, centrally administrated by the IT operations group or outsourced.

Usability: Application usability is a critical issue for successful mobile implementations. In addition to ensuring the applications are easy to use, the data presented and required must be critical to the user and not cluttered by "nice to have" information. The sensitivity to this last issue is dependent on the size of the mobile device's screen.

Security: Concerns were raised by a couple of the companies profiled. The specific concerns raised were with wireless access to e-mail and the need to provide secure access to multiple applications from a variety of mobile devices. Balancing the need for security while maintaining an environment built on open standards that is easily maintained was also noted.

Recommendations

Based on the profiles conducted for this project, iGillottResearch prepared a set of recommendations for vendors offering wireless and mobile application solutions. While some of these recommendations may seem obvious, the profiles show that some vendors in the industry are not addressing these points:

Value Propositions: Many of the case studies indicate payback periods on the initial investment of just a few months. These short payback periods suggest that the industry is leaving some money on the table when working with enterprises. Of course, having said that, we recognize that closing deals in late 2001 and early 2002 has been difficult. However, adopting a fire-sale pricing strategy will be damaging to vendors' long-term profitability.

For those vendors in a position to play for the long term, the answer is to restructure the pricing models to reduce the upfront license payment and add an ongoing enterprise or per seat payment. This will spread the investment required over the length of the contract, lower the upfront investment required, but also, of course, commit the enterprise to frequent payments. Pricing should also be based on the number of users and, where possible, the value of the transactions or application. For example, if possible, tying the price to increased sales revenues would be highly desirable. While determining the sales benefit that can be attributed to the mobile application can be difficult, including bonus payments for the vendor that are tied to increased sales should be possible.

Of course, this is an ideal situation. But the fact remains that more of the value of the wireless and mobile solution can be realized through a pricing scheme that includes frequent payments over a longer period.

For the vendor, the balance must be between an ongoing revenue stream and getting payment upfront. This is a balance – we are not suggesting that an initial payment be

APPENDIX 2

forfeited entirely in lieu of an ongoing pricing scheme. This would then mean that the enterprise has little invested in the project – they need some skin in the game as well!

Ability to Partner: It is clear that mobile vendors must demonstrate a proven ability to partner with other companies to provide the total solution. No one, and we mean no one, can provide a complete solution alone – everyone needs somebody else. The strength of a vendor is therefore measured not only by their solution, but also by the abilities of their partners.

A wide range of partners is not required – what enterprises require is a complete solution. It is therefore important that the partners contribute to the complete solution, while minimizing overlap.

Wireless Devices: Vendor solutions should support as wide a range of mobile devices as possible – several companies commented that they needed to support the existing devices that employees used, both to reduce implementation costs and to improve usability. Microsoft's Pocket PC platform is also becoming more popular and was mentioned by several enterprises as being the mobile computing platform of choice (it should be noted that Microsoft was not a sponsor of this project – in any way).

Browsers: Applications that allow the use of a standard browser on the mobile device were also popular – vendor solutions should therefore be browser-based wherever possible. As well as reducing costs, using the browser also allows the use of multiple mobile devices.

Working While Disconnected: The ability to work off-line, when not connected to the wireless network is critical – this should be a capability of most applications, if it is not already. Having said that, it is harder to implement this type of solution. This is an area where some vendors may need to partner with companies that provide synchronization capabilities.

Open Standards: The use of open standards by vendor solutions is a critical requirement. Several companies noted the use of open standards throughout the solution. Open standards contribute to improved scalability, portability, maintainability, manageability, and operability, as well as a potentially reduced total cost of ownership. If the vendor solution makes extensive use of open standards, promote it. If proprietary standards are used, re-architect the solution.

(Source: http://www.softwaremag.com/l.cfm?doc=2002-SpringEdition/2002Vol22Iss1/2002-Spring-wireless)

285 BPP
PROFESSIONAL EDUCATION

APPENDIX 2

Survey: Information Technology

If in doubt, farm it out

28th October 2004

From The Economist print edition

The ultimate solution to simplifying your datacentre is not to have one at all

EVERY self-respecting technology vendor these days not only vigorously deplores complexity but also claims to have a solution, and a suitably dramatic name for it to boot. Thus, Hewlett-Packard (HP) talks about its vision for the 'adaptive enterprise', helped by HP simplification software called OpenView. IBM trumpets the dawn of 'on-demand' IT for companies through IBM's 'autonomic computing' architecture. EDS, an IT consultancy, offers the 'agile enterprise'. Hitachi has 'harmonious computing'. Forrester, a research firm, suggests 'organic IT'. Sun tempts with a shrewdly mysterious name, 'N1'. Dell has 'dynamic computing' and Microsoft flaunts the grand-sounding 'dynamic systems initiative'.

All these marketing buzzwords imply a promise to hide the complexity of firms' datacentres in the same way that modern cars and planes hide their technological complexity from drivers and pilots. This is hard to argue with. At the same time, the grand titles raise expectations to an exalted level. Words such as 'organic' and 'autonomic' intentionally invite comparisons with biological systems whose complexity is hidden from the creatures living within them. The implication is that digital technology can achieve the same feat.

Take, for instance, IBM's autonomic-computing initiative, launched in 2002 by Alan Ganek, an IBM executive, and now the most ambitious proposal on offer. The label is currently attached to about 50 distinct IBM products with over 400 product features. In the longer term, however, IBM is hoping to bring computing to a level where it mimics the autonomic nervous system of the human body. This is what regulates breathing, digestion, blood-sugar levels, temperature, pancreatic function, immune responses to germs and so on, automatically and without the people concerned being conscious of these processes. It is, in a way, nature's gold standard of virtualisation software and complexity concealment, which is why IBM bagged the metaphor.

What IBM actually means by 'autonomic' in a computing context, Mr Ganek explains, comes down to four technological goals. The first is to make computers and networks 'self-configuring'. Whereas today IT staff walk around and manually perform tasks such as plugging CDs into computers or fiddling with command lines, IBM wants the hardware and software itself to figure out what settings are missing and to install them automatically.

The second step is to make the systems 'self-healing'. Thus, the network should diagnose problems automatically – for example, by noticing a crashed computer and rebooting it. Whereas today IT staff can easily take several weeks to diagnose a problem by manually sorting through logs, autonomic computing can get it done without human intervention in about 40 minutes, says Mr Ganek.

The third goal, Mr Ganek continues, is to make systems 'self-optimising'. This means that

APPENDIX 2

the network should know how to balance processing workloads among the various servers and storage computers so that none is idle or swamped. And the final step is to make the whole network 'self-protecting'. The system, in other words, should be able to anticipate, hunt down and kill computer viruses and worms all by itself; to tell spam from legitimate e-mail; and to prevent 'phishing' and other data theft.

A pinch of salt

The vision is shockingly ambitious. If it ever becomes reality, IBM (or HP, or whoever gets there first) will in essence have achieved what it has taken millions of years of natural evolution to do in the analogue, biological world. Not surprisingly, many experts are sceptical, pointing to the parallel with artificial intelligence (AI), which boffins confidently described as imminent in the 1950s but which remains elusive to this day. Mr Coburn at UBS says the talk of autonomic computing reminds him "of a high-school science fair", and thinks it may be just another one of those things that IT vendors "throw on the wall to see what sticks".

Buried deep underneath the guff, however, there is indeed a technology widely considered to have the potential for radical simplification. Like the wheel, the zip fastener and other breakthrough technologies, it looks deceptively basic at first sight. Even its name, 'web services', is so vague that vendors find it hard to build any hype for a lay audience around it.

The best way to understand web services is to stop thinking of either 'webs' or 'services' and instead to picture Lego blocks. These little Danish plastic toy bricks come in different colours, shapes and sizes, but all Lego blocks have the same standardised studs and corresponding holes that allow them to be assembled, taken apart and reassembled in all sorts of creative ways. The magic of web services, in effect, is to turn almost any fiddly piece in any chaotic datacentre into a Lego block, so that it can snugly fit together with all the other fiddly bits. Thus, datacentres that consist of decades of legacy systems and lots of incompatible machines can now be snapped together and apart, Lego by Lego.

In place of studs and holes, web services use standardised software that wraps itself around existing computer systems. These wrappers do several things. First, they describe what the component inside is and what it does. Then they post this description to a directory that other computers can browse. This allows those other computers – which can belong either to the same company or to independent suppliers and customers – to find and use the software inside the wrapper.

This removes the main bottleneck that scuppered business-to-business computing during the dotcom bubble. "The whole B2B boom died for one simple reason: nobody could get their damn systems to talk together," says Halsey Minor, the founder of Grand Central Communications, a start-up that uses web services to stitch datacentres together. Now, he says, they do talk together.

Imagine, for example, that a company receives an electronic order. The software application that takes these orders must first ensure that the customer has an adequate credit history. It therefore consults a directory of web services, finds an application from an independent firm that checks credit ratings, contacts this application and finds out that the

APPENDIX 2

customer is a reliable debtor. Next, the software consults the directory again, this time to find an internal application that keeps track of inventory in the warehouse, and finds that the product is in store. Now it goes back to the directory and looks for an external billing service, and so forth until the entire transaction is closed.

Making a splat

As a way of simplifying computing, web services have been talked about for some time. Only in the past couple of years, however, has there been real progress in agreeing on the most vital aspect, the standards that will make every system look familiar to everybody else. A major breakthrough came in October 2003, when the industry's two superpowers, Microsoft and IBM, got up on a stage together and stated what protocols they intend to use. Collectively dubbed 'WS splat' in geeky circles, these are now being adopted by the rest of the industry.

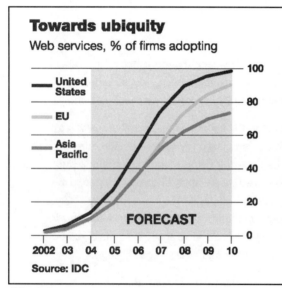

Chart 1

This has raised hopes for a huge increase in their use in the next few years (see chart 1). Ronald Schmelzer and Jason Bloomberg at ZapThink, a consultancy, think that web services are "nearing their tipping point", because they benefit from "the network effect: the adoption rate of the network increases in proportion to its utility." In other words, as with telephones or e-mail, a network with only a few people on it is not very useful; but as more people join it, it becomes exponentially more useful and thereby attracts even more members, and so on.

Taking the idea of web services to its logical extreme, it is reasonable to ask why firms should continue to amass their own piles of Lego blocks, most of which will only duplicate the Lego blocks of business partners. Put differently, why have a datacentre if all you want is the data? This is a fairly new idea in the IT industry, although in many established industries it has been around for a long time. People do not put safes into their basements but open bank accounts. Similarly, "most people shouldn't build their own aeroplanes", says Sun's Mr Papadopoulos. "They shouldn't even own them; in fact, they shouldn't even rent them; what they should do is rent a seat on one."

In IT, the equivalent of renting a seat on an aircraft is to rent software as a service from specialised firms called 'application service providers', or ASPs. These companies build huge datacentres so that other companies do not have to. The best-known ASP today is Salesforce.com, a San Francisco firm that made its debut on the stockmarket in June. As the name suggests, Salesforce.com specialises in software that salespeople use to keep track of their marketing leads and client information. Traditionally, firms buy this kind of software from vendors such as Siebel Systems, then try to integrate it into their own datacentres. With Salesforce.com, however, firms simply pay a monthly fee, from $65 per

APPENDIX 2

user, and go to Salesforce.com's website, just as they go to Amazon's when they want to shop for books, or eBay's to buy secondhand goods.

This arrangement makes a lot of things simpler. Users need to spend less time on training courses, because the interface – in essence, the web browser – is already familiar to them. "I can train the average customer in under 45 minutes on the phone", claims Marc Benioff, Salesforce.com's boss, adding that traditional software packages often take weeks to learn.

The IT staff of the firm using Salesforce.com also have less work to do. They do not have to install any new software on the firm's own computers, and can leave Salesforce.com to worry about integrating its software with the client's other systems. Even upgrading the software becomes much easier. Instead of shipping boxes of CDs to its customers, Salesforce.com simply shuts down its system for a few hours on a weekend night, and when clients log on again on Monday morning they see the new version in their browsers.

As an industry, ASPs got off to a bad start. The first generation, which sprang up during the dotcom boom, had trouble integrating their applications with their clients' legacy systems, and ended up re-creating the complexity of their clients' datacentres in their own basements. When the dotcom bubble burst, says Mr Lane at Kleiner Perkins Caufield & Byers in Silicon Valley, those early ASPs collapsed "because we VCs wouldn't invest in them any more".

The second generation, however, seems to have cracked the problem of integration, thanks to web services, and is now picking off segments of the software market one by one. IDC estimates that ASPs' overall revenues will grow from $3 billion last year to $9 billion by 2008. As Grand Central's Mr Minor sees it, that puts IT today on the same path as other technologies in history, as "complexity gets concentrated in the middle of the network, while the edge gets simple".

© The Economist Newspaper Limited, London (28 October 2004)

APPENDIX 3

Signifo Sales and Marketing Information

Marketing and Sales Data

Average customer size	50 users
Average revenue per user	£6.60 per month
Average customer life	36 months

Marketing and Lead Generation Activities

Activity	Year to March 2005
Direct marketing	
Mailings	20,000
Outsourced telemarketing	15,000
Email marketing	6,000
Pay-per-click advertising	
Google Ads	17,000
Other	8,000
Magazine advertising	
Accounting trade press	21,000
Other magazines	14,000
Other	
Exhibitions	22,000
Public relations	16,000
Taxi receipts	12,000
Website	8,000
Referral scheme (awards)	8,000
Sales Materials	4,000
Directory listings	3,000
TOTAL	**£174,000**

APPENDIX 3

Signifo Accounts

Profit and Loss Account

	Year to March 2005
Ordinary Income/Expense	
Income	
Sales	1499595
Total Income	1499595
Cost of Goods Sold	
Hosting	67471
Related services	893
Total COGS	68364
Gross Profit	***1431231***
Expense	
Employee Costs	592897
Employers NI	57757
Marketing & Advertising	173626
Software Development	127682
Rent	72000
Office Supplies	44920
Professional Fees	25754
Website Costs	23745
Travel and Subsistance	19603
Interest and Charges	14450
Expensed Equipment	12276
Reseller Fees	4839
Software Expensed	3379
Utilities	2979
Insurance	2247
Client Entertaining	1399
Market Research	1308
Entertainment	1183
Subscriptions	470
Exchange Gain/Loss	-509
Total Expense	***1182004***
Net Income	***249227***

Page 40 of Signifo Expenses

APPENDIX 3

Signifo Accounts

Balance Sheet

	March 31, 2005
ASSETS	
Current Assets	
Current/Savings	
Lloyds TSB Current Account	96,835.05
Total Current/Savings	96,835.05
Accounts Receivable	
Euro Accounts Receivable	1,652.79
USD Accounts Receivable	1,890.68
GBP Accounts Receivable	45,702.69
Total Accounts Receivable	49,246.16
Total Current Assets	146,081.21
TOTAL ASSETS	146,081.21
LIABILITIES AND EQUITY	
Liabilities	
Current Liabilities	
Accounts Payable	
USD Accounts Payable	168.51
GBP Accounts Payable	11,549.16
Total Accounts Payable	11,717.67
Other Current Liabilities	
Accruals	850.00
Net salaries control	7,134.81
Payroll Liabilities	3,730.52
VAT Control	2,674.51
Total Other Current Liabilities	14,389.84
Total Current Liabilities	26,107.51
Long Term Liabilities	
Deferred Income	18,443.37
Other Loans	32,706.16
Bank Loan – Lloyds 2102090	24,368.35
Total Long Term Liabilities	75,517.88
Total Liabilities	101,625.39
Equity	
Share Capital	5,753.00
Share Premium	482,529.86
Opening Bal Equity	(503,549.98)
Retained Earnings	(10,139.82)
Net Income	69,862.76
Total Equity	44,455.82
TOTAL LIABILITIES & EQUITY	**146,081.21**

APPENDIX 3

Competitive Matrix

	Website	Size of user base	Notes	Home office/DOB	UK customers	Web Based	Credit card	Offline	Mobile	Multi language
Small and medium market										
Signifo Expenses	www.signifo.com	Medium	Predominately UK user base, although a number of customers based in other parts of the world.	UK - 2000	Yes	Yes	Yes	Yes	Yes	No
ExpensAble	www.expensable.com	Large	Previously owned by Intuit, the owner of Quickbooks. Almost exclusively US user base, most of which are Quickbooks users.	US - mid 1990s	Few	No	Yes	Yes	No	No
Corporate market										
Concur	www.concur.com	Large	The global market leader in corporate market-place. Has an active UK office.	US - 1994	Yes	Yes	Yes	Yes	No	Yes
GEAC - Extensity	www.extensity.com	Large	Largely focused on US market.	US - early 1990s	Few	Yes	Yes	No	No	Yes
Gelco	www.gelco.com	Large	Largely focused on US market.	US - early 1990s	Few	No	Yes	No	No	Yes
Necho	www.necho.com	Large	Recently closed UK office.	Canada - 1995	Few	Yes	Yes	Yes	No	No
SAP	www.sap.com	Large	Expenses module of ERP product.	Germany	Yes	No	Yes	Yes	No	Yes
Oracle/J.D.Edwards /Peoplesoft	www.oracle.com	Large	Expenses module of ERP product.	US	Yes	Yes	Yes	No	No	Yes
Global Expense	www.globalexpense.com	Medium	Offers a service in which the processing of expense claims is fully outsourced. Best suited to large customers.	UK - 2000	Yes	Yes	Yes	No	No	No
Other										
ExpenseWorld	www.expenseworld.net	Small		UK - 2000	Few	Yes	No	Yes	Yes	No
Software Europe	www.software-europe.co.uk	Small		UK - 1989	Few	Yes	Yes	No	No	No
Requisoft	www.requisoft.com	Small		AUS - 1993	Few	Yes	No	No	No	Yes
Resourcing Software	www.resourcingsoftware.com	Small	Specifically focused on the recruitment sector.	UK	Few	Yes	No	No	No	No
Xpensecentre by Ceridian Centrefile	www.ceridiancentrefile.com	Small	Existing customer base	UK	Few	No	Yes	No	No	Yes

Page 42 of Signifo Expenses

APPENDIX 3

Inbound Leads for Signifo 2004-2005

Inbound Leads 2004-2005

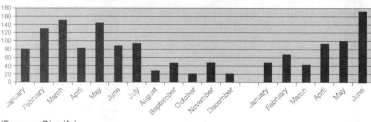

(Source: Signifo)

Inbound Leads Source 2005

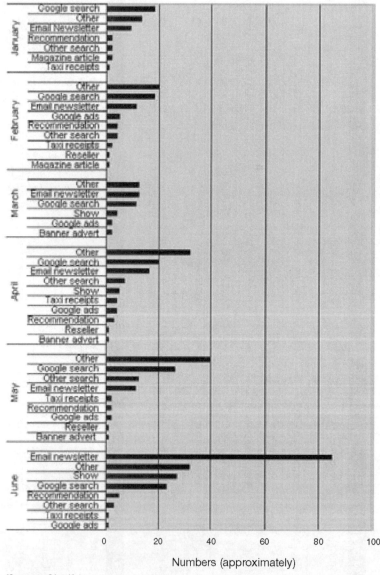

Numbers (approximately)

(Source: Signifo)

The Chartered Institute of Marketing, Professional Postgraduate Diploma in Marketing

APPENDIX 4

Signifo Customer Case Studies

CASE STUDY I
Chivas Regal: Expense processing solutions for global travellers

Industry: Consumer goods

Accounts software: J.D. Edwards

Overview
From its humble beginnings in a grocery store in Aberdeen, Chivas Regal has become the most famous premium whisky and is now appreciated from Tangiers to Tokyo and from Rio de Janeiro to Rome.

Travelling the globe
The Chivas marketing and commercial staff travel the globe, from their home in the highlands of Scotland to distant corners of South America.

Ian Barr, Finance Manager at Chivas, explains how this impacted on their expense claim process:

"Previously, our process was completely paper-based, which led to problems with the paperwork getting lost and an almost complete ignorance over where and when expenses were being incurred."

"Credit card statements were filled in with additional detail by hand, which meant that the accounts department was forever chasing the statements. We needed a systematic way of processing claims with appropriate controls."

A solution is found
Chivas determined that Signifo Expenses was the solution they were seeking and the implementation was completed soon after making the decision to proceed.

"We determined that Signifo Expenses met all our criteria. As the whisky industry is relatively low tech, we were concerned that some of our less computer-literate staff would object to a new system. However, the implementation went very smoothly and any objections soon faded."

"We were pleased that we were able to use the product off-the-shelf, as we'd become used to software implementations for which the changes were so great that by the end of the process you didn't recognise the product as it appeared at the start."

Populating claims with Barclaycard Business Corporate Card data
Most of the staff submitting claims are able to populate their expense claims with expense items incurred on their corporate Barclaycard Business Corporate Cards. This credit card functionality is particularly well received, as there's no thought involved on the part of claimants.

Page 44 of Signifo Expenses

APPENDIX 4

"At the click of a button, an employee populates a claim with the month's credit card data, so there's no thought involved, and that's always a good thing."

Summary

Ian Barr maintains that the benefits have been considerable:

"The benefits for us have been considerable and tangible. We now have visibility over every single expense item throughout the organisation, which allows us the control we sought."

"We saved half a head in the accounts department alone. While we haven't tried to quantify the cost savings outside the accounts department, there's no question that the savings are considerable."

"The interface into J.D. Edwards is such that we consider it a single process, from capturing expense items on credit cards, to posting to the relevant ledgers."

APPENDIX 4

Signifo Customer Case Studies

CASE STUDY II
Financial Risk Management: Expense management in the financial services industry

Industry: Financial Services
Accounts software: Sage Line 50

Overview

The FRM group is an international investment specialist dedicated to maximising hedge fund opportunities and rewards for institutional clients around the world.

With $7.9 billion of assets under management and a large team of professionals with extensive trading experience, FRM's ability to deliver the best hedge fund solutions is internationally recognised.

Chasing the paper trail

FRM, like other organisations in the financial services sector, has high personnel costs and travel and entertainment budgets.

As a result, the finance staff at FRM felt a need to ease the burden on their team of financial professionals by introducing a replacement to the paper-based expense claim process. Rina Kundu, an accountant at FRM, explained:

"Our front office staff travel extensively, and we had separate paper processes for managing cash advances, UK-based claims, overseas claims and expenses incurred on our corporate American Express cards."

"Because the processes weren't standardised, the finance team was investing a lot of time chasing missing claims, amending claim forms and inputting data manually to our accounts system."

Corporate card frustrations

The frustrations with the processing of corporate American Express data were particularly acute.

"Our process required us to distribute the paper-based American Express statements to the cardholders. They would then add the appropriate narrative beside each item, in particular where it involves client entertainment, before having their department heads sign the statements. This was often difficult as the department heads are also typically frequent travellers."

"The burden on the finance team was considerable; we'd have to chase the statements that hadn't been returned, interpret the handwritten narratives and then input the data from the statements manually."

After looking at a number of different automated solutions, FRM selected Signifo Expenses. Rina commented:

Page 46 of Signifo Expenses

APPENDIX 4

"The Signifo Expenses product seemed to fit the process that we had already and addressed each of the issues that we had. It was very easy to use, which is important, as there is always some apprehension when a new process is introduced."

Smooth implementation

Rina Kundu was delighted by how smoothly the implementation was handled:

"The implementation went like a dream. There's plenty of flexibility in the configuration, so it was almost like a bespoke solution developed for our particular needs."

"The only software that we had to install was the interface to Sage Line 50, and that was implemented without any problems. I wish all software implementations were so straightforward."

"I love the fact that it's so easy for me to set up new users and make other changes to the configuration."

Considerable benefits

Rina explains that the feedback from all parties has been excellent:

"I'd say that 98% of the users love it, which is a great hit rate considering the natural resistance that exists against any new system."

"The credit card functionality has been particularly successful, and we have issued more American Express cards to staff as a result."

"For the accounts department, it's been fantastic. It's saved the 2-3 days per month that we would previously spend coding and inputting data. We also like the fact that we now have a standardised process for all expense claims."

"Throughout the business, the cost and time savings have been considerable."

APPENDIX 4

Signifo Customer Case Studies

CASE STUDY III
Genesys Conferencing: Expense claim automation in a global environment

Industry: Conferencing Services
Finance system: SunSystems

Overview

With more than 1,600 employees in 18 countries around the globe, Genesys Conferencing is the world's leading specialist in conferencing services and has earned a reputation as the most innovative company in the industry.

Genesys offers services allowing professionals to conduct effective, efficient virtual meetings and managed events in real-time, reaching participants anywhere in the world.

A global requirement

Because of the international nature of the company, each separate national subsidiary is set up with the appropriate local reporting currency, cost centres and expense categories, under a single company-wide configuration.

The use of different base and reporting currencies, allows, for example, for a taxi fare to be incurred in US dollars but stated in Canadian dollars for local subsidiary reporting, and in Euro for base currency reporting as the parent company accounts are Euro-denominated.

Because Genesys executives are constantly on the move, and are responsible for approving expense claims, a major challenge for Genesys was to improve the expense claims approvals process.

Armelle Koelf, the company's Finance Manager for Europe, describes her need as follows:

"Our top managers move around the world, which made it awkward for people to get things manually signed off. A key factor for us was getting claims signed by the approver wherever they were. And for people on the move, we needed a way to allow them to make claims as well."

Another problem facing Genesys, and other companies operating globally, is the need to convert expense claims in foreign currencies into the home currency. Koelf says:

"With exchange rates changing daily, deciding which exchange rate to use was a problem for the individual making the claim and for us processing the claim. Using Signifo Expenses we get daily exchange rates and automatic translation into each subsidiary's base currency, so we don't have to think about that. This makes our lives much easier, as there's no argument about the rate paid."

Processing efficiencies

Before using Signifo Expenses, Genesys relied on a paper-based system with Excel templates. Koelf says:

APPENDIX 4

"Because everyone is on the same system, we've improved our administration and cost centre management. It's all very clear to everyone where their expense claims are in the system."

Genesys selected Signifo Expenses because of its internet capabilities which give users and approvers access 24 hours a day, seven days a week. In addition, the company didn't simply offer a standard product. Koelf described this flexible approach:

"Signifo were receptive to the problems we might have and any developments we might want to make within the Genesys Group. Price was also a factor; we could install Signifo Expenses relatively cheaply and see the benefits without making a huge financial commitment."

Efficient VAT reclaim

Reclaiming VAT can be a headache for many companies. This is compounded when claiming VAT in EU member countries. Signifo Expenses removes the complexity in dealing with VAT claims outside the UK. Koelf explains:

"The other problem we're using Signifo Expenses to solve is claiming VAT refunds, not only in the UK but also in other European countries. This goes hand in hand with trying to keep the process as tight as possible so we get the most back that we possibly can. We need to be able to isolate the VAT figures from the rest of the information, and the Signifo system is making this possible."

Integration with accounting ledgers

Genesys uses SunSystems as its core accounting system, for which Signifo has developed an interface that allows consolidated expense claim data to be posted automatically to the relevant purchase ledgers.

Summary

Armelle Koelf has no hesitation recommending Signifo Expenses:

"I would certainly recommend Signifo Expenses. Feedback from users is positive and it is very easy to enter expense claims. It's a fully web-based system, and as our accounting is centralised, it is very easy for claimants to obtain approval on their expense claims and for these then to go straight to the accounts team to process."

APPENDIX 4

Signifo Customer Case Studies

CASE STUDY IV
Spring Group plc: Infrastructure for growth
Industry: Recruitment
Software: Coda

Overview
Spring Group plc is one of the UK's leading human capital management companies. The group comprises several businesses specialising in permanent and contract IT recruitment, workforce management services and general staffing. Annual revenues exceed £300 million.

Initially, Spring used Signifo Expenses in a single subsidiary, but then considered that the cost saving benefits and subsequent ROI were such that the product should be rolled out across the other subsidiaries, which involved a rollout to a large number of regional offices.

Efficiencies across the organization
Following a rapid and problem-free implementation, the experience of Signifo Expenses has been very positive. Ruth Schofield, a finance manager at Spring, says:

> "The management information now available to us is substantial and we like the instantaneous nature of the application. From everyone's perspective, it's simplified things. For example, we can immediately inform the claimant that their claim has been rejected, the reasons why, and issue instructions on what needs to be done to correct the claim."

> "This allows us to meet our Friday cut off for reimbursement. If a claim that is submitted on a Thursday requires amendment, we are able to turn it around immediately so that it makes the payment run."

In addition to the efficiencies that have been achieved in the accounts department, she is also pleased at how well the new system has been received in the broader organisation.

> "The feedback from the regional offices has been very positive. It's a quantum leap forward from our previous expense claim process, and it's given our department further credibility in the organization. It's always good to be viewed to be improving systems."

Benefits at the coalface
The benefits are also considerable for the staff overseeing the processing of expense claims. Ruth comments:

> "For the accounts staff, it's the best thing to happen because they're now able to focus on other issues. There's no question that it is labour saving."

> "The upload to our accounts package, which now takes only 15 minutes, was a job that took two days previously."

Page 50 of Signifo Expenses

APPENDIX 4

"However, it's not only in the processing of claims that we're saving time. It's also in dealing with queries and approval limits. There is much less checking and chasing."

"The feedback from the staff is very positive. One of the regional directors called to say that Signifo Expenses 'is a fantastic piece of software'. It's not often that the accounts department gets such praise."

APPENDIX 4

Signifo Customer Case Studies

CASE STUDY V
Taste Connection: Small company expenses

Industry: Consumer goods
Accounts software: Sage Line 50

Overview

Taste Connection supplies the food industry with food ingredients, providing taste packages that bring together precisely the right elements of authentic taste experiences. These range from Mexican, Asian and Mediterranean classics to exotic flavours such as Samarkand Lemon Tagine and Vietnamese Beef Rendeng.

The Taste Connection team consists of the three founding directors and two additional staff members, and is distributed ·across the country, with two team members in Gloucestershire and one in each of Hampton Court, Bristol and Milton Keynes.

Financial control

Taste Connection faced a significant financial control issue, with the directors living in three distant locations and spending on travel, entertainment and related costs as their client and supplier base grew rapidly.

Andrew Sainsbury, a director at Taste Connection, explained:

"I found it hard to believe that the simple issue of processing expenses would cause us such a headache. As we're rarely in the same room and because we incur travel and entertainment costs continuously, this became a major issue, not just from a paper-processing perspective but also from a financial control perspective."

A complete solution

The Taste Connection team members now create, submit and approve expense claims online using Signifo Expenses.

Their claims are populated automatically with their Barclaycard credit card spend and an interface provided by Signifo allows the consolidated claim data to be posted automatically to the relevant ledgers within their Sage Line 50 accounting software.

"The fact that it's web-based made it easy to implement, and because it integrates with both Barclaycard and Sage, it's resolved our issue completely. I'm impressed that such functionality was available to an organisation such as ours with only 5 staff."

Page 52 of Signifo Expenses

The Chartered
Institute of Marketing

Moor Hall, Cookham
Maidenhead
Berkshire, SL6 9QH, UK
Telephone: 01628 427120
Facsimile: 01628 427158
www.cim.co.uk

3   Step 1: Initial overview

Getting started

Tutor Tip

Having read the case study you need to start to understand the broad context in which the business is operating.

What are your first impressions of the business?

The case context

3.1   The Signifo case is about a company rather than a business unit. Therefore, your thinking should be **strategic** both in terms of business growth, and also in **positioning** the business through branding and competitive stance. As the focus is on strategic marketing, you can expect to be advising on where this company should be focusing its growth activities – what services it should be delivering, to which markets and how it should build its brand and competitive position.

In the external environment, there is clearly change in Signifo's favour – increased use of Internet, wider access to IT and wireless connections, the increased importance of **governance** issues driving the need for transparency in record keeping. These all add to the attractiveness of their product.

As always, the challenge is to create information from the narrative data and clues provided. Of course, you will need to tackle the financial data – which can be a particular challenge for marketers.

About Signifo Expenses

3.2   Signifo is a niche 'business-to-business' service provider. It is not a large business – with revenue in the year to March 2005 of approximately £1.5m (page 39). Of course, Signifo only started in 2000 (page 4); is this an acceptable result after five years of trading?

The expense management market potential is enormous and increasing, growing from $700m to $1.8m between 2002 and 2006 (page 7). The danger for Signifo is that it started off with a niche position, but is in danger of expanding into a 'middle of the road position' – unsure of which sectors and indeed which countries to focus its activities in.

Tutor tip

Data health warning!

As you start to familiarise yourself with the case take care to avoid the pitfalls.

■ There is data in both £ and US$.

■ There is external macro info from US and UK and they differ, eg compliance legislation in UK is different from US.

■ There is only one year's financial data so any ratios generated are of limited use as there is nothing to compare them with: we cannot determine what is improving and what is not.

■ The small business sector is more like a 'business-to-consumer' market for selling purposes.

■ The average life time of a client is stated as 36 months. In a five-year old company this is a poor indicator. Most clients will have been with Signifo for less than that time – the business could, in fact, have a very high retention rate.

Your overview

3.3 Take time to complete your case overview and follow through the comments below to help you review your work.

Checking your overview

3.4 The following notes are a guide to help you as you revisit your overview analysis. They are presented to highlight, rather than direct, and you will need to decide for yourself how important each point is. The notes take you page by page through the case, so they help you to review the material in a logical sequence which should reinforce your understanding and build your confidence in the material and your assessment of it.

Page 3

3.5 **The candidate's brief**. Note the role and also the description of the business as 'successful and niche'. It is always worth coming back to the brief at intervals during your preparation to stay on track.

Page 4

3.6 **Introduction**. Note the comments about **unsatisfied need** that led to the company being started. The question is how the company **differentiates** itself as competitors enter the market. We also have very useful opportunity cost figures (£30–£50 per expense report) and the business benefits offered by Signifo Expenses (SE) – again, keep asking which of these are sustainable.

Page 5

3.7 **The market**. This service is an aspect of supply chain management – but a Cinderella aspect, not often considered. SE's importance depends on the nature of the business – those delivering services with large mobile workforces face bigger bills and problems. This page gives us some useful insights into how best to segment this market. If buyer behaviour is the same irrespective of geography, global segments may be a good option – small consultancy businesses and so on.

Pages 6/7

3.8 **The IT service industry**. SE is not alone is being a small firm in this sector. The case also tells you that IT spending from small- and medium-sized enterprises (SMEs) in Europe is expected to be strong, whereas large company spend is slowing down. The market for expenses management is large and growing and expected to reach $1.8bn by 2006. This shows how small a player SE actually is – its global market share is a decimal point.

Pages 7/8

3.9 (a) **Signifo's market position**. A pioneer in the small- and mid-market segments for expense management through organic growth. They had near monopoly position in the SME sector when they started – they boost the sectors they are operating in but there is no real indication that the solution provided has been customised in some way. In fact, this range of sector clients could indicate a lack of focused positioning and reactive marketing as the business has been built.

(b) The diffusion of innovation model might be useful. The firms in an SME market which should be innovators and early adopters are those with the greatest business needs and potential benefits to gain. The comments at the end of the page could imply an 80:20 split in revenue generation between small- and mid-sized firms. Yet the cost of sales and servicing small firms are lower and there are no direct competitors. Penetration into this segment could be why you have been appointed with your B2C background. Mid-sized customers are more costly to service (margins will be lower) and there is head-to-head competition.

(c) The relationship marketing question is key. A retention strategy as well as an acquisition strategy is required for the business.

(d) Note that in terms of the SME market in the UK, SE is a leader in a growing market (a Boston Matrix point of reference).

Build your numbers page as you go:

- 400 clients, with an
- Average of 50 employees claiming expenses in each

Pages 8-11

3.10 **Product overview**. Note that the growth of wireless applications means there will be a lesser need for offline versions of the application. Already, those on the road can use SMS technology.

Notice on page 10 the flow of product releases, each offering improved functionality. This is a good thing, but presentation and communication of these benefits needs care.

Satisfaction ratings seem reasonable but we do not know what these ratios are based on and whether these results represent finance teams or expense claimants etc. Note also the comment at the bottom of page 10 on preparing the product for 'white labelling', an indication SE is considering using third parties to grow the business.

Pages 12/13

3.11 **CSR**. Take care with this section of information. CSR is an added reason for purchasing SE's SAP, *but* CSR is not seen as a differential advantage in SE's branding or marketing. This begins to position systems such as SE's as a 'must have' rather than an optional purchase. This increases the propensity to buy but is also likely to encourage competitors into the market.

In the US, the impact of the Sarbanes-Oxley Act (SOX) is expected to cascade down to the SME sector, but the US and UK markets differ significantly in compliance and governance. SE need a global strategy that thinks global but acts local.

Pages 12-15

Forward plans

3.12 Here the similarities between SE's and the subscription model of business become clear. Direct marketing and database marketing strategies will be critical to success.

The different strategies for lead generation is clear but the level of business generated by each strategy is not. (Note, if you are developing a market map, these are **the channels to market**.)

Notice also the **functionality weaknesses**, as far as mid-sized customers are concerned and the plans to tackle these. Perhaps a mid-market push in the more medium-term is needed.

Pages 15/16

The competitive landscape

3.13 Here we are told the decision to go into the US mid-market has been made, therefore you will need to be ready to make recommendations on how this launch should happen, but might also consider whether the Board should be advised to reconsider this.

There is some discussion of business-to-business (B2B) branding. This needs to be developed as it is a favourite topic with the examiner.

Take time over the summary – international expansion seems to have been based on reactive exporting and an ethnocentric strategy but the company is ready to change this.

The appendices

3.14 **Appendix 1**

Useful product information – but note the ROI comments are about the customers' investment not the company's results. Try to use the Total Product Concept model to build up a picture of core, expected, augmented and potential benefits.

Appendix 2

Find out about ASPs if you are new to the technology – but look carefully at the business model it represents. This is the foundation for our strategy – it is a type of outsourcing model.

The **Business solutions** article is interesting – is **e-Bay** an alternative route to market for small companies? This could suggest that the examiner is interested in SE's e-strategy to grow a 'small client' base. There are also a few comments about web marketing metrics. Remember to add this as a section on your MkIS thinking and recommendations.

The **Jamcracker** article also provides background about the sector and technology – in particular its stage in the technology lifecycle. It stresses the importance of developing new channels. We need to pay attention to the advice given on pages 23 and 24. (Your presentation to the client can be strengthened if you cite examples and cases – this material could provide relevant sources.)

The **business case for wireless software applications** gives us an insight into future developments in the technology and use of the service. Remember, we are planning for the future so forecasting the external environment matters. Do, however, notice the warnings about fast ROI promises on page 32. The pricing strategy requires very careful consideration.

The **'if in doubt farm it out'** article reinforces the willingness of firms to outsource activities related to data management.

As you read these articles pull together a short list of key points.

Appendix 3

The data is a little disappointing. With only one year of information, you will need to make assumptions, but be careful not to draw conclusions without a health warning.

Observations:

- £6.60 per use per month is low, if it costs up to £50 per expense report as the alternative.

- Average life is unhelpful – annual retention or lapse levels would have been more useful as indicators.

- Consider the marketing metrics that can be calculated. What does the data tell you? What do we know and what do we not know? Linked to the source of leads data on page 42, you can estimate cost per lead (remembering that you have one year of costs and six months of leads). Remember that leads do not always generate business, and a low lead source can have a high conversion level.

- Gross margins look good.

- We do not know how many employees there are but the wage bill gives us an indication – if the average pay is £50k+, SE is a team, of perhaps, 10 people. There are a few clues here about the challenges facing a small business – for example, their exchange loss shows a lack of financial planning and treasury function.

- The competitor matrix is helpful. Do a different positioning map for different markets.

- The customer cases give you an insight into buyer behaviour (based on needs). Additional cases can be viewed on the SE site if it helps you get a better picture – but do not import specific data.

3.15 By now you should have a good sense of the case study. Use the following questions to help you to check out your understanding.

Action Programme 1

SO YOU THINK YOU KNOW THE CASE..?

QUESTIONS

1   Who are you and what is your role?

2   What business is Signifo in?

3   What differentiates the Signifo offer?

4   What % of indirect business costs do expenses represent?

5   What competitive and growth strategies has Signifo followed?

6   How old and big is Signifo?

7   What is the Sarbanes-Oxley Act and why is it relevant?

8   What are the implications of wireless devices for Signifo?

9   How big is the marketing spend and does this give you any insight into the business?

10 What is an average customer's life and how reliable is this figure?

Action Programme review

ANSWERS

1   Ed Walker – Marketing Consultant.

2   Management of people's expenses – a B2B services offer.

3   Easy to use, speed of implementation and cost savings – the question is how sustainable are these?

4   20% (page 5).

5   A pioneer following organic growth strategy – a near monopoly position with SMEs.

6   Started in 2000 – turnover is about £1.5m.

7   A major piece of US legislation following Worldcom crash etc – intended to improve corporate governance – it is intended to make all financial information more transparent.

8   It will make their services even more useful to people on the move.

9   1.5% – a bit high – not enough targeting. A further 2,000 spent on HR, hospitality and 4,839 on reseller fees.

10 36 months – not reliable as company is only five years old.

Signifo Expenses: Analysis: Steps 2-4 16

Chapter Topic List	
1	Completing the analysis for Signifo Expenses
2	Step 2: Internal analysis – strengths and weaknesses
3	Step 3: Adding the external analysis
4	Step 4: Summary and critical success factors

Tutor Tip

In this long chapter you need to take your time and work through the various steps and stages of the analysis process. Do the work for yourself and then compare it with the sample analysis provided. Remember you are concerned with process as much as the content – you need to be confident about how to tackle your exam case when it arrives.

Work through the internal and external audits for Signifo Expenses.

Establish the critical success factors for the business.

1 Completing the analysis for Signifo Expenses

1.1 With a broad understanding of the case study you are now ready to tackle the more detailed audits and analysis. This is the time consuming part of your case work and remember, if working with others, you can share the work load.

1.2 For each step in the process you are provided with sample material following a variety of approaches for you to critique after you have applied your own ideas. Tutorial comments will guide you as to the success of approaches demonstrated. We suggest you take this practice case a step at a time; complete one part of the analysis and review the feedback before moving on to the next step. Use tools and models, they will help you to pull material together and effectively communicate your assessment to others.

2 Step 2: Internal analysis – strengths and weaknesses

Financials

2.1 Firstly, let us look at some **financial ratios**.

Financials

(a)	Gross Profit	95.44%
(b)	Net Profit	16.62%
(c)	ROCE	19.29%

Financials ratios

(d)	Current Ratio	5.6:1
(e)	Quick Ratio	1.4:1
(f)	Return on Assets	0.5:1
(g)	Debt to Assets	0.7:1
(h)	Debt to Equity	2.3:1
(i)	Long Term Debt to Equity	1.7:1

Note that the company has few fixed assets.

2.2 Ad spend can be represented in graph form, as below.

(a)

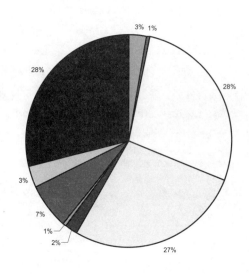

(b)

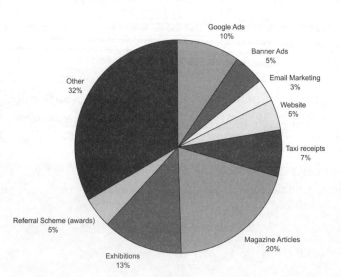

Marketing and sales data

2.3   We can analyse some of the marketing and sales data as follows.

(a)   **Marketing and sales data (1)** – page 38

Average customer size	50	users
Average revenue per user	£6.60	per month
Average customer life	36	months
Average revenue per customer	£330.00	per month
Average revenue per customer	£11,880.00	lifetime
Average gross revenue per customer	£314.96	per month
Average gross revenue per customer	£11,338.41	lifetime
Average net revenue per customer	£54.84	per month
Average net revenue per customer	£1,974.41	lifetime
Average net revenue per user	£1.10	per month
Average net revenue per user	£39.49	lifetime
Average trial to sales conversion	50%+	

(b)   **Marketing and sales data (2) conversion** – (page 14). Some conclusions:

■   SE do not seem to be targeting customers – their approach is unfocused.

■   They do not have an integrated marketing strategy.

■   Unknown lead-to-trial ratio, therefore it is impossible to calculate cost per conversion.

(c)   **Marketing and sales data (3) – Cost per lead**

£ per Lead

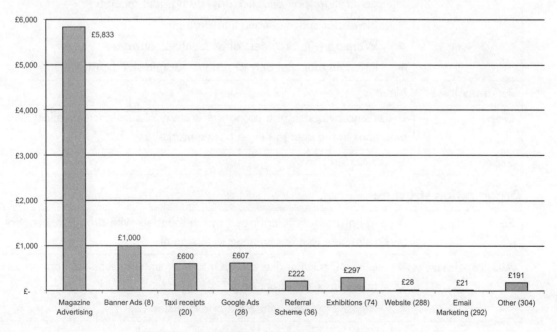

Seven-S analysis

2.4 Shared values and vision

Fact	The leading provider of expenses software to SMEs
Assumptions	■ Original vision appears to have been achieved ■ Core values: belief in the product, leading the ASP revolution, being the best and creating high profits ■ Endemic values transferred from the founders ■ Culture that is high on achievement and innovation
Gap	No information about the founding individuals or the staff
Score	Shared values + 5 Vision and Mission – 5

2.5 Strategy: Medium-/long-term goals

Facts	■ A market pioneer with organic growth targeting the SME market ■ Aiming for expansion in the corporate market and the USA mid sized market sector ■ Building strategic alliances with other foreign suppliers to be more internationally based ■ To increase sales to mid-size customers
Assumption	■ No real strategy to support these objectives
Gap	None
Score	Corporate strategy – 5

Strategy: Short-term goals

Fact	■ Focus on customer retention and procurement strategies, lead generation, pay per click advertising, taxi receipts ■ No sector specific marketing strategy ■ Working with providers of accounting software ■ Improving functionality of product for mid-sized customers
Assumptions	None
Gap	There is no evidence of a corporate strategy of substance to reflect their ambitions to move in to the corporate market or the USA.
Score	Marketing strategy 0

2.6 Organisation structure

Fact	A young organisation managed by the founders with strong cost control and a structure that has sufficed to this point
Assumptions	■ Current structure likely to be informal, small and flexible no formal operations infrastructure ■ Unlikely to cope with a major expansion
Gap	What is the organisational/operations structure?
Score	Structure until now + 8 Structure for the future – 5

2.7 Systems

Facts	■ Strong cost control ■ Systems to measure Customer Lifetime Value (quarterly marketing updates) ■ Use of technology and CRM software ■ ISO 9001 compliant
Assumptions	None
Gap	No evidence of other systems or consistent engagement with customers. No detail behind the user survey or indication how information is used
Score	Systems + 2

2.8 Staff

Facts	■ Insufficient sales resource for face to face meetings to develop into the mid-sized market ■ Outsourcing of telemarketing etc 'virtual team'/partners
Assumptions	■ Small numbers a limiting factor for growth ■ To have achieved what they have to date there is a team that is experienced and works together well
Gap	No information about the staff
Score	Staff + 2

2.9 Skills

Facts	■ Very strong IT skills, good at product development and maximising use of the latest technologies ■ Awareness of quality, legislation and regulations ■ Little apparent investment in training but can adapt flexibly to meet specific requirements ■ They are 'buying in' some expertise. Professional fees are £25k for the year
Assumptions	■ Financial analysis indicates business skills may need development ■ May need to develop relationship building (as opposed to CRM metrics) and softer people skills
Gap	None
Score	Skills + 3

2.10 **Style**

Facts	■ Entrepreneurial
	■ In touch with key technical issues affecting the market
Assumption	Likely to be very technical people with associated thinking and traits. Probably a strong common way of thinking and behaving
Gap	No information as to who the people are
Score	Style + 5

2.11 **Scoring the 7Ss**

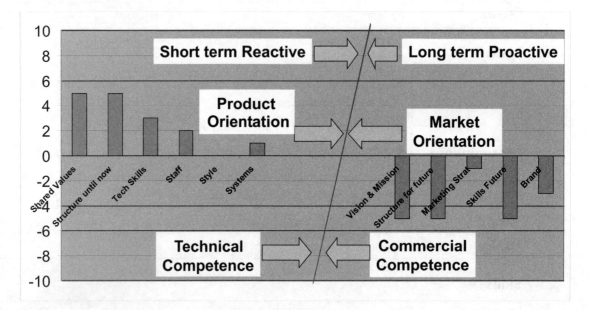

Marketing strategy

2.12 (a)   Marketing strategy involves looking at the following areas.

Segmentation

■ Profitability
■ Sustainability
■ Growth

Position

■ Customer perceptions
■ Comparisons against competitors

Targets

■ Effectiveness of reaching segments

(b)   We can segment the main markets as follows.

Expenses management solutions customer segmentation

Small enterprises		Medium enterprises				Large enterprises			
Office-based, web-enabled	Field-based, offline	Office-based, web-enabled		Field-based, offline		Office-based, web-enabled		Field-based, offline	
UK	UK	UK	Overseas	UK	Overseas	UK	Overseas	UK	Overseas

- Signifo are market leaders in SME category.

- Maximum growth (and revenue) potential sitting in Large Enterprise Segment.

- Signifo has potential point of differentiation in US-based Large Enterprise segment due to imminent Sarbanes-Oxley (SOX) compliance.

(c)   **Product performance: Signifo and the EMS market**

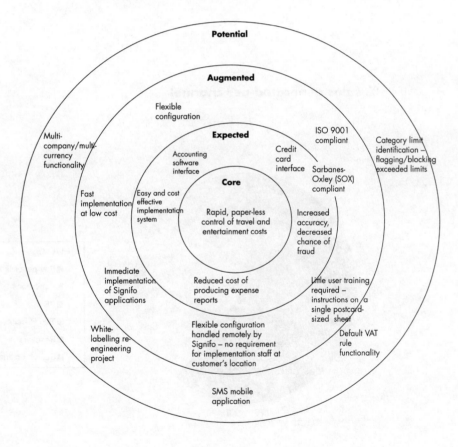

(d) The next two charts show **promotion performance**.

(i) **Promotion performance: revenue per £1 spent, by channel**

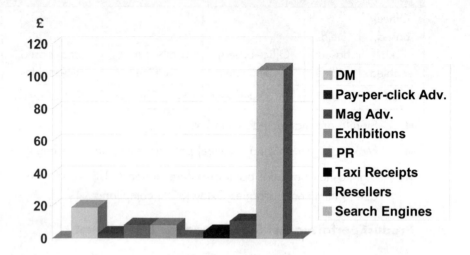

(ii) **% sales generated per channel**

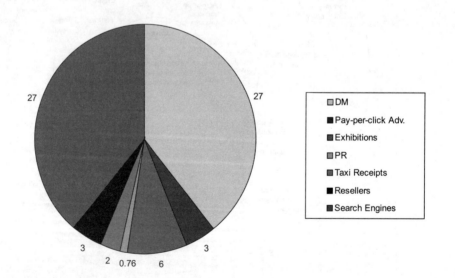

(iii) Place and promotions performance: promotional ROI by channel

Activity	Cost £	% of total spend	No of leads	% of total leads	No of sales	% of total sales	Cost per lead £	Cost per sale[1] £	Average total value of sales[2] £	Average revenue/£ spent/channel[3] £
Mailings	20,000	11%	?	?						
Outsourced telemarketing	15,000	9%	?	?						
Email marketing	6,000	3%	143	27%						
Total DM	**41,000**	**24%**	**143**	**27%**	**71**	**27%**	**286**	**577**	**843,480**	**19**
Google ads	17,000	10%	14	2.6%						
Other	8,000	5%	4	0.76%						
Total pay/click	**25,000**	**14%**	**18**	**3%**	**9**	**3%**	**1,388**	**2,777**	**106,920**	**3**
Trade press	21,000	12%	?	?	?					
Other magazines	14,000	8%	?	?	?					
Total magazine advertising	**35,000**	**20%**	**?**	**?**	**?**					
Exhibition	22,000	13%	34	6.5%	17	6%	1,294	2,588	201,960	8
PR	16,000	9%	4	0.76%	2	0.76	8,000	16,000	23,760	0.48
Taxi receipts	12,000	7%	11	2%	5	2%	2,040	4,800	59,400	3.95
Website (search engines?)	8,000	5%	143	27%	71	27%	56	112	843,480	104
Referral scheme	8,000	5%	16	3%	8	3%	1,000	2,000	95,040	10.88
Sales materials	4,000	2%	?	?	?	?	?			
Directory listings	3,000	2%	?	?	?	?	?			
Misc 'other'	?	?	149	28%	74	29	?			
Reseller	?	?	3	0.6%	1.5	0.6%	?			
Total other	**73,000**	**42%**	**217**	**41%**	**108**	**41%**	**336**	**673**	**1,283,040**	**127.31**
Google search	?	?	117	22%						
Other search	?	?	26	5%						
Total search engines	**?**	**?**	**143**	**27%**	**71**	**27%**				
Total	**174,000**		**521**		**260**		**334**	**668**	**3,088,800**	

1 Assuming all leads convert to trial at 50% conversion rate
2 50 users per sale at £6.60 revenue per user per month × 36 months
3 (Revenue – cost)/cost

Base figures cover Jan-March 2005 inclusive

(e) Finally, to summarise, here are SE's marketing assets.

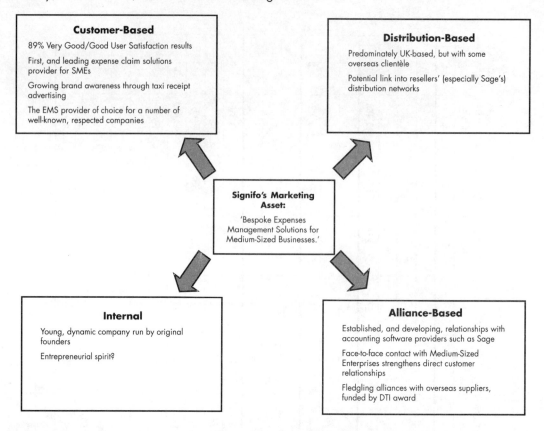

Stakeholders

2.14 (a) The stakeholder map below shows stakeholder components.

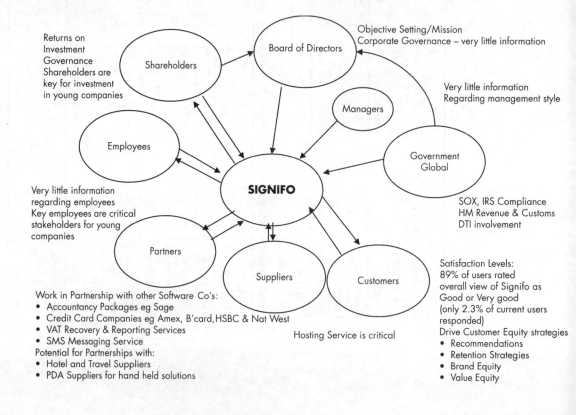

(b)   The table below identifies some external stakeholders, their 'stake' and their power.

<table>
<tr><th rowspan="2"></th><th rowspan="2"></th><th colspan="3">Type of power</th></tr>
<tr><th>Legal</th><th>Economic</th><th>Political</th></tr>
<tr><td rowspan="6">Stake</td><td>Financial</td><td>Shareholders
Board/owners</td><td>Shareholders
Board/owners</td><td>DTI</td></tr>
<tr><td>Economic</td><td>Sarbanes-Oxley (SOX)

Lawyers

HM Revenue & Customs

USA IRS</td><td>Customers
Competitors
Foreign suppliers
Resellers
Banks
Credit card companies</td><td>DTI
HM Revenue & Customs

USA IRS</td></tr>
<tr><td>General</td><td></td><td>Employees</td><td></td></tr>
</table>

■ **Financial/Legal**

The shareholders and board members have a financial investment in the company and are legally responsible for running the company

■ **Financial or Economic/Political**

–   The DTI are prepared to help the company into foreign markets

–   HM Revenue & Customs and the IRS are there to ensure compliance with regulations and political policies

■ **Economic/Legal**

Signifo have invested in ensuring that their software complies with the SOX regulations to enable them to enter the US market and their foreign subsidiaries

■ **Economic/Economic**

All these stakeholders have money invested in supporting Signifo or defending their own business against them (as in competitors), they also expect a return on this investment either as payment for services from Signifo or by successfully competing against them

■ **General/Economic**

Employees have a general stake in the company and expect an economic return on their stake

Source: Marketing Strategies: Ashok Ranchhod

(c) We can then decide the strategy to adopt with each group of stakeholders.

	Power			Strategy			
	High	Med	Low	Pro-active	Accommo-dating	Defen-sive	Re-active
Shareholders	*				*		
Board/owners	*				*		
Banks		*				*	
SOX lawyers	*			*			
Small customers			*		*		
Mid-sized customers	*				*		
Competitors			*				*
Foreign suppliers		*		*			
Resellers	*			*			
Credit card companies		*		*			
Employees	*						?
DTI		*			*		
HM Revenue & Customs		*			*		
USA IRS	*			*			

(Leftmost vertical label: Stakeholder)

- **Proactive Strategies** – SOX, Resellers, Foreign Suppliers, Credit Card Companies, IRS

  External focus on partners for new market entry and product development

- **Accomodating Strategies** – Shareholders, Board Members, Customers, DTI, HM Revenue & Customs

  - There is a willingness to pay attention to the needs of this group of stakeholders but the company does little to anticipate their needs

  - Eg gap in functionality of product for mid-sized customers is now being addressed but wasn't anticipated

- **Defensive strategies** – Banks

  Assumption – have a healthy bank balance, but they did rely on loans for their previous year's growth. They will probably do the minimum they have to, to keep the banks happy

- **Reactive strategies** – Competitors, Employees

  - There is little evidence of an employee strategy, – they may be ignored. However, they are critically important

  - There is no competition from other expense software companies in the small customer segment and they are playing catch up with the bigger players

Source: Marketing Strategies: Ashok Ranchhod

Action Programme 1

You have now seen how student group A used models to tackle the analysis of strengths and weaknesses. As a contrast you now have three models as presented by group B, along with their interpretation in each case.

Put yourself in the role of the examiner. What would your comments be if the three models and discussion below were presented as part of a student's analysis sheets?

Purchase decisions for expense solutions

(a) **Decision making unit (DMU) for expense solutions**

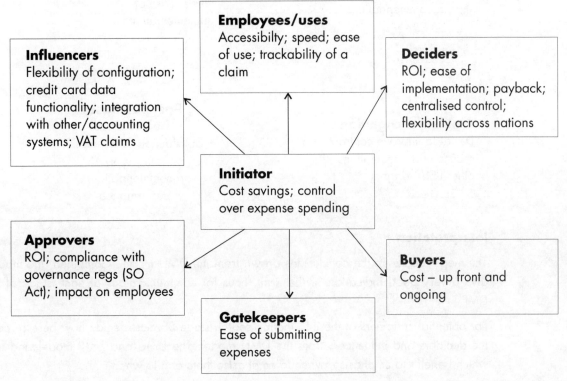

Model may be simplified, or roles combined where smaller organisations are involved.

Interpretation

SE must consider the varying needs of each of the roles described within the DMU. Care must be taken to position SE as providing the right benefits to the right customers. This means varying the focus of communications and positioning according to the stage in the decision-making process the buyer has reached. For example, at the problem-recognition stage, the focus should be on cost savings and control. As a shortlisted supplier, the emphasis should be ease of implementation, compatibility with other systems and ROI. During the roll out of the system, emphasis should shift to accessibility and the speed of claim processing.

(b)   **Decision making process**

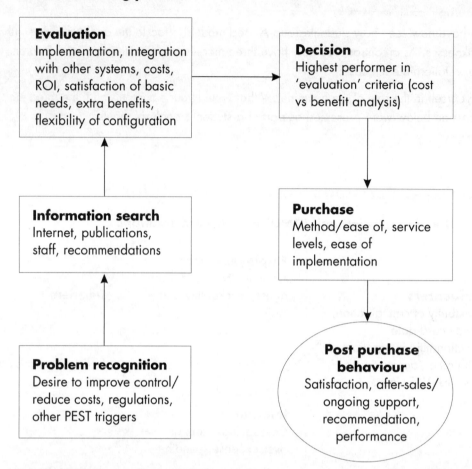

Evaluation
Implementation, integration with other systems, costs, ROI, satisfaction of basic needs, extra benefits, flexibility of configuration

Decision
Highest performer in 'evaluation' criteria (cost vs benefit analysis)

Information search
Internet, publications, staff, recommendations

Purchase
Method/ease of, service levels, ease of implementation

Problem recognition
Desire to improve control/ reduce costs, regulations, other PEST triggers

Post purchase behaviour
Satisfaction, after-sales/ ongoing support, recommendation, performance

Interpretation

The model backs up the conclusions drawn from the DMU model. Combined, the models give a very good indication of the right focus for communications at each stage of the DMP.

For potential customers at the information search stage SE must decide how best to reach the deciders and influencers from the DMU model. The DMU and DMP models indicate which benefits to emphasise, when to emphasise them and to whom.

Pay particular attention to post-purchase behaviour, as this may be an important area for retention or acquisition strategy. There is very little mention of this area in the case study – if the market attracts more competitors, this will become increasingly important.

We'll look at the DMU in Section 3.

(c) **Three phases of customer relationship management** (adapted from Kalokota and Robinson, 1999)

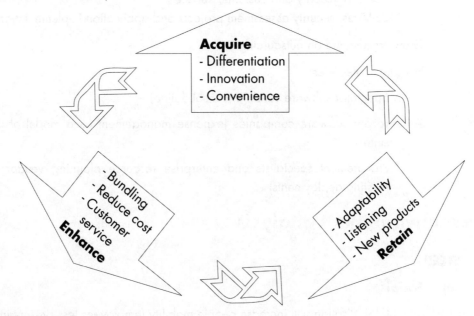

Interpretation

The model provides a framework of how a CRM strategy may help SE to retain existing and attract new clients.

The 'Enhance' area of the model suggests that the company should aim for a greater understanding of clients' needs and move towards mass customisation of products. Flexible configuration and high levels of local control for businesses using the SE product will provide a basis for this positioning based on existing functionality.

3 Step 3: Adding the external analysis

Market set-up

3.1 (a) Signifio competes in the market of IT solutions for increasing SME business process efficiency

(b) Expense management process improves productivity of:

- – employees (time saving in creating and submitting claims)
- – internal accounts managers (approvals possible 24/7, anywhere)
- – accounts clerks (accuracy, time saving in processing)

(c) Dependency on Internet and mobile telephony

(d) Worldwide IT services industry to grow from $536bn (2005) to $707bn (2007), CAGR 5.7%

(e) Expense management market to grow from $ 0.7 bn (2002) to $1.8bn (2006) and to $5bn (when mature, currently 97% of transactions are still on paper)

(f) Application Service Providers (ASP) market growing over the last five years

(g) IT spending appetite of European SMEs strong throughout 2005 (4.6%) – mainly financial services and manufacturing

(h)   2005 spending to be focused on:

- – Tools: IT security and customer service
- – Services: security assessment projects and application implementation

(i)   Growing demand on outsourcing

(j)   Providers categories:

- – Specialist software vendors (consolidating)

- – Larger software companies (expense management as a model of their enterprise suites)

- – Procurement specialists and enterprise resource planning vendors (extension to existing deployments)

Macroenvironment analysis

3.2   STEEP

(a)   **Social**

- – Globalisation will increase people mobility (employees less present in the offices)
- – Social isolation – increased usage of Internet and mobile services
- – Greater social responsibility (CSR)

(b)   **Technological**

- – Cheap broadband
- – Wireless technology
- – Increased standardisation of Internet based applications
- – On Demand Software

(c)   **Economical**

- – Companies focus on increasing business process efficiency
- – Cheap labour countries get access to worldwide services market
- – Credit cards increased usage for travel and entertainment expenses

(d)   **Environmental**

- – Promoting a paper free environment

(e)   **Political/Legislation**

- – Data Protection
- – SOX Act may extend to SMEs
- – Different VAT reclaim regulation across the countries
- – Web environment legislation will become more strict

3.3 The **macroenvironmental analysis** can be carried further to plot the likelihood and significance of likely developments.

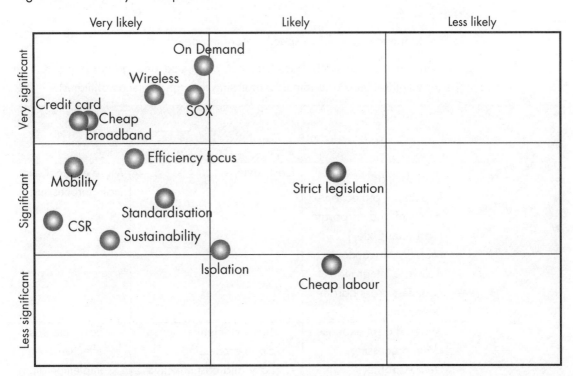

3.4 An analysis of the **DMU** can be useful.

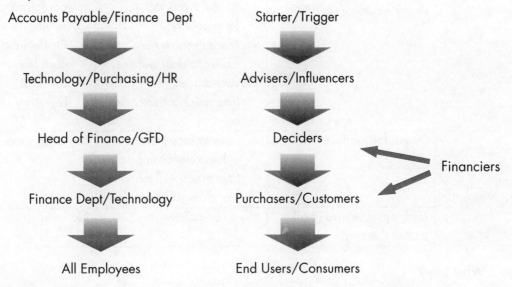

Segmentation

3.5 Segmentation approaches might be as follows.

■ **Company size**

– Large corporates
– Medium-size businesses
– Small businesses
} (analysed in table below)

BPP PROFESSIONAL EDUCATION

■ **Geographic**

  UK, Europe, US (needs IRS compliance)

■ **Industry sector**

  Some like pharmaceuticals have specific reporting needs

■ Signifo segmentation currently based on company size and geography (UK with some Europe largely through UK customers expanding through overseas affiliates)

	The corporate market (largest segment, dominated by Concur)	Medium-size business segment	Small businesses
Benefits sought	– Cost savings – Reputation protection – personal and corporate (Sarbanes-Oxley) – Mobility of workforce – Software integration – Seamless cross border operation	Cost savings	More efficient expense claim processing
Features sought	– More efficient expense claim processing – Demonstrable transparency and good corporate governance	– More efficient expense claim processing – Easy and cost effective implementation – Bespoke product functionality – More likely to need ability to deal with subsidiaries, international currencies, etc	– Easy and cost effective implementation – More willing to accept standardised service – On-demand to help cash flow – Low cost – Low entry price
Purchasing channel	Direct, face to face	– Face to face therefore values relationship – In international markets via strategic alliances	Buy over phone/online
Environment	Highly competitive (market leader Concur)	More competitive	No competition

3.6 **Why buy?**

(a) **What problem are clients dealing with?**

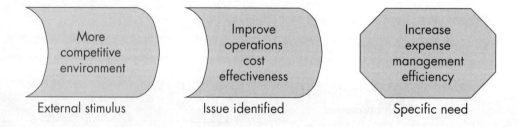

External stimulus — Issue identified — Specific need

(More competitive environment / Improve operations cost effectiveness / Increase expense management efficiency)

Triggers

- Cost analysis outlining expense claim process as a saving opportunity

- Low productivity of employees/accounting because of expense claims paperwork

- The product is part of the package offered by enterprise resource planning companies

- Competitors benchmarking

- Management decision to outsource all non-strategic functions/processes

(b) **Where does the information come from?**

Purchasing decision is made usually by finance/accounting managers, based on information provided by:

- Recommendation of related companies (accounting firms working for the respective company)

- On Demand Software vendors' websites

- Enterprise resources planners already serving the company

- Internet browsers

- Advertising (Internet, financial/accounting magazines)

- 'Other' in inbound leads is very big – it is worth investigating further

ERP and advertising are active sources of information, browsers and websites are passive; recommendation may be either.

(c) **Specific channel patterns**

Payment, level of solution complexity and points of contact with the customer are specific to each channel.

Channel type	Payment	Complexity	Point of contact	Loyalty type
Traditional – Licensed products – One-off purchase	– Fee/user/month	– Complete solutions – Integrated with IT legacy – Customised solution	– Face to face – Help-desk on-line and phone – Online	– Voluntary, based on product and service performance, brand
On demand software vendors – Temporary solutions (usage restricted in functionality/time) – Repeated purchase, irregular	– Pay-as-you-go	– Simpler version of product – Restricted functionality	– Online	– No loyalty, transaction based relationship
ERP – Product as part of a wider package – One-off purchase	– Monthly fee for whole package (not only the expense module)	– Standard package with limited customisation – Highest integration level with IT legacy	– Face to face – Help-desk on-line and phone	– Induced by the high cost of switching (different than the rest of the package)

Market size and potential growth

3.7 (a) The table below shows Signifo's **share of the existing expense management market**.

	Market						Signifo	
	Total IT services market $mn	Total software market $mn	Subscrip. licence revenue $mn	Automated service providers revenue $mn	Managed expenses market $mn	Managed expenses market $mn	Sales $mn	Market share %
2002	536,000	–	–	–	700	448	–	–
2003	566,552	–	–	3,000	886	532	–	–
2004	598,845	–	–	3,737	1,122	606	–	–
2005	632,980	–	–	**4,656**	1,421	810	1.50	0.19%
2006	**669,059**	**–**	**–**	**5,800**	**1,800**	**1,080**	**2.16**	**0.20%**
2007	**707,196**	**–**	**–**	**7,225**	**2,324**	**1,394**	**2.79**	**0.20%**
2008	**747,506**	**126,471**	**43,000**	**9,000**	**3,000**	**1,800**	**3.60**	**0.20%**
2009	**790,114**	**–**	**–**	**–**	**3,873**	**2,324**	**4.65**	**0.20%**
2010	**835,150**	**–**	**–**	**–**	**5,000**	**3,000**	**6.00**	**0.20%**

Note. **Bold** is forecast

(b) **Market size and potential growth**

The graph below shows the value of the managed expense market against the total of IT services market.

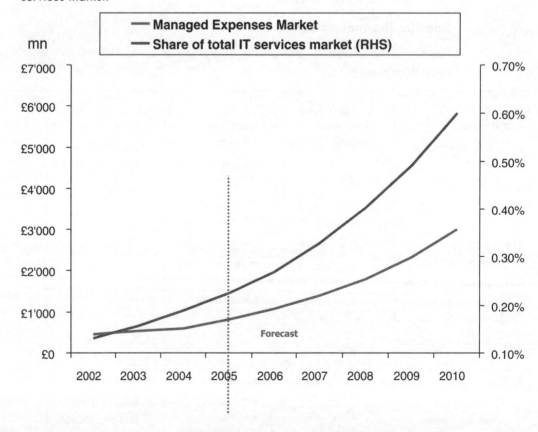

(c) **Managed expenses market map**

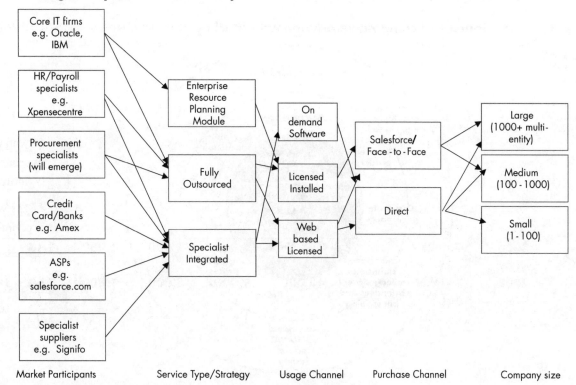

Market Participants   Service Type/Strategy   Usage Channel   Purchase Channel   Company size

(d) **Market/product lifecycle and the diffusion lifecycle**

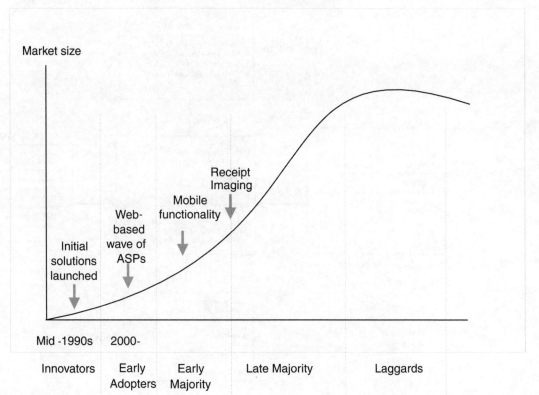

BPP
PROFESSIONAL EDUCATION

Competitive conditions

3.8 Sources of competitive advantage – market

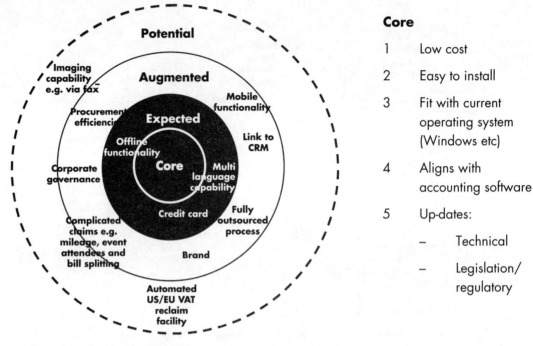

Core

1   Low cost

2   Easy to install

3   Fit with current operating system (Windows etc)

4   Aligns with accounting software

5   Up-dates:

   –   Technical

   –   Legislation/ regulatory

3.9 Porter's five forces in the managed expenses market (version 1)

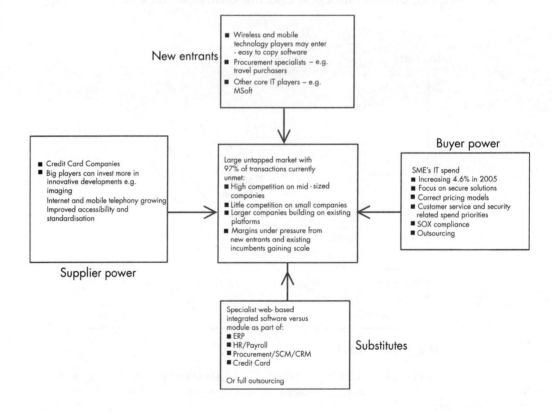

You will find an alternative exposition of this model in paragraph 3.15.

3.10 Competitive forces in managed expenses market

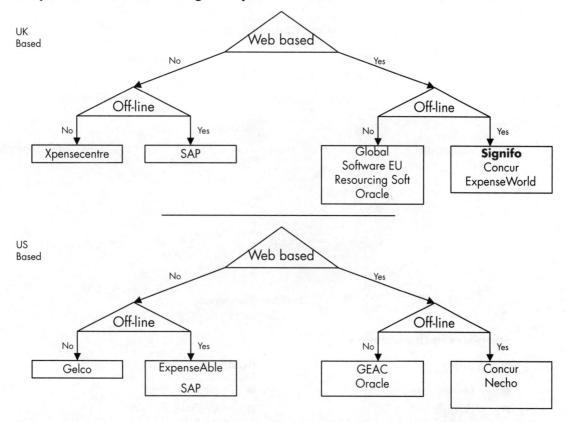

3.11 Competitors' strengths and weaknesses

Competitor	Strengths	Weaknesses
Large ERP	■ Wide range of services ■ Brand equity ■ Customer database ■ Integrative IT platform	■ Lack of focus ■ No mobile service ■ Low customisation ability ■ High complexity
Small providers	■ Low cost ■ Ability to serve small customers ■ Highly focused	■ Limited range ■ Potential lack of compatibility with customer IT systems ■ Low brand equity
Global Expense	■ Expense claims fully outsourced ■ Suitability to large customers	■ No off-line feature ■ No mobile service

BPP PROFESSIONAL EDUCATION

3.12 Positioning of competitors

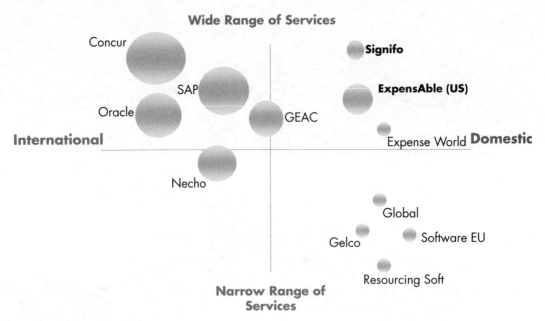

3.13 Suppliers to the industry

Marketing	Business
■ Market research	■ Hosting rental
■ Google	■ Website design
■ Telemarketing	■ Banks – loan
■ Sales collateral	■ Software developing
■ Exhibitions	■ Utilities
■ PR company	
■ Mailing house	

3.14 Opportunities and threats

Opportunities	Threats
■ Outsourcing increasing	■ Slowdown in large enterprises– large players moving into SME
■ IT security	
■ Customer service tools	■ Google, Web browser on demand software
■ Correct pricing models for SMEs	
■ Google web browsers	■ Banks, Credit cards companies
■ Banks, credit cards	■ More owner risk/regulatory environment
■ Open source software	
■ New markets	■ Pricing models
■ Individual modules	■ Ubiquitous software – Free/Open source
■ Outsource hosting and back office work eg, India	■ Web security
	■ Attack from Asian software companies
	■ Vendors offering hosting services need to offer data security

Action Programme 2

In Paragraph 3.9 you can see how one student group completed their Porter's Five Forces model.

Below you can overview the presentation of Porter's analysis completed by a second group.

Take time to compare and contrast the two approaches. What is good and bad about each of them?

Alternative presentation

Porter's five forces in the expense management market – global (version 2)

3.15 Industry competitors

■ The corporate market is by far the largest segment to aim for – Concur is currently the market leader. SE have positioned themselves as 'THE supplier of expense solutions to SMEs' in the UK so far.

■ ExpensAble – focus on SMEs – almost exclusively a US user base (most of which use Quickbooks systems), with a few UK clients. Large US client base – do not offer web-based or mobile functionality – Appendix 3 – Competitive matrix

■ Majority of the major players in the US corporate market have multi language functionality – may be a barrier to entry to US market, or other global markets where multi language is valued by clients – Appendix 3 – Competitive matrix

■ Credit card functionality is offered by most of the key players in both corporate and SME markets – Appendix 3 – Competitive matrix

■ Very little information on SME global market – insights mainly into UK and US – Appendix 3 – Competitive matrix

■ Monica Barron, AMR Research – vendors in the market have merged with and acquired each other – evaluation and selection process quicker for clients

■ SME market – Forrester research – IT spending appetite of SMEs will be strong throughout 2005 (large enterprise segment slowing, SMEs showing healthy 4.6% IT spending increase during 2005 – financial services and manufacturing driving the buying activity). May attract increased composition from new entrants of corporate focused providers

■ AMR Research – expense management market – will reach $1.8bn by 2006 ($700m in 2002). Will attract increased competition in a growing market

Threat of substitutes

■ Some procurement specialists (eg IBM) have treated expense management as part of its overall approach to employee productivity – buyers may opt to go with the expense management services as part of a bigger package, removing the need to select a provider of expense management

■ Many of the vendors have begun offering digital imaging services to scan and store receipts and invoices required by the IRS (Inland Revenue Service in USA)

- Enterprise Resource Planning (ERP) – potentially very significant as clients access expense management as part of a broader solution via ERP providers. More relevant to mid- and corporate-sized organisations – Appendix 3 – Competitive matrix

- SAP and Oracle – provide expense solutions as part of ERP. Both have large client base in corporate market in UK. SAP based in Germany, Oracle in US – Appendix 3 – Competitive matrix

- SE are only firm who offer mobile functionality (apart from ExpenseWorld, who do not have credit card functionality) – potential to develop a barrier to entry or to protect their client base – Appendix 3 – Competitive matrix

- Paper based expense processes – 97% are on paper or on spreadsheets

Power of suppliers

- SE is also trying to build strategic alliances with other foreign suppliers so that they can strengthen their international position vs present situation. UK's DTI will help with this. This will increase the reliance of SE on other suppliers in the global market

- SAP and Oracle – provide expense solutions as part of ERP. Both have large client base in corporate market in UK. SAP based in Germany, Oracle in US – Appendix 3 – Competitive matrix

- Power lies with suppliers of resource management systems (eg ERP). SME market will continue to have very low supplier power (mobile, Internet, wireless etc) as there is little supply to providers other than credit card companies who feed data into the credit card functionality [interpretation from case]

Potential entrants

- Likely to attract new entrants as market is growing and provides good profits

- Barriers to entry low as set up costs low

- Innovation in functionality may raise barriers to entry – protection of innovative functionality key

Power of customers

- Low as there are many clients in SME market (very low with small, slightly higher with mid-sized)

- Higher in corporate market as value of a single customer is greater

Interpretation

Threat of entrants is high, with a very fragmented, very competitive base in a growing market (97%) of current expense claims are paper or spreadsheet based.

SE is fairly well positioned in terms of product functionality and current position in their served SME UK market. Growth of market and healthy profits will attract competitors. SE will need to decide on a deliberate rather than emergent strategy or risk becoming middle of the road as the SME UK market progresses and becomes a market in its own right rather than a niche of a market.

Innovation and positioning is vital, as is segmentation of the market and selection of who to serve, and in turn, who not to serve.

There are broader options open to SE outside of UK and US, as well as a potential focus on the profitable corporate market.

Substitute products in the form of expense solutions as part of ERP or other broader scoped software solutions are a particular threat, especially if SE were to consider the corporate market.

Tutor Tip

(a)   **Tutor comments on internal analysis**

The analysis of marketing and sales data is a good example of how the students took the data from the case and converted it into intelligence.

Some comments lacked evidence, for example under the heading "staff" an assumption was made about "insufficient sales resource for face to face meetings". A perfectly reasonable assumption but it must be backed up by evidence.

(b)   **Tutor comments on external analysis**

Porter's five forces model needed more interpretation of the information for example, what were the barriers to entry? Some comments were in the wrong boxes: eg 'margins under pressure from new entrants'.

Positioning map – 'Wide range of services' was misleading, particularly as the map included a broad range of software providers. It needed to be specific to expenses or the map could give the impression that Signifo were offering a wide range of financial services.

4 Step 4: Summary and critical success factors

■ Marketing orientation
■ Marketing skills
■ Outsourcing (advertising, e-media, research)
■ International development (Strategic alliance, e-supply chains)
■ Competitive positioning
■ Branding communications, values
■ Customer Relationship Management (eCRM)
■ New Production Development
■ Marketing metrics
■ Measurements (what and how)

Action Programme review

1 (a) **The Decision Making Unit**

The case detail does not allow us to identify the job titles or be specific about motives and needs but this is a good effort to apply the model based on reasonable assumptions.

It would be helpful if it was flagged that these were based on assumptions in the commentary.

(b) **The Decision Making Process**

The DMP is a useful model when it comes to campaign planning. Adding a time line is helpful so you know how long the decision process might be in this sector.

Again, the group has made assumptions to populate the model but it is helpful. Linking it to an analysis of the marketing communication activities might have also added some insight.

(c) **Three phases of customer retention**

You should have spotted the difference here. This is a theoretical model (it may help you shape and structure your strategic recommendations) but at the analysis stage models are only valuable if they are populated. You must add data and information from the case for the model to have any value.

2 **Using Porter**

The first Porter example shows the value of communicating your ideas through models. Organising data in this way makes the information easier to absorb and will be useful content for your six pages of analysis.

However, you should have noticed some of the content is in the wrong places. For example, new entrants are included under supplier power. This presentation is data drawn from the case, but to give insight, there must be interpretation. It would be valuable to know, for example, why the barriers to entry are high for new entrants.

Tutor Tip

Remember the examiner wants to know you can interpret models. You must realise the strategic implications of your analysis.

You should aim for a combination of two approaches illustrated in this chapter. Work through the data and organise it like Group B, but make your points succinctly, using frameworks if you can. Hove in on key factors, interpret their implications and work them into a model. Group B's analysis is harder to get your head around than Group A's, but there is more attempt to make sense of the data and very usefully the whole is pulled together with a section dedicated to interpretation.

Do not forget that even on your A4 analysis sheets discussion and interpretation of your models and analysis is expected.

Signifo Expenses: Decision making Steps 5-10

Chapter Topic List	
1	Step 5: Corporate and business decisions for Signifo
2	Step 6: Business implications
3	Steps 7 and 8: Marketing strategy, tactical planning and contemporary issues
4	Step 9: Control
5	Step 10: Final preparation and managing materials

1 Step 5: Corporate and business decisions for Signifo

Signifo decisions

1.1 The next step is to review the nature of decisions that Signifo might have to make and identify the key issues facing the company.

Mission and vision

1.2 What are the strategic marketing planning issues?

Strategic decisions include setting direction, establishing objectives and developing plans. Envisaging the future often involves establishing a mission or vision for the company.

Action Programme 1

Create a mission and vision for Signifo.

Vision What is a realistic ambition for Signifo?

BPP
PROFESSIONAL EDUCATION

Mission

What are Signifo's objectives likely to be?

1.3 Setting objectives and filling the planning gap

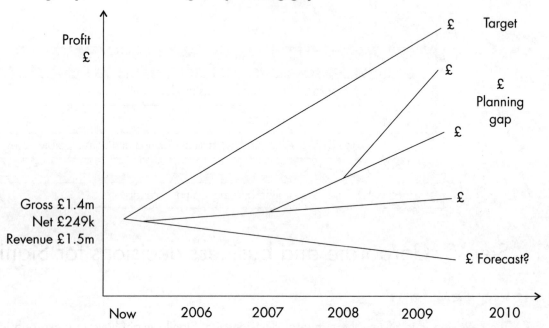

What do you think are realistic objectives for Signifo? Remember, you need to be able to provide an explanation for your forecast (such as internal constraints or external market conditions) and justification for each objective (eg improving marketing orientation, skills, competitive position and so on).

Options

1.4 Product market growth strategies

Action Programme 2

So where will the growth come from? You can use the Ansoff matrix to capture the strategic alternatives.

Products

	Existing	New

Markets — Existing / New

Justification

1.5 You now need to consider the options generated on your matrix against Signifo's strengths and goals. What criteria would you use to help you plan your strategy? Attractive and unattractive options could be plotted on a GE matrix to help support your answer. (A blank grid is given on the next page and our feedback is in the following text.)

BPP
PROFESSIONAL EDUCATION

Evaluation and selection

1.6 (GE) Criteria matrix criteria

Strategy attractiveness	Competitive position
Volume/forecast sales/Profits £	Value for money
Profitability in excess of %	Reputation
Investment required	After-sales service
Utilisation of operational capacity	Quality (relative)
Synergy with range/activities/marketing mix	Back up systems

Strategy attractiveness

	High	Medium	Low
High			
Medium			
Low			

Competitive position

1.7 The model can be adapted to focus on Signifo's key decision on whether to continue to concentrate on their management niche and small organisations or move to the more competitive mid-market sector.

Mid-market specific issues	Small organisation market specific issues
■ Highly competitive – sales to mid-sized constrained by insufficient functionality. ■ See customer endorsements (pages 43 – 51 (Evidence)) ■ **Competitive positioning**: What values differentiate SE from competitors? How do SE handle increasing global competitors/new entrants? ■ CSR Sarbanes-Oxley Act (SOX) and compliance ■ Identification of short- medium and long-term solutions ■ Segmentation positioning and targeting ■ Marketing mix ■ Structure/culture, information systems	■ Pioneer, niche position – mid and corporate market slowing competitors may turn attention to here ■ **Competitive positioning**: What values differentiate from competitors? How do ST handle increasing global competitors/new entrants? ■ CSR Sarbanes-Oxley Act (SOX) and compliance ■ Identification of short, medium and long term solutions ■ Segmentation, positioning and targeting ■ Marketing mix ■ Structure/culture, information systems

In the example we have just included the markets.

Strategy attractiveness

	High	Medium	Low
High	Protect position UK small	Invest to build	Build selectively UK medium UK large
Medium	Build selectively US small	Selectively manage for earnings	
Low			Divest US medium US large

(Competitive position)

2 Step 6: Business implications

2.1 This is a small company with limited resources. The decision it makes about whether to focus on a niche strategy or something broader will significantly affect its business. These are just some of the issues that need to be addressed.

- Structure and entrepreneurial orientation
- Planning and control frameworks, processes
- Information and systems
- Marketing strategies (SPT)
- Outsourcing (advertising, e-media, research)
- Strategic alliances, e-supply chains, evaluation, selection, management
- Competitive advantage
- Sector specific strategies
- Brand architecture
- Stakeholder Relationship Management
- NPD processes, launch strategies and plans
- Innovation
- Sources of funding and budgets
- Measurements (what and how)

3 Steps 7 and 8: Marketing strategy, tactical planning and contemporary issues

3.1 Signifo have been tactical in their approach to marketing and now they need to start thinking and acting more strategically.

Their marketing strategy needs to be based on a better understanding of their customers, better segmentation techniques and clarity as to how to target specific segments for competitive advantage. Positioning must be based on an understanding of what customers value (evidenced by customers' endorsements pages 43 – 51).

There are other issues too.

Communications and brand

3.2 What are the strategic marketing communications and brand issues?

(a) Whether or not you are asked for a formal communications plan, a strategic marketing communications planning structure is useful for ensuring you address all the marketing communications issues.

- Vision for the brand
- Objectives (eg raising awareness)
- Targets whom, nature of relationships
- Strategy – Push, Pull and Profile – what to whom?
- Brand values, positioning and messages
- Promotion techniques and the web

(b) Always look for clues in the case study. For example, Page 15 refers to "Brand architecture" (competency platform), co-branding (joint marketing alliances, market development partnerships, co-branding relationships – licensing, ingredient brand, composite branding, sponsorship). Your notes need to reflect these comments and show how you would achieve this.

Customer relationship managment

3.3 What are the **CRM** and **relationships** issues?

(a) This should be tackled in two ways – (1) relationships with customers (2) relationships with other significant stakeholders.

(b) **Objectives:** what do we want to achieve, what is in it for the customers (and other stakeholders)?

- What do we want from relationships?
- What makes customer attractive eg loyalty, value
- What makes Signifo attractive eg reputation, brand, financial stability, speciality, knowledge?

(c) **Issues** – Defining employee role in customer relationships (link to customers' chain of experience)

(d) **Issues** – Identification of key customers (primary/secondary), nature of relationships.

(e) Role of Internet in building relationships – what and how.

(f) What are the **international market development** issues?

- Structure for international business and planning and control processes
- Which products to which markets? – evaluation of potential products/market attractiveness (match to market opportunities)
- Positioning and the brand (universal appeal?)
- Global segmentation and international e-marketing mix – what does this mean for an online business?

Marketing Information System (MkIS) – design and setting up system, role of website in sourcing of information and gathering, monitoring, intranets/extranets and database management.

4 Step 9: Control

4.1 As well as the usual control mechanisms to implement for various plans (budgets for financial expenditure, schedules for projects and so on), the Signifo case hinted at the need for measures to monitor relationship management. For example:

- Customer retention
- Customer satisfaction
- Communications
- Staff satisfaction
- Customer input

4.2 For an Internet-based business measuring Internet activities is important. For example:

- Banner advertising costs and measurement
- Cost per exposure and length of time user views
- Cost per response

- Cost per action
- Capture – how effectively Signifo are attracting customers to its site
- Content – how well are customers supported with information and ease of use

5 Step 10: Final preparation and managing materials

5.1 Having considered all the possible decisions and actions Signifo might be faced with, your final preparation should be to prepare very brief notes and to annotate your case study, so you have prompts and reminders to help you answer questions in the examination. However, do not be a slave to these notes, they can only be brief; use them selectively and adapt them to the specific requirements of the question. The final stage in preparation is to summarise your analysis.

Six pages of analysis summary

5.2 The following is an example of a summary completed by a student who obtained an A grade pass. What is noticeable is the value of the comments made, they reach conclusions and add insight. The student's notations in places uses too many numbers eg 16.1.2.1, never go beyond three points in business communications. If possible, avoid cramming too much on to a page, it creates a poor impression and makes it harder for the examiner to read (and give marks!).

Purpose of Report

This paper presents an assessment and profile of Signifo Expenses. It focuses on Signifo's current positioning, approach to branding and highlights potential strategic marketing issues.

Structure

Internal Audit

A   Overview of Signifo
B   Financial Analysis
C   Marketing Audit

External Audit

D   Macro-environmental trends
E   Micro-environmental trends

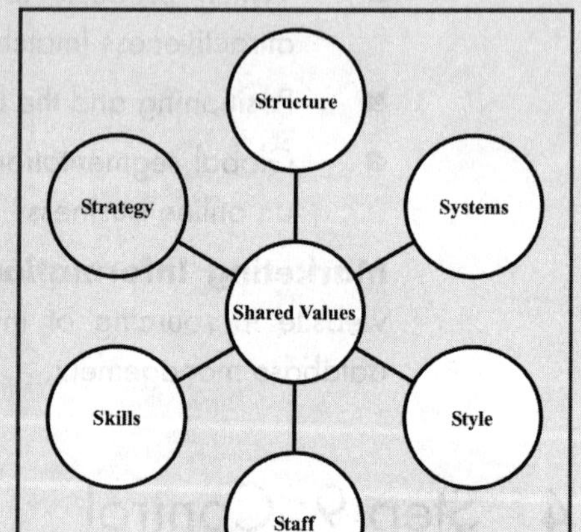

Figure 1
McKinsey
decomposition

I   Internal Audit

A   Overview of Signifo

Signifo is a pioneering automated services provider (ASP) operating in the managed expenses market. This overview is an independent internal profile based on McKinsey's 7S decomposition (Figure 1).

1   Shared Values & Vision

1.1   Vision is to be "*THE provider of expenses software to SMEs*". Unclear if there is an equivalent mission statement encapsulating overarching value proposition to customers.

2 Style

2.1 Entrepreneurial and technology-based approach with little evidence of effective investment in the brand. Customer feedback, eg testimonies, although very positive focused on the software solution rather than Signifo and the service it had provided.

3 Strategy

3.1 Looking to break into US mid-sized market. Potentially incompatible with stated vision to be leader in SME sector.

3.2 Trying to form strategic alliances – one partner will help with automating VAT reclaim across borders. However, relationship with Sage appears ineffective with few and expensive introduced sales (Section Y, PY investigates further).

4 Staff

4.1 Small workforce (appear to be c20 full time employees) brings potential issues around the capacity to expand, particularly as mid-sized firms require salesforce able to spend their time on attracting and retaining mid-sized clients.

5 Skills

5.1 High level of technical expertise allowed pioneering role. Ability to update software for new accounting standards as evidenced by award from Accountancy Age awards 2004.

6 Systems

6.1 ISO 9001 compliant. Advantage as this is usually a requirement if working with public bodies. Good basis for improving quality of service, internal/external service level agreements and business contingency/operational risk management.

6.2 Supply chain management – everything that can be appears to be outsourced and company feels it has a tight grip on costs. Financial Analysis section (Section B) investigates further.

7 Structure

7.1 Likely to be relatively flat structure with little formal operational organisation reflecting entrepreneurial style.

B Financial Analysis

8 Overview

8.1 Signifo is becoming profitable, with net income of c£250,000 in 2005. Retained earnings of –£10,000 suggests this move to profitability is relatively recent.

8.2 Solvency position looks robust, with low interest cover, strong working capital ratio and efficient collection of debts.

8.3 The business model is to outsource as many operations as possible (eg costs of hosting Signifo's website run at c6% of costs). This has kept overheads down, but may inhibit future expansion as there are few economies of scale possible – marginal costs will not reduce as they sell more unless they have contracts with suppliers such as web hosts which build in scale cost reductions.

9 Funding

9.1 Cost of debt capital at 25% is relatively high. This will reflect lack of collateral (there are no fixed assets), short track record of profits and the relative risk of the high tech sector.

9.2 In addition to accessing capital, potential partnerships and alliances may stumble if other companies, as part of the usual due diligence investigations, perceive Signifo as more risky to do business with because they have few assets in the event of becoming insolvent.

9.3 This will also be problematic if additional funding is needed as Signifo has already tapped the DTI and used the Government's small business guarantee scheme.

Figure 2 Customer Profitability	2005
Gross revenue per user	£79
Gross revenue per firm (50 users)	£3,960
Net income per user	£13
Net income per firm (50 users)	£658
	Lifetime
Net income per firm	£1,974
Net income per firm in today's money (discounted @ 2.5%)	£1,926

Figure 3 Aggregate Financials	2005
Profitability	
Gross Profit Margin	95.4%
Net Profit Margin	16.6%
Return on Capital Employed	208%
Solvency/Liquidity	
Working Capital Ratio	5.6
Interest Cover	18
Asset Utilisation	
Net Assets	£119,174
Tangible Assets	£146,081
Debtor Collection Period (days)	12
Creditor Payment Period (days)	13.5
Asset Turnover Ratio	12
Cost Analysis	
Marketing Spend (% of sales)	11.7%
Marketing Spend (% of costs)	14.7%
Software Development (% of costs)	10.8%
Employees (% of costs)	50.2%

10 Customer profitability

10.1 Signifo offering low price service, with gross revenue per firm just £3,960 per annum. Given that the average firm's cost of processing their expenses (£30-50 per month per user) is likely to be c£30,000 per annum; this offers Signifo's customers a return on their investment of around 7 to 1.

11 Investment

11.1 Although high proportionate spend on marketing, audit suggests much of spend is sales focused and may not be particularly effective (See Section Y for analysis).

11.2 As expected, software development accounts for a significant proportion of costs – several product developments took place in 2005 including SMS version, multicurrency/company, category limits and VAT rules. A reengineering project focused on Sarbanes-Oxley compliance and scalability is currently underway.

C Marketing Audit

12 Brand & Marketing Orientation

12.1 It is likely that strategic marketing has been low down on the agenda as befits Signifo's pioneer status. Web-based technology has allowed Signifo to develop an innovative solution to a business need in a market in which the buyers are still in the innovators/early adopters camp. In addition, until recently, with little competition in the SME sector, building a brand has been a less pressing consideration.

13 Segmentation

13.1 Signifo has attracted nearly 400 firms to buy its solution, with a number of well-respected mid-sized players such as Chivas Regal among their customers. Size and geographic location are identified as dimensions of interest to Signifo – as it wishes to expand into the US and to be "THE SME provider".

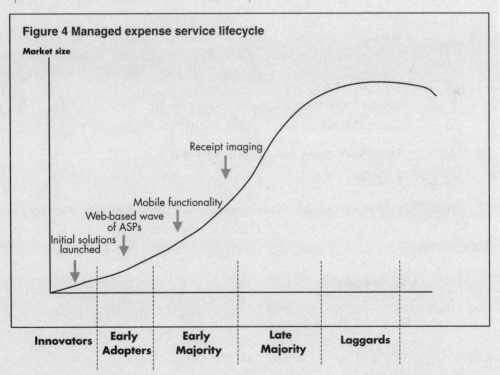

Figure 4: Managed Expense Service Lifecycle

13.2 This segmentation model is likely to prove inadequate as the market for managed expenses begins to mature. Figure 4 shows that the market is embryonic, with those firms buying solutions firmly in the 'innovators' camp. Size and location are unlikely to help predict who the early adopters are – nor whether there are segments within this group.

14 Positioning

14.1 Signifo offers a wide range of standard features on its software (see Product analysis below) and it is largely UK-based. Relatively few of the larger players offer a similarly wide range. However, the larger players tend to offer a more customised service aimed at larger corporates.

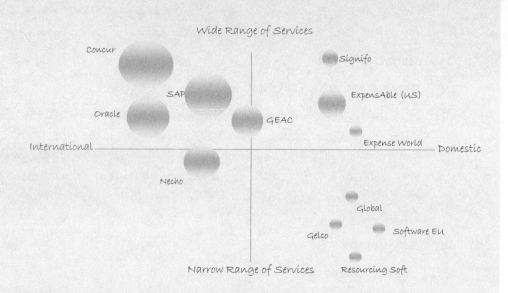

15 Targeting

15.1 It is unclear what approach is being taken. Vision suggests adoption of a concentrated approach with a niche segment being SMEs. However, desired expansion into mid-sized US corporates, using SOX compliance as a source of competitive advantage, contradicts this stance and suggests a differentiated strategy with several different segments.

15.2 Lack of clarity over segment value and selection will hamper the development of clear value propositions and is likely to lead to an ineffective marketing mix.

16 Promotions audit and the marketing mix

16.1.1 Product

16.1.1.1 Figure 6 shows which elements of the managed expenses service currently constitute a differentiated and competitive offering.

Core features

1   Low cost and easy to install

2   Aligns with current operating system (eg Windows)

3   Automatically updated for technical or regulatory developments

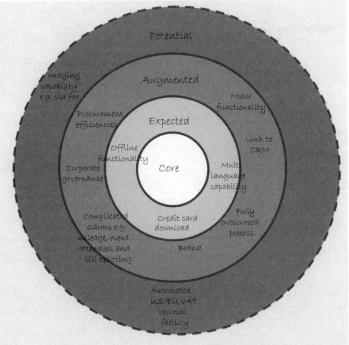

16.1.1.2   Signifo currently has a very competitive offering with automated VAT reclaim, category limits, imminent SOX compliance and SMS functionality.

16.1.1.3   Key issue is how quickly these features become standard. Risk is that larger players invest heavily in matching these product features for smaller firms, while continuing to offer a customised service to mid-sized players who want more complicated claims, mileage and paperless solutions.

16.1.2   Price

16.1.2.1   Figure 7 shows Signifo charges a fee per user licence per month. As described in the financial analysis section Signifo appear to be under-charging.

16.1.2.2   Without significant investment in the brand it is difficult to see how they can now raise prices given competition from ERP providers and other ASPs offering small firms with limited expense claims pay as you go.

Figure 7 Alternative Market Pricing Models   **Signifo**

Monthly fee per user per month	✓ £Y
Free (often as a module of Enterprise Resource Planning suite)	✗
Pay as you go – per transaction (On demand model)	✗

16.1.3   Place/Physical evidence

16.1.3.1   Key marketing asset is the website given that as Figure 11 shows Signifo are a web-based service. Financial analysis showed just 2% of expenses were being utilised to support the website – unclear if this is enough.

16.1.4   Promotional Effectiveness

16.1.4.1   Unclear how accurate lead tracking is. However, lead generation is poor (less than 10 leads in 2005) in a number of areas including banner ads, magazines, taxi receipts and resellers (Figure 8). Analysis of Decision Making Unit (See Figure 11 under 21.1.1) suggests communications targeted at finance departments or in a small company the accountants is likely to be crucial.

16.1.5   People & Processes

16.1.5.1   Limited salesforce

Figure 8 Communications effectiveness evaluation financial year to March 2005

	Spend £		Estimated no of leads	Estimated cost/lead £
Electronic channels				
Pay per click Google ads	17,000	Google ads	19	888
Pay per click other	8,000	Banner ads	5	1,463
Email marketing	6,000	Email newsletter	2000	30
Website	8,000	Google search	174	
		Other search	37	
Above the line				
Taxi receipts	12,000	Taxi receipts	14	878
Accounting trade press	21,000	Magazine article	4	
Other magazines	14,000			
Public relations	16,000			
Through the line				
Mailings	20,000			
Sales materials	4,000			
Directory listings	3,000	Other	208	
Events/sales incentives				
Exhibitions	22,000	Show	36	609
Referral scheme (awards)	8,000	Reseller	4	
Outsourced telemarketing	15,000	Recommendation	21	
Total marketing spend	174,000	Total leads	722	241

II   External Audit

D   Macro-environmental Trends

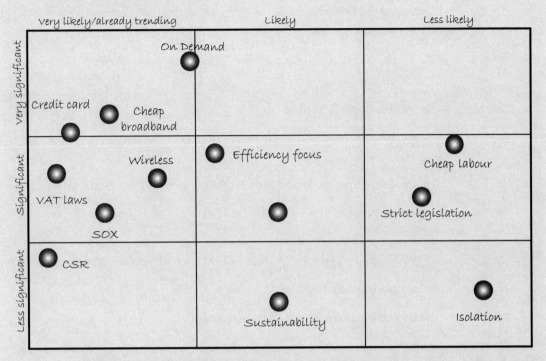

Figure 9 Opportunities and threats matrix for the managed expenses market

There are a number of trends in the external environment which are beyond Signifo's control. Figure 9 shows the significance and likelihood of the following:

17   Social/cultural & Environmental

17.1.1   Entertainment expenses proportionately lower as cost focus impacts on business culture

17.1.2   Flexible working patterns & social isolation to boost usage of Internet and mobile services

17.1.3   More focus on broad range of stakeholder needs – Corporate Social Responsibility (CSR)

17.1.4   Sustainability an increasingly important trend eg promotion of a paper-free environment

18   Political/Legal & Ethical

18.1.1   Legislation to protect Data & ensure web security likely to intensify

18.1.2   Sarbanes-Oxley (SOX) is increasing scrutiny & disclosure costs for large US companies

18.1.3   Complex bilateral international arrangements for tax eg reclaim of VAT across borders

19 Technological

19.1.1 Broadband & Wireless technology becoming cheaper and ubiquitous

19.1.2 Increased standardisation of Internet-based applications eg Msoft & YYY agreement

19.1.3 Fast pace of development in 'On Demand' Software eg ASPs like Salesforce.com

20 Economic Cycle & Trends

20.1.1 Globalisation and cheap air travel suggests increase in growth in overseas travel expenses

20.1.2 Companies focus on increasing business process efficiency & outsourcing

20.1.3 Increased competition in global services market as lower cost countries begin to compete

20.1.4 Credit card usage for travel and entertainment expenses becoming the norm

D Micro-environmental Trends

21 Segmenting customers and stakeholders

21.1.1 Figure 10 shows that the DMU for a mid-sized company is focused around the finance and technology departments. These will be key audiences for brand and sales messaging.

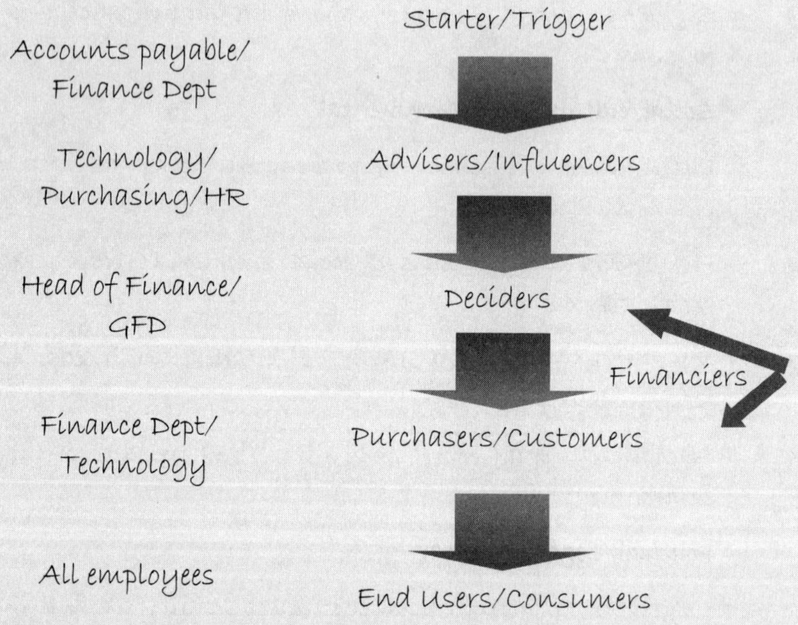

Accounts payable/ Finance Dept — Starter/Trigger

Technology/ Purchasing/HR — Advisers/Influencers

Head of Finance/ GFD — Deciders

Finance Dept/ Technology — Purchasers/Customers — Financiers

All employees — End Users/Consumers

Figure 10 Decision making unit for managed expenses

21.1.2 Signifo is a specialist supplier within the market map in Figure 11. There is a decision to be made regarding competing for the more customised, mid-sized market or to aim for the standardised on-demand market likely to appeal to smaller firms.

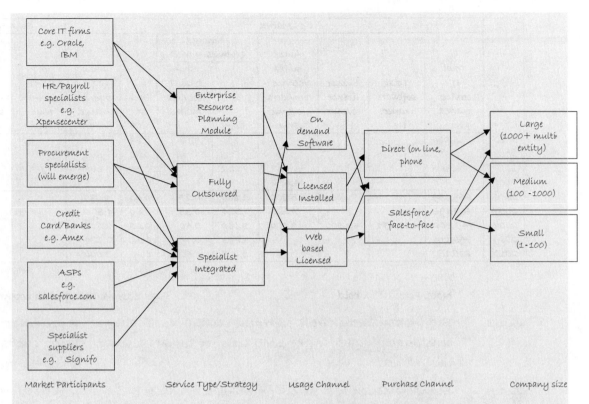

Figure 11 Managed expenses market map

22　Industry, competitors and market dynamics

22.1.1　Figure 12 summarises the competitive pressures that are at play within the market.

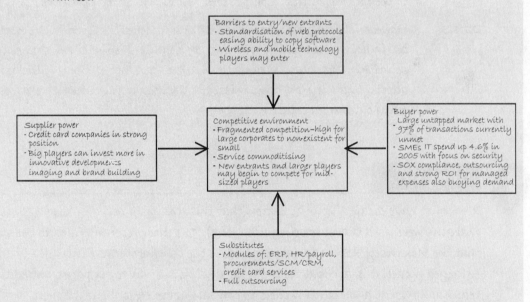

22.1.2　Figure 13 shows estimated market growth through to 2010. It shows the significant growth potential that exists in the managed expenses sector as currently just 3% of expense transactions are automated.

	Market								Signifo	
	Total IT services market $mn	Total software market $mn	Subscr licence revenue $mn	Auto-mated service providers revenue $mn	Managed expenses market		Exch rate £/$	Man-aged expenses market $mn	Sales rev-enue $mn	Man-aged exp-enses market share %
					$mn	Share total IT services market %				
2002	536,000	-	-	-	700	0.13	0.64	448	-	-
2003	566,552	-	-	3,000	886	0.16	0.60	532	-	-
2004	598,845	-	-	3,737	1,122	0.19	0.54	606	-	-
2005	632,980	-	-	**4,656**	1,421	0.22	0.57	810	1.50	0.19
2006	**669,059**	-	-	**5,800**	**1,800**	**0.27**	**0.60**	**1,080**		
2007	**707,196**	-	-	**7,225**	**2,324**	**0.33**	**0.60**	**1,394**		
2008	**747,506**	**126,471**	**43,000**	**9,000**	**3,000**	**0.40**	**0.60**	**1,800**		
2009	**790,114**	-	-	-	**3,873**	**0.49**	**0.60**	**2,324**		
2010	**835,150**	-	-	-	**5,000**	**0.60**	**0.60**	**3,000**		

Note. Forecast in **bold**   **Figure 13 Market growth potential**

22.1.3   Signifo's market share is currently small at c1.5% although it is likely to be considerably higher in the SME sector of the UK given its pioneer status in this market.

22.1.4   Standardisation of protocols for web-based services in 2003 as Microsoft and IBM collaborated has proved to be a convergent breakpoint and paved the way for ASPs like Signifo to provide easy to install, cheap solutions to managing expenses. Given the compelling business case for outsourcing expenses management it is likely that growth will now burgeon with little development to the core proposition. Competitors clearly will enter and drive down pricing.

22.1.5   However, it is likely that there will be another breakpoint in the next few years as imaging capability via fax or scanners enable an entirely paper-free solution. This may mean the market can move from innovator to early adopter/majority as companies of all sizes would then have a cost effective fully outsourced solution.

Tutor Tip

It will not have escaped your attention that this analysis ran over six pages (smaller margins were used than are being used here). The tutor recommended to the student that the McKinsey 7S model was applied, ie the comments were included in an enlarged model. It is difficult to get your analysis down to six pages but editing out redundant words and using models to communicate effectively will help.

Action Programme review

1   There are many possible visions or missions for Signifo. Your statements should be as least succinct, realistic, distinctive and focus on values of differentiations and customer benefits. Ideally, they should possess an inspirational quality to galvanise the company into action.

2

Products

		Existing	New
Markets	**Existing**	Television broadcasting Computer chip manufacture Consumer goods marketing Data storage Engineering consulting Hardware sales Organic food distribution Pharmaceuticals Recruitment consultancy Security systems Public sector	**P10 just completed launched 04** SMS mobile version Nov Multicompany/currency function Dec Category limits Jan 05 VAT rules Feb 05 **To come?** White-labelling capability **P6, 7** Security assessment projects Application implementation Outsourcing **P13** Legal, regulatory req A/C stds guidance Internal ops, mgt
	New	**Geographic** USA, Canada Europe Gulf **Sectors** Financial services Other manufacture Tourism	Consultation applications outsourcing

BPP
PROFESSIONAL EDUCATION

The Signifo Expenses exam

18

Chapter Topic List
1   The exam
2   The examiner's report
3   Reviewing exam answers
4   Examiner's overview and marking scheme

Introduction

In this chapter you will:

- ☑ Work the Signifo Expenses case under exam conditions (allow 3 hours)
- ☑ Have the opportunity to review student sample answers to the exam
- ☑ Consider tutor comments and examiner feedback for Signifo Expenses

BPP
PROFESSIONAL EDUCATION

1 The exam

Tutor Tip

Signifo Expenses exam paper and sample answers

In this chapter, you will have the opportunity to tackle the actual exam paper under exam conditions, at whatever stage you are in your preparation.

We would strongly advise you to take the time to tackle a past paper.

To be of value, you need to practise under exam conditions.

Once you have prepared yourself, make the time to tackle the paper, ideally in:

■ An undisturbed environment

■ A single three-hour sitting

If that is **not** possible, tackle it in two or three timed sessions. Do **not** cheat and give yourself any longer: managing time is one of the biggest obstacles to case success and the more prepared you are, the harder it can become to work within the time constraint.

By the end of this chapter, you will have:

■ Seen the Signifo Expenses question paper and considered the additional information

■ Undertaken Signifo Expenses as a practice exam paper

■ Reviewed your own exam technique and approach

For the examiner's model answers and comments visit the CIM website.

The Chartered
Institute of Marketing

Professional Postgraduate Diploma in Marketing

64 – Strategic Marketing in Practice

Time: 14:00 – 17:00
Date: 9th December 2005

3 Hours Duration

This paper requires you to make a practical and reasoned evaluation of the problems and opportunities you have identified from the previously circulated case material. From your analysis you are required to prepare a report in accordance with the situation below. Graph paper and ledger analysis paper are available from the invigilators, together with continuation sheets if required. These must be identified by your candidate number and fastened in the prescribed fashion within the back cover of your answer book for collection at the end of the examination.

At the close of the examination the student must secure their analysis summary (maximum 6 sides of A4 paper) to the examination booklet with a treasury tag. This will be provided by the examination centre invigilator.

The student must ensure they write their CIM student membership number and examination centre name clearly on the top right hand corner of the analysis summary before the close of the examination.

Read the questions carefully and answer the actual questions as specified. Check the mark allocation to questions and allocate your time accordingly. Candidates must attempt ALL parts. Candidates should adopt a report format; those candidates who do not adopt a report format will be penalised.

CIM reserves the right not to mark any submission that does not comply with the guidelines for this examination.

© The Chartered Institute of Marketing, 2005

364

Professional Postgraduate Diploma in Marketing

64 – Strategic Marketing in Practice

Answer all questions

The board of Signifo has asked you, as the appointed consultant, to address the following questions:

Question 1

Discuss and justify the ways in which Signifo could competitively position itself in its target market.

(25 Marks)

Question 2

Critically assess how CRM strategies can be used by Signifo to enhance Customer Lifetime Value, using relevant examples.

(25 Marks)

Question 3

Recommend ways in which Signifo could develop its brand image and grow its international presence.

(25 Marks)

Marks will be allocated for the prepared analysis and its application.

(25 Marks)

(Total 100 Marks)

2   The examiner's report

As a good marketer you should be instinctively interested in what the customer of your script has to say.

The examiner's report on Signifo is short and to the point but his comments are worthy of reflection. Take a few minutes to review what he has to say.

2.1

Examiner's report

General Strengths and Weaknesses of Candidates

The candidates have improved a lot over the last year. However some concerns remain. Many candidates still try to produce plans into which they would like to squeeze their answers. Some of the analyses are also a cause for concern as some candidates think that they should fill the three pages with pre-prepared answers rather than diagrams and short text. In some cases the analyses are excellent but the application of those analyses to the questions set is rather poor. At some centres, it was clear that the preparation was poor and subsequently the candidates produced rather general answers that were not underpinned by any substantial detail. On the positive side, some candidates are becoming more creative and innovative in the way they tackle questions.

Strengths and Weaknesses by Question

Question 1

Good answers made frequent use of/references to the attached analysis and hence carried good justification for recommendations put forward. They also homed in developing a strategic position for Signifo as opposed to a strategic plan. Some candidates still tried to develop extensive plans without considering the questions set. Good candidates also considered positioning vis-à-vis the competitors.

Question 2

This was a key question related to understanding CRM strategies within a web based company. Good candidates generally tackled the key issues involved in developing CRM and going beyond the technical issues. They also tackled the idea of e-CRM for companies such as Signifo. However, a good number of candidates discussed CRM at a superficial and academic level without applying it to Signifo. In many cases students were not very aware of web-based marketing – which is a worry. Better answers which were relatively few, based their recommendations on a theoretical model of CRM, treated CRM as more than database/direct marketing and emphasised two-way dialogue, mutual trust, customisation, customer research, added value and Key Account Management.

Question 3

Question 3 was closely related to Question 1 and some candidates picked this up well. For Signifo branding has to be achieved through a low budget, PR and the Internet. Good candidates had done good analyses on positioning and competitiveness and used these to justify a branding strategy for the company. They took this further in terms of how the company could internationalise the brand. However, poorer candidates took a superficial view of branding without any real analysis, so the answers were very general and not particularly applicable to Signifo. Good candidates also discussed how the company could 'piggy-back' its PR onto other larger companies.

Future Themes

Future themes are likely to tackle the retailing environment. [As reflected by the focus of the 2006 case, WHSmith.]

2.3 Now look at the more detailed analysis of a good and bad script below. This will have formed part of the examiner's briefing to his examining team.

If you have produced answers to the Signifo questions you might like to try 'marking' your own answers using these script characteristics. Based on the information below how would you rate your script?

2.4 Specimen answers: Signifo, December 2005

(a) **Introduction**

This case study explores the new area of Internet applications marketing within the B2B sector. Signifo is an SME that has made substantial progress in utilising the Internet for marketing and expanding its business. The company has a solid base from which it could build its presence in the larger corporate market and expand internationally. The examiners were therefore not only looking for good application of general marketing thought but also for good understanding of the new Internet marketing rules.

(b) **Marketing scheme: Signifo**

Examiners considered the following criteria in marking **all** three answers.

Good answers	Poor answers
■ Any recommendations will be based on a good analysis of the relevant parts of the case study.	■ Recommendations will be on a partial understanding of the case study.
■ Analysis will be in the form of making sense of the material in the case study rather than the repetition of that material.	■ Analysis will be mainly a repeat of the case study material, and/or will be inadequate.
■ Analysis prepared and attached to the exam script will be no more than six pages long.	■ Answers will not refer/make inadequate references to the attached analysis.
■ Clear references will be made to the relevant analysis which is attached to the script.	■ Analysis will not be based on theoretical models and tools.
■ Clear justifications will be made for recommendations.	■ There will be a lack of adequate justification.
	■ Brief bullet points will be used offering inadequate explanation/incomplete sentences.

Good answers	Poor answers
■ The answers will specifically relate to the question and not include irrelevant material.	■ There will be a lack of theoretical underpinning in the answers.
■ Answers will be based on a strong theoretical underpinning, using relevant theories and models where necessary.	■ Objectives will be vague and corporate and marketing objectives will not be clearly distinguished.
■ Objectives will be SMART and answers will show a separation of corporate and marketing objectives.	■ Answers will be tactical and miss the overall picture/not be synthesised with other answers.
■ Answers will be strategic.	■ The role of marketing research will not be highlighted.
■ Adequate credit will be given to marketing research.	■ There will be a lack of understanding of international marketing and integrated marketing communications.
■ A good understanding of international marketing and integrated marketing communications will be shown.	■ Lack of understanding of contemporary business and marketing issues will be evident.
■ Good awareness of contemporary international business and marketing issues will be demonstrated.	■ Will include unreasonably long or short answers.
■ Answers will be balanced in length.	■ Answers will be patchy and lack cohesion and synthesis.
■ Clear attempt to analysis and synthesis and cohesion in answers will be shown.	

3 Reviewing exam answers

Tutor Tip

Next, compare your ideas and answers with the sample answers provided by the examiners, along with their comments and marking guidance. The two sets of analysis are included at the end of this section.

3.1 Question One

Discuss and justify the ways in which Signifo could competitively position itself in its served market.   **25 marks**

(a) Question one: specimen answer one

To: Signifo Board of Directors
From: Ed Walker
Date: 6.12.05
Re: Signifo competitive position

A Mission

Signifo is a leading provider of expense management software in the UK and the US applying white label variants for the corporate sector to intermediaries and a unique range of sub-bands directly to meet the needs of SMEs.

B Situation analysis

Signifo is currently the UK market leader in the automated expense management market. Signifo's generic competitive position (using Porter's 'Three generic strategies') is niche focus strategy (see 4 (i) on *Analysis Sheets*).

Signifo uses this competitive position to sell to UK SMEs and penetration levels are currently microscopic. UK corporate sales are non-existent and sales to the US and other foreign markets are occasional and accidental (just 7% accounts receivable in 2005) (see 5 on *Analysis Sheets*).

The replicable nature of Signifo's current single product makes the organisation vulnerable to existing competition and hostile acquisition activity. In addition, the market is an attractive growth market characterised by low entry and exit barriers and bolstered by the political and legal environments.

C Objectives

Given the above situational analysis and the key issues (see Analysis 1) it is clear that Signifo must address their competitive position in order to meet the mission.

The objectives are:

- To survive as an independent entity
- To increase turnover by 10% per year (£1.5m in 2005; £1.8m in 2007)*

*If turnover increases by 10%/year gross profits will also increase by 10%. However, other expenses can be controlled at 4.5% increase per year (2% above inflation) so this allows marketing expense to increase by 15% per year of turnover and still equate to more profitable business (net profit: 17.4% in 2005; 30.3% in 2010 etc).

D Strategies – the potential competitive positions

Signifo could continue to operate as a niche player. However, while this competitive position is preferable to 'being stuck in the middle' it will not be sufficient to meet the stated growth objectives.

The advantages of this competitive strategy are:

- As a small organisation with limited financial and human resources (see Analyses 3 and 5), Signifo must not overstretch itself.

- A niche strategy can aid segmentation.

- There are many examples of highly profitable niche players but the disadvantages include:

  (i) Signifo's web-based product is part of the new economy, which can transcend traditional boundaries. A niche competitive position may deter potential customers from other countries.

  (ii) New entrants and existing competitors could jeopardise Signifo's success.

Alternatively, Signifo could pursue a cost leader strategy.

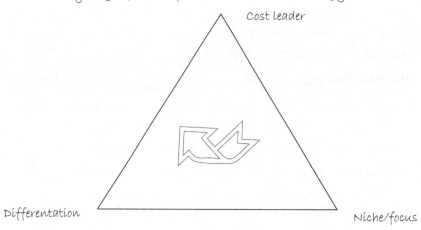

(Porter)

Cost leader advantages

- Signifo has grown to date partly by controlling costs.

- As expenditure (excluding marketing expenditure) does not increase at a rate commensurate with sales for Signifo's business model (see 5), reducing costs simultaneously while increasing sales could radically affect profitability.

- The cost of goods sold is low (gross profit = £1.4m in 2005, turnover = £1.5m). There is good growth potential here.

Disadvantages

- This is not a sustainable competitive position as competitors can emulate the strategy and erode its position.

- It is unlikely to generate the returns required to meet organisational objectives, as increased marketing expenditure will be necessary to take advantage of the open market.

Differentiation is the third possible generic competitive strategy.

Advantages

- The situation analysis makes it clear that Signifo is vulnerable because of the replicability of the product so it should arguably look for means of differentiation.

- The distribution analysis also reveals that the attractive nature of this growth market (see analysis 1) means that new entrants and existing competitors could easily replicate Signifo's current product. This is a further argument for differentiation.

Disadvantages

- Differentiation can only be a successful competitive position if it is based on attributes, which are desired by the target market, and if these attributes are effectively communicated.

E Conclusion

It is clear that either a niche or a cost leader will prove a sustainable competitive position enabling Signifo to reduce its vulnerability and meet its objectives. A strategy of differentiation, however, offers serious potential as a way by which to position the organisation to the target market.

Figure 9 on the analysis sheets shows how Signifo could segment the market based on 'organisational hierarchy of needs'. This is an adaptation of Maslow's hierarchy of needs, which analyses the level of need that organisations seek to address from Signifo's product.

As part of a broader branding strategy (see question 3), Signifo can use these 'organisational buying needs' as the target market, whilst differentiating themselves from the competition, eg:

Convert expenses into profits   = Organisational buying need

The first choice for expense re-charging = Positioning statement

↓

Source of sustainable differentiation

Signifo could also use this competitive strategy when positioning itself to the intermediary target market (who in turn can resell Signifo product to the lucrative corporate market).

Figure 11 shows how Signifo can differentiate them from other niche ASPs (represented as single jigsaw pieces) when targeting intermediaries.

With white label variants for re-sale by positioning themselves as a unique 'fit' to the already complex intermediary (represented as a larger jigsaw),

Signifo can offer a tailored, differentiated service that is an exact fit for the pre-existing products and services that are offered.

By seeking to differentiate itself, Signifo will be in a sustainable competitive position to target both their end-user and their intermediate markets. This strategy will enable the corporate objectives to be met.

Comments

This was essentially a good answer concentrating on the question set. Although the candidate has tried to slip in some strategic plan ideas, he/she has concentrated on positioning and offers very cogent arguments for why Signifo should follow a differentiated strategy. Differentiation, however, would require significant investment, both from a new product development perspective as well as the development of a comprehensive communication strategy. This needed to be further discussed in the answer. The analyses support the answer quite well.

(b)   **Question one: specimen answer two**

1.0   Introduction

Signifo has built a strong position for itself and established leadership in the UK SME market in just five years. However, as the market forces analyses shows (Appendix – figure 3), competition is likely to heat up over the coming years and differentiation will be key to the company's long term prospects.

2.0   Options for differentiation

Signifo can choose to differentiate in a number of different ways.

(i)   Technological leadership

The company has already been successful in developing innovative features for its product and the 7S analysis shows that development expertise is one of its core assets (Appendix – figure 10). Competitor mapping (Appendix – figure 6) shows that its mobile capabilities are ahead of the market, with only one competitor able to offer functionality in the same area. Nevertheless, caution needs to be exercised in relying on technological advantage as a sole differentiation. Signifo is a small company with limited resources and risks it R&D effects being copied by competitors.

(ii) **Customer base**

To date, Signifo has sold its product to the broad SME market for expense management. Figure 5 in the Appendix indicates that there are a number of ways of segmenting the market and building more targeted offers and products that would be more difficult for competitors to imitate. For example, Signifo's ability to support project-based expense claims would make the product very attractive to the consultant sector and a product tailored for their specific needs could do well.

(iii) **Services**

At the moment, Signifo provides services based around the product for expense management. Building value-added service, such as advice on dealing with SOX, or consultancy on minimising travel costs would help build a brand image of 'trusted advisor' and would further differentiate from competitors.

(iv) **Alliances**

Signifo has already been successful in building relationships with accounting software providers such as Sage, and other partners such as VAT reclaim specialists. Further development of complementary relationships would increase the value of its offer to the customer and increase switching costs. For example, it could ally itself with payroll providers, HRM applications or procurement application specialists.

3.0 Recommendations

(i) Monitor mobile development as a key technological differentiator, extending mobile support to a full browser-based mobile application.

(ii) Extend alliances to provide a 'one-step-shop' of resource management applications to customers.

4.0 Justification

(i) Mobile development builds on Signifo's technical skills and supports a brand image as an innovative company. It positions Signifo to exploit the growing market for mobile applications.

(ii) Developing alliances builds on Signifo's strength in developing partnership (Appendix – 27). It offers more value to customers and positions the company to move into new markets as competition in expense management solutions increases.

5.0 Implications

A focus on technological innovation has major implications for HR management given the size of the company. Retention of key R&D staff must be a major priority, for example through career development opportunities and incentives such as share ownership. Success in basing differentiation on alliances will depend on identifying appropriate partners and putting resources behind making the alliance work. I would recommend that a senior member of staff is assigned the responsibility to make this work.

6.0 Control measures

Appropriate metrics could be:

- 95% retention of key R+D staff over three years.

- Development of full mobile application by end of 2006-02-09

- Partnerships in place to cover full suite of "Resource Management" applications by mid-2007.

Comments

This is a very clear concise answer, supported by the material in the analysis section. However, from an implementation point of view, there may well be problems that have not been fully addressed in the answer. On the other hand, developing a unique advantage in mobile technology may well be a sensible solution. The diagrams in the analysis section are quite sensible and creative.

(c) **Examiner's overview and marking guidance**

Below is an overview of the examiner's comments and marking guidance.

This is a young company that has specialised in a particular Internet Applications Software that is now a burgeoning market globally. In terms of competitive positioning the company has to address many questions:

- What level of resources are likely to be needed to expand into the larger FTSE companies?

- Should the company stick to its niche SME market – if so how can it continue in such a manner that it has the major market share?

- Within a GE Matrix where does the company stand with regards to its products?

- How can it globally position itself effectively?

Students will be expected to utilise some of the various portfolio matrices such as the GE Matrix and even consider SPACE analysis.

GROWTH VECTOR ANALYSIS

| | **product alternatives** | | |
	Present products	Improved products	New products
Existing market	Market penetration	Product variants imitations	Product line extension
Expanded market *(options)*	Aggressive promotion	Market segmentation product	Vertical diversification
New market	Market development	Market extension	Conglomerate diversification

The growth vector analysis will help students to think through the product and its application and then the GE matrix helps with positioning.

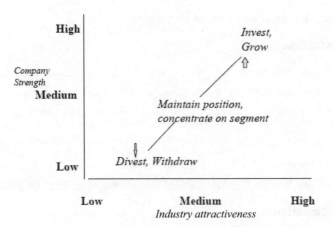

Industry attractiveness/company strength matrix

Students should also utilise the data provided to see how the company is positioned vis-à-vis the competitors. In this instance, a range of diagrams could be used depending on how the data is accessed. Finally students should consider how the company can position itself within a single market.

Different product strategies in a single market

	Product Alternatives	Relative Advantage
Range of Product Strategies	Present Product	Builds distinctive competence Economies of scale Clarity and unity of purpose Efficient utilisation of resources
	Related products	Broader product appeal Better use of salesforce and distribution network Motivation from doing something new Flexibility to respond to changing market conditions
	New products	Reduced competitive pressure Reduced risk of market saturation Smaller fluctuations in overall sales

Mark Allocation

Analysis and understanding of position	10 Marks
Number of alternative ideas for positioning	15 Marks
	25 Marks

BPP
PROFESSIONAL EDUCATION

3.2 Question Two

Critically assess how the concepts of Customer lifetime Value and Customer Relationship Marketing can be adopted and implemented by Signifo, taking into account the information that has been provided. **25 Marks**

(a) **Question two: specimen answer one**

Re: A critical Assessment of CRM strategies

A An Introduction

CRM Strategies are born out of increasing competition, globalisation and buyer power. They are bolstered by technological advances which facilitate the gathering, storing and analysing of massive amounts of customer data.

The aim is to:

Ensure long – term profitability through building and sustaining mutually satisfying relationships with key parties (including customers, distributors and suppliers).

B Current Situation

The online nature of the business, coupled with the technical expertise of the staff means that Signifo has developed a CRM database. Recently this has been put to use segmenting email bulletins (so that existing customers are at least recognised). However, much more can be done in term of 'Customer Profitability Analysis' (see 8).

Signifo also list 'retaining customers as a key objective, though in reality a transaction – based approach to marketing in still the norm (see 7 – AUDIT of MARKETING STYLE, WHEN Signifo scores 23/60).

In addition, not all customers are likely to prove profitable (see 8)

C Objectives

If Signifo is to pursue CRM strategies this must be to address specific objectives:

- Identify the potential top 20% customers generating profits and manage them with good key account strategies.

- Identify the 20% least profitable customers and ensure marketing expenditure is commensurate.

- Retain customers through better identification and service of their needs (Increasing value from £11,880 to £34,000 – see 3)

If these objectives are achieved, customer lifetime value will increase.

D Deciding when to use CRM strategies

A CRM strategy incurs costs and must therefore only be used if the profit potential exceeds both the initial and the ongoing costs. Barbara Jackson argues that RM is not effective in all situations as much depends on time horizons and switching costs, whereas Anderson and Narus argue that it depends on the customers competitive strategy – if they seek a cost leader position they may favour a transactional approach.

Using this information, Signifo can ensure there a CRM strategy is only used where it will enhance CLTV. This 'segmentation' technique was successfully employed by Hewlett Packard.

'Trusted advisor' Add value with CRM strategies → High-value long-term clients

HP

Transactional approach to setting systems → Low-value customers

(i) Top 20% Profit Generating Customers

These are the customers which Signifo must seek to build long-term relationships with. However, such relationships must be sincere and two-way; Signifo must avoid the pitfalls prevalent in business-to-consumer markets where direct mail is frequently perceived as junk mail; for example, Tesco are criticised for their open exploitation of the depth and breadth of knowledge that they possess on their consumers' buying behaviour.

- The first stage is obviously to identify who these customers are (potential and active). This is where Signifo's CRM database can be mined to great effect.

- The second stage is to organise and motivate all employees so that they understand the long-term benefits of CRM. This will entail a culture change, so that face-to-face partnering prevails.

- The third stage is to assign Key Account Managers who are targeted with increasing the revenues and profits generated from each relationship.

(ii) Bottom 20% Customers

Conversely, Signifo must also identify where profits, both now and in the future, are unlikely to come from.

These will typically be:

- Small organisations
- Not dealing with expense recharging (see 7)
- Not operating in different geographical regions (see 9)

These customers must be allowed to continue, but on a transactional basis. Processes should be automated so that contact both in person and over the telephone is reduced. This way, potential returns will be commensurate with organisational expenditure.

E Maximising CLTV through CRM strategies

Clother's customer profitability pyramids (see 8), can be used to demonstrate how the above strategies will enhance CLTV.

- If customers identified as lacking profit potential (A), receive a similarly low level of investment (B), than the CLTV is greatly enhanced than if all customers were treated equally.(C).

- If potentially very profitable customers (D) are imbued with a similar level of marketing expenditure (E) then:

- This may cost more than opting for the mid-point (C) in the short-term, but provided such accounts are properly managed, they will increase profits in the longer term.

- This will be because by entering into a naturally beneficial partnership with a client Signifo will be more likely to retain them (it costs between 5 and 15 times more to acquire new customs than retain existing ones).

- Signifo will be on hand to deliver bespoke solutions, which will differentiate their offering from that of competitors.

- Signifo will be able to focus on technological solutions (where their expertise lies), rather than in converting cold leads (currently conversion rates are 5:1 for inbound leads: trialists and 2:1 for trialists to customer- (see 6)).

- Signifo will be more likely to win new associated business, for example to help different sites/SBUs.

F Control

CLTV will only grow if Signifo segment their customer base and invest in relationships accordingly.

Key Account Managers will themselves incur additional expenses for Signifo. With this in mind I recommend the adoption of what Gummerson terms 'Return on relationship objectives; Key Account Managers will need to meet six monthly and yearly (Return on Relationships) ROR targets.

Low value customers should incur costs of no more than 20% of the value of their contract in acquisition and retention (the low cost of goods sold (see 3) make this possible).

High value customers must be retained beyond the 36-month average client life.

Comments

This is a well-balanced answer taking into account the best way to develop CRM strategies for Signifo, supported by some fairly incisive analysis. The idea of developing grades of customers and also looking at how CLV dovetails into this is good. The candidate would have benefited from developing more ideas on e-CRM and how this would fit in with the company's current knowledge base. This area is weak, whereas the segmentation, targeting and retention issues are well handled. Overall this is a very good answer that could have been improved by paying more attention to the changing nature of e-CRM.

(b)   **Question two: specimen answer two**

To: Board of Directors, Signifo
From: Ed Walker
Date: 9th December 2005
Subject: Enhancing Customer Lifetime Value Through CRM Strategies

1.0   Introduction

CRM strategies have a key role to play in building profitable, long-term customer relationships for Signifo and supporting differentiation strategies have been outlined in question. 1. Figure 23 in the appendix shows that while some customers are very profitable for Signifo, others are losing the company money. To achieve profitable growth, it needs to focus its limited resources on the 20% of customers generating 80% of revenues and profits. The objective is to move customers up the 'ladder of loyalty' to become supporters, advocates and partners.

2.0   Current Situation

Appendix figure 24 demonstrates Signifo's current CRM positioning. It has a good quality product and convenient delivery mechanism via the web which puts it in a relatively good position in terms of acquiring customers. Acquisition will also be supported by a stronger brand image, which will be discussed in question 3.

There are lots of opportunities to develop retention and enhance the relationship, which are not being exploited, and these will be discussed in the next section.

3.0   Developing appropriate CRM Strategies

The first stage to developing a CRM strategy is to analyse the customer base. Appendix, figure 5 shows that this is currently being done on only a limited basis. Customer database analysis will indicate:

■   Revenues per customer

■   Length of time as customer

■   Costs to service customer

■   Penetration of customer site, ie what proportion of the full employee base are using Signifo

From this information Signifo can do a more detailed per-customer CLV analysis, which will provide a more accurate picture than that provided in the summary analysis.

This will indicate:

■   Key accounts
■   Potential key accounts
■   Loss making accounts

CRM strategies should be developed for each individual class of customer.

These should include, but not be limited to:

(i)   Involving key accounts in decisions around new products development to ensure future enhancement meet their need and encourage dialogue.

(ii) Consideration for assigning key account managers for top accounts based on value to Signifo and opportunities to grow the business, as well as the potential impact of the loss of an account.

(iii) Reviewing customer service levels provided and consideration for having tiered service levels depending a customer value, eg web support only for low-value accounts and a telephone hotline for key customers.

(iv) Personalisation of the website to greet key customers by name and then push information of value to them based on pre-defined areas of interest.

(v) Extend "loyalty" email marketing, which has already seen success, leading to a big rise in leads during the month following its implementation in 2005. Use email to add value to the customer base by providing information on how to best use new features, provide value-add content such as advice on implications of changes in business tax rules, and encourage feedback from customers.

(vi) Build a community via the website, using tools such as forums and blogs, to encourage users to register their details and revisit the site. Appendix figure 22 outlines some of the tools that are available and are not currently being utilised by Signifo.

(vii) Build customised solution through partnerships as outlined in question 1.

4.0 Implication

To support its CRM strategies, Signifo will need to invest in CRM software to enable it to analyse its customer base and track key customer interactions. An increase in marketing investment in the website will be needed to support personalisation and development of community and other value –added services. I would recommend that Signifo increases its marketing spend on the website from its current level of £ 8k per year to £20k, funded through a reduction in off-line activities, eg by cutting its spending on taxi receipt advertising which Appendix figure 14 shows is not effective.

There are the implications of assigning key account managers and providing telephone support that must be considered.

Finally, Signifo may need to consider using an external agency consultant to support their efforts in this area. Given my area of expertise, I would be more than happy to make myself available to assist.

5.0 Control Measures

To ensure the success of its CRM initiatives Signifo should set clear objectives and measures for success. Suggested targets could be:

- Reduce customer churn by 5% by end of 2006.

- Extend average customer life by 5% per year to end of 2009.

- Achieve customer satisfaction rating of 85% and above for 'Good' or 'Very Good' in satisfaction surveys the company is already conducting.

Comments

Another very clear concise answer supported by good analyses. This candidate has also spent some time considering the value of e-CRM and has homed in on software development and community building. Some more discussion of CLV, following on from diagram 23 would have made some sense in the actual text. The candidate has tried to follow a strategic plan formula, but fortunately has managed to avoid the traps. It is important that candidates answer the question set, rather than following their own pre-conceived ideas, as this can often create a straitjacket for creative thinking.

(c) **Examiner's overview and marking scheme for question two**

The CLV format has already been given in the case study, therefore students will be expected to look at the figures supplied in the appendix of the case study and to apply them to developing a CLV strategy. Students should then link CLV to CRM and understand how CLV can be enhanced by using CRM strategies.

CLV implementation strategies

Strategy	Tactics	Operation	Requirements
Conquer – increase C – – the number of customers	– improve the existing offer in order to attract the potential customers close to the existing customer segments	– improve: – product – price – distribution – promotion	Research Segmentation Investment
	– diversify the offer in order to attract new segments of customers	– increase the product/ service portfolio	Research Segmentation Investment
Increase RR – recurring revenues	– increase the volume of sales	– diversification – stimulate the demand	Research Segmentation Investment
	– increase the value of sales	– upgrade the offer	Research Segmentation Investment
	– increase both the volume and the value of sales	– diversification – stimulate the demand – upgrade the offer	Research Segmentation Investment
Reduce RC – recurring costs	– reduce general costs (admin, maintenance, etc)	– increased efficiency	Research Segmentation Investment
	– reduce cost of: product/service distribution communication	– cheaper supplies – cheaper outsourcing – increased efficiency	Research Segmentation Investment

Strategy	Tactics	Operation	Requirements
Retain – increase Y	– increase customers' loyalty maintaining and/or increasing customer satisfaction	– improve present offer – better targeting – score better than competition	Research Segmentation Investment
Reduce AC – acquisition costs	– better targeting of potential customers	– improve offer – improve targeting – use the same resources more efficiently	Research Segmentation Investment

CRM strategies

CRM is defined as IT-enabled relationship marketing. The company can use IT to build and maintain relationships with smaller customers. For larger customers it may adopt Key Account Management strategies.

Students could look at the six markets model and also take into account the following issues:

- Long-term orientation
- Communication and achievement of mutual objectives
- Fulfilment of promises by all the parties involved
- Creating trust and commitment

Towards the end of the answer students should take into account how CRM can help build CLV and how this can help the bottom line.

Mark Allocation

Discussion of CLV	10 Marks
Discussion of CRM	10 Marks
Linking the two together	5 Marks
	25 Marks

3.3 Question Three

Assess the ways in which Signifo could develop its brand image and grow its international presence. **25 Marks**

(a) **Question three: specimen answer one**

Re: BRAND IMAGE AND INTERNATIONAL PRESENCE

A   CURRENT SITUATION

Signifo currently operates a non-differentiated product, sold under the company name. Its international presence is limited to occasional and 'accidental' export primarily to SBUs of UK customers (see question 1).

B   OBJECTIVES

Developing brand(s) and growing the International presence are essential if Signifo is to meet the mission statement and corporate aims outlined in question 1.

Specific related objectives are:

■ Increase income from United States Dollars from 3.7% in 2005 to 15% by 2007 (bearing in mind that turnover will be growing by 10% per annum as a total to £1.8m in '07, therefore USA must equal £270,000 income).

■ Increase income from UK SMEs from £1.5m to £1.6m by 2007.

C   STRATEGIES

■ Signifo will adopt two branding strategies

(i)   One promoting a differentiated range to UK SMEs primarily.

(ii) One promoting white-label variants to UK and US intermediaries.

These will be resold to the larger SMEs and corporate sectors.

■ These strategies will allow Signifo to meet stated objective, but will signal a move to a differentiated competitive position (see 4);

■ Strategy (i) is a market penetration strategy aimed at increasing revenues from Signifo's existing UK SME customer base.

■ Strategy (ii) is a market development strategy, whereby Signifo's existing product will be branded to target a new market – the US.

■ The strategies will not try to build a wider International presence for Signifo as given the limited resources, this is too ambitious for the next two years.

■ The strategies will not aim to sell directly to small business in the USA recent product development (see 4ii) means Signifo is ideally placed to its product to the larger businesses already effected by the SOX Act. Longer-term this can be broadened to include smaller SMEs.

■ The strategies do not intend to develop brands to sell directly to the corporate markets in either the US or UK as Signifo is not equipped to compete in their markets and lacks the field force necessary to do so.

■ Diversification strategies will also not be pursued at this juncture as the risks and costs prove positive (see 5).

To reiterate, the chosen brand strategies and International strategies are:

Market \ Product	New	Existing
Existing	Market Penetration * Sub brands for UK SMEs	Market Penetration Utilise existing product (See 4ii)
New	Diversification avoid	Market Development *White Label variance for UK Corporate and USA Corporate/ Large SME markets

D TACTICAL IMPLEMENTATION –SUB-BRANDS FOR UK SMES

- A unique array of 'Sub-brands' will enable Signifo to increase profitability by adding value, differentiation (see question 1), reducing the importance of price in buying decision and helping Signifo's pull strategy
- Signifo could develop sub-brands using any of following brand strategies:
  - Company brand – Rejected – no source of differentiation
  - Range brand – Rejected – Signifo have essentially one product which can be positioned differently, too costly.
  - Individual brand name – Rejected see above
  - Umbrella brand – Accepted. This strategy is realistic given the size of the organisation and its financial resources.
- Under question 2 Signifo looked at segmenting customers based on the need they address by purchasing from Signifo (see 9).
- This should be used as the basis for segmenting customers eg professional service firms are motivated by the red to re-charge clients for project work.
- A positioning statement can then be developed accordingly, eg The first choice for expenses re-charging.
- Umbrella sub– brands can then be developed eg Signifo Professional. (see 10)
- This method of Segmentation links it at the level at which the sub-brands can be positioned.

BRAND PYRAMID

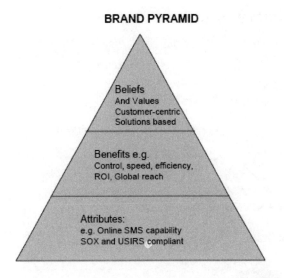

(Scott-Davis)

- As Signifo operate in the business-to-business market they should position the sub-brands at the 'Benefits' level as this concisely communicates the rational benefits sought by organisational buyers – Signifo Globetrotter, Signifo Professional etc (see 10).

- Signifo must promote these sub-brands to the target audience – for example Signifo Professional could be advertised on online accountancy and law sites and at key industry event.

E   **White – label's brand to the UK and the USA.**

- To become a 'White-label' intermedia Signifo must ironically develop a non-branded brand, which communicates their ability to 'fit-in' with other organisations, hence, the 'jigsaw' motif employed in 11.

- The positioning will vary between the US and the UK.

In the US the benefits of a SOX compliance and IRS compatible expense management tool will sway third parties, whereas in the UK the existing track record of successfully servicing clients will prove more enticing.

- The important universal benefits to emphasise are the willingness to be flexible in order to meet the intermediary organisation's own objectives.

- Following from the example on figure 10 the following platform could be addressed to increase business in both the UK and US.

POSITIONING STATEMENT

The flexible expense solutions partner

SEGMENT

UK/US Information (eg: large software companies or alternative business service providers)

BRANDING

Signifo perfect fit (TM)

F   CONTROL

The following time line must be adhered to if Signifo are to generate sufficient profits to meet the organisation's objectives.

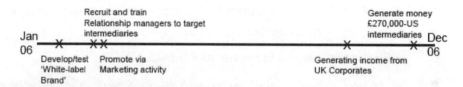

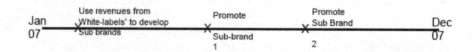

Comments

This is a very good answer taking into account the problems of creating an international presence and taking the company forward with regards to its brand image. The models used to develop the ideas are good, as is the notion of collaboration and working with resellers. Developing differentiated products under an umbrella brand also make sense. Some interesting and creative ideas have been put forward.

(b)   **Question three: specimen answer two**

To: Board of Director, Signifo

From: Ed Walker

Date: 9th December 2005

Subject   Developing Signifo's Brand Image and International Presence

1.0   Introduction

Given the competitive forces shown in Appendix figure 3, building a strong brand image for Signifo will be a key weapon in fending off competitive threats. Brand is important in creating trust and confidence in the B-to-B market in which Signifo operates and this is particularly true on the web. Businesses are unlikely to entrust confidential expense information to a company about which they know nothing! Development of a brand will also support Signifo in its ambition to develop its international presence.

2.0 Developing a Brand Image

Figure 25 in the Appendix shows that Signifo's brand is made up of not just the tangible aspects such as its name, logo and website, but also its culture, values, skills and knowledge.

The first step to building the Signifo brand is developing a clear set of brand values that will be consistently communicated. These should be developed from the company's mission. I would recommend that Signifo's mission should be "to help fast-moving, agile companies manage their resources effectively through innovative, highly-reliable and cost-effective solutions."

Brand values could then be "innovation," "reliability" and "trusted advisor."

In developing brand values, it is important to consider where expenses management is on the technology adoption curve (Appendix – figure 8).

"Crossing the chasm" will emphasise the need for "trust" and "reliability" as brand values.

Using Aaker's elements of brand equity, I would recommend the following steps:

■ Build awareness and interest through: influence programmes, case-study-based PR and industry analyst programmes using key industry commentators and gurus such as Gartner and IDC. Such programmes are relatively cheap to run and Signifo's position in the two growing markets of expense management and ASP (Appendix figures 1 and 2) provide a good hook to engage interest. These influences will also play a key role in persuading the early majority to adopt the technology.

■ Current off-line and on-line marketing activities (Appendix – figure 11) must be integrated and support the brand image consistently. The CRM strategies outlined in question 2 will also support the development of the Signifo brand.

    (i) Build brand loyalty through the CRM strategies already discussed.

    (ii) Perception of brand quality is already good since we have a high-quality, highly-reliable product but this must be clearly communicated.

    (iii) Brand associations will be supported though the differentiation strategies of innovation and partnership outlined in question 1.

3.0 Developing an International Presence

Appendix figure 20 shows that Signifo's current level of internationalisation is reactive. It has built a multi-national customer base through extension of UK customer installations to overseas offices and through proactive contact from customers overseas.

Appendix figure 6 shows that Signifo's UK market is still relatively open at the moment but competition will increase and internationalisation is key to achieving its growth ambitions, spreading its risk and meeting the needs of its international customer base.

The Harrell and Keifer matrix in the Appendix provides a method for determining market attractiveness based on environmental issues and Signifo's care capability and prioritising opportunities.

4.0 Recommendations

Based on my analysis, I would recommend that Signifo first enters the German market using a local reseller as a partner. The next stage of internationalisation should be US market entry, into a strategic alliance partner. Further detailed analysis will be needed before final decisions are made.

5.0 Justification

Signifo has limited international experience to date. The choice of a market close to home, in a similar time zone, will make management easier, and provide an opportunity for Signifo to develop experience. Germany makes a attractive prospect because it has a large number of mid-sized companies-the "Mittelstand," and a German-language version of the product will also open up opportunities in Switzerland, Austria and Eastern Europe.

The US is an attractive future prospect because Signifo's product is well-suited to the market, it is English-speaking and the opportunity is huge. Nevertheless, the competitive rivalry in the US market and the danger of Signifo spreading itself too thin means that the company should obtain maximum information before moving ahead.

Possible opportunities to consider are white-labelling the Signifo product, in a stripped-down, simplified form through special agents within eBay or Google who could operate as resellers to the low-end of the market, which we have seen can be costly to service in return for value provided. These portals are keen to add value to their sites through new services and this has the added benefit of squeezing out ExpenseAble which does not currently have a web interface.

6.0 Issues to Consider

Success will depend an identifying the right partners for international expansion and this role should be part of the remit for the resource indicated in question 1. My recommendation would be that one of the three founders takes responsibility for both developing the international business and the appropriate alliance.

Expansion into Germany will require a multi-language version of the product. If a suitable partner is identified, they may even be able to assist with the translation.

7.0 Control Measures

Control measures should be put in place to set objectives and measure performance with both brand building and internationalisation.

Suggested targets would be:

- Unaided brand awareness of 20% by end of 2007. This will be dependant on Signifo setting up a brand tracking and measurement programme and targets should be finalised once base measures are known.

- International revenues of 60% of total revenues by end of 2010.

Comments

A very good answer again, unfortunately following a set pattern. The candidate has some interesting ideas, such as entering the German market because of a preponderance of small businesses. This makes sense as it is also much nearer the home market and part of the EU. The brand awareness issues are discussed well and are supported by some very good analyses (Figures 22 and 21).

Summary of candidate one

This is a well-presented coherent paper, where each of the answers builds on the other. If presented to the board this would make a lot of sense. However, more discussion of financial issues would have helped. The analyses are generally very good and some interesting branding and segmentation ideas have been put forward. There is a tendency to veer into too much discussion on some of the diagrams in the analysis section, otherwise generally sensible utilisation of diagrams. The application of the analyses to the general text is very good and supportive of the arguments that the candidate is putting forward.

Summary of candidate two

Both these papers take a different view of the way the market should be tackled. In both cases, the candidates have given good justification for their strategies, from differing perspectives. This is healthy. In SMIP, we are trying to reward creativity and innovation and it is important that this trend continues. In each case the level of analytical thought and application is very good, making them good papers in their own right.

4 Examiner's overview and marking scheme

4.1 Answers should address the following issues:

- The brand name

- The possible B2B branding strategies

- Brand values, associations, personality and image

- Additional services to enhance the brand image

- Problems of global branding (universal cultural values, service level, country of origin effect, etc)

- Issues relating to standardisation Vs adaptation and effects on the global image of the brand

- Possibility of re-branding and re-positioning the company within a global context

4.2 **Note**. The company are contemplating a re-branding, for example from 'Signifo Expenses' to 'Web Expenses by Signifo'. This would allow us greater flexibility in aligning ourselves with their partner brands, such as 'Web Expenses for Sage users'.

Considering co-branding strategies, the company believes that the following initiatives will increase business from outside the UK:

- Alignment with other foreign suppliers: join programmes (QuickBooks, MYOB and others), get a case study for each, advertise when able to do so.

- Build the product to reflect foreign needs – eg US IRS data capture (business purpose, attendees).

- Concerted effort to generate business in foreign markets by replicating the UK plan in these markets.

For General Analysis and Application of the Analysis the marks will be as follows:

Mark Allocation	
Analysis	10 Marks
Application of analysis in the answers	15 Marks
	25 Marks

4.3 Candidate 1

Below is reproduced **how it appeared** the six pages of analysis submitted by the first candidate.

1., Resume and Key Issues

Signifo is the UK market leader in the niche SME automated expense management market. The market, both within the UK and globally, is growing rapidly and penetration levels are currently very low. The attractive nature of the market, coupled with the replicability of Signifo's single product means that the organisation is vulnerable and that future growth cannot be relied upon unless changes are made. Moving forward, Signifo need to increase market share and profitability by addressing some key issues:

A. **Emphasis on product features**, (add value through customer-centric strategies)
B. **Profitability of transactions**, (analyse using Customer Profitability Analysis or enhance via Relationship Marketing or Key Account Management)
C. **Replicability of the product**, (not factored on balance sheet, could be reproduced by new entrant)
D. **Segmentation of the market** (develop relevant positioning strategies and then branded accordingly)
E. **Global market wide open** (US in particular)
F. **Corporate market open** (potentially lucrative)

2.) Index of Analysis

In order to address these key issues, Signifo must develop and use **company** strengths to differentiate themselves from **competitors** and better satisfy **customer** needs. Ohmae's *Strategic Triangle* reflects the importance of these three areas and therefore serves as an index to position the analysis on the following pages. Each 'bubble' details the title of the analysis and its section number:

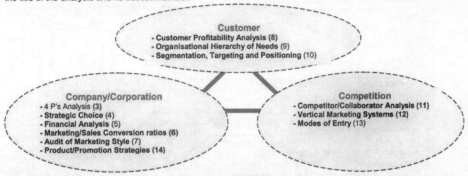

Customer
- Customer Profitability Analysis (8)
- Organisational Hierarchy of Needs (9)
- Segmentation, Targeting and Positioning (10)

Company/Corporation
- 4 P's Analysis (3)
- Strategic Choice (4)
- Financial Analysis (5)
- Marketing/Sales Conversion ratios (6)
- Audit of Marketing Style (7)
- Product/Promotion Strategies (14)

Competition
- Competitor/Collaborator Analysis (11)
- Vertical Marketing Systems (12)
- Modes of Entry (13)

3.) Internal Product, Price, Place and Promotion Analysis

Product
- Replaces paper based systems and takes advantage of Internet and mobile telephony advances
- Growth market, which taps into outsourcing, global operating and home working trends
- Web based application with credit card and accounting software interface. SMS version. Multi-company and multi-currency functionality.
- Compliant with SOX, USIRS and ISO9001
- Degree of bespoke functionality available
- Rated good/very good by 89% users
- Benefits for businesses = cost + speed + control

Price
- Simple 'pay-as-you-go' model; customers pay per user per month
- Average revenue per user is £6.60/month
- Average revenue per customer is £330/month
- Average customer life is 36 months, therefore average Customer Lifetime Value is £11,880
- High Return on Investment; payback period typically less than 3 months.

Place
- Majority of customers UK based
- Global customers are subsidiaries of UK customers
- Product sold and delivered via web therefore global reach
- Remote product training – postcard sized instruction manual.

Promotion
- Costs rise in line with size of customer's user base: small customers accessed by phone/web, mid-sized customers require face-to-face meetings
- Email bulletins, pay-per-click google advertising, direct mail employed
- Advertising on taxi receipts, banner adverts, trade press adverts,
- Work with providers of accountancy software to reach end-users.

4.) Strategic Choice
4i.) How to compete (Porter)

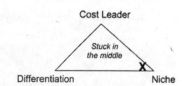

Cost Leader

Stuck in the middle

Differentiation   Niche

4ii.) Directions of Growth to Date (Ansoff)

PRODUCTS

		Existing	New
MARKETS	**Existing**	**Market Penetration** - Enhance life time value of existing customers - Increase number of customers (increase advertising)	**Product Development** - SMS service - US IRS Compliant - SOX Compliant - Re-engineering project to draw together the above.
	New	**Market Development**	**Diversification**

4iii.) Review of Potential Future Methods of Growth

KEY: RED = 'No go' in light of current information AMBER = Viable options – additional research required GREEN = Viable options to pursue								
OPTIONS	Feasibility	Knowledge	Risk	Profit Potential	Cost	Potential Gains	Competitive landscape	**TOTAL SCORE (out of 70)**
1. Increase penetration of UK SME market	8	7	7	5	7	6	7	
2. Enter UK corporate market	6	5	5	8	5	8	4	
3. Enter US SME market	7	5	5	8	4	8	3	
4. Enter US corporate market	5	4	3	9	2	8	1	32
5. Enter Global markets	4	3	3	7	1	8	3	
6. Merge with fellow specialist software vendor	4	3	3	4	4	5	4	
7. Acquire fellow specialist software vendor	1	2	2	4	8	5	3	
8. Form joint venture with fellow software vendor	6	3	6	4	5	5	5	34
9. Promote white-label variants to intermediaries	7	5	5	5	7	7	5	
10. Develop sub-brands to target key segments	7	6	6	6	6	7	7	
11. Develop alternative APS services	5	3	2	3	2	5	3	

Judging Criteria and Score (1=extremely unfavourable, 10=extremely favourable)

5.) Financial Standing
The above matrix ranks the methods of growth available to Signifo in terms of the risks posed versus the likely return. However, decisions can not be made without first considering the financial standing of the organisation:

Current Situation
- Turnover ~£1.5m
- Gross profit ~£1.4m (cost of goods = low)
- Marketing spend (~£174,000) = ~12% turnover
- Net profit (~£250,000) = ~17% turnover
- 93% Accounts Receivable GBP, 3.3% Euros, 3.7% USD
- £40,000 hard cash in the business
- £57,000 loans (£97,000 total)
- Debtors worth £49,000 (11 debtor days)
- No fixed assets - software not reflected in balance sheet

Potential Sources of Funding
- Additional bank loan
- Floatation and sales of stocks/shares
- Acquisition by Venture Capitalist/Private Equity House
- License the intellectual property of the software to competitors operating in different markets (e.g. overseas)

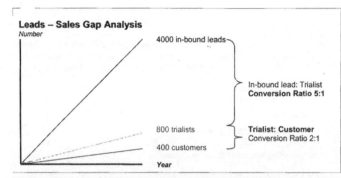

Leads – Sales Gap Analysis
Number

4000 in-bound leads

In-bound lead: Trialist
Conversion Ratio 5:1

800 trialists

400 customers

Trialist: Customer
Conversion Ratio 2:1

Year

6.) Conversion Ratios
According to the information supplied, Signifo has generated ~4000 in bound leads in the last five years. ~800 of these have resulted in a trial, which in turn has generated ~400 customers.

Analysis of these conversion ratios reveals that Signifo must focus on transforming a significantly higher proportion of in-bound leads into active trialists.

7.) An Audit of Signifo's Marketing Style: Transaction versus Relationship

Transaction Marketing
Characteristic

Score (1-10)

Relationship Marketing
Characteristic

Transaction Characteristic										Relationship Characteristic
Single sale						7				Retention
Product features			4							Product benefits
Short time-scale				5						Long time-scale
Little customer service	2									High customer service
Limited customer loyalty	2									High customer loyalty
Moderate customer contact		3								High customer contact

Adapted from Kotler

Analysis of Signifo's existing marketing style reveals that the organisation is currently too focussed on a transaction based, product orientated approach. Signifo is vulnerable because the lack of customer service and only moderate levels of customer contact engender limited customer loyalty. This is particularly dangerous as the market is attractive to new entrants and is characterised by low switching costs. As Signifo's single product could be swiftly and easily replicated then the active pursuit of Relationship Marketing strategies is essential in order to illicit a degree of loyalty.

8.) Customer Profitability Analysis
In addition to concerns about conversion rates and customer retention, Signifo must also be sure that the customers that they do have are generating significant returns, once the cost of the initial acquisition and the ongoing servicing and retention costs have been factored in. This is particularly important for a couple of reasons:

- The fact that the automated expense management market for UK SMEs was previously untapped (thus enabling Signifo to avoid head to head competition) is surprising given the buoyancy and attractive nature of the market. CPA analysis is necessary to assess whether the segment was avoided because the costs of acquiring and retaining such small players proved prohibitive.
- Signifo's low over-heads and fixed costs (gross profits = ~95% turnover) means that Signifo could service significantly more clients, without incurring additional costs in the same proportion. The end result would be improved margins, providing the new customers generate more profit, than they require in investment.

Kotler's CPA model is a useful tool for making decisions regarding future strategies:

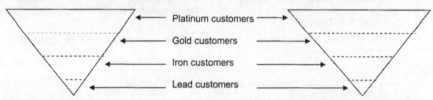

Platinum customers

Gold customers

Iron customers

Lead customers

Profit Tiers　　　　　　　　**Marketing Investment Pyramid**

The key point illustrated by this model is that investment must be commensurate with expected returns: Signifo can continue to attract SME's on relatively low value contracts, but ONLY IF the costs of acquisition and retention are also relatively low. It is a balancing act.

9277196

9.) Organisational Hierarchy of Needs

The following adaptation of Maslow's *Hierarchy of Needs* shows the level of organisational need addressed by automated expense management solutions. Different organisations will buy to satisfy different needs. An understanding of this can help Signifo develop segmentation and positioning strategies and to brand accordingly.

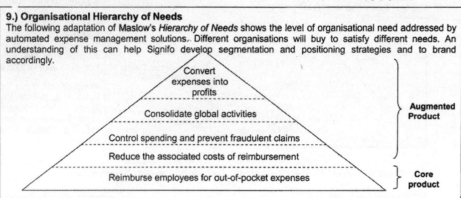

Convert expenses into profits

Consolidate global activities

Control spending and prevent fraudulent claims

Reduce the associated costs of reimbursement

Reimburse employees for out-of-pocket expenses

Augmented Product

Core product

10.) Segmentation, Targeting and Positioning

SME Market

It is possible to segment the Signifo's existing market using the factors identified in the above the 'Hierarchy of Organisational Needs'. Indeed, it is from this point that Signifo should start:

Step 1: Segment the market according to the organisational need answered by Signifo's existing product.
E.g. professional service firms (marketing agencies, accountants etc.) will be motivated by the need to re-charge clients for monies accrued against projects, whereas firms operating in multiple regional locations will be driven by the need to simplify proceedings, in particular with regard to foreign tax and VAT regulations.

Step 2: Select the segment (s) to target based on research into how they score in terms of cohesive needs, size of segment, attainability, measurability etc.

Step 3: Tweak the product to emphasise the core need of each sector.

Step 4: Develop positioning statements for each of the segments to be targeted.
e.g.   *The* first choice option for expense recharging

The first choice option for global expense reimbursement

Step 5: Develop strong umbrella sub-brands based on these positioning statements.
e.g.   Signifo Professional

Signifo Globetrotter

Differentiated Positioning Statements	Market Segments	Branding
• *The* first choice option for expense recharging →	Accountancy/Law practises →	Signifo Professional
• *The* first choice option for global expense reimbursement →	Corporate frequent flyers →	Signifo Globetrotter

11.) Competitor/Collaborator Analysis

Given the characteristics of the market (fragmented, young, growing, attractive, source of frequent merger and acquisition activity) and of Signifo (small player, approximately 20 members of staff, turnover of £1.7 million, reliant on one product), it is recommended that Signifo view other players not only as competitors, but also as potential collaborators.

The new economy encourages organisations to adopt leaner structures and to focus on core competencies, while out-sourcing (ideally to single sources of supply) wherever this proves financially beneficial. Acting alone limits Signifo's ability to exploit this trend, so collaboration must be considered in certain circumstances.

The following model outlines ways in which Signifo could collaborate with **fellow specialist software vendors** to win and retain lucrative contracts (examples 1 and 2). Alternatively, Signifo could look to collaborate **with larger software companies or business service providers, by providing the/an expense management module** to enhance their enterprise suite (example 3):

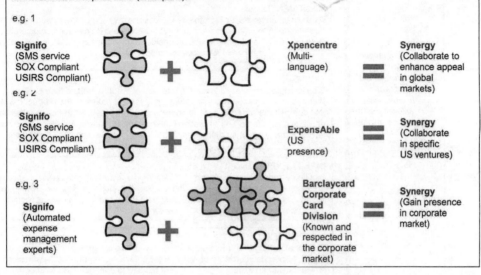

e.g. 1

Signifo (SMS service SOX Compliant USIRS Compliant) + Xpencentre (Multi-language) = Synergy (Collaborate to enhance appeal in global markets)

e.g. 2

Signifo (SMS service SOX Compliant USIRS Compliant) + ExpensAble (US presence) = Synergy (Collaborate in specific US ventures)

e.g. 3

Signifo (Automated expense management experts) + Barclaycard Corporate Card Division (Known and respected in the corporate market) = Synergy (Gain presence in corporate market)

12.) Vertical Marketing Systems

The options for collaboration outlined above would necessitate a variety of supply chain relationships. These, in turn impact on branding decisions. The model below outlines three options, which are not mutually exclusive:

Signifo ——— *'own brand variant'* ——→ End-user (e.g. UK SME)

Signifo ——— *'white label variant'* ——→ Intermediary —— *'own brand variant'* —→ End-User (e.g. UK Corporate)

Signifo
↓
Strategic Alliance ——— *'dual brand variant'* ——→ End-User (e.g. US SME)
↓
'Competitor' ASP

Adapted from Hooley et al.

13.) Deciding How to Enter New Markets – Kotler's *Five Modes of Entry*

As an online business, operating without substantial overheads and fixed costs, Signifo follows a non-traditional business model. This affects the decision making process when considering entry modes to new markets, and means that long-held and widely accepted models must be re-considered:

Assumed level of **commitment**, **risk**, **control** *and* **profit potential** *for businesses following a* **traditional model**

DIRECT INVESTMENT
The Internet breaks down traditional global barriers and Signifo's product is available worldwide without costly foreign assembly or manufacturing facilities. However, the larger, more lucrative larger contracts (often involving a degree of product bespoke functionality) would require investment in field sales personnel.

JOINT VENTURES
As a small, niche player Signifo's resources are dwarfed by the opportunities opening up in the global market and must therefore consider such collaborations. When selecting partners they must consider organisational culture, comparative strengths and sources of synergy *(see model 11)*.

LICENSING
Signifo could potentially license the intellectual property behind their product features to foreign competitors. However, given the nature of the product it is likely that competitors would choose to develop additional features in-house rather than pay to license them. The exception could be larger organisations who have not developed any expense management software, but see it as a viable add-on.

DIRECT EXPORITNG
Signifo currently undertakes passive 'occasional exporting' primarily in response to requests from subsidiaries of existing UK based customers. Active exporting would not necessarily require significant investment in the product, but would require major additional promotional spend *(see model 14)*.

INDIRECT EXPORTING
Indirect exporting of a 'white-label' variant would be an appropriate strategy for Signifo to pursue in order to provide 'larger software companies or business service providers with an expense management module to enhance their existing enterprise suite' *(see models 11 and 12)*.

14.) Product/ Promotion Strategies for Foreign Markets – Keegan's *Five Adaptation Strategies*

		Product		
		Do Not Change	**Adapt**	**Develop New**
Promotion	**Do Not Change**	*Straight Extension* Cheapest option. Possible in markets where Signifo's segmentation model works.	*Product Adaptation* E.g. re-engineer inline with US SOX and IRS laws. Consider expected returns vs. costs.	*Product Invention* Due to limited resources this option hould not be considered purely on grounds of enabling access to foreign markets.
	Adapt	*Communication Adaptation* Necessary if organisational buying motivation differs *(see model 11)*. Costly.	*Dual Adaptation* Best avoided as this would drain Signifo's limited resources.	

4.4 Candidate 2

Below is the six page analysis submitted by candidate two.

To: The Board, Signifo
From: Ed Walker
Date: 9 December 2005
Subject: Analysis of Signifo
Overview
Signifo has established itself as the leading UK provider of expenses management software for SMEs in just five years. It is profitable and liquid, with a customer base of approximately 380 companies, including some well-known brand names. It has tiny market share in both the expense management and ASP markets, but with substantial growth opportunities. All analyses refers to the expense management market unless otherwise specified.

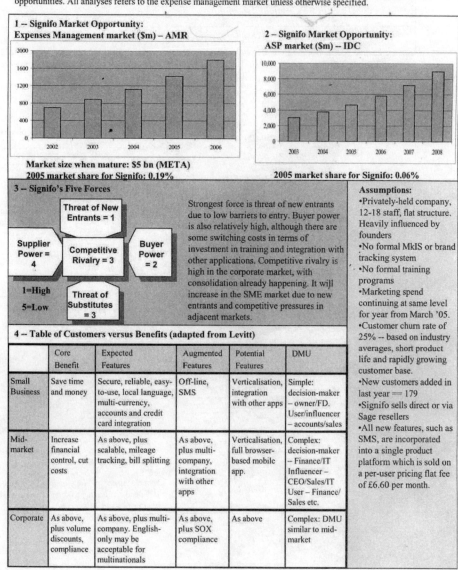

1 -- Signifo Market Opportunity:
Expenses Management market ($m) – AMR

2 – Signifo Market Opportunity:
ASP market ($m) – IDC

Market size when mature: $5 bn (META)
2005 market share for Signifo: 0.19%

2005 market share for Signifo: 0.06%

3 -- Signifo's Five Forces

Threat of New Entrants = 1

Supplier Power = 4

Competitive Rivalry = 3

Buyer Power = 2

1=High
5=Low

Threat of Substitutes = 3

Strongest force is threat of new entrants due to low barriers to entry. Buyer power is also relatively high, although there are some switching costs in terms of investment in training and integration with other applications. Competitive rivalry is high in the corporate market, with consolidation already happening. It will increase in the SME market due to new entrants and competitive pressures in adjacent markets.

Assumptions:
•Privately-held company, 12-18 staff, flat structure. Heavily influenced by founders
•No formal MkIS or brand tracking system
•No formal training programs
•Marketing spend continuing at same level for year from March '05.
•Customer churn rate of 25% -- based on industry averages, short product life and rapidly growing customer base.
•New customers added in last year = 179
•Signifo sells direct or via Sage resellers
•All new features, such as SMS, are incorporated into a single product platform which is sold on a per-user pricing flat fee of £6.60 per month.

4 -- Table of Customers versus Benefits (adapted from Levitt)

	Core Benefit	Expected Features	Augmented Features	Potential Features	DMU
Small Business	Save time and money	Secure, reliable, easy-to-use, local language, multi-currency, accounts and credit card integration	Off-line, SMS	Verticalisation, integration with other apps	Simple: decision-maker – owner/FD. User/influencer – accounts/sales
Mid-market	Increase financial control, cut costs	As above, plus scalable, mileage tracking, bill splitting	As above, plus multi-company, integration with other apps	Verticalisation, full browser-based mobile app.	Complex: decision-maker – Finance/IT Influencer – CEO/Sales/IT User – Finance/Sales etc.
Corporate	As above, plus volume discounts, compliance	As above, plus multi-company. English-only may be acceptable for multinationals	As above, plus SOX compliance	As above	Complex: DMU similar to mid-market

5 – Signifo Customer Segmentation

Basis for segmentation	Possible Sub-segments	Current Segment Focus
Type of industry	Pharmaceutical, IT services etc.	Broad – customers drawn from number of industries
Size of company	1-20, 21-100 etc.	Customers vary from single user to 1000-person firm.
Type of organisation	Proportion of home-vs. office-based; proportion of field workers; no. of branches; degree of internationalisation etc.	Not known
Geographic location	UK, US, Europe etc.	Majority UK. Few non-UK customers acquired reactively
Usage type	Light, medium, heavy users	Not known
Primary benefits sought	Increased productivity; reduced costs, cost control, compliance etc.	Not known
Feature use	SMS, VAT reclaim, multi-company/multi-currency, category limits etc.	30 SMS customers globally. Others not known.

6 -- Competitor Mapping

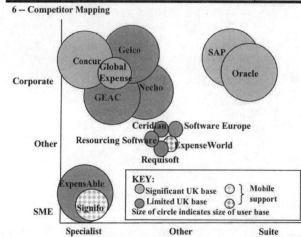

Positioning derived from Signifo Competitive Matrix.

No major direct competitors in UK SME market although threat from corporate players moving down. Corporate market very over-crowded which may drive major players into new segments.

Small "other " players pose a potential threat, particularly to domestic UK market. Two (Requisoft and Xpensecentre) also provide multilingual capabilities.

Some key functionality missing from Matrix, e.g. support for mileage, maximum number of users supported, provision of additional applications such as HR management or procurement.

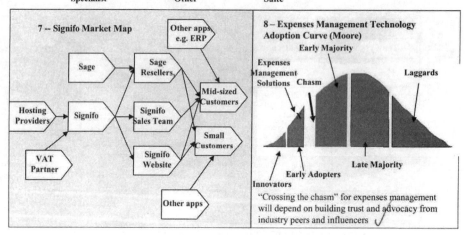

7 -- Signifo Market Map

8 – Expenses Management Technology Adoption Curve (Moore)

"Crossing the chasm" for expenses management will depend on building trust and advocacy from industry peers and influencers ✓

9 – Signifo Financial Performance		
Performance Ratios	Value	Implications
Gross Margin	95%	Good
Net Margin	17%	Low for software business. Need to review costs
ROCE	208%	Good due to low capital requirement for business
Gearing	63%	High: major investment may need to be funded through non-loan sources, e.g. VC, IPO
Quick ratio	5.6	High: capital may not be being used effectively
ROI	561%	Good

Caution must be used in drawing conclusions from financial analysis because no trend information available

10 -- 7S Model for Signifo

Strategy: Signifo has targeted UK SME market and is positioning for move into US. It plans to leverage strategic alliances to build international presence. No evidence of strategic marketing planning.

Systems: Regular reporting of marketing activities and leads. No formal MkIS. ISO 9001 compliance: systems in place for customer feedback/complaints. Needs CRM system to support customer retention and CLV objectives. No brand tracking.

Structure: Flat structure due to size; UK office only; privately held, funded through loans

Staff: 12-18 staff; lack of international experience; multi-skilled. Experienced services team. Use of outsourced staff for telemarketing. 45% of costs so need to be carefully managed. Staff retention, particularly R&D talent, a key issue.

Skills: Software/web/mobile-development & apps integration. Accounting/ compliance knowledge. Building alliances. Cross-industry implementations. No formal training program.

Style: Heavily influenced by founders. Tight cost control. Some evidence of customer focus. Quality important

Shared Values: Strong shared commitment to grow business

Soft elements (style, skills, staff, shared values) in particular need to be carefully considered and managed with any expansion of the business internationally.

11 -- Marketing Spend for Year to March '05

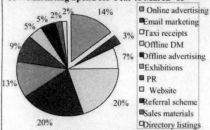

- Online advertising
- Email marketing
- Taxi receipts
- Offline DM
- Offline advertising
- Exhibitions
- PR
- Website
- Referral scheme
- Sales materials
- Directory listings

12 -- Source of Leads: Jan – Jun '05

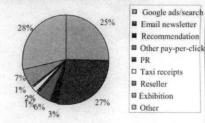

- Google ads/search
- Email newsletter
- Recommendation
- Other pay-per-click
- PR
- Taxi receipts
- Reseller
- Exhibition
- Other

13 -- Lead Generation Q1 04 to Q2 05

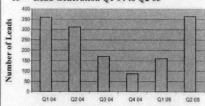

Leads in decline throughout 2004. Upswing in Q2 '05 due to high response level to email marketing campaign in June.

Significant volume of leads generated by "other" activities which are not measured separately.

14 -- Budget versus Lead-Generation

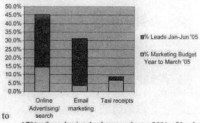

- % Leads Jan-Jun '05
- % Marketing Budget Year to March '05

17% of marketing budget produces 59% of leads

Cost per Lead:
Email marketing = £21
Online advertising/search = £153
Taxi receipts = £600

BPP
PROFESSIONAL EDUCATION

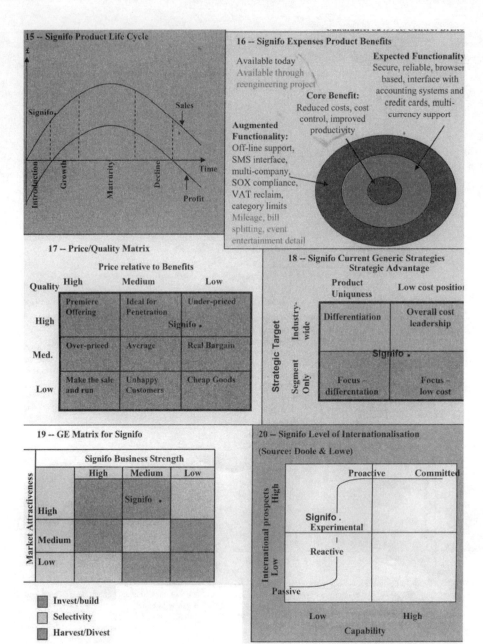

15 -- Signifo Product Life Cycle

16 -- Signifo Expenses Product Benefits

Available today
Available through
reengineering project

Expected Functionality
Secure, reliable, browser
based, interface with
accounting systems and
credit cards, multi-
currency support

Core Benefit:
Reduced costs, cost
control, improved
productivity

**Augmented
Functionality:**
Off-line support,
SMS interface,
multi-company,
SOX compliance,
VAT reclaim,
category limits
Mileage, bill
splitting, event
entertainment detail

17 -- Price/Quality Matrix

Price relative to Benefits

Quality	High	Medium	Low
High	Premiere Offering	Ideal for Penetration	Under-priced
		Signifo .	
Med.	Over-priced	Average	Real Bargain
Low	Make the sale and run	Unhappy Customers	Cheap Goods

18 -- Signifo Current Generic Strategies
Strategic Advantage

Strategic Target		Product Uniquness	Low cost position
Industry-wide		Differentiation	Overall cost leadership
		Signifo .	
Segment Only		Focus – differentation	Focus – low cost

19 -- GE Matrix for Signifo

Market Attractiveness	Signifo Business Strength		
	High	Medium	Low
High		Signifo .	
Medium			
Low			

Invest/build
Selectivity
Harvest/Divest

20 -- Signifo Level of Internationalisation

(Source: Doole & Lowe)

Proactive — Committed

Signifo .
Experimental

Reactive

Passive

International prospects (High / Low)

Low — High
Capability

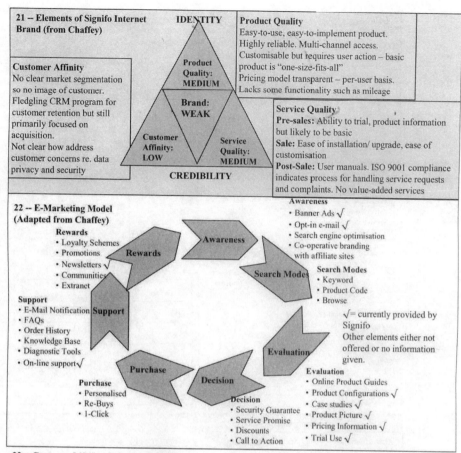

21 -- Elements of Signifo Internet Brand (from Chaffey)

IDENTITY

Product Quality: MEDIUM

Brand: WEAK

Customer Affinity: LOW

Service Quality: MEDIUM

CREDIBILITY

Product Quality
Easy-to-use, easy-to-implement product. Highly reliable. Multi-channel access. Customisable but requires user action – basic product is "one-size-fits-all"
Pricing model transparent – per-user basis.
Lacks some functionality such as mileage

Customer Affinity
No clear market segmentation so no image of customer. Fledgling CRM program for customer retention but still primarily focused on acquisition.
Not clear how address customer concerns re. data privacy and security

Service Quality
Pre-sales: Ability to trial, product information but likely to be basic
Sale: Ease of installation/ upgrade, ease of customisation
Post-Sale: User manuals. ISO 9001 compliance indicates process for handling service requests and complaints. No value-added services

22 -- E-Marketing Model (Adapted from Chaffey)

Awareness

Awareness
• Banner Ads √
• Opt-in e-mail √
• Search engine optimisation
• Co-operative branding with affiliate sites

Search Modes

Search Modes
• Keyword
• Product Code
• Browse

√= currently provided by Signifo
Other elements either not offered or no information given.

Evaluation

Evaluation
• Online Product Guides
• Product Configurations √
• Case studies √
• Product Picture √
• Pricing Information √
• Trial Use √

Decision

Decision
• Security Guarantee
• Service Promise
• Discounts
• Call to Action

Purchase

Purchase
• Personalised
• Re-Buys
• 1-Click

Support

Support
• E-Mail Notification
• FAQs
• Order History
• Knowledge Base
• Diagnostic Tools
• On-line support√

Rewards

Rewards
• Loyalty Schemes
• Promotions
• Newsletters √
• Communities
• Extranet

23 -- Customer Lifetime Value

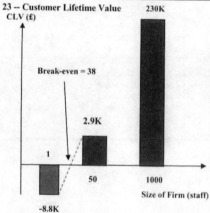

CLV (£)

230K

Break-even = 38

2.9K

1

-8.8K

50   1000

Size of Firm (staff)

Calculations based on estimate of total recurring expenses of £1m per year, and total acquisition costs of £180K

For 50-staff firm:

Change	CLV(£)	Break-Even
Reduce acquisition costs by 10%	3K	37
Reduce costs by 10%	3.7K	34
Increase average customer life by 10%	3.3K	38
Increase prices by 10%	4.1K	34

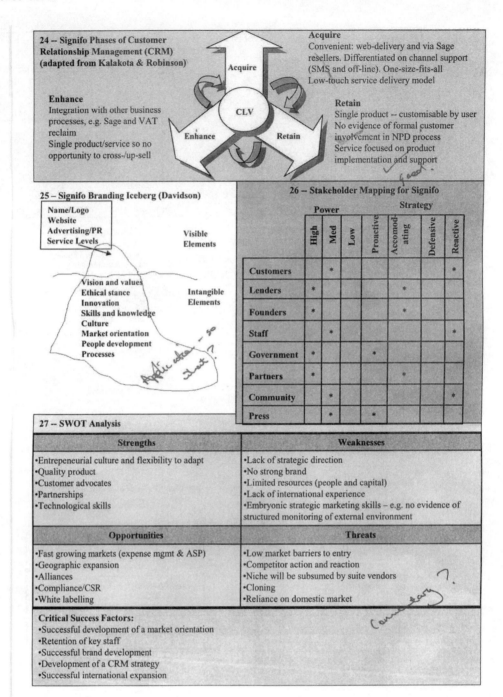

24 -- Signifo Phases of Customer Relationship Management (CRM) (adapted from Kalakota & Robinson)

Acquire
Convenient: web-delivery and via Sage resellers. Differentiated on channel support (SMS and off-line). One-size-fits-all Low-touch service delivery model

Enhance
Integration with other business processes, e.g. Sage and VAT reclaim
Single product/service so no opportunity to cross-/up-sell

Retain
Single product -- customisable by user
No evidence of formal customer involvement in NPD process
Service focused on product implementation and support

25 – Signifo Branding Iceberg (Davidson)

Name/Logo
Website
Advertising/PR
Service Levels

Visible Elements

Vision and values
Ethical stance
Innovation
Skills and knowledge
Culture
Market orientation
People development
Processes

Intangible Elements

26 -- Stakeholder Mapping for Signifo

	Power			Strategy			
	High	Med	Low	Proactive	Accomodating	Defensive	Reactive
Customers		*					*
Lenders	*				*		
Founders	*				*		
Staff		*					*
Government	*			*			
Partners	*				*		
Community		*					*
Press		*		*			

27 -- SWOT Analysis

Strengths	Weaknesses
•Entrepeneurial culture and flexibility to adapt •Quality product •Customer advocates •Partnerships •Technological skills	•Lack of strategic direction •No strong brand •Limited resources (people and capital) •Lack of international experience •Embryonic strategic marketing skills – e.g. no evidence of structured monitoring of external environment

Opportunities	Threats
•Fast growing markets (expense mgmt & ASP) •Geographic expansion •Alliances •Compliance/CSR •White labelling	•Low market barriers to entry •Competitor action and reaction •Niche will be subsumed by suite vendors •Cloning •Reliance on domestic market

Critical Success Factors:
•Successful development of a market orientation
•Retention of key staff
•Successful brand development
•Development of a CRM strategy
•Successful international expansion

A Final Practice Case: June 2006: WHSmith

19

Chapter Topic List

1	Introduction
2	June 2006 case: WHSmith
3	June 2006 exam
4	Marketing in the retail industry
5	Templates

Introduction

In this chapter you will work through a final practice case, further developing your own skills and case technique in advance of the exam.

Tutor Tip

You can download sample answers to the exam from CIM's website as well as the examiner's report and feedback.

1   Introduction

1.1   In this chapter you will find a final practice case study – WHSmith set in June 2006. This is a contrast to Signifo, based on a well-known UK retailer facing the many challenges besetting that sector today.

Tutor Tip

You might find it helpful to create templates of tools, checklists for each stage in the process which will provide you with your own customised DIY guide to help you when the final case arrives.

1.2   You will find in this section:

- The June 2006 case – WHSmith
- Some guidance notes to get you started

Action Programme 1

Start by reading the case as far as the end of the narrative and turn the pages to see what is included in the Appendix. You will see this is quite a different case context.

Tutor Tip

The case studies will always vary in context and whether or not you are familiar with the sector the case process remains consistent.

1.3   If you have the time, work through the whole case again in as close to exam conditions as you can.

2   June 2006 case: WHSmith

The Chartered
Institute of Marketing

Professional Postgraduate Diploma in Marketing

Strategic Marketing in Practice

Case Study June 2006

WHSmith

Strategic Marketing in Practice – Case Study

Important notes for candidates

The examiners will be marking your scripts on the basis of questions put to you in the examination room. Candidates are advised to pay particular attention to the mark allocation on the examination paper and budget their time accordingly. Your role is outlined in the Candidate's Brief and you will be required to recommend clear courses of action.

Candidates are advised not to waste valuable time collecting unnecessary data. The cases are based upon real-world situations. No useful purpose will therefore be served by contacting companies in the industry and candidates are strictly instructed not to do as it may cause unnecessary confusion.

As in real life, anomalies will be found in the information provided within this Case Study. Please simply state your assumptions, where necessary, when answering questions. The Chartered Institute of Marketing is not in a position to answer queries on case data. Candidates are tested on their overall understanding of the case and its key issues, not on minor details. There are no catch questions or hidden agendas.

Acquaint yourself thoroughly with the Case Study and be prepared to follow closely the instructions given to you on the examination day. To answer examination questions effectively candidates must adopt a report format.

As part of your preparation for the examination, you need to carry out a detailed analysis of this Case. You will then need to condense your analysis into a 6-page summary (a maximum of 6 sides of A4, no smaller than font size 11). This summary, and how you use it to answer the questions set, will be awarded marks and should be attached, with a treasury tag, to your answer booklet at the end of the examination. Your tutor should provide you with guidance on how to compile your summary 6-page analysis.

The copying of pre-prepared 'group' answers, including those written by consultants/tutors, is strictly forbidden and will be penalised by failure. The questions may demand analysis in the examination itself and individually composed answers are required to pass.

From time to time case studies will contain excerpts from company reports. The views expressed within these company reports fall within the jurisdiction of the given company and are not the responsibility of the CIM. Information is openly provided for the purposes of the case study examination only.

Important Notice

The following data has been based on a real-life organisation, but details have been changed for assessment purposes and do not reflect current management practices. Candidates are strictly instructed NOT TO CONTACT WHSmith or any other companies in the industry. Further copies may be obtained from: The Chartered Institute of Marketing, Moor Hall, Cookham, Berkshire SL6 9QH, UK or may be downloaded from the CIM student website www.cimlearningzone.com

---

Candidate's Brief

Assume that you are Gary Ross, an experienced marketing consultant who, until recently has worked within the garment retailing business in Europe. You have been appointed as a consultant to WHSmith (WHS), a very old established retailer with a strong presence on the High Street in the United Kingdom (UK). The company has undergone many changes as it has grown. It is now a major force in stationery and book retailing.

Over the years, it has acquired and divested itself of different types of retail outlets. It also has a presence internationally, mainly at airports; however, this strategy is also under review. The beginning of the 21st Century has not been a happy one for many retailers and WHS was no different. However, the arrival of a new CEO in the form of Kate Swann, and a new Chairman, Robert Walker, have seen major changes taking place within the organisation. The City has met the changes with approval and the company is enjoying a revival in its fortunes. However, this momentum has to be maintained, and new and creative approaches to retailing are needed, especially with the onward march of technology in all its guises.

The Board is particularly keen to develop a sensible approach to marketing, to understand its segments and to work on the revival of the brand. As a consultant you have undertaken considerable work in different areas of the corporation and have come up with the following report that you will present to the Board on the 9th June 2006. At the meeting, you will also be asked questions related to your report.

WHSmith

Introduction

Having started off as a small newsagent/retailer in 1792, WHSmith (WHS) is now one of the leading High Street retailers in the UK. In general, over the years, the company has made moves into publishing, music and the travel industry, but the greatest strength of its business has always been stationery, books and magazines sold through various outlets. Figure 1 outlines the various landmarks for the company since it was founded. The WHS family no longer has majority shareholding within the group.

In terms of retailing, WHS faced difficult times in 2003 and 2004 owing to generally poor sales within the British retail environment (see Appendix 1). The appointment of Kate Swann as Chief Executive Officer (CEO) heralded a new era for the company. Nonetheless, in 2004 the company received a preliminary approach from Permira, a Venture Capitalist Group, regarding a possible offer for the company. The offer was later withdrawn. In 2004, WHS sold the Asia Pacific Retail Consortium (ASPAC) business to the private equity group Pacific Equity Partners. This business consisted of retail outlets in Australia (Angus & Robertson), New Zealand (Whitecoulls) and Hong Kong. The Singapore Airport retail outlet was excluded from this deal and later sold to TimesNewsLink. Hodder Headline, WHS's publishing business, was sold to Hachette Livre, a wholly-owned subsidiary of Lagardère SCA. Recently, Robert Walker was appointed non-executive Chairman of WHS PLC. The organisation has three strategic business units, predominantly active in the UK:

a) UK Retail
b) News management
c) Travel management

Key facts about the company:
- WHS has stores in 399 out of the top 400 High Streets in the UK
- The company has 542 High Street stores and 200 Travel stores across 125 airports and railway stations
- WHS employs 24,061 people across the UK
- Every year, 70% of the UK's population visit a WHS store
- On average, just over 1.2 million people visit a WHS High Street store every day of the year
- Every year, 125 million travellers pass WHS's busiest Travel store at London's Victoria Station (Source: Network Rail)
- WHS sells 1.5 million magazines every week - 24,000 every hour they are open.
- Every year, WHS sells in excess of 40 million books
- On average, the company sells 3,000 A4 note pads a day
- End to end, the sales of the company's 3 best-selling rulers would stretch from London to Spain

The current structure of the organisation is shown in figure 2.

Figure 1: WHSmith Historical Landmarks

1792	HW and Anna Smith open a small newsvendor in Little Grosvenor St, London
1848/50	Opening of bookstalls at railway stations; becomes principal newspaper distributor in the country
1905	Railway franchise dispute means shops opened near railway stations
1920	Bookshop in Brussels
1928/29	PLC formed to avoid death duties - partners become directors
1939	5000 men and women from WHS go to join the war effort
1990	WHS and Boots form Do it All
1991	Disposes of WHS Travel Agencies and the television services division. Waterstone's store opens in Boston, USA
1992	WHS 200 years old. Acquires 50% of Virgin Retail Ltd. to operate Virgin's chain of 14 Megastores and 12 computer games centres. WHS Music Inc acquires 59 stores from Record World and 20 stores from National Record mart - Wall music retailer formed
1994	Our Price and Virgin Retail are merged with WHS establishing a 75% share of the business
1995	Waterstone's 100th branch opens in Reading, UK
1996	Major strategic review of the company. Sale of WHS Business Supplies to a french office supplier and also WHS's 50% holding in Do it All
1997	UK Travel Retail created as a separate business. Core business emphasised: WHS High Street, WHS Europe International Travel Retail, WHS News. Music business divested
1998	Waterstone's is sold to EMI/Advent International. WHS's shares in Virgin Our Price sold to Virgin Retail Group for £145m. Purchases John Menzies Retail chain and the leading European internet bookshop www.bookshop.co.uk
1999	Purchases Hodder Headline, a leading education and consumer publisher. WHS online www.whsmith.co.uk is launched
2000	Acquires Hazelwood Enterprises Inc for $19m and Benjamin Company Inc for $19m
2001	Acquires Blue Star Retailing Group (leading bookseller in Australia and New Zealand) for £38m
2002	Sells Helicon and acquires a leading educational and consumer house John Murray (Publishers) Ltd. WHS TXT launched to help literacy in schools
2003	WHS TXT - finalist in Business in the Community Awards. Kate Swan appointed as Chief Executive. Sells US airport and hotel retailing businesses for £41m and £8m

Boots – retail chemist; Our Price and Virgin – record retailers; Do-it-All – a Do it Yourself (DIY) retailer; Waterstone's – book retailers

BPP PROFESSIONAL EDUCATION

Part C: Practice cases

Page 6 of WHSmith

Figure 2: The current structure of the organisation

UKR Retail Management Executive

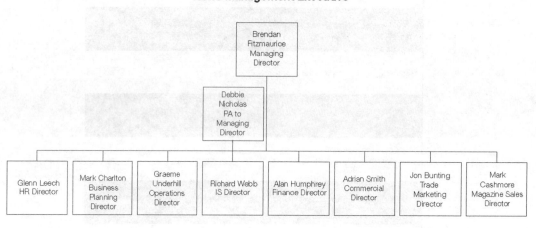

News Management Executive

Travel Management Executive

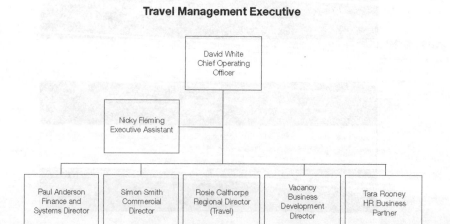

Values

Within the last year, the company has emphasised the importance it places on values and the drive to be customer focused. All employees are judged according to their progress on the Values in Practice (VIP) scheme (Figure 3). This scheme is also kept alive by good communications and engagement with staff at all levels within the organisation. This has been an important aspect of the turnaround strategy at WHS.

Figure 3: WHSmith values

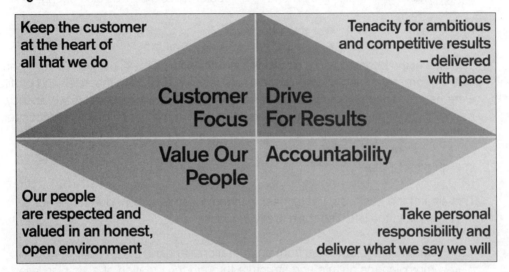

As part of its values, WHS has also chosen to behave ethically and responsibly towards the community it serves. It is regarded as one of the most ethical companies in the country, with strong community-based activities and supporting cause-related marketing. Recent research carried out in 2005 by the Guardian newspaper indicated that WHS is one of the most generous companies when it comes to the amount of charitable donation allocated per Christmas card. Much of the detail on Ethics and Corporate Social Responsibility is shown in Appendix 2.

Turnaround

In 2003/2004, the new CEO, Kate Swann, carried out a strategic review of the business and felt that certain changes needed to be incorporated in order to return WHS to profitability. It was clear that the company had a good strategic position in the High Street, but whether this position was leveraged to the best possible extent was under question. (Appendix 3 contains more situational analysis). Also under question were the various acquisitions that had been made over the years, as indicated in Figure 1. In order to understand the strengths and weaknesses of each area, the strategic review looked at the following:

Page 8 of WHSmith

a) Publishing

Hodder Headline, which was acquired during the dot.com* era, was delivering good sales and profit growth with strong market share positions in fiction and the high-margin areas of education. Hodder Headline was number 2 in fiction and secondary education, and number 1 in consumer education and further education. Given this position, the response to market challenges was to diversify the education portfolio, reduce high-risk products, manage promotional spend effectively and tighten financial controls. The emphasis on customer service was also strengthened.

b) UK Travel

This area of the business had a clear position within the UK travel market. The company was well organised and offered tailored services to clients, and the sales and profits were healthy. The main areas targeted for improvement were operational efficiency, partnerships with landlords, better productivity within the space that was occupied, better customer conversion and an improved service proposition to the customer.

c) High Street Retail

This area of the business, the biggest, needed much attention, due to the weak retail market in the UK. The main areas of focus were:

i)   stabilising the business from an operational angle
ii) improving the culture and structure through the creation of a simpler, less bureaucratic organisation
iii) finding areas of growth for the long-term health of the business

Performance in this area was weak because of the pressure on sales and margins from the changing competitive environment and changing customer behaviour. The Internet was also taking customers away. WHS was losing its authority on the High Street. To the customer, the value proposition of WHS was not clear, as it offered a very wide range of products, including music. At the same time, costs were rising and the operating performance was poor. Complex structures were partly to blame, as well as lack of clarity of purpose. As the cost base was rising faster than sales in all key areas, and central office costs were higher than other retailers, initially 250 roles were cut from the central offices, giving savings of £8.5m.

The other area that was looked at seriously was the speed at which goods were moved into the shops. Inventory levels were never properly assessed, resulting in poor availability in the shops for certain products. It was recognised that managing the inventory levels and the supply chain required better information management. In order to facilitate this, a new Information Services Director was appointed.

* The dot.com era (1999-2001) – when funding for e-commerce-based companies in the UK and the USA grew unsustainably high, resulting in many companies going out of business

The Retek (Retail Tracking) system was overhauled and IT management was outsourced to the Fujitsu Corporation – a contract worth £50m. In addition, to improve the efficiency of WHS's information sharing, communication and knowledge management, Fujitsu developed and implemented a UK-wide intranet system and managed the service for WHS's 530 High Street stores and headquarter offices. This project alone generates savings on paper usage and distribution costs of some £200,000 a year.

Fujitsu has also begun to refresh and standardise WHS's infrastructure through a comprehensive programme of server rebuilds, PC upgrades and complete migration to a managed Microsoft Exchange email environment. The service operates on a 24/7 basis (24 hours a day, seven days a week).

The Benefits

The outsourcing of its IT operations to Fujitsu has enabled WHS to realise significant business benefits:

- the ability to focus on its core business activities and the achievement of business targets
- standardised office systems enabling greater productivity and easier communication
- reduced 'down time', due to proactive fault diagnosis and centralised system management
- increased customer service, with less store staff time taken up on IT problems
- more accurate budgeting with predictable base costs
- reduced training costs, with no requirement to train and maintain IT infrastructure staff skills
- rapid access to a comprehensive set of technical and business skills if required
- strategic input of new ideas and the latest technology through Fujitsu's relationships with other leading IT companies

Through the outsourcing agreement, Fujitsu has enabled WHS to move forward from the previously complex infrastructure to a simpler, more standardised set of systems. The availability of Fujitsu's skills and personnel was crucial in lessening the risk of the change programme for WHS. This type of investment is very important for a company that relies on critical information to manage a complex range of stores and stocks. In the retail environment, such information is vital for the profitability of companies. Appendix 3 shows how well the stores were performing compared to competitors in 2003/2004.

Marketing Strategies

WHS actively monitors the various strands of its marketing strategies in order to assess their effectiveness. The next section assesses the various areas of interest, including retail performance, brand performance, and advertising and Public Relations (PR) effectiveness.

Retail

As the company offers a range of products to consumers, its performance needs to be tracked against various other retailers (who may specialise in one or more of the product categories). Figure 4 gives a snapshot view of WHS's performance in comparison to other retailers in 2004. The table indicates that WHS retains a strong market share for stationery and books, but generally struggles to make an impact in other categories. WHS is doing better on cards but it still remains well behind Clinton.

Figure 4: WHS's share versus leading competitors in certain product categories

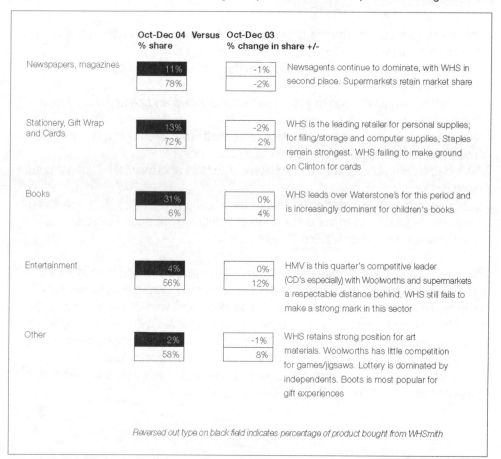

Reversed out type on black field indicates percentage of product bought from WHSmith

Figure 5 indicates that WHS remained the preferred retailer for children's books, with a comparable share to Waterstone's for adult books, although this has seen some decline. WHS also retains preference as a stationery supplier, although this has also marginally declined, giving some cause for concern. As more supermarkets enter these product areas, the company is being 'squeezed' between these low-cost suppliers and specialists such as Waterstone's, HMV, Staples and Clinton.

Figure 5: WHS's status as preferred retailer to leading competitors (LC)

	Oct-Dec 04 % share		Versus		Oct-Dec 03 % change in share +/-
Children's Books	31%			Rank 1	4%
	14%	LC	Waterstones		2%
Adult Books	24%			Rank 2	- 8%
	31%	LC	Waterstones		8%
Magazines	28%			Rank 2	-5%
	11%	LC	Local Newsagent		1%
Stationery	21%			Rank 1	-1%
	49%	LC	Staples		0%
Gift Wrap and Cards	11%			Rank 2	1%
	15%	LC	Clinton		-2%
Videos and DVDs	5%			Rank 5	-4%
	21%	LC	HMV		-1%
CDs	5%			Rank 6	-3%
	26%	LC	HMV		0%

Reversed out type on black field indicates percentage of preference for WHSmith

Part C: Practice cases

Figure 6: WHS Sector Penetration by Customer/Consumer Socio-economic Grouping – shows the key segments that are willing to shop in WHS

	Buyer Profile	WHS Customer/Consumer Profile
Stationery	* Fewer DEs buy * Women buy more than men	* Penetration high among those in education * ABs likely to buy from WHS
News and Magazines	* ABs more likely to buy (90% Vs. 82% DEs)	* Older customers DEs least likely to buy from WHS * Local outlets preferred
Children's Books	* Mainly bought by family gatekeepers (57%) and browsing husbands	* Under 25s unlikely to buy here * Browsing husbands more likely to buy
Adult books	* More likely to be bought by ABs (63%, vs 30% DEs) * More likely to be bought by women (47% vs 39%)	* Middle aged more likely to buy from WHS * Middle aged most likely to buy from WHS
Entertainment	* Aged up to 45, all groups are active in this sector * Under 35s more likely to buy CDs/Computer games	* Pre-family is least likely to buy from WHS, but penetration is poor for all segments
Gift Wrap/ Cards	* Women and family gatekeepers most likely to buy 85% and 85% respectively	* WHS has low penetration amongst the 'discerning' young traditionals/family gatekeepers * Time poor FT/PT employed more likely to buy

Other key findings were:

a) Local independents continue to dominate for newspapers, taking a 70% share, with WHS at 6%, Tesco and other major retailers trailing behind

b) Local independents also dominate for magazines, with 40% purchased from this sector and 20% from WHS. Tesco, Asda and Dillons have shares of 10%, 8% and 4% respectively. The supermarkets pose a real threat in this area

c) There is strong rivalry between WHS and Waterstone's for leadership in the adult book category, with WHS at 18% compared to 19% share for Waterstone's. WHS does not fare as well as Waterstone's during the busy Christmas period

d) For children's books, WHS retains the lead, with around 18% purchasing from the stores and 7% from Waterstone's during the Christmas period

e) Figures 7 and 8 show that WHS remains behind the specialists for satisfaction and the likelihood to be recommended for books

f) WHS's share of video purchase is negligible for adults and around 9% for children. Although one in ten purchasers have visited WHS for these products, the specialists and supermarkets continue to lead. Many consumers would not recommend WHS as a retailer of CDs

* A, B, C, D and E refer to socio-economic groupings within the United Kingdom, with A being the top group.

g) WHS remains the first choice for stationery, although Asda and other supermarkets are posing a threat. WHS's share is around 19%, with convenience stores at 12%. Asda and Staples command a share of 8% each, with Woolworths at 7%. The company is also a favoured location for calendars and diaries. In general, customer satisfaction for WHS stationery remains high (around 49%)

h) For Christmas card and card purchase in general, Clinton has the largest market share at around 22%, with local newsagents at around 17%. WHS has a share of around 3%. For cards and gift wrap, WHS scores better and is in second place at around 11%, tying with Woolworths, with Clinton at 15%. However, in a recent Guardian article*, WHS had a good write-up regarding its policy on cause-related marketing through Christmas cards

i) For games and jigsaw puzzles, WHS and Asda (owned by Walmart) tie in second place with a 7% share, whereas Woolworths takes the lead with a 24% share

j) Local newsagents lead the pack for lottery tickets, commanding a 53% market share, with the supermarkets hovering around 6% each. WHS has a share of 2%

k) Appendix 4 contains some of the reasons why consumers think that WHS has become a better or worse retailer

l) In general, the larger stores sell more items per square metre than the smaller shops. The smaller shops, however, give WHS a presence in small towns

All the points made above and the ones featured in Appendix 4 are based on a market research survey carried out by BDRC on behalf of WHS.

The Guardian 29th November 2005 – WHSmith really scores with its Children in Need Christmas Cards where the full £4.99 price will go to Children in Need

Figure 7: Percent of customers delighted/very satisfied Jan-Dec 2004

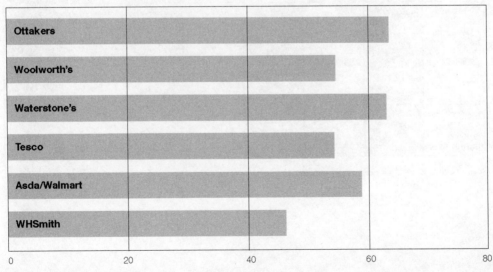

Percent of customers

Page 14 of WHSmith

Figure 8: Percent of customers extremely/very likely to recommend Jan-Dec 2004

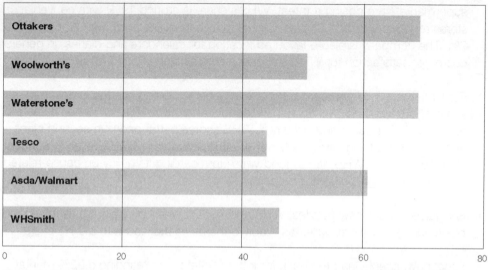

Percent of customers

Advertising Strategies

The company constantly reviews its media spend to look for the most effective ways of attracting customers to spend their money at WHS. WHS's media spend is much smaller than that of many of its competitors, as shown in Figures 9 and 10. However, their TV ads have been quite effective.

Figure 9: Overall media spend by key retailers in the UK during the last quarter of 2004

All Data in GBP Sterling (£)	WHSmith (includes Travel)	Woolworths	Argos	Boots	M&S	Waterstones	HMV
2004 total advertising gross spend (000s)	15,422	33,325	34,052	33,188	35,956	4,875	15,899
2004 total sales (000s)	1,374,700	2,284,900	3,384,000	4,475,700	7,159,800	429,700	930,000
2004 advertising spend as % of 2004 sales	1.12%	1.46%	1.01%	0.74%	0.5%	1.14%	1.7%

Retailers account for the largest industry advertising within this quarter (17%) and increased their spend by 16.5% year on year (YOY)

Figure 10: Retailer rankings in terms of spending on TV advertising in 2004

Ranking	Retailer	Annual TV spend	Weeks on air p.a.
1	B&Q	£32.1m	50
2	Tesco	£24.7m	39
3	Argos	£16.3m	31
4	Asda	£23.7m	51
5	Sainsbury's	£23.5m	52
6	PC World	£15.2m	26
7	Woolworths	£19.2m	49
8	Currys	£19.6m	49
9	Boots	£18.4m	46
10	Homebase	£21.1m	41
11	Comet	£10.7m	25
12	Iceland	£7.7m	42
13	Phones 4 U	£5.8m	15
14	Dixons	£5.3m	16
15	WHSmith	£8.2m	15
16	Debenhams	£7.7m	36
17	M&S	£7.9m	15
18	Morrisons	£7.9m	23
19	Somerfield	£5.1m	24
	AVERAGE	£15.6m	34

The main areas where the company advertises are indicated in Appendix 4, Figure 4.3. The company adopts a mix of strategies, as follows:

a) The company spends around 1.1% of its sales on advertising

b) The Christmas period sees the highest advertising spend

c) TV remains the dominant medium of activity across all retailers, especially at Christmas

d) The company has shifted from weekly newspaper editions to having the widest possible mix of national dailies compared to its competitors. WHS tends to use mono-colour ads that generally work well but are not so effective for gift products, cards and wrap, or children's books

e) The company has a strategy of dropping leaflets through people's doors, and this has had a sufficiently useful impact on sales. The company has shifted from dropping expensively produced catalogues to smaller ones that depict offers, prices and Gift Ideas. However, research has indicated that the company needed to show more stationery offers and provide more clarity on pricing. The Christmas catalogue was distributed to more homes in 2004 and a similar strategy was followed in 2005

f) The company's Christmas Clubcard mailing programme generated £2m in incremental profits. Higher value customers tend to spend more with the Clubcard. The company also holds special Sunday events such as children's reading clubs

g) On the creative side, the company utilised an ad campaign on TV called 'Bookworm and friends'. This had good recall and was seen as distinctive and different, but many customers felt that it lacked warmth. 'Bookworm' is generally liked, so it has some potential for development

h) The company decided that it would withdraw from radio advertising. (Details of advertising spend and media placement are in Appendix 4, Figures 4.4 and 4.5)

Summary

WHS has clearly not only addressed the main issues for surviving the generally dismal retail environment, but has also embraced a successful turnaround strategy under the leadership of the CEO, Kate Swann, and the Chairman, Robert Walker. The company is a major player on the High Street in Britain and has excellent exposure within the travel network in the UK, servicing most railway stations and airports. However, there is growing competition for the retail market from online providers, and most retailers now have excellent websites for the Internet shopper. WHS also faces competition from specialists such as HMV for CDs and DVDs and the supermarkets for cheaper books, magazines and stationery. The company has responded by offering customers better gift vouchers, such as music downloads. The main challenges facing WHS are the same as those facing many High Street retailers, such as store layout, product offerings and range, brand image and the continuing growth of Internet shopping.

Appendix 1: News Articles

Newsagents on the rack
Publishers and shopkeepers are united in fighting OFT proposals that could make buying a newspaper at a local shop a thing of the past

Jane Martinson, Media Business Editor
Wednesday July 13, 2005

Guardian

Former cabinet minister Michael Heseltine is spearheading a united industry campaign against Office of Fair Trading[1] plans to shake up the way newspapers and magazines are distributed in Britain.

Lord Heseltine, Chairman of the Haymarket publishing group, is campaigning against possible OFT plans to open magazine distribution up to full competition. In a meeting with OFT officials tomorrow he is to present alternative proposals for a code of conduct for magazine and newspaper distributors.

The proposals, which include the appointment of the industry's first independent ombudsman, unite independent retailers, much of the publishing industry and some wholesalers.

Alongside the former trade and industry minister will be representatives from the Periodical Publishers' Association, the Newspaper Publishers' Association, the National Federation of Retail Newsagents and the Association of News and Magazine Wholesalers. The united approach is an attempt to head off what they see as a threat to the universality of newspaper and magazine purchases.

The so-called "Heseltine group" hopes to persuade the OFT to change its controversial draft ruling, published in May, when it issues its final opinion towards the end of the summer. In the draft the OFT argued that the current system, in which a handful of distributors have exclusive rights to deliver magazines in a certain region, contravened European competition laws.

The draft exempted newspapers, partly because of their time-sensitive nature, but most newspaper publishers, with the exception of News International and the Express group, have also joined the Heseltine campaign. Newspapers argue that taking away magazines would make their distribution arrangements uneconomic, especially to small rural areas.

David Daniel, trade relations manager at the NFRN, which represents 20,000 independent retailers, welcomed the push for a new code. "Most people are beginning to realise that this offers a workable solution. Nobody ends up as a massive winner but we have to move forward at the same time as complying with the law as laid down by the OFT."

[1]The authority that administers UK competition policy

Page 18 of WHSmith

Under the proposals, independent retailers would be able to seek redress or change supplier if they had poor service from wholesalers or publishers. They would be able to hold wholesalers and publishers to account for missing or late deliveries or giving the wrong magazines.

In the past year, independent retailers have been highly critical of publishers' efforts to gain a bloc exemption for the industry, which they felt supported the status quo. "Rather than embracing the fact that change was inevitable, they wasted well over a year with that stupid campaign," said Mr Daniel.

A spokesman for the Periodical Publishers' Association confirmed that the bloc exemption initiative had been shelved as the industry focused on backing a combined code.

Haymarket, which publishes more than 100 specialist magazines, such as Practical Caravan and Packaging News, readily admits that it depends on small local newsagents. Large retailers, which tend to stock more celebrity and mass-market titles, have little demand for The Gramophone or Young People Now.

Alan Kemp, business development director of the group, said his boss approached independent retailers as an "honest broker" to reach cross-party agreement. The move was inspired partly by the understanding that retailers' complaints about the service needed to be addressed. "As we live with an increasingly ageing population, there really is no substitute for such retailers in terms of home delivery," he said.

The Tory peer[2] is also understood to believe the campaign fits his political support for small, rural businesses and concerns about the environment if the supply of newspapers and magazines was split.

Lord Heseltine's involvement comes as the issue looked set to fall foul of political infighting. Dylan Jones, president of the British Society of Magazine Editors and a Guardian columnist, had accused the OFT of "intransigence" and of denying press freedom. The OFT, for its part, accused the industry of scaremongering.

But the Heseltine group may face an uphill struggle. An OFT spokeswoman said it would consider all proposals before giving its final opinion. But she said the existing system of absolute territorial protection was unlawful. "And so far, the response from the industry to a bit more competition has been to suggest more regulation."

Other government departments have left the matter largely to the OFT, raising concerns among publishers that public interest issues will carry less weight than competition ones.

Plans for a new voluntary code of conduct have yet to be finalised, but the outline plan to be put to the OFT tomorrow suggests beefing up the newspaper code introduced in 1993 after an inquiry by the Monopolies and Mergers Commission. The trade and industry minister at the time was Lord Heseltine.

Independent retailers believe the existing code is weak and outdated, as it simply prevents wholesalers from cutting off supply to any suitable retailer. Since it was introduced, the number of newsagents has increased from 45,000 to 54,000, mainly as a result of garages and supermarkets starting to stock papers and magazines.

[2] i.e. Lord Heseltine

Industry analysts believe that the OFT's draft ruling, if adopted, would benefit large supermarkets and any organisation with ambitions for a national network.

Publishers have cited a study by Professor Paul Dobson of Loughborough University that warns that up to 20,000 newsagents could fold as a result of the ruling. They have also pointed to the experience in the US, where a similar ruling benefited large retailers such as Wal-Mart at the expense of smaller rivals.

The PPA has claimed that 32,000 independent retailers have closed since US distribution was opened up a decade ago. It also claims that the number of magazine titles published fell from 9,311 to 5,340 in the four years to 2002, although the figures are disputed.

The issue has long divided large and small retailers here. Large retailers have said little publicly about the OFT ruling this time round, but in 2000, supermarkets pushed for a national distribution network with an exclusive deal by trying to sign a deal with WHS wholesalers.

The move prompted the Sun to run a picture of Terry Leahy, the Tesco boss, with the headline: "Is this the most dangerous man in Britain?"

MediaGuardian.co.uk © Guardian Newspapers Limited 2005

WHS sees profits surge

Mark Tran
Thursday October 13, 2005 Guardian

The high street retailer WHS today said its recovery programme was on track as it reported annual profits of £64m after having made a £135m loss in 2004.

The company, battling a consumer slowdown and competition from supermarkets and online retailers, said it had improved its performance through cutting costs and offering more choice in books and stationery.

However, same-store sales dropped 2% over the 12 months to the end of August as WHS, like other retailers, fell victim to the consumer slowdown.

Kate Swann, who was appointed as the company's Chief Executive two years ago, said the company's recovery plan did not depend on sales growth.

"Our plan was not based on sales growth, it was on getting the cost base of the business in good shape and changing the mix [of products]," she said.

At the same time, the 203 year old retailer stopped attempting to compete with supermarkets by offering discounts that ate into profits.

Despite the profits turnaround, Ms Swann warned that trading conditions on the high street remained challenging. "As we approach Christmas, we remain cautious about consumer spending and have planned accordingly," she said.

Page 20 of WHSmith

With its return to profitability, WHS announced a 14% increase in dividend payments to shareholders.

The company said it had found £18m of extra savings that would shield it from cost pressures such as rising salaries and energy bills until 2007, on top of the £30m of savings over three years identified in the initial recovery plan.

Investors welcomed signs of a turnaround at WHS, which operates 669 stores. Its shares were up 3.3% at 352.68p in early trading.

WHS extends Tiscali deal
Thursday June 16 2005

Two year contract to distribute ISP[3] services

Tiscali and WHS have announced a new two-year exclusive deal to distribute consumer ISP and fixed line services through WHS stores.

WHS has offered Tiscali ISP service to customers since 2003. The success of the ISP distribution has led to its extension to include fixed line telephone services, including exclusive offers to WHS customers.

The new deal will begin this month, with the launch of Tiscali Smart Talk. The campaign will be supported by a POS[4] campaign across the 700 WHS high street and travel stores.

Mary Turner, CEO of Tiscali UK said: "We are delighted to be working with WHS for a further two years. Both businesses have derived huge value from the relationship and it has helped us deliver great value to both our customers. We will be working closely to ensure that we continue to build sales and continue to bring innovative packages to our customers."

Ian Sanders, head of commercial development at WHS, said: "Over the past two years, Tiscali has proved that we can offer our customers the best value, quality and choice when choosing either a narrowband or broadband package. By extending this offer to include fixed line, we hope to be able to fulfil all of our customers home telephony requirements and offer genuine savings against BT."

http://www.theretailbulletin.com/?page=5&i=311&id=6776&keys=WHSmith&cat=news&action=login&

[3] Internet Service Provider

[4] Point of sale

Research shows extraordinary impact of In-store music on sales
Thursday November 3 2005

New research by DMX MUSIC and Vision One Research, has shown extraordinarily positive results for retailers.

The research, carried out in Principles[5] stores earlier this year, revealed that when a specially created customer focused music channel was playing, sales averaged double digit growth over the times when no music was playing.

The study (carried out through a new, innovative research approach developed by Vision One) highlighted the importance of playing the right music.

Findings also showed that 90% of customers like having music in-store (the remaining 10% mainly consisted of no opinion) and, crucially, 60% said that music made them stay longer in store.

Shoppers were also asked to rate each store against a range of key attributes. Stores that were playing the customer focused music channel were rated, on average, 15% higher against those attributes than stores with no such music playing. On the key attribute 'welcoming', the rating showed an increase of over 40%.

Julia Haynes, Marketing Manager of Principles said, "We are very excited about the results of the survey and in particular the enhancement it has made to our customers' shopping experience."

Tony Lewis, Director of Vision One Research commented, "This study demonstrates how research can bring retailers closer to their customers, with an innovative approach that enables retailers to enhance their customers' shopping experiences profitably."

Alex Martin, Marketing Director of DMX Music added, "This research has shown even more significant results than we expected, particularly regarding sales uplift. It further reinforces our experience of the power music has to enhance the retail environment, create a great shopping experience and ultimately boost sales."

www.theretailbulletin.com/index.php?page=5&cat=rese&id=7458

[5]*Women's clothing chain*

Retail websites surpass the Christmas 2004 peak
Tuesday November 29 2005

With retailers in the throes of the busy Christmas shopping season, Hitwise reports that UK visits to retail websites have already surpassed last year's peak.

Visits to retail websites ended last week 5% higher than the week ending 4th December 2004, the strongest week for visits to retail websites in 2004. "In August, Hitwise predicted that visits to retail websites would peak the week ending 3rd December 2005, and with two weeks to go until the projected peak, retail sites have already passed last year's high" said Heather Hopkins, Director of Research for Hitwise UK. "At the current rate of growth, online retailers are set to have their best year yet."

Hitwise Search Intelligence reveals that Apple's iPod is set to be a big hit again this Christmas, with searches for 'ipod' and 'ipod mini' among the top 20 search queries. Searches for 'ipod' increased 8% in the week ending 19th November 2005, compared with the previous week.

Bratz and Barbie are also set to be popular gifts this Christmas, holding their own amongst the top 20 product search terms, alongside the latest games and gadgets. Bratz seems to be gaining in popularity, with searches for 'bratz' overtaking
searches for 'barbie' for the week ending 19th November 2005. Searches for 'bratz' increased 41% compared with two weeks earlier.

http://www.theretailbulletin.com/index.php?page=5&cat=rese&id=7567

E-Christmas shopping soars 50 per cent
Tuesday December 27 2005

Internet shopping is growing at its fastest rate for 22 months, as millions more shoppers migrate online to buy their Christmas goods.

The IMRG Index recorded that November's UK internet sales exceeded £2 billion in one month for the first time ever, a staggering 50% higher than was reported for the same month last year, then an all-time high. Meanwhile, high street annual sales for the same period grew by just 0.9%, according to ONS[6].

Britain's 24 million internet shoppers spent £2.253 billion online during November, an average of £94 each. November's annual growth rate is more than double the 22% recorded a year ago, and the fastest increase for the month since November 2002, when shoppers spent just £864 million online. IMRG Index participant, Firebox, reported sales up over 80% against the same period last year. Managing director, Christian Robinson, commented: "Firebox re-launched its catalogue just two years ago and has seen a dramatic rise in sales coinciding with the launch of each new edition. For us, it's all about driving traffic online - we haven't included a paper order form in our catalogue for years." IMRG's CEO, James Roper, commented: "The best e-retailers, such as Firebox, Comet, the Co-Op, JD Williams and dabs.com, tend to prominently display the ISIS trust scheme logo on their homepage because they recognise that the safety of shopping online continues to be a major concern to many consumers, especially the millions of novice internet shoppers. Some online shopping services are much better than others. An ISIS logo displayed on their website remains the best indicator that a retailer is taking internet shopping seriously and is confident that they consistently provide good service.

www.theretailbulletin.com/index.php?page=5&cat=news&id=7701

[6]*Office of National Statistics*

Appendix 2:
Highlights from the Company Report

Detailed notes for the accounts have been removed and information that is likely to be most useful for the case examination has been retained.

Corporate Responsibility Review

Community

Our community investment continues to focus on supporting education and lifelong learning. This year, in line with our Per Cent Club commitments, we continued to invest over 1 per cent of our pre-tax profits in charity and community projects. We joined the London Benchmarking Group (LBG) and have adopted the LBG reporting model which provides a standardised way of managing and measuring our community involvement.

Our community investment falls into three areas:

Partnership with the WHSmith Trust

WHSmith provides essential management, marketing, communications and fundraising support for the WHSmith Trust. This year, the Company has worked in partnership with the Trust using our combined resources and skills to leverage greater community benefit.

During the summer we worked with the WHSmith Trust and the National Literacy Trust to deliver the Reading is Fundamental 'Summer Read', aimed at maintaining literacy levels and making children enthusiastic about reading. Over 2,500 children took part in the 39 'Summer Read' events across the country.

An evaluation of the project's achievements is available at www.whsmithplc.com/grp/cr. The WHSmith Trust and the Company want to build on the success of this year's scheme and will provide funding and support for 'Summer Reads' in 2006 and 2007.

Employees making a difference in their local communities

Our staff play a vital role in supporting the local communities in which we operate. Actions are often on a small scale, but the cumulative effect is significant. Typical examples include the donation of Christmas gifts to a local shelter by our Leeds store and the donation of stock to a local school by our Minehead store.

Products to support charity and education

We sell a number of products, ranging from Christmas cards to DVDs, which provide customers with a convenient way to support their favourite charities, as well as giving the charities an opportunity to reach a new audience. These products have raised money for charities including Cancer Research, the RSPCA and Children in Need. Our charity toner cartridge recycling scheme is raising money for Tommy's the baby charity. In addition, WHSmith Educational Achievement Rewards provide a tool for teachers to recognise pupils' achievements and encourage good behaviour. More details are available at www.whsmithplc.com/grp/cr.

Targets for 2005/06 include:
— Work in partnership with the WHSmith Trust to deliver two significant education and literacy projects.
— Establish a scheme to recognise and reward staff for outstanding work in the community and to share best practice.
— Increase the range of products we sell which support charities.

WHSmith community contributions 2004/05

1. Cash (£613,810)
2. Gifts in kind (£25,640)
3. Staff time/ management costs (£245,000)

WHSmith has adopted the London Benchmarking Group (LBG) reporting model which provides a standardised way of managing and measuring our community involvement.

The WHSmith Trust is an independent registered charity (registered charity no. 1013782). This year the Trust adopted a new strategy to deliver two objectives:
— to support the local communities in which WHSmith staff and customers live and work; and
— to support education and lifelong learning, helping people of any age to achieve their educational potential.
For further details of the Trust's work, see www.whsmithplc.com/grp/trust.

The National Literacy Trust is an independent charity dedicated to building a literate nation.

Over 2,500 children took part in the 'Summer Read' events this summer, a partnership between the National Literacy Trust, the WHSmith Trust and the WHSmith Group.

Investor engagement on ethical trading

We met with Insight Investment to discuss our management of ethical trading issues. The winter 2004 edition of the *Insight Investor Responsibility Bulletin* included the following report on the meeting:

WHSmith 'has good governance, policy and systems in place to manage ethical trading issues, which have not been compromised despite recent restructuring … its extensive sourcing from China will likely continue to pose significant ethical trading challenges. The company's active involvement in the ETI and commitment to proactive engagement with suppliers should go some way to addressing them.'

← The WWF-UK Forest & Trade Network works with UK companies to improve forest management around the world.

↑ This year we introduced new recycled stationery ranges in-store including writing paper, notepads and envelopes.

Marketplace

WHSmith takes its responsibility for the products it sells seriously. We aim to supply high-quality products that are produced by people working in decent conditions with minimal possible impact on the environment. This is the focus for our supply chain management activity.

We are committed to making our Supplier Code of Conduct and Forest Sourcing policy an integral part of our buying decisions. This year, we trained buyers on the role they should play, notably the need to consider ethical trading issues in critical path planning. We also established a review group, comprising senior buyers, quality and corporate responsibility functions to oversee performance and agree actions on ethical trading and forest sourcing.

Ethical trading

We continue to engage with our suppliers to promote improved labour standards and better environmental management. Our 24 month rolling audit cycle monitors supplier compliance with our Code of Conduct. This year, 64 supplier factory audits were carried out by an independent third party, the majority of these in China. After each audit, we agree a corrective action plan with the factory management. Resources and engagement focus is on suppliers in the Far East who provide us with WHSmith branded product, with priority given to suppliers rated high and medium risk.

Twenty six high-value own-brand UK suppliers were also assessed to check they have a process in place for monitoring labour standards in their own supply chains.

As members of the Ethical Trading Initiative (ETI), and specifically through the ETI China Working Group, we continue to work with other members to share best practice and develop solutions to the challenges we all face.

Forest sourcing

Our revised Forest Sourcing policy was approved by the Board. The policy sets out our objective that all virgin (i.e. non-recycled) material used in our products should come from known, legal, well-managed and credibly certified forests. To achieve this objective, we have:
— Continued our membership of the WWF-UK Forest & Trade Network that works with UK companies to improve forest management around the world.
— Extended our annual supplier survey on forest sourcing to cover key suppliers of paper and wood products in the Far East as well as in the UK. This year's return covered over 70 per cent of the volume of the own-brand paper and wood products we sell and helped us identify the suppliers to prioritise for engagement.
— Provided suppliers with guidance notes outlining the issues to consider when sourcing timber or paper from China, Finland and Russia.
— Increased the number of recycled and Forest Stewardship Council (FSC) certified products we sell in-store.

Corporate Responsibility Review

Customer service standards

'Customer Focus' is one of our core business values and underpins everything we do. Increased focus on retail standards in our High Street business has translated into improvements in our mystery shopper scores and a reduction in the number of customer contacts into our central customer service centre.

Our News business carries out twice yearly customer surveys to assess customer service standards. We publish the findings alongside details of the actions we will take in response. The survey results can be found at www.whsmithnews.co.uk and form the basis of the customer service action plan with performance incentives for individual employees based on delivery of the required improvements.

Targets for 2005/06 include:

— Incorporate ethical trading and forest sourcing into the job specifications of key buyers.
— Appoint a specialist internal audit team in our Asian sourcing operation to strengthen our engagement with suppliers on labour standards and forestry issues.
— Work with two key Far East suppliers to improve the way they manage health and safety and human resources.
— Hold workshops for 15 key UK own-brand suppliers to raise awareness of WHSmith's ethical trading and forest sourcing requirements, providing practical tools to help them improve standards.
— Maintain the data coverage of our forest source survey at 70 per cent of the volume of all own-brand paper and wood products or increase coverage further.
— Pilot at least three new lines of recycled or FSC certified stationery to test the commercial opportunities.

Workplace
Embedding our values within the business culture

Last year, we adopted four key business values: Customer Focus, Drive for Results, Value Our People and Accountability. As part of our three year plan to embed the values fully throughout the business, this year we focused on raising awareness, helping staff understand what the values mean and how to apply them in their role.

In November we launched the 'Values in Practice' or VIP scheme for all High Street, Travel and Group head office employees to recognise individuals and teams who are demonstrating the values in their work. Awards were also made to those store staff who are outstanding role models in living the values.

The values are used as a key part of our recruitment and training programmes and our performance management process. Every member of staff, from Board level down, has their performance assessed against the values.

Communicating with and engaging our staff

Recent changes within the business make it more important than ever that all employees feel engaged in delivering our turnaround plan. We have substantially improved the quality and effectiveness of our internal communications to update and inform staff on business performance.

We collect feedback to measure the effectiveness of every communication event we hold so that we can continue to make improvements.

The Forest Stewardship Council (FSC) is an international network to promote responsible management of the world's forests. Its product label allows consumers to recognise products that support the growth of responsible forest management.

WHSmith values

Keep the customer at the heart of all that we do	Tenacity for ambitious and competitive results – delivered with pace
Customer Focus	Drive For Results
Value Our People	Accountability
Our people are respected and valued in an honest, open environment	Take personal responsibility and deliver what we say we will

Eye-catching posters raise staff awareness of the Company's values.

Diversity profile: WHSmith Group

All employees

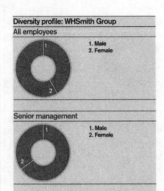

1. Male
2. Female

Senior management

1. Male
2. Female

Training and developing our staff

The specialist training and development team in WHSmith Retail focuses on helping staff develop the skills to deliver their objectives and help people to reach their potential.

Highlights from 2004/05 include:
— Training provision doubled within WHSmith Retail.
— Launch of an easy-to-use training and development intranet site to raise staff awareness of the resources available, so they can take an active part in requesting training.
— Launch of a Career Development Framework for High Street store staff to support succession planning and provide a clear route map showing how a member of staff can progress from one role to another.
— Development of a 360° feedback process for our top 100 leaders which is aligned to our Values and Leadership behaviours.

Valuing diversity

We want all our employees to contribute as much as they can to the business and its success. Our equal opportunities and diversity policies outline our commitment that all employees should be treated with respect and dignity with people's differences valued and recognised in everything that we do.

Targets for 2005/06 include:
— Further embed the values in our business culture in head office and stores through the launch of a tool for managers to send an immediate message to positively recognise staff who demonstrate the values.
— Launch a Fast Track Development programme for store supervisors.
— Develop a Coaching and Mentoring programme for senior executives.
— Fill 50 per cent of the store manager vacancies in our high street stores with internal candidates.
— Set up a Diversity Working Group to develop initiatives and policies concerning gender, sexual orientation, ethnicity and disability.

Health and safety

The Board is committed to maintaining high standards of health and safety in the business.

Management teams in each business, supported by professional safety advisers from the Group Risk and Occupational Health department, monitor key safety performance indicators and an annual report of each business detailing trends, performance and recommendations is presented to the Board. Each business also has a properly constituted health and safety committee that comprises employees' representatives, management, trade union representatives and officials.

	Accidents and injuries (Rate per 100,000 employees)		
	2005	2004	2003
Major injuries	86	76	132
Injuries resulting in over 3 days' absence from work	557	628	439
All RIDDORS*	643	704	571

*The number of accidents legally reportable under the Reporting of Injuries, Diseases and Dangerous Occurrence Regulations.

BPP
PROFESSIONAL EDUCATION

Corporate Responsibility Review

This year, the total number of reportable accidents across the Group reduced by 19 per cent which is a good result and is in line with the Health and Safety Executive's 'Revitalising H&S' strategy for businesses to significantly reduce workplace accidents. This result must be tempered by a reported increase in major injury accidents. This equates to 30 such injuries throughout the year and, although a small number, each incident is taken very seriously and measures introduced to avoid similar occurrences. This will be an area for focus in the coming year.

During the year over 1,100 managers have been trained so they can cascade safety training to their staff. Additional training to support the Health and Safety Executive's 'Mind your Back' campaign will be launched next year with the aim of further reducing the number of accidents following manual handling operations.

Targets:
By the end of August 2010, we aim to:
— Reduce reportable accidents in WHSmith Retail by 5 per cent from September 2004 levels.
— Reduce reportable accidents in WHSmith News by 50 per cent from September 2004 levels.

Environment
The environmental impacts of WHSmith's businesses fall into three main areas:
— Energy used to operate our stores, offices and distribution centres.
— Fuel used to distribute our products.
— The production, use and disposal of our products and packaging.

We are committed to energy and fuel efficiency, waste reduction and recycling, recognising that as well as reducing our environmental impact this can also contribute to greater business efficiency.

Energy
During the year, we have reduced energy consumption across the Group by 1.2 per cent (see table). Fifty per cent of the electricity we purchased came from renewable sources helping us to reduce the associated emissions of carbon dioxide from 56,597 tonnes to 23,258 tonnes.

We targeted the 40 stores with the highest levels of energy consumption, developing an improvement plan for each. A checklist of energy-saving measures is now also included in routine maintenance.

Steps have been taken to increase energy awareness including training for High Street store managers, supervisors and all new starters. Store managers now have visibility and direct accountability for energy consumption in their store, with energy costs applied to the store's profit and loss account.

Transport
Through the introduction of Ideal Delivery Frequency routing, we have reduced fuel usage in our Retail distribution fleet by 12.1 per cent with vehicles also travelling less distance (see chart). Other factors include more effective management of vehicle fill and introduction of new vehicles.

Within WHSmith News, we now operate from fewer locations and make greater use of large vehicles. We achieved a 3 per cent reduction in the distances travelled by our own fleet, however we saw an increase of 8 per cent in the distance travelled by our contractors' vehicles, with the whole News fleet covering a total of 49,361,393 km. We continue to work on optimising the efficiency of our distribution network.

Accidents by type 01.09.04 – 31.08.05
1. Manual handling
2. Striking fixed objects
3. Struck by moving/falling object
4. Slip/trip/fall
5. Fall from height
6. Hand tools

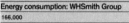

Energy consumption: WHSmith Group

166,000
162,500
159,000
155,500
152,000

2002 2003 2004 2005

— Energy consumption (in 000's, MwH)

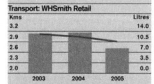

Transport: WHSmith Retail

Kms		Litres
3.2		14.0
2.9		10.5
2.6		7.0
2.3		3.5
2.0		0.0

2003 2004 2005

■ Total fuel used (in millions)
— Total km travelled (in millions)

WOODLAND
TRUST

↑ ←
WHSmith remains a key
partner in the Woodland
Trust Christmas Card
Recycling Scheme. In
2005 the Scheme recycled
over 58 million cards.

Packaging and waste

Transit packaging, namely cardboard and polythene, is a major waste stream
for our business and has been a focus for our waste reduction and recycling
programmes this year.

We have been rolling out a cardboard recycling scheme to those high street
stores that have sufficient space to accommodate cardboard collection bins,
resulting in a reduction in the volume of waste sent to landfill.

Our News business has now successfully implemented recycling programmes
at larger locations and this is already helping us achieve significant reductions.

Data on our waste reduction and recycling programmes is available at
www.whsmithplc/grp/cr.

Working with suppliers to reduce transit packaging

An over-packaged product places a burden on the environment, costs more
to transport and takes longer to unpack. We are working with key Far East
suppliers of own-brand products to reduce transit packaging. To date we have
saved 45 tonnes of transit packaging. We are now looking at opportunities to
reduce packaging in a wider group of suppliers, both in the UK and the Far East.

Encouraging customers to recycle

Wherever we can we will encourage our customers to recycle our products
after use.

WHSmith remains a key partner in the annual Woodland Trust Christmas
Card Recycling scheme. Now in its eighth year, the 2005 scheme broke all
previous records to recycle over 58 million cards.

All own-brand toner cartridges include a recycling bag providing our
customers with a convenient way to recycle their old cartridges. This year, we
have collected 22,000 cartridges, raising money for Tommy's, the baby charity.

Targets for 2005/06 include:

— By August 2008, reduce energy consumption by 5 per cent per square
foot from September 2004 levels.
— Establish an Environmental Champions scheme to help deliver
continuous improvement in energy efficiency and waste minimisation.
— Reduce fuel use in the WHSmith Retail distribution fleet by 15 per cent
from September 2004 levels.
— Work with our top 20 own-brand suppliers in the Far East to reduce the
amount of transit packaging by 10 per cent from September 2004 levels.
— Extend cardboard recycling to 150 WHSmith High Street stores.

A full CR review is available on our website at www.whsmithplc.com/grp/cr.

Group Profit and Loss Account
for the 12 months to 31 August 2005

£m	2005			2004		
	Before exceptional items and goodwill amortisation	Exceptional items and goodwill amortisation	Total	Before exceptional items and goodwill amortisation	Exceptional items and goodwill amortisation	Total
Turnover						
Continuing operations	2,497	–	2,497	2,520	–	2,520
Discontinued operations	11	–	11	314	–	314
Group turnover	2,508	–	2,508	2,834	–	2,834
Operating profit / (loss)						
Continuing operations	81	(1)	80	51	(93)	(42)
Discontinued operations	–	–	–	21	(10)	11
Group operating profit / (loss)	81	(1)	80	72	(103)	(31)
Net loss on sale of discontinued operations	–	(8)	(8)	–	(101)	(101)
Profit on sale of fixed assets – continuing operations	–	–	–	–	2	2
Profit / (loss) on ordinary activities before net finance charges	81	(9)	72	72	(202)	(130)
Net finance charges	(8)	–	(8)	(5)	–	(5)
Profit / (loss) on ordinary activities before taxation	73	(9)	64	67	(202)	(135)
Tax on profit / (loss) on ordinary activities	(18)	–	(18)	(23)	10	(13)
Profit / (loss) on ordinary activities after taxation for the financial year	55	(9)	46	44	(192)	(148)
Dividends (equity and non equity)	(166)	–	(166)	(24)	–	(24)
Retained (losses) / earnings	(111)	(9)	(120)	20	(192)	(172)

Headline earnings per share[1]		
Basic – continuing operations	*31.6p*	*14.3p*
Basic	*31.6p*	*19.2p*
Diluted	*31.3p*	*19.2p*
Earnings / (loss) per share[2]		
Basic – continuing operations	*30.5p*	*(20.5)p*
Basic	*26.0p*	*(60.7)p*
Diluted	*25.7p*	*(60.7)p*
Equity dividends per share	*13.7p*	*12.0p*
Fixed charges cover – times	*1.4x*	*1.3x*
Equity dividend cover – times	*2.0x*	*–*
Equity dividend cover before exceptional items and goodwill amortisation – times	*2.4x*	*1.5x*

1. Headline earnings per share excludes exceptional items, goodwill amortisation and FRS 17 pension interest.
2. Earnings per share is calculated in accordance with FRS 14 'Earnings per share'.

Group Balance Sheet
as at 31 August 2005

£m	2005	2004
Fixed assets		
Intangible assets – goodwill	14	164
Tangible fixed assets	231	237
Total fixed assets	245	401
Current assets		
Stocks	162	184
Debtors due within one year	111	187
Debtors due after more than one year	21	25
Cash at bank and in hand	46	64
	340	460
Creditors due within one year		
Debt	(48)	(17)
Other creditors	(346)	(397)
	(394)	(414)
Net current (liabilities) / assets	(54)	46
Total assets less current liabilities	191	447
Creditors due after more than one year		
Debt	(46)	(2)
Other creditors	(1)	(2)
	(47)	(4)
Provisions for liabilities and charges	(31)	(38)
Net assets excluding pension liabilities	113	405
Net pension liabilities	(71)	(149)
Total net assets	42	256
Capital and reserves		
Called up share capital	4	139
Share premium account	17	93
Capital redemption reserve	218	156
Revaluation reserve	3	3
Other reserve	(34)	(27)
Profit and loss account	(319)	(110)
Equity shareholders' (liabilities) / funds	(111)	254
Non equity share capital	153	2
Total shareholders' funds	42	256

Approved by the Board of Directors on 13 October 2005.

Kate Swann
Chief Executive

Alan Stewart
Finance Director

Notes to the Accounts
for the 12 months to 31 August 2005

1 Segmental analysis of results
a) Segmental analysis of Group turnover

£m	2005	2004
Continuing operations:		
Retailing		
High Street Retail	**1,112**	1,152
Travel Retail	**311**	301
Total	**1,423**	1,453
News Distribution		
Total turnover	**1,187**	1,182
Internal turnover	**(113)**	(115)
Total	**1,074**	1,067
Turnover – continuing operations	**2,497**	2,520
Discontinued operations:		
Retailing		
USA Travel Retail	**–**	49
Aspac Retail	**–**	132
Total	**–**	181
Publishing business		
Total turnover	**14**	155
Internal turnover	**(3)**	(22)
Total	**11**	133
Turnover – discontinued operations	**11**	314
Group turnover	**2,508**	2,834

Notes to the Accounts
for the 12 months to 31 August 2005 continued

1 Segmental analysis of results continued
b) Segmental analysis of Group operating profit / (loss)

£m	2005			2004		
	Before goodwill amortisation	Exceptional operating items and goodwill amortisation	Total	Before exceptional items and goodwill amortisation	Exceptional operating items and goodwill amortisation	Total
Continuing operations:						
Retailing						
High Street Retail	43	(1)	42	23	(77)	(54)
Travel Retail (note a)	26	–	26	21	(5)	16
Total	69	(1)	68	44	(82)	(38)
News Distribution	37	–	37	35	–	35
Trading profit	106	(1)	105	79	(82)	(3)
Support functions	(16)	–	(16)	(15)	(11)	(26)
Pension service costs (note b)	(10)	–	(10)	(14)	–	(14)
Internal rents (note c)	1	–	1	1	–	1
Operating profit / (loss) – continuing operations	81	(1)	80	51	(93)	(42)
Discontinued operations:						
Retailing						
USA Travel Retail	–	–	–	(5)	–	(5)
Aspac Retail	–	–	–	7	(1)	6
Total	–	–	–	2	(1)	1
Publishing business	–	–	–	20	(9)	11
Pension service costs (note b)	–	–	–	(1)	–	(1)
Operating profit / (loss) – discontinued operations	–	–	–	21	(10)	11
Group operating profit / (loss)	81	(1)	80	72	(103)	(31)

a) Travel Retail includes profits of £1m (2004: £1m) generated in Continental Europe.
b) The annual pension service costs in respect of the defined benefit scheme, if allocated between the businesses based on pensionable salaries, would be as follows: High Street Retail £5m (2004: £8m), Travel Retail £1m (2004: £1m), Publishing £nil (2004: £1m), News Distribution £3m (2004: £4m) and Support functions £1m (2004: £1m). In addition to these pension costs, £3m of contributions has been charged to the individual businesses in respect of the defined contribution pension scheme.
c) The results for the Retailing businesses are reported after charging an internal arm's length market rent on freehold and long leasehold properties owned by the Group. The internal net income generated of £1m (2004: £1m) is shown as a separate credit to the profit and loss account.
d) Exceptional operating items and goodwill amortisation includes goodwill amortisation for the following businesses: High Street Retail £1m (2004: £1m) and Aspac Retail £nil (2004: £1m).
e) On 1 September 2004 WHSmith Online was integrated into the WHSmith High Street Retail business, the comparable results for the year ended 31 August 2004 were turnover: £7m, operating loss before exceptional items and goodwill amortisation: £2m, exceptional items and goodwill amortisation: £10m, operating loss after exceptional items and goodwill amortisation: £12m.

Detailed notes for the accounts have been removed and information that is likely to be most useful for the case examination has been retained.

1   Segmental analysis of results continued
c)   Geographical split

£m	Turnover 2005	Turnover 2004	Profit / (loss) before taxation 2005	Profit / (loss) before taxation 2004	Net assets 2005	Net assets 2004
Continuing operations before exceptional items and goodwill amortisation – UK / Europe	**2,497**	2,520	**73**	46	**167**	139
Exceptional items and goodwill amortisation			(1)	(91)		
Continuing operations – UK / Europe	**2,497**	**2,520**	**72**	**(45)**	**167**	**139**
Discontinued operations before exceptional items and goodwill amortisation:						
UK / Europe	9	110	–	16	–	205
USA	–	49	–	(5)	(6)	11
Asia / Pacific	2	155	–	10	–	5
	11	314	–	21	(6)	221
Exceptional items and goodwill amortisation			(8)	(111)		
Discontinued operations	**11**	**314**	**(8)**	**(90)**	**(6)**	**221**
Net (debt) / funds					(48)	45
Net pension liabilities:						
Continuing operations					(71)	(132)
Discontinued operations					–	(17)
Total Group	**2,508**	**2,834**	**64**	**(135)**	**42**	**256**

Turnover is disclosed by origin.

2   Group operating profit

£m	2005 Continuing	2005 Discontinued	2005 Total	2004 Continuing	2004 Discontinued	2004 Total
Turnover	**2,497**	**11**	**2,508**	2,520	314	2,834
Cost of sales	(1,790)	(4)	(1,794)	(1,882)	(146)	(2,028)
Pre-exceptional operating items	*(1,790)*	*(4)*	*(1,794)*	(1,836)	(146)	(1,982)
Exceptional operating items	–	–	–	(46)	–	(46)
Gross profit	**707**	**7**	**714**	638	168	806
Distribution costs	(501)	(4)	(505)	(531)	(99)	(630)
Pre-exceptional operating items	*(501)*	*(4)*	*(505)*	(517)	(90)	(607)
Exceptional operating items	–	–	–	(14)	(9)	(23)
Administrative expenses	(126)	(3)	(129)	(149)	(58)	(207)
Pre-exceptional operating items and goodwill amortisation	*(125)*	*(3)*	*(128)*	(116)	(57)	(173)
Exceptional operating items	–	–	–	(32)	–	(32)
Goodwill amortisation	*(1)*	–	*(1)*	(1)	(1)	(2)
Group operating profit / (loss)	**80**	–	**80**	(42)	11	(31)

Detailed notes for the accounts have been removed and information that is likely to be most useful for the case examination has been retained.

Appendix 3: Performance data in 2003

Figure 3.1: Increasingly complex Group – inconsistent performance

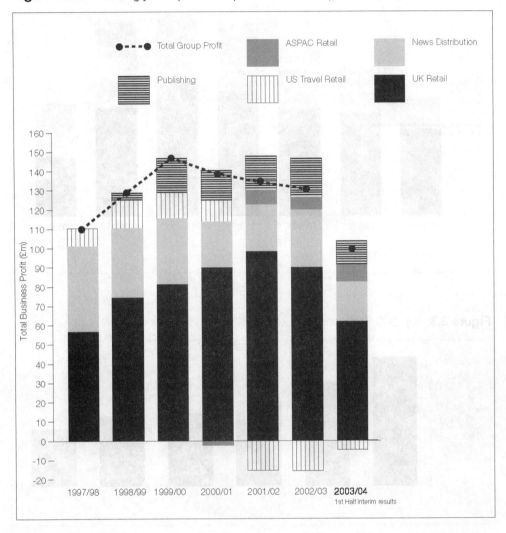

Page 36 of WHSmith

Figure 3.2: Underlying profit performance poor

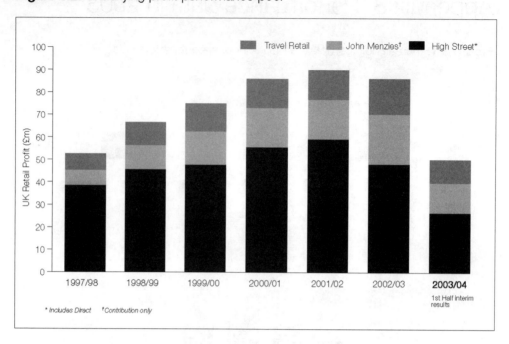

* Includes Direct   †Contribution only

Figure 3.3: Top 200 Stationery SKUs*

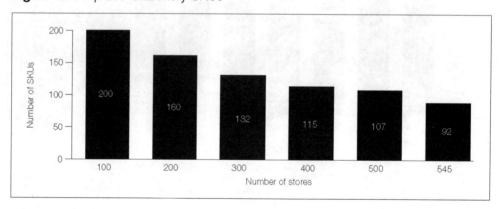

SKU stands for "Stock Keeping Unit." It is a common term for a unique numeric identifier, used most commonly in business to refer to a specific product in inventory or in a catalogue. This means that the larger stores have more variety of SKUs and also seem to do better in terms of sales.

Figure 3.4: WHS foot print: display space ratio below competitors

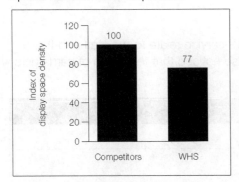

Figure 3.5: WHS SKU density per square foot below competitors

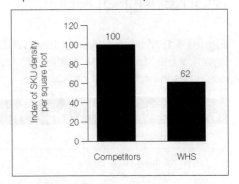

Figure 3.6: Average store sizes of various competitors on the high street (competitors not identified)

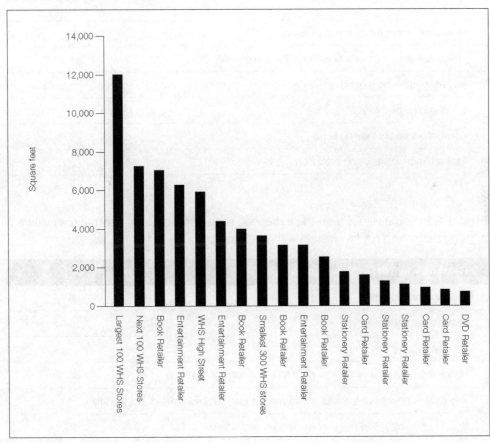

Appendix 4: Details of Market Research and Marketing Spend

Figure 4.1: Main improvements in WHSmith's service relate to the staff and the layout of the store. Some customers have also noticed that the range of cards/gifts items has improved (not ranked)

Reasons why WHSmith has got better
Staff are more courteous
Layout of the store is better
A better range of and more offers
Seems to be more choice
You don't wait as long to be served
Better displays
Store looks more modern and pleasant
Layout has improved and till systems have improved
Seems to have more gift items
Wider choice of cards
Good offers on best selling items
Staff are more friendly and efficient

Figure 4.2: Some issues with the increased range of products – sometimes viewed a 'piling them high'. A few issues with staff and price.

Reasons why WHSmith has got worse
Staff are very unhelpful
Prices have got worse
They cram too much stuff in
Range too limited. They do a lot of things, but none of it well
The store is better, but the staff are worse not qualified, not trained, not friendly
Seem to have a limited range of magazines and videos
They are piling things high which makes things less easy to find

Figure 4.3: WHSmith Advertising Strategy

Media Targeting	Housewives with kids	All adults
Media Type	• Wide range of magazines and selected newspapers • Fractionals, full pages mix • All colour • TV • Radio	• Mono press in national dailies and 9 Sundays • All full page or page dominant • All mono • TV
Creative	• "WHSpecially for Christmas • Development of 2002 Brand Campaign • Pulled back through the store window	• "Bookworm and friends" • Supported 'home of popular culture' • 'More of what you really want' • All-action set in store

Figure 4.4: Retailers' Media Spend Oct-Dec 2004

	TV	Press	Radio
Argos	60	40	0
Boots	72	7	21
Clinton	82	18	0
HMV	61	38	1
M&S	64	22	14
Ottaker's	0	100	0
Virgin	69	30	0
Waterstone's	62	38	1
WHSmith	73	27	0
Woolworths	78	21	1

Figures indicate percentage spend in each media format

Figure 4.5: Media Delivery by WHS Xmas Periods

	2003 Coverage	2004 Coverage	2003 Cost	2004 Cost
TV (TVRs)*	2,469	4,692	£4.9m	£5.8m
Press (GRPs)*	1,180	1,479	£1.7m	£1.8m
Radio	2 ads	0 ads	£0.3m	nil
Advertising production	4 TV executions 94 press ads 2 radio ads	13 TV executions 189 press ads 0 radio ads	£2m	£1.5m
Mailing	Oct to 1m homes Nov to 1m homes £0.6m net profit	Oct to 700k homes Nov to 700k homes £2m	£0.6m	£0.4m
Catalogue	100 page 3.7m in-store 1m via Mail Order Service	16 page 2m in-store 10m via door drop	£2.4m	£0.8m
Totals	TV cover: 96% Press cover: 82% Cat/Mail cover: 10% Total: 98%	TV cover: 98% Press cover: 87% Cat/Mail cover: 26% Total: 99%	**£11.9m**	**£10.3m**

* Television rating. One TVR=1% of a specified target audience group
* A Gross Rating Point (GRP) is one percentage point of a specified target audience

Page 41 of WHSmith

Figure 4.6: Marketing

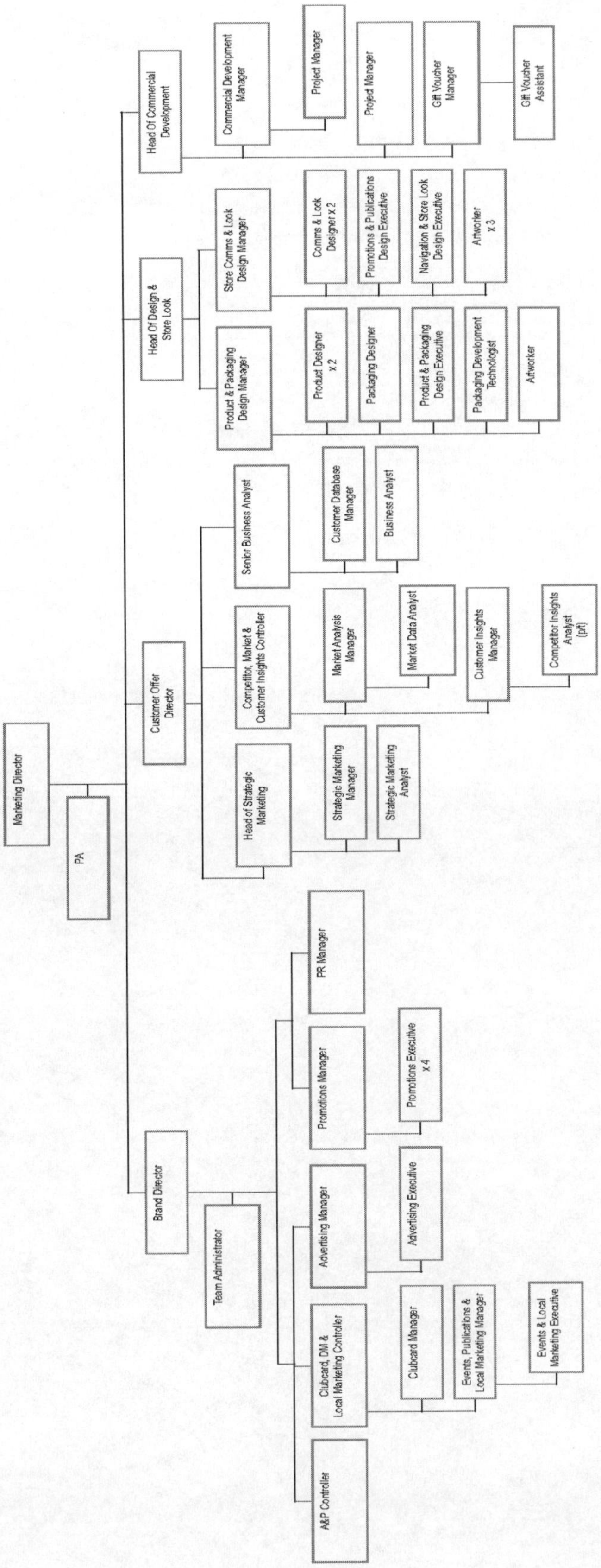

3   June 2006 exam

The Chartered
Institute of Marketing

Professional Postgraduate Diploma in Marketing

Strategic Marketing in Practice

Time: 14.00 – 17.00

Date: 9th June 2006

3 Hours Duration

This paper requires you to make a practical and reasoned evaluation of the problems and opportunities you have identified from the previously circulated case material. From your analysis you are required to prepare a report in accordance with the situation below. Graphing sheets and ledger analysis paper are available from the invigilators, together with continuation sheets if required. These must be identified by your candidate number and fastened in the prescribed fashion within the back cover of your answer book for collection at the end of the examination.

At the close of the examination the student must secure their analysis summary (maximum 6 pages of A4 paper) to the examination booklet with a treasury tag. This will be provided by the examination centre invigilator.

The student must ensure they write their CIM student membership number and examination centre name clearly on the top right hand corner of the analysis summary before the close of the examination.

Read the questions carefully and answer the actual questions as specified. Check the mark allocation to questions and allocate your time accordingly. Candidates must attempt ALL parts. Candidates should adopt a report format; those candidates who do not adopt a report format will be penalised.

CIM reserves the right not to mark any submission that does not comply with the guidelines for this examination.

© The Chartered Institute of Marketing 2006

BPP
PROFESSIONAL EDUCATION

Professional Postgraduate Diploma in Marketing

Strategic Marketing in Practice

Answer ALL questions

As the appointed consultant to WHSmith (WHS), the Board has asked you for responses to the following questions:

Question One

Outline a strategic marketing plan for WHSmith (WHS) for the next two years.

(25 marks)

Question Two

Critically assess the key segments (both product and market) that the company is dealing in, and develop a product/service proposition for these segments.

(25 marks)

Question Three

Utilising the data given in the case, formulate a one-year marketing communications plan to enhance the competitive position of the WHS brand.

(25 marks)

In addition, 25 marks will be allocated for the prepared analysis of the case and its application to the questions above.

(25 marks)

(Total 100 marks)

The Chartered
Institute of Marketing

Moor Hall, Cookham
Maidenhead
Berkshire, SL6 9QH, UK
Telephone: 01628 427120
Facsimile: 01628 427158
www.cim.co.uk

4 Marketing in the retail industry

4.1 This is an easy industry and market for us all to understand whether in the UK or in other countries. The products and service are simple but perhaps developing strategies in an increasingly competitive market less so. This industry is mature and fragmented making competitive advantage difficult to build and sustain.

4.2 As well as the large warehouse style office suppliers and bookshops that have revitalised themselves and evolved into new forms, the Internet is now providing greater choice and new purchasing and retail opportunities. The threat made to traditional retailers by the growth in online sales (growing at a pace predicted prematurely in the 1990s but now here for real) cannot be ignored. New market entrants and pioneers are poised to exploit these opportunities to their advantage. Having been a sluggish industry for a very long time, this environment is moving into a new and dynamic era. The challenge will be to recognise what the dynamics are and how the competition will respond.

W H Smith case overview

4.3 W H Smith (WHS) has a long established history and is a familiar brand in the UK. While its brand and products are well known, its competitive position has become less clear. Diversification and various ventures have not been successful and have done nothing to reinforce a clear competitive position.

4.4 WHS are in the B2B wholesale and distribution business and B2C retail. The case seems to be focused on the retail high street but it is important to try to understand all the SBUs. A lack of clear purpose is evident from the way SBUs and products are described and one of your challenges will be to establish a clear purpose.

4.5 WHS has a 216-year history, evolving from a small newsagent/retailer to one of the leading high street retailers in the UK. Over the years, the company has been involved in publishing, music and the travel industry. After facing difficult times, WHS started the turnaround in 2003/04 by restructuring the business. Now they want to develop a sensible approach to marketing.

4.6 WHS have had a strong product orientation but faced a period of financial crisis which forced them to be finance-driven and concerned with operational efficiency. There appears to be no clear mission and vision to reinforce company values and to give direction. The bureaucratic style and the hierarchical, silo type of organisation structure are significant obstacles to becoming a market-orientated company, even thought the need for this change is acknowledged by the senior management. There is a lack of effective MkIS and poor marketing skills. Apart from the focus on operational efficiency, the only other area that is driving improvement is their CSR programme.

4.7 Some of the key developments and issues appear to be:

- Establishing a clear purpose and distinct business portfolio
- Formulating strategies and competitive positioning
- Segmentation and understanding customers
- Communications and building a brand
- Supply chain management, alliances and partnerships

4.8 These areas are interrelated and your analysis needs to reveal a good understanding of the issues so strategy development and planning is credible. There are numbers to extract which will be useful for helping you understand current conditions and for setting objectives in the exam. Fortunately, there is nothing daunting or difficult about the numbers and you can work them to provide a fuller picture.

4.9 The data on competitive forces and trends and customer data is rather patchy, but your interpretation of what you do have (and your general knowledge) can provide real insights that will add value and guide strategy development.

4.10 Remember, in a retail context, to check how you are using 'place' (where products/services can be accessed) and 'physical evidence' (retail environment).

Your role and challenge

4.11 You are Gary Ross, an experienced marketing consultant with a background in European garment retailing and your key challenges are to develop a 'sensible approach' to marketing, good segmentation techniques and revitalise the brand.

4.12 The most significant industry developments taking place at this time are the Internet, competitive alliances, strong brands moving into non-core competence areas and possible changes in news distribution.

4.13 Customer shopping behaviour is changing. Online shopping has increased dramatically. More aware customers are more demanding.

4.14 WHS has set many goals around their CSR strategy and supply chain management. Less evident are any growth and marketing strategies and this is clearly the area you will need to focus on when you reach decisions.

4.15 These are some of the models and techniques we used during our analysis task.

- McKinsey's 7Ss
- Value chain
- Porter's generic competitive strategies
- PLC and total product concept
- Brand pyramid
- PEST framework
- Porter's five forces
- Positioning map
- Market map

At the conclusion of your analysis you will be able to decide what the critical success factors are. Compare your list with those below.

4.16 Critical success factors

- Marketing orientation, structure and corporate social responsibility
- Competitive position
- Financial performance
- Internal marketing
- Communications and branding
- Segmentation
- Supply chain management
- Marketing information
- Partnerships/alliances

Exploring solutions and options

4.17 In preparation for the exam, you can spend a little time thinking about how you would address the CSFs. For example, what structure would you have for a strategic marketing plan (which would cover some of the above issues) and what very brief notes would you need to make.

4.18 Remember to address the issues raised in the case study.

- No clear competitive position
- No revenue or profit growth from product market opportunities

4.19 Another issue to prepare for is how to use communications to build the brand.

What are the WHS values? It is not just their new corporate values – customer focus, results driven, value people, accountability. These are not necessarily meaningful to customers. What values could WHS build that are meaningful to customers? You also need to think whether they need to change their current promotional mix and media strategies to build brand and, if so, how?

4.20 Segmentation was clearly flagged as an issue to address on the first page.

How could WHS improve their segmentation? Their current poor customer segmentation and research suggests they do not have good enough information to be able to segment their markets. Therefore, what information is on offer (eg MOSAIC or ACORN or psychographic or behavioural)? All sources need to be considered in order to select the most appropriate and useful to WHS. In the longer-term, how can WHS improve their segmentation? What information they choose to collect and build customer profiles will be essential to future segmentation.

4.21 Other issues that may be included in the above notes or have separate notes include:

- Marketing information and marketing metrics
- Supply chain management and relationships with suppliers
- Internal marketing

5 Templates

McKinsey's 7Ss

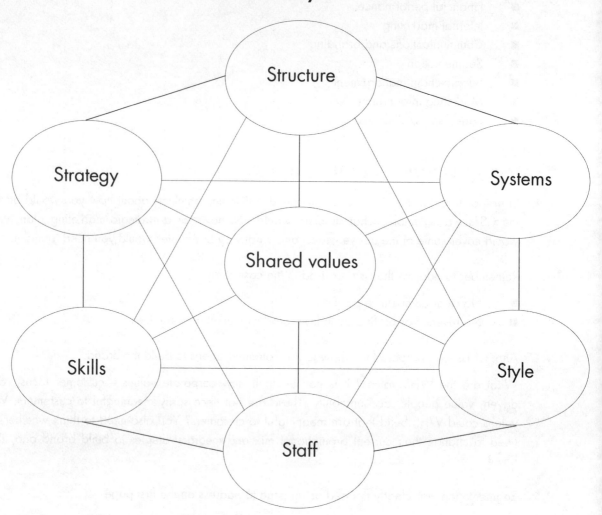

SUPPORT ACTIVITES

PRIMARY ACTIVITES

The Value Chain

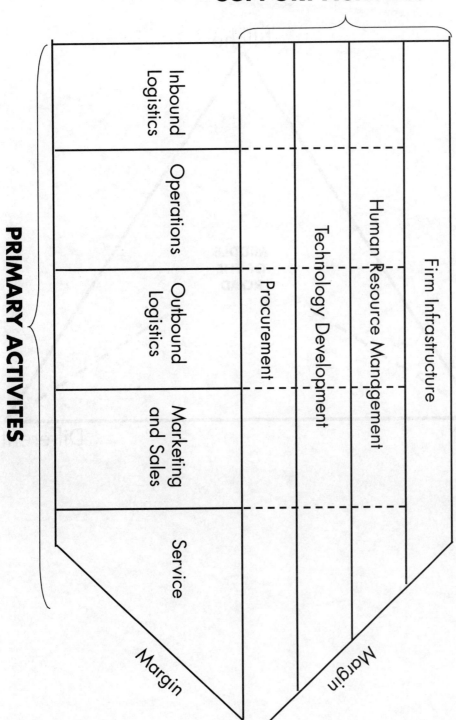

Porter's generic strategies

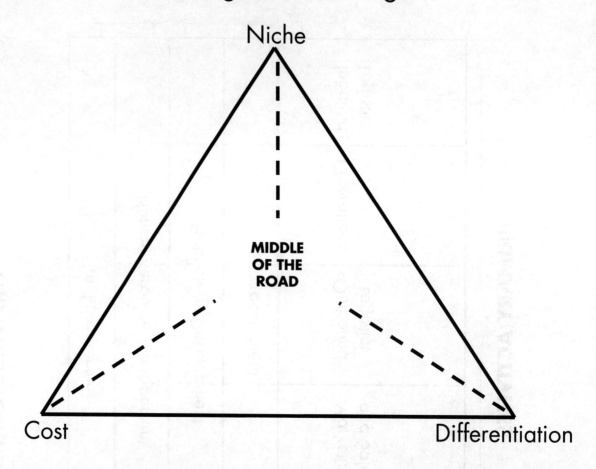

Product life cycle

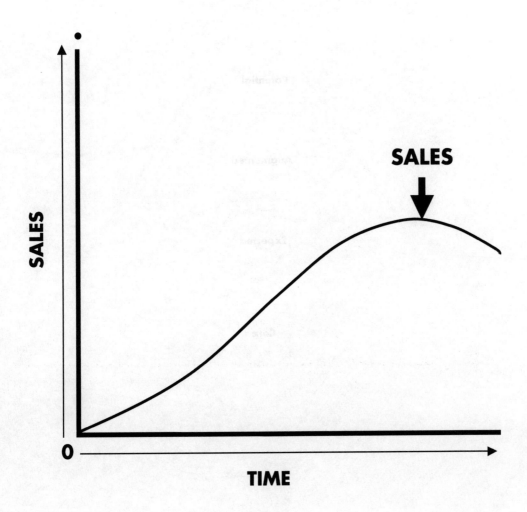

Total product concept

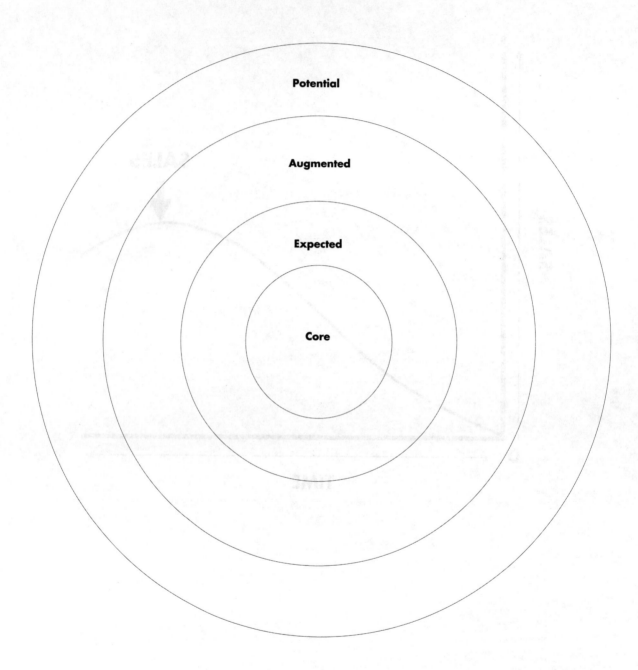

Building brands

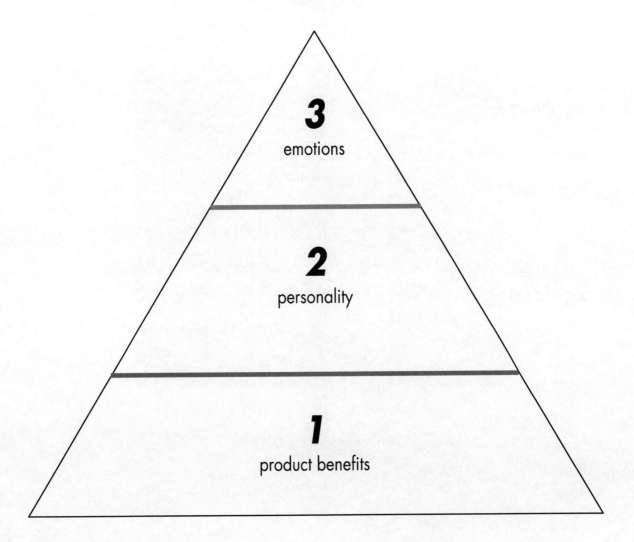

Opportunity/Threat Matrix

To happen

	Very likely	Likely	Less likely
Very significant	Plan	Contingency Plan	Scenario Plan
Significant	Plan	Monitor	Reject
Less significant	Monitor	Reject	Reject

Porter's Five Forces

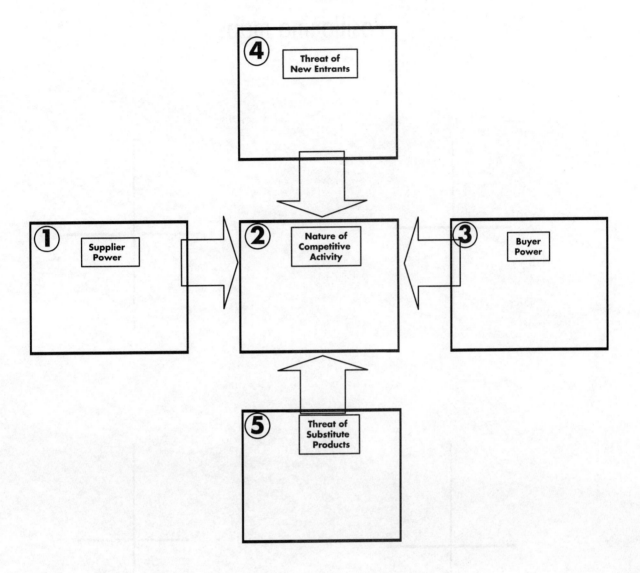

Positioning maps

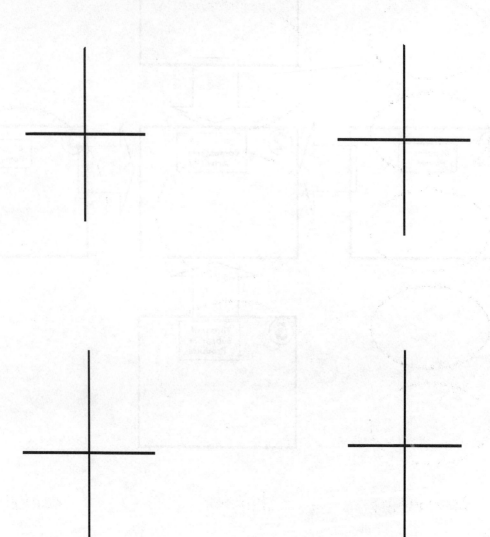

A market map

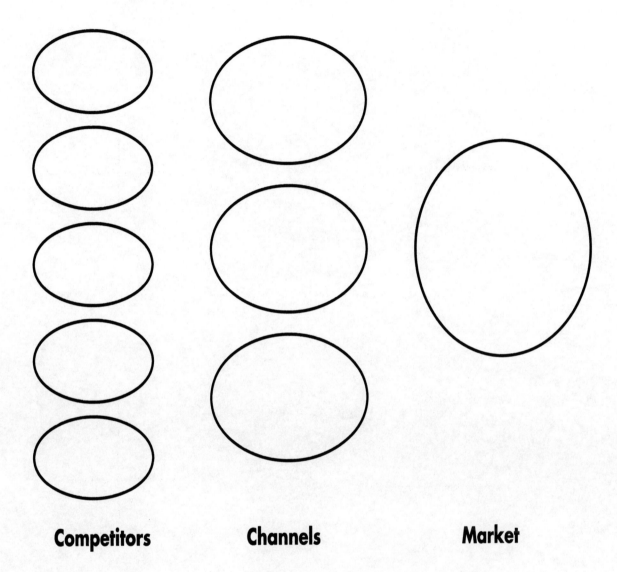

Competitors   **Channels**   **Market**

BPP
PROFESSIONAL EDUCATION

Part D

Exam notes

Exam preparation

20

Chapter Topic List	
1	Exam technique
2	Report format

1 Exam technique

1.1 You have probably already sat successfully a number of CIM examinations, and the general tips on exam technique all remain equally valid. The following notes will provide you with the opportunity to remind yourself of best exam practice to ensure you do not throw away a case study through poor presentation or exam technique.

1.2 Get organised

Make sure you have space and materials e.g. files, dividers etc so you can get down to organizing your notes and analysis as soon as the case comes.

Exam Tip

You may have found the idea of having blank templates of key models helpful. If you have Ansoff, PLC, market maps etc. you can simply add the case detail to these as you come across them. Templates for use in developing your A4 × 6 analysis sheets could help save time immediately prior to the exam. Aim for a maximum of 3 per side.

1.3 Developing an exam timetable

You are now ready to make your final exam preparations. You should already have planned to make time available for the case study preparation. Use the attached timetable to help you plan your case preparation.

Step	Timing
Case Step 1 Read and overview case	
Case Step 2 Complete internal inview analysis	
Case Step 3 Complete external inview analysis	
Case Step 4 Prioritise and identify critical success factors and prepare analysis summary	
Case Step 5 Establishing the strategic direction	
Case Step 6 Consider marketing management and business implications	
Case Step 7 Develop marketing strategies and marketing mix plans	
Case Step 8 Develop contemporary issues and management plans	
Case Step 9 Develop controls	
Case Step 10 Preparing for the exam	

2 Report format

2.1 You **must** work in report format for this paper.

You **must** answer the questions in the order set.

Report format requires the following:

- Title and contents page
- Numbered sections and sub-sections

  Treat Q1 as Section 1
  Treat Q2 as Section 2
  Treat Q3 as Section 3

- Use bullet points rather than a, b, c or numbering

- Include diagrams and tables within your content and where relevant refer specifically to the analysis appendix.

- Add that white space and colour to highlight your work

2.2 You will only convince the Examiners if your approach is clear and decisive with your assessment and recommendations justified.

2.3 Wait until the end of your preparation to annotate your case study. Keep your notes simple with key numbers/prompts etc. Finally put together your analysis appendix as described earlier.

Time management will be critical and you will not be able to have a minute over your allocated time – the responsibility to manage that time against the marks allocated is yours.

Look at the mark allocation and be prepared to plan a finish time for each question accordingly.

Marks

Question 1	finished by	
Question 2	finished by	
Question 3	finished by 5 pm	
	180 minutes	100

Remember your analysis is worth up to 25%

Exam Briefing and Tutorials

If you are working alone and independently on the case, you may be glad of some final help and advice. Angela and Juanita working through Tactics for Exam Success, and Juanita, working through the Marketing Studio (Juanita@marketingstudio.org) (www.tacticsforexamsuccess.co.uk) produce case guidance notes, final briefings and offer workshops and one to one tutorials for Case.

To find out availability and prices, please contact Angela on 020 8313 9317 or Juanita on 01732 750887.

REVIEW FORM & FREE PRIZE DRAW

All original review forms from the entire BPP range, completed with genuine comments, will be entered into one of two draws on 31 January 2007 and 30 July 2007. The names on the first four forms picked out on each occasion will be sent a cheque for £50.

Name: _____   Address: _____

_____

_____

How have you used this Text?
(Tick one box only)

☐ Self study (book only)

☐ On a course: college_____

☐ Other _____

Why did you decide to purchase this Text?
(Tick one box only)

☐ Have used BPP Texts in the past

☐ Recommendation by friend/colleague

☐ Recommendation by a lecturer at college

☐ Saw advertising in journals

☐ Saw website

☐ Other _____

(Tick as many boxes as are relevant)

☐ Our advertisement in *Marketing Success*

☐ Our advertisement in *Marketing Business*

☐ Our brochure with a letter through the post

☐ Our brochure with *Marketing Business*

☐ Saw website

Which (if any) aspects of our advertising do you find useful?
(Tick as many boxes as are relevant)

☐ Prices and publication dates of new editions

☐ Information on product content

☐ Facility to order books off-the-page

☐ None of the above

Your ratings, comments and suggestions would be appreciated on the following areas.

	Very useful	Useful	Not useful
Introductory section	☐	☐	☐
Methodology	☐	☐	☐
Biocatalysts	☐	☐	☐
Reiss	☐	☐	☐
Centrica	☐	☐	☐

	Excellent	Good	Adequate	Poor
Overall opinion of this Text	☐	☐	☐	☐

Please note any further comments and suggestions/errors on the reverse of this page.

Please return to: Glenn Haldane, BPP Professional Education, FREEPOST, London, W12 8BR

REVIEW FORM & FREE PRIZE DRAW (continued)

Please note any further comments and suggestions/errors below.

FREE PRIZE DRAW RULES

1 Closing date for 31 January 2007 draw is 31 December 2006. Closing date for 31 July 2007 draw is 30 June 2007.

2 Restricted to entries with UK and Eire addresses only. BPP employees, their families and business associates are excluded.

3 No purchase necessary. Entry forms are available upon request from BPP Professional Education. No more than one entry per title, per person. Draw restricted to persons aged 16 and over.

4 Winners will be notified by post and receive their cheques not later than 6 weeks after the relevant draw date. List of winners will be supplied on request.

5 The decision of the promoter in all matters is final and binding. No correspondence will be entered into.